Fashion for Profit

A Professional's Complete Guide to Designing, Manufacturing, & Marketing a Successful Line

By

Frances Harder

Everything you need to know when starting your own business. Reviewed and validated by experts from within each specific crucial area of design, product development, finance, production, through to sales and marketing of a product.

6th Edition, July, 2004

"An ancient fashion remains a curiosity,
a fashion but lately gone by becomes an absurdity, a
reigning mode, in which life stirs, strikes us as the
very personification of grace."

Author Unknown

Harder Publications

3402 Tanglewood Lane,
Rolling Hills Estates
CA. 90274
USA
Tel: 310 541 7196
Fax: 310 541 3436
www.HarderPublications.com
www.FashionForProfit.com

Editor: Suzanne Gross
Technical Editor: Evan Smith
Cover Design: Angelena-Simpson Wentzel

Copyright © 2000
ISBN: 0-9727763-1-1

Fashion for Profit

Preface

*"**Fashion for Profit**" was first conceived for the many talented students that I have had the pleasure of teaching who want to achieve their dreams of one day owning their own company and producing a successful line of clothing. The apparent lack of business information for start-up apparel manufacturers motivated me to provide this critical education and business training. I developed a class for the continuing education department at Otis College of Art and Design in Los Angeles. This hands-on, how to class, provided the one-on-one which assisted entrepreneurs develop a small, workable clothing line and get the business training needed to become successful in a business well known for its failures.*

The classes were filled and proved to me there was a need for such courses. Some participants had the design talent and training but no business skills; others had business skills, but no idea where to begin when planning a line of clothing. It was stimulating to assist these talented individuals achieve their dreams by providing a solid business base and expertise on the various aspects of owning a small apparel company.

*The fundamental material for "**Fashion for Profit**" has evolved over the many years that I have been involved with the fashion industry, both in the U.S. and in Europe, where I received my degree and began my design and teaching careers. My experience as a teacher, and twice owning and operating my own business, has provided me with much information and experience.*

*"**Fashion for Profit**" has been developed to cover all the important aspects of going into business: licenses, business plans, bookkeeping, financing, costing, fabrication, contracting and the every day logistics of running a small apparel manufacturing company, plus the marketing (including E-commerce) and sales. (The design information in this book is minimal, as there are plenty of other books and courses offered which cover this information).*

*There have been many textbooks written about the fashion industry, but "**Fashion for Profit**" is a unique book that fills an educational and information gap. The book will provide critical help to a start-up apparel manufacturer, as well as resource information the manufacturer needs to operate a small business successfully. The book has been planned in four main informational sections to enable users to get immediate help on topics of importance to them. Starting with Product Development and Financing* your business, which lead the reader to the production section and all its various stages. The final part is devoted to sales and marketing of the product, including Catalog Sales, E-Commerce, E-Tailing and M-Tailing plus a new chapter on the major steps involved in opening your own retail store.

In the day-to-day operations of running any business, there are always forms necessary: from licenses, specification sheets, pattern cards, purchase order forms, shipping forms, etc. All these various forms can soon be downloaded from the web site (*www.FashionforProfit.com*) or you can use the blanks provided with the purchase of this book. In order to customize these forms, manufacturers can print their own business head on the top, then they will be ready for immediate use. This will save immeasurable time and energy in finding these "must have" forms and applications.

I am not a writer, an accountant, a banker, or a sales representative; I am a trained designer, and educator. Most of the information in this book has been put together with the help and advice of many experts, much reading, and my own expertise and experiences. To give the book more validity I asked a number of professionals from their own field of expertise to review and up-date the material covered in certain key chapters. This gives the book a solid basis of **"real"** material and expertise. However, I would still recommend that a start-up company find the best experts available in their own area, who will help steer and guide them through the rough waters of this industry, which are not easy sailing but never boring. Towards the back of the book, there is a list of industry resources, which can assist entrepreneurs with more detailed information. There is also a glossary of fabric information included and a vocabulary list to educate the reader with necessary industry related terminology.

"Fashion for Profit" has led me to a new venture The **Fashion Business Incorporated, a 501 c3 educational non profit,** which was previously named the **Fashion Business Incubator (FBI)** (LA). I developed and co-founded the FBI with Sandy Bleifer, artist, and realtor in 1999. (Sandy has since moved onto other ventures.) It was already apparent to me while teaching, that the link most needed by emerging designer-driven manufacturers was business education and training, or fashion economics, plus networking opportunities, promotion and resources. (*www.FashionBizInc.org*)

The Fashion Business Inc. has recently moved in to a newly renovated 5,000 square foot training facility housed in the **New Mart Building**, in the heart of the fashion district in down-town Los Angeles. This state-of-the-art center has been funded by the City of Los Angeles and the Los Angles Department of Water and Power, Economic Development Department. The FBI has also been fortunate to have the support and backing of Joyce Eisenberg-Keefer, the New Mart Building President, who realized the need for our educational resource and who has agreed to house our new FBI center rent-free for a period of *five years. The center has been designed to provide an educational space that will give apparel manufactures a state-of-the-art training facility. Housed within the 5,000 square feet, is a co-op showroom that will house six new emerging designers until they have found their own representatives, classroom space, a photo studio and computer lab, plus general office space and conference room. It is the first of its kind in the States and indeed the World. I am proud and humbled by the support and friendships that have grown from my vision! Many supporters have helped to turn a great idea into a wonderful resource for growing apparel manufacturers within the LA area.*

Since the FBI's inception, some of our FBI members have grown and become successful designer/manufacturers. Others have chosen to remain on a more secure level and keep their sales small and manageable. Unfortunately, others have fallen by the wayside or chosen to go in other directions. But whichever type or size of business, the Fashion Business Inc. will benefit the industry and the community as a whole.

I am convinced and committed to what we have developed here in LA. I know we will continue to grow and eventually prosper. I believe we have a collective responsibility to create the infrastructure, community, educational resources, and the opportunities that will enable the next generation of new entrepreneurs to spring up and blossom right here on the west coast of America, or where ever they happen to be on this planet.

Frances Harder

www.FashionForProfit.com
www.Fashionbizinc.org

"PLAN, PREPARE, PRODUCE AND PERSEVERE"

Dedication

I dedicate this book to all the talented students that I have been fortunate enough to instruct and influence in my career. I may have forgotten your names, but I will never forget your dreams and your desire to succeed in this perilous business. By reading this text I hope that it will relieve some of the worries and anxieties involved with starting an apparel manufacturing company. Without the business skills to operate a company, it is like playing Russian roulette with bullets in every chamber but one! Take the time to read and learn all about the business side of doing business. You can be the best designer in the world but without business skills you will be a bad investment.

In Appreciation

This book would not have been possible without my wonderful family, for whom I will always be most grateful. To Helmut (my husband), for his loving support. To my two children, Hans and Erika for keeping me grounded. I love you all!

WITH SPECIAL THANKS

There have been many wonderful people who have spent their time in reviewing and giving helpful expert advice in getting this book finished. Below are some that deserve a special mention and my appreciation.

George Ackers for his "Design Today For Tomorrow" advice to designers.

Dr. Alyssa Dana Adomaitis (Cal Polly Pomona), for her professional advice and help with editing Chapter 18

Henry Cherner for his support and advice. Aims software forms taken from their program. EDI Information.

Diane Company from X-Y Axis, Inc., for reviewing Samples, Patternmaking, Grading, Marking and Cutting. (Chapter 10)

Robin Cornwall (Consultant from USC Business Fast Track), for reviewing the "Business Plan." (Chapter 3)

Kathy David – Managing Director of JbK Design Internet Website Development. Reviewing Chapter 16

Louise Farr for her contribution in editing parts of the book.

Professor Jean Gipe (Cal Polly Pomona), for reviewing the chapter, Production, Quality Control and Shipping. (Chapter 13)

Suzanne Gross for the update and re-edit of 5th edition of Fashion for Profit.

Brian Kaster from Gerber Technology for the Spec Pack and for his assistance.

Professor Kathrine Hagen (Otis College of Art & Design), for allowing me to use her croquis and illustrations. (Chapter 7)

Neil Hofman (Ex-President, Otis College of Art & Design); you are an inspirational leader.

Leonard Horowitz (TALA, Textile Association Los Angeles), for his time reviewing "Finding Fabric and Trims." (Chapter 8)

Peter Linington (CIT Group), for his time, and for helping me with the "Financing Your Business." (Chapter 5)

Richard Littman (friend and Tax specialist), for his friendly and helpful advice with "Bookkeeping for a Small Business." (Chapter 4)

Peter Jacobson (Creative Concepts), for his time and advice on the Marketing & Sales chapter. (Chapter 14)

Ayse Oge for reviewing Chapter 17 Producing and Selling Abroad.

Joe Rodriguez (Garment Contractors Association), for his kind help and advice on Finding a Contractor. (Chapter 11)

Antonio R. Sarabia Attorney at Law for his expertise and legal advise on Chapter 2.

George Schmid for his friendly help and expertise on "Producing and Selling Abroad". (Chapter 17)

Evan Smith for his hard work in getting the book formatted and getting the book completed for every edition.

Joel Stonefield for his help and advice on "Chargebacks" and "Accounting" information. His many hours of giving, to both me and the members of FBI, have been a true example of "giving back" to the industry in which he was so successful.

Richard Swanson, U.S. Department of Commerce, for his efforts and input on "Producing & Selling in a Global Market". (Chapter 17)

Kathy Swantko (American Sportswear & Knitting Times), for her kind help with my fabric information "Understanding Textiles" (Chapter 9) and "Glossary of Fabric Terms." (Appendix)

Arnie Wachman (Webmaster) for his time in reviewing information in Chapter 16 and his hard work on my two websites www.Fashionforprofit.com and www.fashionbizinc.org

Angelena Simpson-Wentzel for the great book cover design and for being the cover girl!

Ginny Wong for reviewing the chapter, Marketing & Sales. (Chapter 14)

Adrienne Zinn (Dept. Chair, Fashion Merchandising, LA Trade Tech), for the "Introduction" to **Fashion for Profit**.

DESIGN TODAY FOR TOMORROW

"A new year, a new decade, a new century, a new way to design. You are living in a time where you can make a difference: you can lead the generation that stopped taking more than it replaced.

The 20th century brought us tremendous advances in medicine, agriculture, technology, and lifestyle, but these advances did not come without their costs: polluted land, water, food and air as well as a rapidly depleting ozone layer that we need to maintain life on earth.

Knowing all this, the 21st century promises to be a wonderful time to be a designer. The secret to success is "find a need and fill it." Everything we consume needs to be responsibly re-designed to deliver quality and at the same time be produced, keeping in mind a sustainable balance with nature. This is a "need."

Change is the only constant on earth, and designers - whether they know it or not - decide how much impact their creations will have on the next generation. Today's designers are very special people because they have inherited a polluted world (from designers who did not know any better) and have been given the task of re-designing our way back to sustainability. This is a "need."

Fashion promotes change and the educated consumer today wants goods that are made better and more responsibly, as well as being fashionable. The successful designers of the future will add impact to their thought patterns. They will use the Internet and technology to research and produce goods with the hidden value of responsibility in their products. Strive to be this kind of modern designer and research the materials, the dyes, the trims and makers. Choose the path with the least impact on our future. Be a responsible designer and you'll fill a "need." And if you fill a "need," you'll be successful."

George Akers

"Britannia Jeans" and "Union Bay" founder
January 1, 2000

TABLE OF CONTENTS

CHAPTER 3 31

BUSINESS PLAN 31

CHAPTER 4 47

BOOKKEEPING FOR A SMALL BUSINESS 47

INTRODUCTION

Welcome to the Fashion Business! This is a unique industry: artistic and creative, profit-driven and demanding. **_Fashion For Profit_** will take you to the heart of Fashion and give you the real facts.

This may be the place that you always wanted to be.

Now is the time to learn about Fashion and make your mark on it. This is where your sense of style and knowledge of financial planning can bring great financial and personal rewards. This will be the place that will support your ideas and reward your hard work.

Fashion research will teach you about the cultural impact on apparel and accessories. You will learn about sketching as well as figuring. You will understand all about the processes of manufacturing and the thrill of marketing. You will not only learn what you need to know but about what you want to know.

As you browse this book you will note that you will get more and more excited. Every chapter brings the definitive information about each specific area of Fashion Design and Merchandising. You will find that many of the questions you thought would never be addressed anywhere are answered here in clear and understandable terms.

One of the great things about the fashion Industry is that one person can make a difference. There is always room for those who want to work and plan and organize and design and market a product at a profit. If it doesn't sell, we learn to get over it and go on to another success.

Enjoy this book and let it guide you and your dreams to fulfillment.

Adrienne B. Zinn

Adrienne B. Zinn B.A., M.A., M.F.A.,
Dept. Chair, Fashion Merchandising
Los Angeles Trade-Technical College
January, 2001

CHAPTER 1

MAJOR STEPS IN

MANUFACTURING A GARMENT

Fashion, like all the arts, serves as a release from the humdrum in life. Part fantasy and part romance, it turned Princess Diana, Jackie Kennedy, Cinderella, Beau Brummel, and Elton John into legends. There are many pleasures in life; fashion being one that is enjoyed by many who are fortunate enough to have the time and the money available to do so! To the designer, it is an art form and more; it is also an exciting and unpredictable business.

To become a fashion designer, then an entrepreneur in the apparel business means being aware of all the important new changes happening around you, and being able to predict new trends of tomorrow. It is being able to create a simple little dress, which to your amazement breaks all records for sales. Fashion is a continual gamble, but owning a company can be rewarding, though sometimes a stressful experience.

You may have been thinking about going into business for some time and just didn't know where or how to begin this daunting undertaking. Or, you may already have begun to realize your dream, but need extra help and advice from someone who has been in the fashion industry for many years, someone who can predict some of the potential difficulties that may occur, and most importantly help prevent them for happening.

This introductory chapter presents a brief description of the many roles an apparel manufacturer will have to become familiar with in order to run a business efficiently. Manufacturing consists of several interrelated processes, explained in this first chapter; from the basic theory of garment design, through the production stage, to the marketing and selling of the line. This is an overview of most of the components that are involved in running and operating a small clothing company. Starting with design and development, financial organization, marketing and sales, production, quality control and shipping. A more in depth explanation of these steps will be covered more thoroughly in the following chapters.

Product Development

Product development is the first step in the manufacturing process. This involves lots of research and inspiration. For the start-up entrepreneur it will mean a great deal of research and market analysis in order to come up with a product which will be in demand. Manufacturers and even large retailers such as The Gap, J.C.Penney, Sears, and The Limited all spend a great deal of money on product development and formulating new ideas. This could mean a trip to Europe to view the collections and research ideas in European stores and on the streets. It may involve exhibits and professional trend services that predict styles, fabrics and colors for the next season. Design is an on-going process and as soon as one line is complete, the designer will have to begin on the next season's designs, producing four to six collections each year.

(As a start-up manufacturer developing a first line, coming up with fresh ideas for the next line can often be problematic. Remember that you will never have as much time to develop a future line as you have had for the first line you produce and market).

Each garment must be individually styled. Although it may be similar to other garments in the line, and similar to garments in the preceding line, it will still need new individual features of its own. These similarities represent the signature "look" for your company, one which retailers and customers come to recognize and return to buy. This is called "**Branding**". It is important that a manufacturer achieve a look that is recognized as its' brand image. To achieve this goal, the designer starts with structure, trims and fabric. The necessity for balanced proportions, good fit and quality for the money paid by the customer, is another important aspect of producing a saleable line of clothing.

The number of "pieces" in a line depends on the size of the company and the price range of the product. For a start-up manufacturer, keeping the line small and manageable is important. Finding a product that can fill a need in a market that is saturated with old styles and with a price ticket that will allow the start-up to provide product and make a profit, will make the difference between success and failure. Some successful companies have started with one item, sold it in large quantities, which made it possible for them to grow slowly. Of course there are many manufacturers who have been "one trick ponies" that have not been able to develop another successful item. They are gone within a few short months of starting their business. Product development is where it starts and finishes.

Fashion Trends

In the fashion industry there is a constant flow of information about what the customer is buying. Information about customer preferences, as expressed in customer purchases, flows in several directions. One example is when information flows back from the manufacturer to the retail store, via the manufacturer's sales representative. This alerts the store to trends they may not have noticed. Sales representatives are constantly analyzing the fashion trends, and a good sales representative can help a manufacturer with such key information. From the records of an individual store, the retailer can discern sudden or gradual changes in the preferences of the customer and is able to spot new trends. Another flow of information is from the manufacturer to the fabric producers. This is often in the form of the garment manufacturers' fabric reorders for the most popular materials, patterns and colors. In addition, there are professional trend services that provide manufacturers with future trends in design, fabric, and trim likely to be in the stores in the upcoming seasons. These trend services can be expensive, but many manufacturers feel they are worth it.

Fabric

As a designer it is important to find the right fabrics for your first line. This could mean a trip to see fabrics at a textile show. Textile shows will inform you of new trends and colors for the following seasons. Finding your dream fabric on your first line can be a problem for a start up business. Most mills want you to buy minimum yardage, which could be as much as thousand yards. It takes patience to fabricate your line and find the best choice at the right price. Plan on using just a few fabrics at first: no more than three. Using more fabrics than three will cost too much to produce. Do not give up; use all the resources mentioned in Chapter 5. There are great fabrics available, and with the Internet, finding the right fabrics has become easier.

Usually a designer plans a certain number of garments for each type of fabric and color selected; this is called a story. A certain proportion of the line could be high-end fashion, with some styles designed in more basic styling and fabric, which would complementing the more extreme styles. Price as well as the design influences the choice of fabric and trimmings. If the fabric is on the more expensive end of the budget, then a simpler design will be necessary in order to keep the garment within the price range required for the line. A more reasonably priced fabric can be cut in a more elaborate style that will allow the major cost to be in labor.

First Pattern and Sample

Once the sample yardage is acquired, the first pattern must be made. In order to produce a good first pattern, the patternmaker must be able to understand the design that is to be translated into a pattern, and then into a first sample. A flat (technical drawing) of the garment is sketched with finished dimensions and sewing details, topstitching, zipper length, etc. If you are trained in draping, and are able to make your own patterns, this will obviously save you a great deal of money. You will then be more likely to achieve your vision of how you would like your garments to look and be produced, without having the garment remade a number of times before it is to your satisfaction. The next step is to have the first sample sewn. The contractor that you plan to use for your production, (not necessarily a sample maker) can often make samples. This has the added advantage of the contractor being able to cost the garment for production. Contractors like to sew the first sample, as they hope that they will then be able to sew your production orders. Using this method allows the contractors to become aware of any problems involved with sewing a particular style, and enables them to give a fair estimate of the costing. As a rule of thumb, sewing the first sample is usually two to three times the price of sewing a garment in production.

Will the garment stay in the line? What changes should be made to keep it saleable for the right price point? Often you have to switch fabric or take fewer markups to make a garment sell. Other times the trim will be reduced or eliminated or the pattern adjusted so it will take less fabric. All these are tricks of the trade to make a garment sell, and sell at the right price point.

Product Costing

It goes without saying, the simplest garments cost less to make. As styling details are added; pockets, fancy seaming, linings and trims etc, the cost of the finished garment will increase labor cost in production. If you have chosen an expensive fabric for one of your designs, it would be wise to keep the details to a minimum. Using expensive fabric and many styling details often makes the finished cost of the garment too high for the market which it has been targeted. Costing a garment is a mathematical formula:

Costs of fabric + trims + labor+ business overhead + profit= Garment Cost

Overhead costs are affected by such factors as design research, markdown sales losses, brand advertising, promotions, rent, and everything else that goes along with owning and running a business. This all has to be calculated into the costing of a garment. The cost of piece goods (fabric) is generally about one-third the initial production cost of a garment. For the small company, the mark-up will be higher than for bigger mass-producing companies that have a lower mark-up percentage due to the volume they manufacture.

Ultimately the final figures may be a subjective call of what the market will bear. If you price your garments higher than comparative garments sold in the same stores as your product, you will find that your clothes will be left on the rack!

Editing the Line

Designing for the most part is experimental, and there will be a number of first samples that will not make it into the line. Editing the line or weeding out is a very important stage and it takes someone with experience to pick the potential good sellers. The approved sample for the line will have the right combination of fabric, styling, and trims, and can be sold for the right price with the appropriate profit margin. It takes only a few really good styles for a company to have a successful season. It takes only a few bad styles to close a company or make for an unprofitable season.

Sales Representative

Now the samples can be shown to the sales representative or "rep". Sometimes they will ask that you make certain changes in order for a better presentation. Experienced sales representatives can be informative, and give helpful advice. They meet with the buyers and have an eye for what will sell well. Buyers from retail stores all over the country are invited to visit the sales representatives' showrooms in one of many fashion Marts across the country for presentation of the season's collections. Sales reps will show lines at trade shows, which occur at various times each year. Some sales reps also travel to show the line to individual stores. This type of rep is known as a road rep. For a start-up company, it is always a good idea to show a first line and sell it yourself. It is important to see the reaction to the product and to learn something about selling.

Selling Online

Selling on the Internet is a fast growing business. For a new company it could be a good idea to set-up a web page to see if there is any reaction to your product. Of course there are drawbacks to this method because the buyer needs to find the product on the Internet. With E-Commerce, the right links, and the right product it is possible that a new company could be very successful with on-line selling either direct to the customer or to the retailer. There are buying offices that have virtual showrooms, which show the product and sell to the customer without ever having direct contact. Just as mail order is an important sales method, the Internet will continue to grow as a major sales outlet available in everyone's home.

Production Pattern, Marking and Grading

Once the line is edited and the sales representative has the line, then the first pattern is made into a production pattern. The **Production Pattern** is a perfected first pattern. This means that the first pattern is corrected for fitting and sewing details and the lay of the fabric is tested for an economical marker. The production pattern is then given to the **Grader and Marker Maker** to be graded into sizes. These days the computer is mainly used to perform these two steps, although there are still hand graders and markers who do an excellent job.

Grading is taking the first production pattern, which is normally a middle size, like a size 8, and grading it up and down into other sizes. Grading is an important part of production, so the grader must be experienced. Production samples of these graded sizes are sometimes made to test the fit, and specifications are written for each garment and each size. This ensures that in production the garments are sewn exactly as the approved production samples. **Duplicate samples** are usually made at this stage. **Duplicates** of the line called **Sales samples** are sent to the various sales representatives to show to buyers all over the country. The larger the company, the more sales reps you have to represent you and therefore more sales samples will be required.

The **Grader** usually makes the **marker** as part of their service. The marker is made for the complete pattern, using as little fabric as possible and interlocking the pattern pieces together to ensure there is no wasted fabric. It is printed out onto paper that is the same width as the fabric. The marker is used by the cutter who will follow it while cutting out the pattern pieces. It is laid over layers of fabric that have been rolled out onto large cutting tables. The fabric is some times rolled out and layered to thirty layers of fabric or more.

Fabric & Trim Ordering

As soon as the line is completed, **duplicates** are made for the sales reps to show to buyers to write orders. An estimate of how much fabric will be needed to produce the line is usually done at this time. This step should be given close consideration. Ordering too much fabric will result in waste and will take away from the profit. Ordering too little will result in losing orders and profit margin. These days it is best to be conservative and to order on the safe side. If there are more orders and not enough fabric, then you can explain the problem to the retailers, and if you are lucky they may be willing to wait for a reorder of fabric to fill their orders.

Building a Cutting Ticket

Once the sales representative starts to write orders, the manufacturer will begin to write **cutting tickets**. This will give a good idea as to what items in the line are going to be good sellers, and what will not. An estimate of the yardage will then be made and the fabric will then be ordered. As soon as the fabric arrives for production it must be checked for flaws or shading. If this is done as soon as the fabric is received, there maybe time enough to return any damaged goods and receive replacement fabric.

Cutting

Having in house cutting demands a higher volume of sales in order to justify the cost of employing a full time cutter. Therefore, **start-up businesses** usually give the fabric to a cutting service to cut the garments. Often, the cutter and the contractor are under one roof and will be responsible for both cutting and sewing the complete garment. The cutting is done on large, long **cutting tables** that are the full width of the fabric rolled out on to them. The paper marker (as explained earlier) is placed on top of the fabric and the piece goods are then cut for production with **band knives** that vibrate up and down, cutting through the numerous layers of fabric at one time. Larger manufacturers use computers to grade, make the marker, and cut out the pattern from the fabric. The cut garments are then separated and **bundled** into lots to be sewn together by the sewers.

Production of the Garment

Usually the **Contractor** is responsible for taking the cut goods and sewing the garments for production. Larger companies may sometimes have their own in-house sewing operators, and still contract out some of their work. Some larger companies cut in the U.S. and then ship the cut garment to an off shore contractor to sew together. Or, they may have the total production produced abroad, will enables the manufacturer to produce at a more competitive price point. There are pros and cons for producing offshore. Some manufacturers would rather pay more and have their garments produced domestically where they are able to keep better control over the quality of goods, have a faster turn around in production, and not have to contend with the customs and shipping costs.

Contractors generally work in **piece goods**, this means the garment is sewn piece by piece. For example: one operator is responsible for sewing a collar, another is responsible for setting the sleeves and another will complete the whole garment by sewing the finished pieces together. Each worker is paid depending on the number of pieces he or she has sewn.

Operators who show exceptional ability are frequently promoted to produce the first sample and responsible for the prototype samples. This **Sample Hand** position requires a person that has a number of years experience and who can produce a good looking garment. They are generally assured steady employment at a regular weekly salary. A good sample maker is hard to find and well respected.

Betterwear companies have their garments sewn completely by one operator to assure a better quality garment; these operators are paid by the hour and not by each piece produced.

It is a common practice these days for a group of operators to be responsible for one garment, working as a team to sew the complete garment.   This induces a sense of pride in the operators as their finished product is recognized as their own work. This is known as the **modular method**.

Quality Control and Distribution

It is important for the manufacturer that the quality of the goods be carefully controlled. In the beginning this will be done by you. It is your responsibility to check with the contractor to ensure that he is following the construction methods used in the production sample and that the quality remains constant. This is achieved by going to the contractor's factory and inspecting for yourself the quality of goods produced. Once the contractor finishes the garments they are delivered for final quality inspection and shipping, or the contractor himself could be responsible for shipping the garments when completed. These days the industry is using more technology, which makes for better quality in production, increased efficiency and faster movement of goods from factory to store. The use of coding tickets sewn into the garments makes tracking the garments from cutting through to the final sale an efficient method of keeping a record of production. Even cash registers can be coded to send reorder information to suppliers as stocks drop. The garments will be shipped either on a hanger or flat in plastic bags depending on what arrangements were made with the retailer. The garments are grouped depending on the customer and the dates to be shipped. An order always bears two dates: the **ship** date after which shipping can begin and the *cancel* date when all shipping must be completed to avoid cancellation. Late shipping must be avoided at all costs as the store could cancel its order.

Buyer Reaction

When the ordered garments arrive at the receiving department of the retail store, they are checked in, examined and delivered to the correct department of the store. The retailer will cost the garments with their own mark-up costs. The norm for most department and specialty stores is to double the manufacturer's price plus an additional 20 to 30 percent, or what the industry refers to as "2.2." If a garment costs $100 from the manufacturer, it will be $220 on the retail floor.

An initial order may not be very large. **Buyers** often check how the stock comes through, which means how the manufacturer produces the finished garments. Buyers will also watch for public reaction to those garments. The styles that prove popular are reordered in greater quantity, whereas styles that do not sell satisfactorily go on the mark down rack. How long a garment stays on the floor before it becomes sales merchandise varies with the store and the competition. Retailers soon learn what types of garments sell best, and which manufacturer made them. The stock is analyzed each day, and records show how many of each size, color, and styles are sold. Armed with this information, a buyer will return to a manufacturer for reorders or returns.

Selling to large department stores has become a very risky business and new companies should be aware of canceled orders and **charge backs**. These can occur when the store wants part-payment for any of your garments that have not sold and end up on the mark down rack, or if you should ship late. In reality charge backs are much more complex, and are explained later in this book. Mark down money adds to the manufacturer's overhead costs and may boost the original retail price of the garment. Manufacturers who want to keep the stores as customers try to cooperate. Unfortunately, it has become such a contentious issue that some manufacturers refuse to sell to certain retailers because of these charge back issues. This is one reason why so many manufacturers are opening their own retail stores in recent years. For start up manufacturers, it is best to avoid the large department stores. They can break a small company in one order. Diversify your orders to a variety of smaller stores.

Financial Organization

This part of your business must be carried through with much planning and with as much advice as is available. The first step is the **business plan**. This can be an arduous task, but by carefully following the simple directions laid out in this book, you will complete a business plan in less time than you may think possible. Next, the **bookkeeping** should be set up, to allow the business to flow smoothly and efficiently. Arrange bank accounts with business checking, make company business cards, and apply for licenses. Use the many free forms of help that are available to new companies, including the forms that have been included with the purchase of this book. The forms can also be downloaded from the Internet site. It is in your interest to use this readily available help. Remember that without good financial planning you are basically wasting your time and money! It is here that most businesses fail. By not paying attention to this part of the business there is no business. Out of ten businesses that start, one may make it. The first two years are critical.

Apparel Retail Store

Opening a retail store in order to sell directly to customers is attractive to many designers, lured by the promise increasing sales and building a brand. However, like manufacturing it should be fully investigated before making a final commitment. Many fashion designers, both large and small, have become successful retailers. With the addition of a retail store the business now becomes a vertical operation; from the first sketch to the point of sale, the designer/manufacturer has control. Once you open your store, it may also be a good idea to include other product lines within the store, which would complement your own creations. These other lines could be sold on consignment, which would help cut back on the direct costs of investing in inventory. Having several options will empower you and help you to make the right decisions. Opening a retail establishment demands a significant amount of time to properly oversee every aspect of the fledgling business. (As a designer/manufacturer do you have that time available?)

Finding the right location and understanding your customers' needs are key elements of owning a retail store. It is helpful to sell what you know! However, if you are not familiar with basic marketing principles or the fashion industry, it will be critical to learn about and investigate the market. Becoming profitable will require continual upgrading on a weekly basis to improve and refresh your retail operation. All of the information in **Fashion for Profit** is valuable to you when planning to open a vertically operational retail store. Even if you are not going to manufacture clothing yourself, it is important to understand all aspects of producing a garment, from concept to the consumer. Some of the most important issues that will influence your success as an apparel store owner will be the same as the components necessary in becoming a successful designer/manufacturer; both your discerning good taste and your business expertise.

As the head of your own company you must direct the general operations necessary to run the company smoothly. By following the outline set forth in this book you will be able to setup your business in a logical, straightforward and successful way. This will result in a profitable conclusion for you and your start-up company enabling you, the entrepreneur, to turn your dreams into a realistic small business. There will still be many hurdles to negotiate, but by using this book, you will prepare yourself for most of the challenges ahead. Get as much help as you can afford and use all the free help that is available to small businesses. Keep your objectives in mind. Do not lose your focus. Stick to your original plan. Visit my website **www.fashionforprofit.com**

Product Cycle

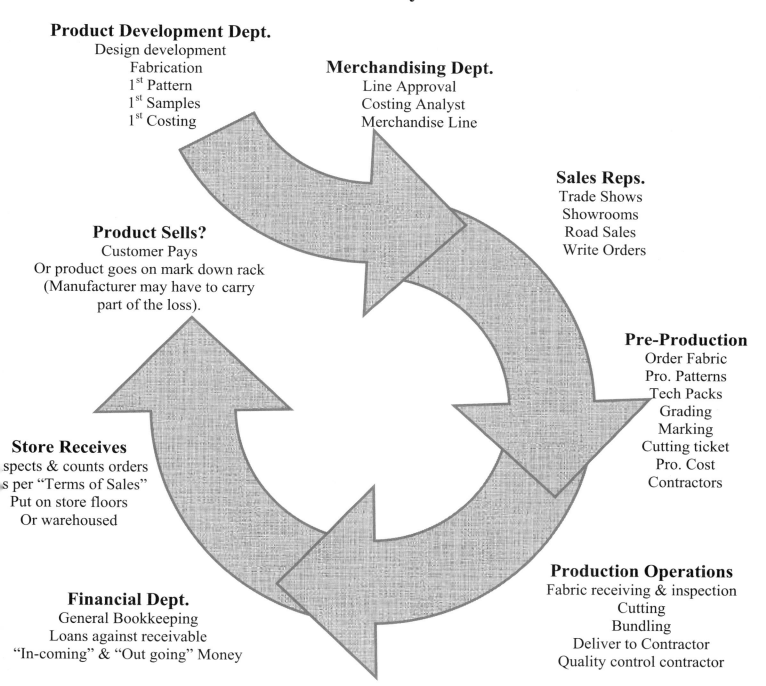

Product Development Dept.
Design development
Fabrication
1st Pattern
1st Samples
1st Costing

Merchandising Dept.
Line Approval
Costing Analyst
Merchandise Line

Sales Reps.
Trade Shows
Showrooms
Road Sales
Write Orders

Product Sells?
Customer Pays
Or product goes on mark down rack
(Manufacturer may have to carry
part of the loss).

Pre-Production
Order Fabric
Pro. Patterns
Tech Packs
Grading
Marking
Cutting ticket
Pro. Cost
Contractors

Store Receives
Inspects & counts orders
as per "Terms of Sales"
Put on store floors
Or warehoused

Financial Dept.
General Bookkeeping
Loans against receivable
"In-coming" & "Out going" Money

Production Operations
Fabric receiving & inspection
Cutting
Bundling
Deliver to Contractor
Quality control contractor

Quality Control & Shipping Dept.
Check Production from Contractor
Trim & Tag
Pull Orders
Bundling
Pack & Ship as per term of Sales
Invoice with shipment

CHAPTER 2

GETTING STARTED

"Enthusiasm – Nothing great was ever achieved without it". Emerson

Having an idea for some new revolutionary design is an exciting experience, but to follow through and run a successful company takes creativity, along with good business skills. Having both these qualities is essential to you and your company. In this chapter, we will cover the nuts and bolts of setting a company up and making it fully operational.

Questions to ask yourself before starting a business

There are numerous questions to ask yourself before you undertake a venture involving the fashion industry, which is famous for its complexities. You should try to answer these questions and analyze the answers with a trusted friend or family member. It is important to you in your new venture that you feel confident that all these questions are fully understood and researched. Answering these questions will prepare you for the next important step: writing a business plan. Many of the answers to the questions will be covered in this book, but some of the questions will be quite taxing.

Do I have what it takes to own and to manage a small business?

You will be your own most important employee, so an objective appraisal of your strengths and weaknesses is essential. Some questions to ask yourself are:

- Am I a self-starter?
- How good am I at making decisions?
- Do I have the physical and emotional stamina to run a business?

- How well do I plan and organize?
- Are my attitudes and drive strong enough to maintain motivation?
- How will the business affect my family?

Have I researched the market completely?

You may have developed your new product due to the realization that there is a need for this product and that's a good start. You should still spend the time to research the stores or markets you wish sell. Manufacturers and designers are constantly "shopping" the stores. They are checking how their garments fit into the wide variety of department and specialty stores. Talk to the sales people and check customers' reactions to garments, fit and quality. Check mark down racks for the mistakes. Visit the higher priced stores for the innovative firms and fashion trends. Do they look worth the money? Check garments for construction and finishing details. Take notes of this shopping report and to refer to them when writing your business plan and designing your line. Shop in a variety of neighborhoods and compare the customers. Keep a record of your research, as it will be needed when you develop your business plan. Investors will want to see that you have done your homework and that you know and understand your target market.

What price bracket will my clothing line fall into?

After researching the market, you will have a better comprehension of this question. It goes without saying that starting any business requires money. It costs money to develop the product and it requires money to produce the product. You may think that once you have the product developed then it would be wonderful to get a huge order. **Wrong!** In order to meet a large order you will have to outlay funds for all the fabric and production before you l receive your payment. You may be lucky enough to get a loan from somewhere, but loans are not easily come by for a new company. There is no history of past success to evaluate whether your new company will be able to repay a loan. Also you do not want to put yourself into too much debt at the start of your new venture. Plan to build slowly and with as little borrowed money as possible. The higher priced market is the most recommended and easiest to succeed in. Higher profits and smaller orders for your new company make better business sense.

What legal aspects do I need to consider?

A bank account with company checks will be the first thing to consider. There will be licenses required, zoning laws and other regulations varying from business to business, and state to state. You will need to consult your attorney or **SBA** (Small Business Association) for advice specific to your business arrangement and State. You must also decide about your form of organization (corporation, partnership or sole proprietorship) for your tax status. You will have to register your fictitious name, which is the new name for your company, if other than your own name.

Would a partner(s) make it easier to be successful?

A business partner does not necessarily guarantee success. If you require additional management skills or start-up capital, engaging a partner may be a good decision. The ultimate success of a partnership will be determined by its ability to give technical or financial assistance as well as personality and character.

If you have a partner, do you know him or her well enough to operate a business together?

Like any close relationship working in close proximity can often lead to conflict between *"good friends"*. Define the jobs to be done by each partner by making a list of jobs, and dividing them up. It is better to choose a partner who has other skills from yours and who can complement your own skills.

Should I hire a family member to work for me?

Frequently, family members of the owner "*help out in the business.*" For some small business owners, it is a rewarding experience; for others it can cause irreparable damage. Carefully consider their loyalty and respect for you as the owner-manager.

Is it possible to keep family and business decisions separate?

If you borrow money from a family member remember that they are loaning money because of their relationship with **you,** and not because of the products worth. When you borrow money from an institution they loan money on the product developed by you, and the collateral that you provide. (*When dealing with a family member you are their collateral! They are investing in the person, not the product.*)

How much money do I need to get started?

One of the leading causes of business failure is insufficient start-up capital. If you can begin to produce a small line of no more than ten items it may be possible to continue your normal day job and start your new venture on the side. This way you will not be relying on having to make a profit on your first line, and taking a loan. If you do not intend to have a second income, then you must plan on having enough money in the business to cover operating expenses for one year, maybe two. Sometimes using a credit card with a low interest rate will enable you to finance some of the start-up costs and cover some production costs for your first line. If you do use your credit card, paying it back in a timely manner will be important.

What do I have to do to get a loan?

For women and minorities there are loans available and the SBA can be very helpful. There is a SBA in most towns around the US. When applying for a loan, here are three of the most important questions that will be asked:

- How much do you need to borrow?
- How will you spend the loan?
- How do you intend on repaying the loan?

When you apply for a loan, a clear description of your experience and a cohesive business plan will be required.

What kind of a profit can I expect in the first two years?

Consider that for the first two years of business there could be very little profit. However, after the first couple of seasons there should be enough money coming into the business to at least cover operation expenses. The cash flow will improve as your business grows, with good financial planning.

What should I know about accounting and bookkeeping?

The importance of keeping adequate records cannot be stressed enough. Without records, you cannot see how well your business is doing, and where it is going. At a minimum, records are needed to substantiate:

- Your tax returns under Federal and State laws, including income tax and Social Security laws.
- Your applications for credit from vendors or for a loan from a bank.
- Your claims about the business, should you wish to sell it. But most importantly, you need to keep records to run your business successfully and to increase your profits.

Can I operate my business from my home?

Yes. In fact, experts estimate that as many as 20 percent of new small business operate out of the owner's home. With increased use of the computer and cyber space, home-based business owners are able to access all types of information without ever leaving the comfort of their home offices. Organize your workspace and your work hours. It is hard to run a successful business from your home with all the distractions. You must stay focused on your goals and objectives. If there are members of the family using the phone, get a designated line for your business. This is to prevent sweatshop operations from being run from homes.

(*It takes self-discipline, timing and, if you're lucky, a caring partner. Manufacturing from your home is against the law in most states, and can have a high penalty for abuse*).

Contact your nearest SBA and state chambers of commerce who can provide pertinent information on how to manage a home-based business. Each city has its own variances; so it is also advisable to call your local city hall for information pertinent to your local area.

How do I find out about suppliers, manufacturers and sales representatives?

Most suppliers want new accounts. There is a variety of trade lists and directories available in each main city and State. Your local library, Chambers of Commerce, or SBA would be a good start. Trade shows and trade papers are other means of finding the right company for the right job. (*Finding the right sales representative is covered in Chapter 14 of this book*).

How do I market my product?

Marketing is one of the most important operations involved in promoting the finished product. Whether you are selling direct, mail order, on the Web, or selling through a sales representative the objective is the same; **reaching as many people as possible.**

Worksheet for Estimating Your Basic Financial Needs

"ONE-TIME" START-UP EXPENSES	START-UP ESTIMATES	TO DO LIST
Fixtures and equipment		
Decorating and remodeling		Talk it over with a contractor
Installation of fixtures and equipment		Talk to suppliers
Starting inventory		Suppliers will probably help you estimate this
Deposits with public utilities		Find out from utility companies
Initial legal and other professional fees		Lawyer, accountant, and so on
Licenses and permits		Find out from city offices what you have to have
Advertising and promotion for opening		Estimate what you'll spend
Accounts receivable		What you need, to buy more stock, until credit customers pay
Cash		Have on-hand for unexpected expenses or losses, special purchases, etc.
Other		Make a separate list and enter total on this list
TOTAL ESTIMATED START-UP CASH REQUIRED	$	Add up all the numbers in the second column

Marketing

Marketing encompasses much more than just advertising or selling. For example, marketing involves researching your customers and competitors.

- What does the customer want?

- What can the customer afford?

- What does the customer think of your product?

- Who are your competitors?

- What will you provide that will give you higher sales? Your ability to learn faster than your competitors maybe your only competitive edge and ultimate advantage.

- Are you able to define your market share?

  (Seniors are the fastest growing group who are living longer and remaining more active. This new crop of seniors wants active sportswear and play clothes. They have the time and for the most part better health to enjoy and use of such clothing).

- Do you plan to eventually sell internationally, and can you define the global market? Developing countries are creating middle class consumers rapidly. In eleven years the Pacific Rim will have a larger market than the US! China will be the number one middle class market by 2010.

Here are the "five P's" of marketing

Product The item you sell.

Price The amount you charge for your produce.

Promotion The way you inform your market as to what you sell.

Provision The channels you use to take the product to the customer.

PR Few start-up companies can afford to pay a pubic relations firm to publicize their product. Finding ways to get free publicity is always a good idea. Sending out a press release about an up coming event where your product will be highlighted is one way to promote your product. Having your garments in fashion shows that will be raising money for a charity is another means of free publicity.

Your understanding of the answers to such questions plays a major role in the success of your business.

Deciding on the "Right" Business Structure

Tony Sarabia contributed material to this portion of the chapter. He is a principal in the law firm IP Business Law Group, Inc. which specializes in counseling apparel companies about laws applicable to the industry and retail store operations. A particular focus of the firm is the protection of intellectual property - trademarks, copyrights and trade secrets. Mr. Sarabia has negotiated contracts for all phases of the apparel business. He is intimately familiar with the vast array of legal problems which fashion companies face.

When starting your own business you will have to choose a legal structure, or business entity. Your choice will affect different aspects of your business and its operations. It is, therefore, important to understand your basic goals and financial outlook when choosing a business structure. Several basic structures are available for organizing your business:

Sole Proprietors (1 person or husband/wife)

Sole Proprietorship is not a real legal entity, as the term refers more to the person who is directly responsible and liable for the business. While all the profits belong to the owner (sole proprietor) so to do all the debts and this can put their entire estate at risk. If the sole proprietor is married, any community property can be put in jeopardy. If the **DBA** (Doing Business As) is other than the owner's full name or surname, be sure to file the fictitious business name.

- Simplest paper work
- Lower taxes than corporations or LLC
- Personal assets can be seized to pay business debt.

Partnerships (2-35 people)

General partnership and limited partnerships have some of the attributes of a separate legal structure but do not have as much protection as a Limited Liability Corporation (LLC). A partnership can hold legal title to real estate property in its own name (rather than the names of the partners). The partnership can be sued and any debts and assets are usually split, unless the partnership agreement provides otherwise. A limited liability partnership provides protection against loss of personal property. As co-owners, each general partner has equal rights to participate in management and control of the business. They are also liable for each others misapplication of moneys and debts incurred in the operation of the business. If a partner should choose to leave the partnership the other may buy-out the rights of the leaving partner.

- Paperwork only slightly more complicated than sole proprietorships
- Lower taxes than corporations or LLCs
- Partners are responsible for the actions and debts of each other, (even if they were unaware of them.)
- Personal assets can be seized to pay business debts

Corporations and Limited Liability Companies ("LLC")

Both a corporation and a LLC are separate legal entities. Each has its own identity, separate and apart from the persons who created it. As a separate entity, each has the power to act in any way permitted by the law that created it and by its own charter; e.g. to contract, to own and convey real estate, to sue and be sued. A company is responsible for its own debts and normally the directors, officers, and shareholders are not responsible for company liabilities. However, a director or shareholders may be held personally liable for company obligations if they have personally guaranteed them and under a few other limited circumstances. A company is capable of continuing indefinitely and as such is generally not affected by the death or incapacity of its directors, officers, or shareholders, or by transfer of its shares from one person to another. Having a company substantially increases the paperwork to operate a business. In addition to reducing personal liability it may offer tax benefits.

Corporation

Must treat offices as employees, which creates a significant amount of paperwork

- $600 minimum tax must be paid upon incorporation, $800 in four months, and $800 every April 15th
- Personal assets protected from business debts

Limited Liability Company

- Less paperwork than corporations
- Paperwork only slightly more complicated than sole proprietorship, but same as a partnership

- $600 less start-up costs than corporations
- $800 minimum tax every April 15th
- Personal assets protected from business debts
- Conversion can have tax consequences.

Whichever business structure you choose, your initial choice of a business form is not permanent. You can start out as a sole proprietorship or partnership and convert to a corporation later as your company grows.

Regardless of the business structure you choose, it is important to keep your business documents in a safe place. They will be required for opening bank accounts and other business matters. *(Some laws may differ from state to state so it is important to investigate your own state's requirements before going into business. There is free advice readily available to help you put your business structure together. Your local Small Business Administration office will have consultants to assist with advice and they have a website worth a visit* **www.sba.gov**). Attached to SBA is **SCORE**, the Service Corps of Retired Executives. SCORE includes more than 13,000 volunteers, who provide training and one-on-one counseling at no charge, in 389 of their offices all over the country. You can inquire about the SCORE program at **www.score.org.** If you do not have Web access, call their SBA Small Business Answer Desk at **800 U ASK SBA (827 5722)**. Also your local Chambers of Commerce will help and they have a webpage to assist with which business structure is best for you and your company **www.products.calchamber.com.**

Fictitious Name

A fictitious name is the name that you have chosen for your new company, (*if other than your own name. Choosing your own name for a company is not a good idea).* If the company should fail and close due to financial problems you will find that it will be hard to get a good credit rating due to having the same name as your folded company.

You will have to file a **Fictitious Business Name Statement**, which will be published in newspaper classifieds. It must be listed four times in the classified section of any newspaper. Using a local paper is the cheapest method, rather than using a national paper. If there are any other businesses with this same name, they can notify you. Of course this does not guarantee that there is not another company with your chosen name. A good way to investigate the use of your name before registration is to look in the phone books at the library. You can also look it up on the Internet and search to see of your fictitious name is used by another party. One company to offer this service is "**Identity Research Corporation**" at **www.idresearch.com,** or you can call them at (800) 689 6223. Forms are available at the County Clerks Office or contact your local neighborhood newspaper.

DBA "Doing Business As"

You will need your fictitious name statement in order to open a business checking account at the bank of your choice. The bank will then refer to your business name **(DBA)**, which will be connected to your name. **Example: Frances Harder, dba "Fashion for Profit".**

As stated above, it may seem logical to use your own name for your new company but it is not advisable. If for any reason the company should fail, then you are left with a bad name, which will have to be changed for your next business venture!

Licenses

Licenses are needed to comply with local laws. Each city and state has its own rules and it is best to call your local city hall and Chambers of Commerce to inquire, about the exact licenses needed in your area. There are, however, certain licenses that will be necessary no matter in which state or city you intend to set-up business.

Resale License

The first license to apply for is a Resale License, from the State Board of Equalization. There will be an office in your local town and you can call and apply over the phone. This license is required of all businesses engaged in the sale of tangible personal property. No fee is necessary, although monthly or quarterly tax returns (depending on the company size) must be filed to remit sales tax. If incorporated, a copy of your Articles of Incorporation is required. When selling directly to a customer, tax must be collected and forwarded to the state. The State Board of Equalization will want to know how much money you expect to make in the first year of business. Keep your expectations minimal, as they will be looking for resale taxes. Your suppliers will require the resale number on your license when buying from them. . No tax is paid on your wholesale purchase, but you must keep records of all purchases using the resale number. You will also require the resale numbers of the stores you sell goods to, if within the same state. For questions on state sales tax contact the **BOE – Board of Equalization at 800 400 7115 or www.boe.ca.gov.**

Business License

You will need a Business License from your local city hall in the city where your business is located. If you are working from the home, your fee will be minimal. The larger the company becomes and the more personnel, the more regulations and licenses that are required. When you describe the type of business you are operating from the home, remember to specify that it is to be used as an office or design studio, and that the manufacturing will be done elsewhere.

Garment Manufacturing License

This license is required of all apparel manufacturing businesses in California and New York State and is obtained from the Department of Labor. A registration fee of $750-$2,500 per year and proof of Workers' Compensation Insurance is required. The owner of the company must sign this application, and must take a brief test on labor laws. It is law that a manufacturer must obtain this license before they begin to manufacture. If you have not obtained this license and you are a manufacturer you will be subject to fines and confiscation of your goods. See **www.calgold.ca.gov**.

Employer Identification Number

All businesses must have an **Employer Identification Number**, *(abbreviated as an EIN)*. If you are the sole proprietor, and are the only employee, it is possible to use your own Social Security Number as your EIN. However it is strongly recommended to obtain a separate EIN, because your future activities may require one. For example, if you hire other employees, you must have an EIN. The EIN is free. To request an EIN application, contact the **IRS** by telephone, mail or fax and ask for a **SS-4 Form**.

Registration Number

As soon as you start to manufacture your own clothes, each garment will need a **R.N.# Registration Number**. The **R.N. number** is used to identify the garment's manufacturer. There is a copy of the form in the Appendix. You can use it to apply for your RN #, or you can go to their web site **www.ftc.gov** and find information on labeling requirements. If you are not yet hooked to a computer, call your nearest **U.S. Federal Trade Commission**, or **202 326 3553**; everything can be sent by mail.

As your company grows here is a list of some of the other licenses that you will have to apply for, and other issues to address, in order to comply with local regulations:

Public Health License

Obtained from the County Department of Public Health Services. All garment manufacturers require this license for employees. This license is renewed June 30 of each year with payment of an annual fee.

Insurance Issues

When doing business from the home, it is a good idea to talk to your insurance agent to inquire about special issues pertaining to a home office.

Dun & Bradstreet Number

This is not a license, but a service that is worth checking out, they check the credit of your customer for a fee. You can sign on with them and you will also get a credit rating, so that vendors can check your credit. If you are a new company it will be unlikely that you will be able to get a rating. It is however, an important institution that you must be educated about. Check out their website **www.dnb.com** for further information or call toll free **800 234 3867.**

Taxes

The IRS and the state taxing agencies produce many free publications to help you fill out your tax returns, and to answer your tax questions. All publications and forms can be ordered by telephone from the **IRS - Internal Revenue Service, 800 829 3676, www.ustreas.irs.gov**
FBT -Franchise Tax Board, 800 338 0505, or 800 852 5711, www.ftb.ca.gov

Registering a Trademark

Disclosure Agreement

Start-up companies tend to worry about having their business ideas stolen. Successful entrepreneurs, however, have mixed feelings about the importance of protecting their ideas. Do not worry about protection so much that it interferes with your test marketing and business development. But, you have to be discrete about revealing details of your business plans, or showing your line particularly to competitors. If you think your designs qualifies for legal protection, you can ask that the persons involved sign a Disclosure Agreement, which will hopefully help protect you from being knocked-off. These agreements can be found in stationary stores, or from any library and can be used **"as is",** or re-worded to suit your own needs. Never leave your designs with any company.

Example

This business plan is the property of (insert name here) and is considered strictly confidential. This business plan contains information intended for the person to whom it was given. With the receipt of this business plan, the recipient acknowledges and agrees that:

- *In the event that the recipient does not wish to pursue this opportunity, this document will be returned immediately to (insert address and phone number here)*

- *The recipient will not copy, fax, reproduce in any way, divulge, or otherwise distribute this confidential plan, in whole or in part, without the express written consent of (insert name here)*

- *All of the confidential information contained herein will be treated with the same care as afforded their own confidential material.*

Trademark

A trademark can be defined as symbol, word, phrase, or design of some kind, which is used to identify a company. We are all aware of some of the more familiar trademarks that identify a particular brand. Generally, a trademark appears on the goods themselves, or on the packaging. Federal and state trademark registrations provide much more protection for your trademark than use alone. In most countries in the world, without a registration there is no protection. To file a federal trademark application go to **www.uspto.gov**.

Protecting your business identity, or trademark by registering is not a must. The use of a mark in the marketplace is all that is required. As soon as consumers perceive a name associated with a product or service as indicating its source, that name is entitled to legal protection as a trademark. Once you have settled upon a proposed trademark it is a good idea to do a trademark search to determine whether your trademark will conflict with another mark that is already in use. As mentioned in the fictitious name section there is a service which will provide a search to see if the name or trademark you choose is already used by another manufacturer. Their Web page is **www.idresearch.com** or call **800-689-6223**. This is a great service and it will help speed up the process. In the mean time, you can use your new logo with TM symbol next to your mark, which will **"defend"** it. The fact that you are using and producing the new logo copyrights it in the same way as the written word has a copyright as soon as it is written.

Once your registration is issued you can and should use the ® seen next to almost every well-known label and brand name. Best of all, it allows you to safely invest time and money in the name and label, without worrying about losing it to another manufacturer in a costly legal battle.

Establishing Copyright

Copyright protects art, music, books, films and videos among other things. Copyright establishes the right of the author to control the use of his creation. Copyright cannot protect functional items. Common uses of copyright in the apparel business are to protect logos and prints on fabric. Copyright protection is significantly expanded by registration. It is very important to register company logos, assuming the logos have some design, as opposed to only plain letters. A copyright application is cheap. Visit **www.copyright.gov** and use form VA to protect your logo.

You can establish copyright by mailing the item you wish to copy to yourself by Certified Mail. Once you receive the certified mail, keep it unopened and tape the postal receipt to it and file it away. *(This is called a poor man's copyright.)* If the envelope is opened the copyright becomes invalid. However, it is advisable to make sure that you are not infringing on any other company's copyright or trademark. A mark will be protected only if it is not confusingly similar or identical to a mark that is already in use. If another business has prior rights to a name, it is often wise to discover this before you invest any money in promoting your product. To protect your logo, it is best to have it federally registered as your trademark, which protects your mark in all states, plus all U.S. territories. It also allows you to file a suit in Federal court, and gives you a presumption in court that the mark is yours. To obtain U.S. copyright forms, or for more information about copyright protection, contact: **Copyright Office, Library of Congress, Washington, D.C. 20559**. For more information about patents and trademarks, log on to the **U.S. Patent and Trademark Office at www.uspto.gov**.

Once your registration is issued you can and should use the ® seen next to almost every well-known label and brand name. Best of all, it allows you to safely invest time and money in the name and label, without worrying about losing it to another manufacturer in a costly legal battle.

Trade Dress

What, you may ask is Trade Dress?

Trade dress is the nonfunctional appearance of a product. It can apply to ornamental elements of clothing or even retail store decoration. It is entitled to the same protection as a trademark. However, unlike a trademark it is necessary to prove that the trade dress has become recognized by the public as associated with a particular manufacturer. The distinctive shape of the Coca-Cola bottle is a classic example of packaging trade dress.

Infringement and Fashion

While it is permissible to get ideas from any source, when one copies a trademark, trade dress or the expression of an idea which is protected by copyright (such as a fabric print), the originator or owner may sue the copier. Suits are very expensive, regardless of whether one is right or wrong.

What of the fashion business?

Most people in the Industry know the problems of copyrights for clothing designs. In the past it has been possible to copyright textile designs, but to copyright clothing has been a hard case to prove. However, there have been some interesting cases in the Federal Court of Appeals that may make knocking-off a garment more difficult than it used to be. Changing the details of the knock-off to a different look and using alternative fabric, is still within the law. But piracy, with intent to deceive consumers as to the source, is now something to be avoided.

Addition Information:

Library of Congress (202) 707 9100

Washington, DC 20559

U.S. Department of Commerce

Patent & Trademark Office

Washington, DC 20231

General Trademark or Patent Information (703) 557-INFO

Status Information for Particular Trademark Application   (703) 557-5249

General Copyright Information: (202) 479-0700

United States Trademark Association

Six E. 45th Street, New York, NY 10017

Contracts

Commission agreements with sales representatives in California and New York must be written. If they are not, you are exposed to double damages in case of a dispute. Each of these states has laws listing what must be in the commissions' agreement.

While it is not possible to explore the aspects of the many contracts you will encounter, there are some simple principals to keep in mind. First, if it is important to you - such as delivery on time - it should be clearly stated in writing and there should be some consequences for failure by the other party (such as your right to cancel or a percentage reduction). Second, as a small fish you may not always be able to get what you want, but if you do not ask to have it in writing you will never know. An effective technique is simply to write in what you want in plain language. Third, to be enforceable both sides must sign. So if you add a provision, such as a delivery deadline, get the person you are negotiating with to sign. Fourth, always make sure you have a complete copy, (don't forget the back of the form which often has important terms on it) and then make sure you file it some place you can find it months later. Fifth, if there is a problem start by looking at the written agreement to see if there is something that supports your view. If there is, you will start from a much stronger position.

Business Cards and Stationery

Business cards were first used in Europe in the 1600's and were used by tradesmen as calling cards. They are the least expensive and most used form of advertising in today's business world. Choosing a name for your new company is a challenge, and should be considered with care. As previously discussed it is not advisable to choose your own name when starting your first venture. Once the name is decided then you should design your own business card. Remember, your business card is an important marketing tool because it is often the first thing a customer sees, so do not put odd graphics on the business card, e.g. rolls of fabric, dummies or scissors. Using these types of graphics make you look like a home sewer, amateurish and unprofessional. The trick is to design a card that is distinctive and practical. Too much information is also a problem; names, telephone numbers, fax numbers, e-mail address's all on one card can add up to, too much information. Think of using a color stock paper but make sure that the paper is not too flimsy and cheap. *(Elvis had a pink card, Al Capone's said he was a used furniture dealer, William Jefferson Clinton, has only his name. Keep it simple and clear).*

Business cards will be needed for a variety of business reasons:

- **They will be required for entrance to trade shows**
- **To prove that you have a legitimate business**
- **Vendors will also require them when you wish to purchase from them.**

Cards can be designed on a computer, and the cost will be minimal. Most computers have a program that enables you to design and print your own business cards. If, however, you do not have the time or the desire to design your own cards, most large office supply stores offer business card printing for a very nominal fee. If you are told that you have a great business card then you have a winner. Stationery is not really necessary; it can be created on a computer and save printing costs. *(Company labels will be covered in Chapter 13).*

Telephone Messages

If you are running your business from home make certain that your telephone message is professional, and if possible, have a dedicated line for your company. If you are unable to financially justify a dedicated line, include in your message your company name and your full name. Do not have music or your children on the machine. It is really annoying to people trying to contact you for business reasons.

Toll-Free Numbers

If you plan to sell directly to your customers via the Internet, catalogues or other means, having a toll-free number for your business could make good marketing sense. *(See Chapters 15 & 16)*

Toll-free numbers are now much more affordable, even for the home-based business. Phone companies can add a toll-free number to your regular phone line without requiring on-site hookups. There maybe a monthly cost, plus the cost of the incoming 800 number calls.

Each incoming call is listed on your monthly statement, along with the date, and time people call, plus their phone number. It is a good idea to keep a record of all the toll-free calls you receive, as you will be billed for wrong numbers. Keeping a record of your in-coming calls will allow you to check the bill and save money at the end of the month. *(If you don't keep a record you will never know how much money you are losing!)*

Web Page

With commercial users logging in at record rates, the Web has become **"the in-place to be"** for business. The use of a web page is dependent on whether or not you intend to do business on the Internet. Having one has no disadvantages, and could help circulate your company name if it can be found in cyber space! Setting up a good web site isn't expensive so small company sites can look just as good, if not better than, larger company sites. Smaller companies can in fact move faster than their larger counterparts, because they are able to make changes without calling endless meetings or securing department approval. It is important to realize that a web page is like a storefront and should be changed regularly. Customers will return if there are new and interesting things for them to see. *(For more on selling on the Web look at Chapter 16).*

Internet Business Information

Using the Web for business information will help you with running your business. There is a lot of information available on the Internet. Electronic Commerce, the electronic exchange of business and technical information using Electronic Data Interchange (**EDI**), e-mail, and Electronic Funds Transfer (**EFT**), is a powerful tool for your business. To find out how to use e-commerce, there is a free site which is federally funded. **The Electronic Commerce Resource Center (ECRC)**. Regional ECRC offices include:

- **Georgia: www.ecrc.gatech.edu**
- **Cleveland: www.ecrc.camp.org**
- **Bremerton, Washington: www.ectag.org**
- **San Antonio: www.saecrc.org**

(See Selling on the Internet in Chapter 16).

Management Plan

Understanding all the pieces involved in running an apparel company is one thing, pulling them all together is another. Good management coordinates all business functions and makes them work. Deciding on a management style will be the first important step. Identifying who will be responsible for the overall management, or who will take control of what part of it will be essential to the success of the company. A plan will be necessary to accomplish your goals and objectives. The management plan should be written to cover a specific time period. The plan will be added to your business plan as an important indication of forethought. A plan must be reviewed regularly and be flexible enough to allow for change, yet keep the objectives clearly defined. *(Profit and planning are directly related).* Companies that plan and have a clear understanding of their goals are much more likely to succeed.

A plan is the backbone of success! Creative people tend to skip over areas of operating and managing an apparel business, as it does not interest them. If this is the case, it will be very important to find a partner who can compliment the design talents you have with the all important business skills.

Identify management duties and assign responsibilities

Decide who will be responsible for:

- **Product development**
- **Production**
- **Finance**

- **Marketing**
- **Office management**
- **Personnel**

Reporting and recording all plans will help to supply feedback to evaluate current plans and develop new plans. (*Beware of people who provide excuses and not answers*). Reports should contain facts and figures. Not knowing can lead to problems for which solutions are too little, too late. Review key areas daily and establish a regular reporting procedure. Communication is the key.

Know what you want and understand what you are getting. Recognize everyone's individual part in the success of the company. It goes without saying that problems get worse, not better when not identified. Assess your strengths honestly and improve your weaknesses. Planning the various elements of operating your business will be essential. **Management will be the key to your overall success.**

Pitfalls of Self-Employment

When you are employed by a corporation health insurance, social security and taxes are partially or fully paid by your employer. However, when you start your own business, you are responsible for paying your own social security and taxes. Remember also that if your employer provided life insurance, a prepaid legal plan, and dental and optical coverage, you will either have to go without such benefits, or purchase them yourself. Health insurance is always a problem for the self-employed. If you have had a major medical problem, you might find insurance prohibitively expensive, although things are changing for the better in the States. Self-employment can be especially attractive if you have a spouse whose job provides the security of a steady paycheck as well as medical insurance and other benefits.

Once the business is up and running, you should consider disability insurance. Most of us are more likely to become disabled than killed, which is one reason disability coverage usually costs more than life insurance.

Advantages of Self-Employment

Start-up businesses manufacturing clothing are, on the whole, cheaper to start than most other companies. Wholesale priced goods, credit, and short-term loans allow start-ups to enter the business for a relatively low cost. With technical know-how, business savvy, available funding, an entrepreneurial spirit, and lots of good luck you can make it.

In conclusion, here are some things you should try to remember when going into business for yourself:

- **Prioritize and plan. Make time for yourself. Everyone needs down time to refuel and reflect. Set limits on work time.**

- **Manage and delegate. Do what you are good at and leave the other stuff to someone that can do it better.**

- **Most successful business people love their work.**

- **Remember to make time for a smile and a good laugh! If you have stopped smiling you could be in the wrong business. Life's too short!**

CHAPTER 3

BUSINESS PLAN

"Plan: A devised scheme; a way of executing an act" (Webster Dictionary)

Reviewed by: Robin Cornwall Business Consultant at University of Southern California.

Mapping out a strategy for a successful business can be a difficult step, but it is a step that shows that the entrepreneur has done his or her homework. Hopeful entrepreneurs anxious to be their own boss, see business ownership as their road to freedom. They often fail to realize that their brilliant concept is only the first of many steps that must be taken if they are to transform their brainchild into a profitable venture. Think of it as being invited to a wonderful and exciting event that you have wanted to attend for a long time. The event is in a part of town that you are unfamiliar with, and has a reputation for being dangerous. Would you start the journey without first checking the map?

Business planning is about execution

A business plan forces you to evaluate whether your product will satisfy a need and provide a guide for exactly how you will operate your company. Most people have an idyllic notion of running their own business. Moreover, after going through the process of creating a plan, some actually decide against starting a company. This exercise saves them from wasting a lot of time and money. For other people, the planning process serves as an inspiration for an even better planned business.

What is a business plan?

A business plan defines your business, identifies your goals, and serves as your firm's résumé. Its basic components include a current balance sheet of your financial situation, an income statement, cash flow analysis, description of the product, market to be targeted, projected sales and executive summary. It helps you allocate resources properly, handle unforeseen complications, and make the right decisions. Because it provides specific and organized information about your company and how you will repay borrowed money, a good business plan is a crucial part of any loan application.

Additionally, a business plan can tell your sales personnel, suppliers and others about your operations and goals. Work on the assumption that whoever reads the outline plan will be completely unfamiliar with the business, and will seek answers to relatively basic questions. Critically appraise each draft of the outline and allow someone with experience to review the final drafts. Anticipate many hours of hard work and several drafts of the emerging plan to get the job right. A well-prepared business plan will demonstrate that the managers or entrepreneurs know the business, and have thought through its development in terms of product, management, finances, and most importantly, markets and competition.

Strategic Plan (The preparation for a Business Plan)

A short strategic plan (2-3 pages) can provide a very useful foundation on which to base a much more detailed and comprehensive business plan. If you do not have a sensible strategic plan, how can you realistically write a sensible business plan? Ask these four basic questions:

- **What is your product and your market?**
- **Where is our company today?**
- **Where do we want to be in two years time?**
- **How will we get there?**

Here are two key elements in a business plan:

Executive Summary: this gives an overview of the entire company by the executives of the company. It will include the company's current status and future plans.

The Marketing Plan: is the most important aspect of the whole plan. What is the company's game plan, and how it will market its product? How will it identify the market place? Who will buy from it and why?

Research is an essential part of the planning process. Research your market thoroughly and scrutinize your business idea. How does it fit into today's taste? Are you venturing into something that was popular five years ago and is no longer appealing? Read everything you can about your field of interest. Attend trade shows and talk to people in the industry and do not be shy about asking for tips. Pay attention to new technological developments in the apparel industry and think how they can be applied in your business.

Above all, size up your competitors. Rather than trying to beat them on their terms, identify ways to beat them on your terms.

Funding If you are looking for backers, or planning to borrow from a bank or other source, it is important to demonstrate that you have the experience and desire to make your business a success. Even if you plan to fund your venture yourself, this process helps you take a realistic look at whether you have the skills and knowledge you need to be successful.

On the following pages I set forth a business plan outline to follow. It will help you to focus on the specific kinds of questions that you need to ask yourself. Try to answer as many as possible. If you find writing the answers to the outline difficult, you could try having a friend interview you. Use a tape recorder for your answers.

How to prepare a Business Plan

Cover Page and Table of Contents

- **Include the company name**
- **Address**
- **Phone number**
- **Name of contact person for your company**

Introduction

Introduce the plan. Explain who wrote it, when and for what purpose. Give contact details.

Executive Summary

Write in a narrative fashion with no sub-headings, a brief two-page overview of your entire business plan. This section is designed to entice readers to read your entire plan, so summarize the key points in each section of your plan. It may help to write this section last when you have a clearer picture of the overview.

Mission Statement and Strategies

What are the central purposes and activities of the planned business? What are its major objectives, key strategies and prime goals?

Company Description

- What type of business entity are you?
  Sole proprietorship
  Partnership
  Corporation
- When was your business formed?
- What general business are you in?
- Who are the owners?
- What is your present situation? (pre-start-up, start-up, young, operating, or mature)

Products

- What types of product are you selling/producing?
- What are the key features that make your product different to the customer?
- Do you enjoy a proprietary advantage?
- Is it protected? (i.e., trademark, patent, copyright, licensing)
- How does your product or service compare with other competitors?
- What are manufacturing processes for the product? Will the work be contracted out? Will you need to buy any equipment to produce your product?
- Explain the quality control aspect of producing your goods.

Marketing Plan

- What are the industry trends?
- Who are your chief competitors and what are the demographics of your customer?
- Who are your target markets?
- In order to penetrate your target market, how will you coordinate product, price, promotion, distribution, and sales issues into an effective overall strategy?

The sales plan is the foundation of all businesses. Nothing happens without a sale. What methods will be used to sell your product; direct sales to the customer, sales representative, trade show, mail order, Internet etc? What type of store and client will be your target? Pricing structure and profit margin should be outlined. Your pricing policies are intended to produce the maximum amount of profitability with a quality product.

Financial Plan

- How much will it cost to start up or expand your business?
- How much financing do you need and what kind are you seeking?
- What are your projections for years one, two and three for sales, expenses, profits, cash flow, assets, liabilities, and net worth? Use charts, graphs, tables and other visual aids for this section whenever possible.

This area is difficult if you are not familiar with financial data. It is recommended that you hire an accountant to help with your financial report. Be sure that you fully understand it before you submit it to anyone.

Operating Plan

- How are you going to get the work out?
- Will you perform work in house or subcontract?

- How much equipment, labor and physical plant will you need?
- Who is responsible for quality control and how will it be maintained?

Management Plan

- Who are the key executives?
- What are their job responsibilities?
- What is their work experience and education?
- Who are your important outside advisors?

Contingency Plan

List the five risks that your company will be exposed to, and outline your plan to combat them if they materialize.

Appendix

Include any information that you believe will help explain the nature of your business and present it favorably. Include financial statements, copies of patents, newspaper articles, company brochures, etc., in this section.

If you seek outside investor financing, what will their return on the investment be? When and how do they get paid?

When you are finished

Your plan should look professional, but the lender needs to know that you did it. A business plan will be the best indicator to judge your potential for success. It should be no more than 30 to 40 pages long. Include only the supporting documents that will be of immediate interest to your potential lender.

These documents would be:

- **Personal resume** Limit to one page. Include work history along with education and special skills.

- **Personal financial statement** A statement of personal assets and liabilities. For a new business, this will be part of the financial section.

- **Credit reports** Business and personal from suppliers or wholesalers, credit bureaus and banks

- **Copies of leases** All agreements currently in force between your company and a leasing agency.

- **Letters of reference** Letters recommending you as being a reputable and reliable businessperson worthy of being considered a good risk. (Include both business and personal references).

- **Press coverage** Include any press that would be applicable to your new venture.

Be sure to number the pages of your plan. It is a good idea to use section numbering and number each page within each section. Keep all other information with your copy where it will be available on short notice. Have copies of your plan bound at your local print shop, with a blue, black or brown cover purchased from the stationery store. Make copies for yourself and each lender you wish to approach. Do not give out too many copies at once, and keep track of each copy. If your loan is refused, be sure to retrieve your business plan. Number each business plan handed out so you have a record of to whom, and where the copies went. You may want to include a disclaimer that assures you of the reader's confidentiality.

Keep in mind who will be reading your business plan. If the plan is going to be read by a loan committee it must address the purpose for the funds.

Ten Most Common Mistakes Found in a Business Plan

1. **Too Long** Reviewers of business plans look for concisely written plans in bullet form that do not read like term papers.

2. **No Competition Indicated** Too little competition may indicate that there is no market for your product.

3. **Unreasonable Expectations and Projections** Grandiose estimates regarding sales projections or money requested can be disastrous.

4. **Unreasonable Financial Assumptions** Financial assumptions do not match data in the financial statements.

5. **Unrealistic Profitability for Investors** Business does not provide a realistic exit for investors.

6. **Management Skills** Firms fail to demonstrate that they have the necessary management skills to operate the business.

7. **Unrealistic Projections of Products** Unrealistic projections that the product can be produced in a reasonable time period.

8. **Lack of Knowledge** Little business knowledge demonstrated.

9. **Inadequate Calculations** Inadequate pricing or cost ratio.

10. **Not Clear To Reader** The plan describes a product or manufacturing process with technical jargon only experts can understand.

There are many ways of putting a successful business plan together. You will have to design your own plan and tailor it to your own company's needs. One resource available to you on how to put the plan together is your local SBA (Small Business Administration). They provide this service free of charge and can be of great assistance to a start-up company. There are also many good software programs that can help you map out a good plan. Many companies require that the plan be e-mailed, so be prepared for that request.

Remember that no two businesses are alike and therefore no two business plans will be the same. Although there is some very helpful material available, both from text and from software programs, do not expect to copy your business plan. It is your vision of how the business is going to be run and it explains how your business is different from all the other businesses that already exist. It is your road map to success.

"You've got to be careful if you don't know where you're going because you might not get there."
Yogi Berra

Example of a Business Plan in Progress

The following is an example of a sample business plan that will help you understand how the above process should look when finished. This is a good start for a business plan, and it will help you to build a more in depth plan, which will be needed in order to find financial assistance.

Millinery Proposal
By Anita Hopkins

Background

Hats designed by Anita Hopkins can be found in international markets such as Paris and Madrid, as well as domestically in New York and Los Angeles. They are sold in upscale boutiques such as Shauna Stein and Maxfield. Celebrities such as Jada Pinkett-Smith and Claudia Schiffer have been seen wearing *Anita Hopkins* hats and Anita designed a one-of-a-kind hat for Tom Bradley, the now deceased, ex-mayor of Los Angeles.

Anita designs her hats using Coco Channel's original hat blocks. In doing so, she is carrying on the Channel tradition of creating hats that are elegant without being formal.

Anita's interest in hats started while she was modeling on the catwalk in Europe, working for designers such a Zandra Rhodes, Jean Muir, Jasper Conran and Christian Dior. It was then that she realized one of the biggest voids in the fashion industry was the lack of accessories, such as hats, to make individual statements and to fashionably stand out in a crowd.

Anita has now been designing hats for twelve years. She began working with straw for spring and summer fashion and moved to felt for autumn and winter. Throughout the years, she has traveled world wide in search of malleable materials and has experimented with a variety of raw goods, including paper, to create an elegant look for the modern woman. She has found the right blends of shape and color that result in a hand made, one-of-a-kind hat, wearable in all situations and conveniently portable. "My hats aren't too precious," says Anita "They are designed for convenience and the unpredictability of any situation."

Anita has designed two collections for the house of Jean-Louis Scherrer of Paris. She currently teaches the art of Millinery at Woodbury University in Burbank, California.

Company Summary

MISSION STATEMENT

To create elegant accessories, primarily hats, for the fashion conscience modern woman in the international and domestic arenas, while elevating the status of designer, Anita Hopkins, to world prominence.

OBJECTIVES

The primary objectives of the *Anita Hopkins Company* are as follows:

- Generate a minimum of *$1* million in gross sales within 3 years.
- Increase name recognition of designer Anita Hopkins and the *Company* throughout the fashion industry and the purchasing public.
- Create a sample line of fall and holiday hats for the upcoming *1999* trade shows.
- Create a line of spring hats for the year 2000 and secure the appropriate distribution outlets for this high-end product.
- Diversify the product line to include accessories such as scarves, bags, belts, and shoes. This may occur after sales have been realized or used as a strategy to enhance sales.
- Add a product line of men's hats once the *Company* is established in the women's arena.
- Create a line of women's hats and accessories to introduce to the middle market and secure the appropriate distribution outlets. This may become a subsidiary of *Anita Hopkins Company* to maintain a distinction between the high-end and middle market products.

KEYS TO SUCCESS

- Expedient advertising in the trade publications and industry related retail magazines to establish name recognition for *Anita Hopkins Company.*
- Representation at the appropriate trade shows.
- Commitments from high-end distributors with multiple outlets to carry *Anita Hopkins Company* products
- Maintenance of the up-scale status of the designs as it relates to raw material and the distribution outlets.
- Establishment of a showroom in the Los Angeles Mart. Initially this space could be rented from an existing showroom to minimize the expense.
- Economical purchase of quality raw materials.
- Efficient production of the product lines.

Products

PRODUCT LINES

The primary product will be upscale women's hats. These can be packaged as a line (fall, winter, spring or summer) for distribution through high-end department stores.
They can also be packaged as a limited edition or one-of-a-kind for specialty boutiques or specific individuals.

The company will eventually diversify by offering other accessories such as scarves, bags, belts, shoes and a line of men's hats. Fashion trends of the past indicate that men wearing hats drives up the popularity of women wearing hats, therefore developing a men's line may be used as a strategy to market the women's hats.

PRODUCT OPERATIONS

Ms Hopkins will be the sole designer of hats and accessories and she will train individual(s) of her choosing to produce the products. There will be an operations officer to assist the production staff when Anita is unavailable.
Initially, there will be 2 production periods lasting 3 months each to complete the fall and spring lines. Eventually production will become a year-round necessity.

Marketing

SEGMENTATION

The primary market segment of *Anita Hopkins* hats is the upscale outlets such as Saks Fifth Avenue, Maxfield, Neiman Marcus, Barney's of New York and Giorgio, which will generate a volume in sales as these distributors have multiple locations. *Anita Hopkins Company* will also target smaller high-end boutiques and individuals through advertising for the one-of-a-kind hat or limited edition lines.

STRATEGY

It is imperative to develop name recognition as quickly as possible. Even with commitments from the upscale outlets mentioned above, the demand for the product must come from the public, as the stores do not actively promote all the individual merchandise they sell. Name recognition can be gained through advertisements in fashion magazines and media coverage.

It is also important to contact as many upscale outlets as possible and this can be achieved through trade shows, company representatives (one each in Los Angeles, New York and Miami), a showroom and a CD-ROM modeling show which can be mailed to prospective distributors.

COMPETITION

There are other hat designers, but none that have the uniqueness and diversity of *Anita Hopkins* hats.

Operations

LOCATION AND FACILITIES

The production facility should be approximately 2,000 square feet. The area should have appropriate utilities, sufficient storage, and an efficient working section.

The administrative location of Ms. Hopkins and her assistant can be housed at the current location of *Anita Hopkins LA* in Pasadena.

The showroom for *Anita Hopkins Company* should be located in the Los Angeles Mart area. Initially space can be rented from an existing showroom to minimize cost and piggyback on their established connections.

RESPONSIBILITIES

Augustine Hyun
- Provide raw materials that are consistent with high quality merchandise.
- Complete all accounting functionality and generate the financial reports.
- Set up and maintain the production facility.
- Assist in lead generation for distribution outlets that deal in up-scale products.
- Provide an operations officer, with the approval of Ms. Hopkins, for the general operations of the *Company*.
- Finance the start-up and marketing of *Anita Hopkins Company*.

Anita Hopkins
- Design high-end women's hats packaged as a line, limited edition or one-of-a-kind.
- Design other accessories such as scarves, bags, belts and shoes.
- Design the men's hats.
- Approve all raw materials for quality.
- Approve all distributors to assure that the products are reaching the up-scale market.
- Oversee the production of all product lines
- Represent the company at trade shows with the help of an assistant.
- Approve the creation of advertising ventures and selected publications.
- Conduct the sales efforts through direct contact with the prospective distributing outlets.
- Manage any representatives sanctioned to work on a commission basis to secure distributors.
- Monitor the growth and profitability of *Anita Hopkins Company*.

NEEDS

To initiate a successful strategy, which will result in growth and profitability, the following will be needed:

Staffing
- A fulltime administrative assistance for Ms. Hopkins.
- Part-time production employee(s).
- Part-time management consulting assistance.

Marketing and Sales
- Showroom space.
- Capital for advertising, trade shows, public relations and a CD-ROM show.
- Travel expense for the sales effort.

Production
- Hat blocks, irons, presses and steamers.
- Quality raw material.
- Production facility.
- Telephones, Computer, and a Fax Machine.

Anita Hopkins
- Base Salary.
- Percent of Net Profit.
- Leased automobile.
- Health insurance.

Management

OWNERSHIP

The *Anita Hopkins Company* will be a partnership, whereby Anita Hopkins owns 51 % and Augustine Hyun owns 49%. The name *Anita Hopkins* will always be owned by Anita Hopkins one-hundred percent.

STRUCTURE AND MANAGEMENT TEAM

Anita Hopkins Company will be run by a Board of Directors. The Board will make up the management team and will include Augustine Hyun, Philip Young, Anita Hopkins, Paul McAtee and the Operations Officer.

When possible the board will meet monthly to review the progress, financial reports, and plans and to discuss strategies and make *Company* decisions.

PERSONNEL PLAN

There will be three fulltime staff: Anita Hopkins, her administrative assistant and the operations officer. On a part-time basis the *Company* will employ production staff and a management advisor.

Financial Plan

FIRST YEAR ASSUMPTIONS

Sales and Cost of Sale

Gross Sales	Assumes that 200 outlets are secured (about 5-10 companies with multiple outlets) and that 20 hats are sold to each outlet. This results in the sale of 4,000 hats, the average price per hat is assumed at $75
Direct Labor	Assumes that 10 hats can be made per day at a rate of $15 per hour.
Raw Material	Assumes winter material is $15 per hat and summer is $5 per hat. This can be reduced if the *Company* is able to buy in volume to secure lower rates.
Commission	Assumes 15% commission on half of the hats sold the first year.
Rent-Production Area	Assumes $50 per square foot for 2,000 square feet (triple net)
Production Equipment	One time expense. 100 hat blocks at $100 apiece, 2 steamers at $100 apiece, I iron at $50, and one press at $1,000.

Sales and Marketing

Salary	Anita Hopkins base salary.
Advertisement and Promotion	Estimated magazine ad campaign in noteworthy fashion magazines, 3 trade shows and a showroom (initially rented space in an existing showroom).
Travel	Includes necessary trips to New York and material purchase trips to Czech Republic, China, Ecuador and Africa.
CD-ROM Modeling Show	This will cut down much of the travel expense visiting prospective distribution outlets.
Brochures and Marketing Literature	These expenses are merely an estimate.
Direct Mailings	This is an estimate.

General & Administrative Expenses

Administrative Salaries	This is for the fulltime administrative assistant to Anita Hopkins.
Office Equipment	Includes a one-time purchase of a computer and a fax machine and on-going expense for telephones.
Insurance	Health and other potential insurance needs.
Automobile	Lease of an automobile for Anita Hopkins, plus gas and maintenance. Lease assumed at $500 per month.
Professional Services	Monthly retainer for Paul McAtee, management consultant, to formally plan and monitor progress of *Anita Hopkins Company*. Also assumes some legal contractual help.
Miscellaneous	This is an estimate.

PRO FORMA

Three Year Profit & Loss Statement

	Year 1		Year 2		Year 3	
		%of		%of		%of
	Amount	Sales	Amount	Sales	Amount	Sales
Gross Sales	$300,000	100.0	$600,000	100.0	$1,000,000	100.0
Direct Cost of Sales						
Labor	6,000	2.0	12,000	2.0	20,000	2.0
Material	40,000	13.3	72,000	12.0	110,000	11.0
Commission	22,500	7.5	90,000	15.0	150,000	15.0
Rent	12,000	4.0	12,000	2.0	12,000	1.2
Prod. Equip.	11,250	3.8	0	0.0	0	0.0
Total Direct Costs	$91,750	30.6	$186,000	31.0	$292,000	29.2
Gross Margin	$208,250	69.4	$414,000	69.0	$708,000	70.8
Operating Expenses						
Sales & Mkt'g						
Salaries	100,000	33.3	100,000	16.7	100,000	10.0
Adv/Promo	50,000	16.7	50,000	8.3	50,000	5.0
Travel	30,000	10.0	30,000	5.0	30,000	3.0
CD-ROM	5,000	1.7	1,000	0.2	1,000	0.1
Brochure/Mkt'g	5,000	1.7	2,000	0.3	1,000	0.1
Mailings	5,000	1.7	5,000	0.8	5,000	0.5
Other	5,000	1.7	1,000	0.2	1,000	0.1
Total Sales & Mkt'g	$200,000	66.7	$189,000	31.5	$188,000	18.8
General & Administrative						
Office Equipment/Telephone	5,000	1.7	3,000	0.5	3,000	0.3
Administrative Salaries	24,000	8.0	25,920	4.3	27,994	2.8
Insurance	4,600	1.5	4,600	0.8	4,600	0.5
Automobile	12,000	4.0	12,000	2.0	12,000	1.2
Professional Svcs	14,000	4.7	14,000	2.3	14,000	1.4
Miscellaneous	10,000	3.3	4,000	0.7	4,000	0.4
Total General & Admin.	$69,600	23.2	$63,520	10.6	$65,594	6.6
Total Operating Expenses	$269,600	89.9	$252,520	42.1	$253,594	25.4
Total Net Profit/Loss	($61,350)	(20.5)	$161,480	26.9	$454,406	45.4

Three Year Profit & Loss Statement

Summary

	Year 1		Year 2		Year 3	
	Amount	%of Sales	Amount	%of Sales	Amount	%of Sales
Gross Sales	$300,000	100.0	$600,000	100.0	$1,000,000	100.0
Total Direct Costs	$91,750	30.6	$186,000	31.0	$292,000	29.2
Gross Margin	$208,250	69.4	$414,000	69.0	$708,000	70.8
Operating Expenses						
Total Sales & Mkt'g	$200,000	66.7	$189,000	31.5	$188,000	18.8
Total General & Administrative	$69,600	23.2	$63,520	10.6	$65,594	6.6
Total Operating Expenses	$269,600	89.9	$252,520	42.1	$253,594	25.4
Total Net Profit/Loss	($61350)	(20.5)	$161,480	26.9	$454,406	45.4

CHAPTER 4

BOOKKEEPING FOR A SMALL BUSINESS

"Every debit must have its credit. It is essential that you should be able to see at a glance, at any given time, exactly what you owe and what is owing to you. That is the object of properly kept books." Penelope Fitzgerald "The book shop"

Reviewed by Dick Littman financial specialist

Importance of good booking skills

By becoming an entrepreneur, you have chosen to be a business owner, which means you will be your own boss. To achieve your dream by doing something you love, and to make enough money to live comfortably means you have to understand something about finance! You must pay attention to the business of doing business. In other words, you must understand where the "out-going money" is going to, and where the "incoming money" is coming from. However, to many hopeful business owners this is a major pitfall on the way to success. This chapter will explain some simple bookkeeping skills (accounting) to monitor your cash flow, both for running the business efficiently, and to prepare you for the dreaded end of the year tax forms.

To a creative person, bookkeeping is a boring prospect. It would be ideal to have a partner who is able to take care of this particular part of running the business. However, if this tedious job of bookkeeping falls on your shoulders, there are several basic rules you can follow. When you can afford to, hire help! Keep this in mind; bookkeeping is similar in principal to balancing your checkbook, but a little more paperwork and additional detail! Once you have set-up a business account at a bank and have business checks ready to write you must start to put into place your bookkeeping systems. You are not expected to be an accounting wizard, but you need to be comfortable with certain financial terminology. When in doubt, engage a reputable accountant, or a bookkeeping service.

The first important step in setting up your accounting or bookkeeping system is to sit down and project your yearly budget. How much will you need to run and operate your new company? (See cash flow chart) More importantly, this will determine how much money you need available to put into your business. Knowing how much money is available before the orders are written will be a very important planning strategy.   Once the orders are written and you have a problem finding the funding for production, you will have lost your first customers! Remember it is common to take at least two years of hard work before you will see any financial returns. *(See Chapter 3 Business Plan).*

Questions that need to be answered

- *Can you afford to work for very little for two years?*

- *What are your basic set-up costs for a small apparel business?*

- *Are you going to apply for a loan to finance your new venture, borrow from family or friends, or do a combination of both?*

Costs that will have to be thought about in advance:

- Licenses (both local business and state licenses)

- Incorporation of your business or other partnership agreements (legal fees)

- Product development costs; fabric, patterns, samples etc.

- Business cards and stationery

- Trade shows

- Production costs, fabric, grading, cutting, sewing etc.

- Sales Representative, commission (plus possible rent for show rooms)

- Studio or office space

It is most important to remember that you have a lot of money going out before there is any coming back to you. A new line is being developed while you are in production on your previous line. Retailers will not be paying for the goods for 30-60 days after you have shipped. So, from the time the order is written, to the time you receive payment could be up to 90 days. You will need a plan before you begin production.

Computer Use

Although you can start a business without a computer, it is hard to imagine anyone operating for long without one. More than any other single tool, a computer will help you keep accurate records, increase your productivity and stay competitive. A computer should be one of your first important investments. There are good bookkeeping software programs available once you have invested in a computer. These programs are user-friendly and make bookkeeping more of a clerical task. When doing the books without the help of a computer, you have to be certain you are saving money, and not doing more harm than good. It could end up costing you more money than you had hoped to save. Some software packages on the market are:

- **Quick Books**
- **Quicken**
- **Turbo Tax (primarily tax oriented)**
- **Dac Easy**
- **M.Y.O.B**

They make the basics of keeping the books a much easier process. There are however, some very good outside bookkeeping services that can help you perform this part of the business for a small weekly or monthly fee. Ask your local Better Business Bureau for advice on good accounting services in your area.

Important! You should never give up control of your finances. If you find a good accounting service, make certain that they do not have the power to sign your checks. Have the bank statements sent to your own home and verify all checks written.

Who are the checks made out to? Make sure that they have been written to a real person, and not a family member or a friend of the accountant for some service, which was never performed. Like all professions, there are some disreputable services that can bring about the downfall of your business unless you are careful in reviewing all bank checks. Take precautions in dealing with any accounting service.

Financial Statements

The three basic financial statements that you will need to understand and be able to produce are:

- **Balance Sheet** Shows how much you own and how much you owe at any particular time. This is usually calculated on the last day of the year or month, if necessary.
- **The Income Statement** Shows how much money is brought in and spent during a specific accounting period. This is also usually done yearly or monthly, if necessary.
- **Cash Flow Analysis** Shows exactly how much cash you received in revenue and how much cash you spend on a monthly basis.

Cash Flow

The cash flow statement should be watched carefully, it shows how much money you have in the bank account to pay the bills. When running your business, remember that cash in the bank is the only true indication of your cash balance. Too many businesses have run out of cash before all the bills have been paid. Cash flow control begins with the cash flow budget. If you don't have a cash flow budget, you will have cash flow problems. You will also need a sales budget, or its equivalent, to monitor the sales level and where it should be. Small sales lags can add up to big problems, ranging from a sluggish sales representative, to a less interesting line of clothing for the season. Pinpoint the problem as soon as possible, and try to correct it. To have a very successful season, your sales should greatly exceed previous seasons. A word of caution, this could be too large for your budget or resources, and could mean trouble.

There is a variety of ways to set up a businesses bookkeeping system, and if you are unfamiliar with how to keep the books and records, the simpler the method the better.

Using the Cash method The cash method of accounting is simple enough. When the garments are complete and shipped, you bill the customer. In this industry you normally have to wait for 30 days or longer to receive payment, unless you can get CODs. To keep track of who owes what, just create a sales file of all the invoices sent out. As the invoices are paid, you take their invoice copies out of the file and stamp "**paid**". These should then be maintained by a "**paid invoice**" file system. If you have to wait for a late payment, then you can call the customer and inquire about it. It is important to stay on top of the incoming money, as you will need every payment to be paid on time.

Cash Flow Budget Your cash flow budget is a tool for keeping overhead costs down. You have a degree of control over costs that you don't have over sales, while you can almost always cut costs, you cannot generate sales whenever you need them. If that were possible, you would never have a cash flow problem. Tightening controls on the cash flow means always asking whether this or that purchase or expenditure will have a positive effect on your business. If there is no clear answer, examine the expenditure closely.

Elements of Cash Flow

- **Starting Cash** (or Starting Balance) Each monthly projection begins with the amount of cash you have on hand at the start of the month. Your starting cash is the same number as the previous month's ending cash.

- **Cash Received** This section of the statement is also called "Sources of Cash." It includes all cash received during the month. There are several possible sources:

- **Sales** are a primary source of cash, but remember to include only cash sales. Sales that have been invoiced do not represent money you can spend this month (it takes approximately 30 days for payment). So list only the cash sales you expect to have.

- **Paid Receivables** are those sales that were previously invoiced and have been paid this month. It is important to project accurately when you expect to be paid, 30 days, 60 days, etc. If a sale, made in January, is actually going to be collected in March, you want your projections to be realistic and to reflect that time lag.

- **Interest** is paid on any money you should be fortunate enough to have in the bank.

- **Other Sources** of cash might be a bank loan, sales of stock, or other loans or sale of an asset such as a company car.

- **Cash Out** This section is also referred to as "uses of cash." Cash leaves the business in two basic ways: fixed expenses and variable expenses.

- **Fixed expenses** Are incurred regularly, and are not easily controlled. Generally, they do not fluctuate with sales volume. They are "fixed" from month to month: rent and payroll, taxes, estimated taxes, utilities, interest on loans, and insurance payments.

- **Variable expenses** Change from month to month and often vary with sales volume or production volume. They are more flexible than fixed expenses. Some examples: cost of labor, supplies, commissions, advertising, raw materials, consulting services and promotion.

- **Ending Cash** (Ending Balance) is how much cash is left at the end of the month. It is a balance of the numbers in Cash In, and Cash Out. Simply add the Starting Cash to Total Cash In, and then subtract Total Cash Out. The cash you end the month with, is the cash you have to start with the next month. The number for Starting Cash is the previous month's Ending Cash.

- **Cash Flow** The amount of cash that has flowed through the business (see example of Flow chart). It is a measure of what has happened that month. If nothing has happened for the month it would look as follows: Starting Cash was $1,000 and nothing went out as payment and nothing came in as payment, so your cash flow would

be $0. To calculate Cash Flow, subtract the Ending Cash from the Starting Cash. *(The secret to success is positive cash flow. See Chart, page 67).*

This is the simple day-to-day business of bookkeeping and necessary in running a successful business. Once you have understood these principles it is important to project your sales, and to understand how an order will impact the Cash Flow on a larger scale.

Example If on your first line you receive a large order of $50,000, you will think that you have made it to the big time until you run the numbers. To manufacture an order of this size you must have around $25,000 in cash available. That may seem fine if you have an abundance of ready cash or you are prepared to borrow against your house. The big problem occurs when you have to begin the next line, and need more money before you have been paid for the first production line. This problem with ready cash compounds itself, the further you get into production. *(See graph of sales growth and money crunch problem)* Many companies have gone bust because they have been successful, but too greedy! This may seem odd, but it is a fact worth remembering: You must plan and budget ahead of time.

Cash Crunch Timing the payment of bills will be an important procedure. As the money comes in, are you able to pay the bills? This may seem simple enough, but think again. If you have 30 days in which to pay the vendors for fabrics and trims and the merchandise will be shipped in another 30 days, then if you're lucky the retailer will possibly pay you in another 30 days, **cash crunch!** This will leave you without money for 60 days or so, and you still have to pay the contractor. You need some money coming in before it goes out.

Remember that a new company will be unlikely to obtain ready cash on an unproved business unless you take a loan out on your house. You need collateral to borrow money. Rapid growth and large orders can put you out of business. Slow and steady wins the race.

Short-Term Loan

Assuming that you have done all you can do to control your cash flow, you will still face occasional periods of cash shortfalls. To tide you over these periods, you have to borrow from an outside source; e.g. a commercial bank or a credit card company's line of credit. *How do you go about preparing a financing proposal?* Begin by focusing on your receivables and inventory. Chances are they are your largest current assets against which you might borrow. *(More on Loans and Factors in Chapter 12)*

To manage your working capital properly, you must know:

- The age of your receivables and inventory

- The turn of your inventory and receivables, how long it takes to sell your inventory and how long it takes to convert a sale to cash

- The concentration of your receivables (how many customers comprise the majority of your receivables, what amount of receivables they represent, what category

these receivables represent i.e. prime, good or other).

Using a Credit Card

Try to pay for some things with credit cards, which delays payment for 30 days. This is just like obtaining a line of credit from the bank, in other words, a loan! Remember not to delay repaying the credit card beyond the grace period or you will have to pay interest. In case you do, make sure that the credit cards you hold have the lowest interest rate possible. There are all kinds of credit card deals out there that you should inquire about; some are better than the bank for a short-term loan. Word of caution; credit card use can be very risky. If your business should fail, you are personally responsible for the repayment of the credit and not your business. Even if you have a LLC or have incorporated your company, the repayment of a credit card is a personal responsibility. Unpaid credit cards could impact your business along with your own personal credit and your personal assets or personal collateral.

Trade Credit

It is important for a start-up to try to establish trade credit from your suppliers. For your first line they will all require you to pay for the goods as you receive them, COD. However, on your next line ask for a grace period of 30 days, and settle for 15 days. Every bit of time allowed you before you have to pay will help in the cash flow crunch. .

Management of Receivables

Four Steps to Managing Receivables

1. **Age your receivables.**

2. **Identify slow-paying customers.**

3. **Identify fast-paying accounts and try to increase their number of sales.**

4. **Calculate your collection period and apply the 40-day/30 day rule of thumb to see if you have a problem.**

To control your receivables, check each week for the slow paying accounts. Then try and collect before the accounts eat into your profits. Aging receivables are simple: Separate invoices into, Cash-on delivery (COD), and 30-day credit sales. Then calculate your collection period; divide annual credit sales by 365 to find the average daily credit sale. Next, divide your current outstanding receivables total by the average daily credit sales. This yields your collection period. A good rule of thumb for your receivables management; if your collection period is more than one third greater than your credit terms (for example, 40 days if your terms are net 30), you have a problem.

Example

- **Annual credit sales**......................................**$270,000**
- **Average outstanding balance**......................**$35,000**
- **Credit term**...**30 days**

Calculate

- **Average daily credit sales:**   **$270,000 ÷ 365 days**   **= $740. per day**
- **Average length of collections:**   **$35,000 ÷ $740**   **= 47.3 days**

Note: Your problem is that the actual credit term exceeds the 30 days by 17.3 days. This float is an interest free loan, which most small businesses cannot afford!

Slow Paying Customers

All too often small-business owners mistake sales for profits. They extend more and more credit, pursue lax collection policies, and end up financing their customers to increase their sales. Most businesses cannot afford to provide interest free loans to customers that do not pay on time. Slow-paying customers must be subjected to profitability analysis, which takes in their carrying costs. Sales increases should translate into profit. It is difficult to increase profits when you are carrying *"receivables"* from customers who habitually stretch their payments. Staying on top of this problem will save you time and money. Follow-up on lagging accounts with a phone call and make sure to document the conversation on a standard form (see sample form). The completed slip will provide back-up information and should be filed for reference on further calls. **Ask for specific payments on specific dates.** If payment is not received, call back and ask again.

Divide your customer list into three groups**: Prime, Good, and Other**. **Prime** customers always pay within term; **Good** usually do; **Others** seldom do. Look for similarities within the groups. What kinds of customers are Prime or Good? How do they differ from "Others"? Try to think of ways to upgrade as many customers as possible to Prime or Good. (*Remember, you don't have a sale until you are paid*).

Keep a visual account of the incoming monies and the out going payments, on a calendar. It will help you see the big picture and allow you to plan your finances. The first two or three years need very careful consideration and planning. As the company grows and funds are freed up, you will be able to pay yourself. But for the first year of your business, paying an employee will be more important than paying yourself. (*You have to be sure there is enough money to pay all the bills before you can get paid*).

Managing Inventory

Inventory management, like receivables management, is often overlooked as a source of operating profits. Careful attention to how you manage these two areas can often free up cash, and improve operating profits without resorting to bank borrowing. If you are managing both of these areas well, congratulate yourself as you are in a distinct minority.

Carrying costs of inventory can run high and can be a substantial drain on working capital. Consider the costs of storage, spoilage, pilferage, inventory loans, and insurance. They all add up faster than you realize. Inventory control is a balancing act and determining the right level of inventory to carry can be difficult. On one hand you want to avoid unnecessary expenses, while on the other you want to avoid carrying too much stock. If your inventory gets too high, you can run out of cash. If it is too low, chances are you are buying in uneconomical quantities, a danger sign to bankers. Meaning, you are too under capitalized to ever become profitable which is another danger sign, or your business is being bled. Bankers are increasingly interested in the quality of inventory as well as the more standard indications of good management, liquidity, profitability, and a good track record.

Contingency Plan

Having a contingency plan in place should there be a money crunch, or a bad selling season, is a good idea. You are then prepared for the worst. It does not have to be lengthy; one page would be fine. The contingency plan should provide answers to these questions:

- **What suppliers would give you extended terms or carry you in case of a crunch?**
- **Why would they carry you and for how much, and for how long?**
- **Would you refinance personal assets to provide a cash cushion for your business, and could you? Do you have any other cash assets that could be used?**
- **Does your company have any other assets that could be used to turn into cash if necessary, lease back or sale?**
- **How will you keep your banker and major trade creditors on your side?**
- **Would it be possible to speed up orders if it would help?**

The purpose of a contingency plan is to make sure, before a crisis is at hand, that you do not panic. This form of planning is evidence of thoughtful business management, which more and more creditors are seeking from apparel manufacturers.

Business Terms and Definitions

Account: A formal record of a transaction with a customer or vendor.

Accounts Payable: Amounts owed to vendor, *(usually paid within 30 days)*.

Accounts Receivable: Amounts due to the company from customers, *(usually paid within 30 days)*.

Asset: Any owned physical objects or intangible with probable economic value to their owner (Furniture, equipment, cars, trademarks, patents, bank accounts etc.).

Balance Sheet: A financial statement that shows a company's assets and liabilities. It also reflects your business "*net worth*" at a point in time.

Break Even Point: The anticipated amount of sales revenue necessary to equal the fixed and variable expenses of the business. Amounts in excess will be profit.

Budget: A forecast of revenues and expenditures for a specific period of business activity.

Cash Flow: Usually refers to net cash provided by operating activities; any cash from investment earnings, i.e. interest, should also be included.

Cash Flow Statement: A report on cash receipts and cash payments for a particular period.

Chart of Accounts: A list of accounts in the general ledger, which lists all the possible categories of transactions and organizes them to make producing financial statements easier. Accounts that summarize the assets and liabilities of the company will be grouped together to form the balance sheet. Accounts that summarize the sales and expenses of the company will be grouped together to form the income statement.

Collection: Money owed that must be collected, usually performed by a third party whose business it is to collect outstanding debts.

Collection Agencies: A company who collects money on outstanding invoices. The fee is usually one third of the outstanding bill. Additional legal bills can also be involved in the collection of outstanding money.

EDI: Electronic Data Interchange; shared information network between suppliers, manufacturers and retailers.

General Ledger: A record containing the group of accounts that supports the amount shown in the financial statements.

Gross Profit: The difference between sales revenue and cost of goods sold.

Net Profit: This is the gross profit minus expenses, including taxes

Income Statement: A report of all revenues and expenses pertaining to a specific period.

Inventory Turnover: The number of times during an accounting period that a business sells the value of its inventory. Turnover is calculated by dividing the cost of goods sold, by the average inventory during the period. Average inventory is figured by adding beginning and ending inventory, then dividing by two.

Invoice: A bill, which will include all the details of a sale. The quantity of goods sold, sizes, cost, and method of shipment. The invoice should be shipped with the goods and a second copy sent by mail to the customer.

Line Of Credit (LOC): An agreement by which a financial institution (usually a bank) holds funds available for a business's use, ordinarily renewed annually.

P.O. (Purchase orders): provides a record of all purchases made. Each purchase order has a number, that number will be used to refer to that particular order. A purchase order is the source of such important control information as:

- Date of order
- Classification of merchandise ordered
- Vendor's name and address
- Cost

Profit: The amount over the basic cost of producing and marketing an item.

Accrual Basis of Accounting

As clothing manufacturers accumulate an inventory, the IRS requires the accrual basis of accounting be used. The accrual method recognizes sales and expenses when they are incurred, rather than when they are paid.   This also entails the setting up of an inventory account. *(The accrual basis also matches expenses incurred to sales generated in the period in which the income is reported).*   This may seem confusing to you, as it is a more complicated and a more costly method of accounting.   So, for the first year since you will have little or no inventory it would be fine to use the cash basis method of accounting, or use one of the many software programs available.   After the first year, hopefully you will be able to afford help with this part of running a business, or take some accounting classes.   You must project your spending and your gross profits.   In short, **budget, budget, budget!**

Taxes

Taxes are another hurdle for the self-employed.   When you work for a company, you and your employer each contribute 7.65% of your paycheck *(up to a ceiling of $76,200 for the current year)* for Social Security and Medicare.   But when you are self-employed, you will pay both portions.   Currently, 12.4% of the first $76,200 you earn goes for Social Security and an additional 2.9% on all wages *(no limit)* to Medicare.   Although some of this is tax deductible, it still takes an enormous bite out of self-employment income and is the bane of many budding entrepreneurs.   Do not think you can postpone the pain until April 15.   The government wants its cut four times a year.   If you are self-employed, get used to paying quarterly estimated taxes not just to Uncle Sam, but to your state as well.

Deductions

Self-employed people gain access to deductions usually unavailable to employees.   Your home office, business telephone, office supplies, business meals, and trips to the post office to buy tax-deductible stamps all generate tax savings.   Your health insurance premiums are also partly tax deductible. The key to these tax savings is good record-keeping.   Here are some of the important records you will be required to show when applying for these tax deductions:

- **Income (wages, alimony, etc.)**
- **Charitable contributions**
- **Taxes and interest**
- **Child care**
- **Home improvements, sales and refinances**
- **Inherited property**
- **Un-reimbursed business expenses (office supplies, postage, meals, travel, etc.)**
- **Investment purchases**
- **IRA contributions**

Track every possible expense for tax purposes, even nickels and dimes.   **The small things add up!**

It is generally recommended that you should keep all tax records for seven years after filing date. Record keeping may not be the most enjoyable task, but organized tax records will make it easier for you to prepare your tax returns and provide the necessary documentation if you are audited.

Laws for home based business

In recent years the computer has made it possible to conduct business using a relatively small office space. Entrepreneurs are now running very successful businesses from their own homes. In the last year the IRS has redefined the allowable deductions to those who use their home as an office. The home office need not be a whole room or even marked off by a permanent partition. It needs only to be an identifiable, dedicated space. Under the old rule the space must be used for business exclusively. If you worked off a dining table, you could not serve dinner on it!

Deduction amount Home office workers can deduct part of the expenses of the entire house or apartment, e.g. rent or depreciation, utilities, housekeeping costs, home insurance and general repairs. To compute the deductions; comparing the business area to the area of the whole house or apartment. Consider either the number of rooms or square footage, e.g. if you have seven rooms in your home and you use one room exclusively for business, then the deduction is one-seventh of the allowable household expenses. (*Make certain to back up home office deductions with records*).

Taxpayer ID number

Contact the Internal Revenue Service to obtain a Taxpayer Identification Number. You will also need to figure out how best to report earnings and pay your business taxes. The IRS is a large bureaucracy and may seem like a complicated maze. However, there are numerous publications, councilors and workshops available to help you sort out your tax situation. **Call 800 829 1040** or visit any office of the **U.S. Internal Revenue Service** for more information.

Insurance Coverage

Many small business owners fail to realize just how quickly they could go out of business if other risks, such as fire, natural disaster, theft, vandalism or even their own disability, prevented the enterprise from operating for a period of time. It is therefore important to consider the risks to your company and talk to an insurance broker about the best type of insurance for you and your company. Here are some types of insurance that you should consider buying, either within a single "business owner's policy" or as individual coverage items added to basic property/casualty:

- **Comprehensive property/casualty and liability** The property/casualty is given, but the key is making sure the policy provides for full replacement, not just "cash value" coverage. It is also important to maintain sufficient *"liability"* coverage. This would be for 3ʳᵈ party damages and injuries.

- **Business Interruption coverage**   Small business owners often overlook this one, because they don't expect anything short of a large-scale disaster will force them to cease operations. This coverage, also called "business income" or "business overhead" insurance, covers such items as net profits, cost of renting temporary space if necessary, taxes, employee payroll and other operating expenses.

- **Records coverage**   This is not a big item for a small business but if complete accounting is housed in a single computer system that fails, the cost of reconstructing lost data can be significant.

- **Auto insurance**   Make sure that whoever uses your car for business purposes is covered on your insurance policy.

- **Worker's compensation**   This will apply as soon as you employ one employee. It is a good idea to use a payroll-processing firm to avoid any liability for faulty tax reporting, to keep up with the ever-changing state and federal payroll issues.

- **Health and disability coverage**   It is critical to have both good health insurance and disability coverage. Also, have a plan of action for running the business if you are temporarily indisposed.

- **Retirement accounts:** One of the biggest financial advantages of self-employment is the ability to save more of your pretax earnings in retirement accounts, where money will grow sheltered from income taxes. Consider putting money away in an IRA, 401(k) or other retirement plan as early as possible.

Choosing the Right Financial Advisor

Because self-employed people face more complicated taxes, you will need to start looking for a capable accountant (CPA) before tax time. If your business takes off and begins to prosper your accountant might suggest incorporating your company. Incorporating permits even more aggressive retirement savings and also provides some insulation from lawsuits. Besides, no one can deny that putting Inc, after the name of your business looks more professional. *(See Business Plan chapter)*

The trick is finding someone who will advise you wisely and be sensitive to your financial needs and personality. Begin by asking professional colleagues who have similar needs. Identify a handful of CPA's and call them with a few preliminary questions to get a feel for their personalities and experience. Ask for references, check their credentials, and call the Better Business Bureau for references or referrals. Always spend the time to check them out. They may seem nice and trustworthy on the outside, but so do most scam artists! Just because they have a license to be a CPA does not mean they are right for you and will have your best interest at heart. This is of course true with any services or agents that you should choose to do business with.

Accountants in the Apparel Industry

By Joel Stonefield CPA
Founding Partner, Stonefield and Josephson, LA

Who are they and how do they do it?

These are people holding the professional designation **Certified Public Accountant (CPA)**, upon passing a tough academic exam. They are universally known in our society for their integrity and intelligence. (This is true, usually.) Stereotypically, they are known as bloodless and humorless. (This is false, usually.)

CPAs serving the apparel industry are the financial experts who provide their clients with the necessary guidance to survive the many perils present in their industry. Each of them has general expertise in financial statement preparation and in tax practice. Beyond that they have acquired specific knowledge in many aspects of the industry of their clients, giving them insight into the mechanics of apparel manufacture and the ability to give advice for improving their client's business.

Just as importantly, they know the people who serve the financial sector of the apparel industry. And they are known by their counterparts in these other professions – banking, factoring, credit granting, law. The point is if people who lend money trust you; you can maximize money flow.

What do they do <u>inside </u>your business?

In a few words, your CPA <u>does or oversees everything financial</u> in your business. Examples:

1) The proper financial structure for your business
2) Your books and your accounting staff – when you have one
3) Taxes. Income, payroll, etc. Planning and compliance.
4) Computers and software used in the office
5) Costing merchandise manufactured
6) Merchandise purchasing budgets
7) Inventory control
8) Operating budgets
9) Financial statements

What do they do <u>outside</u> of your business?

In fewer words, the Apparel Industry CPA <u>gets you money</u>. Here's how:

1) With the items prepared in 6) and 7) above, your CPA can explain to your factor, your bank, and to your credit grantors the progress and financial condition of the company, giving to it all the aura of credibility that he/she (the CPA) has worked so hard to create.

2) By legally minimizing your taxes on your returns and defending them upon audit, the CPA makes money available for your business, which in less expert hands might be wasted on unnecessary taxes.

What do they cost?

Your prospective accountant may be persuaded to accept a low fixed monthly fee from a client whose business is in its infancy.

Remember, CPAs cannot ethically accept an interest in your business.

How do I find one?

Your bank, factor, lawyer, or business incubator will be pleased to refer a CPA to you..

A last reminder…

Always use a CPA who has experience in the apparel industry and who has achieved acceptance by the various lenders.

Leasing or Buying Equipment

Small businesses have difficulty raising capital, so leasing equipment maybe the logical alternative to buying the required equipment. All types of equipment leasing options have become more and more attractive, from motor vehicles to computers.

What is a Lease?

A lease is a long-term agreement to rent equipment, land, buildings or any other asset. In return for most, (but not all) the user (lessor) makes periodic payments to the owner of the asset (lessor). The lease payment covers the original cost of the equipment and provides the lessor with a profit.

Types of Leases

There are three major kinds of leases:

- **The financial lease,**
- **The operating lease**
- **The sale and lease back**

Financial Lease This type of lease is the most commonly used. A financial lease is usually written for a term to exceed the economic life of the equipment. You will find that a financial lease usually provides the following:

- **Periodic payment is made.**
- **Ownership of the equipment reverts to the lessor at the end of the lease term.**
- **The lease is non-cancelable and the lessee has a legal obligation to continue payments to the end of the term.**
- **The lessee agrees to maintain the equipment.**

Operating lease Sometimes referred to as a "maintenance lease," can usually be canceled under conditions spelled out in the lease agreement. Maintenance of the asset is usually the responsibility of the owner (lessor). Computer equipment is often leased under this kind of lease.

Sale and leaseback This type of lease is similar to the financial lease. The owner of an asset sells it to another party and simultaneously leases it back to use it for a specified term. This arrangement frees the money tied up in an asset for use elsewhere. Buildings are often leased this way.

Net lease or gross leases Under a net lease agreement the lessee is responsible for expenses such for maintenance, taxes, and insurance. Under a gross lease the lessor pays these expenses. Financial leases are usually net leases.

Full payout lease Under a full payout lease the lessor recovers the original cost of the asset during the term of the lease.

Kinds of Lessors

As the use of leasing has increased as a method for businesses to acquire equipment and other assets, the number of companies in the leasing business has increased dramatically. Leasing is now Big business! Commercial banks, insurance companies, and finance companies do most of the leasing. Many of these organizations have formed subsidiaries primarily concerned with equipment leasing. These subsidiaries are usually capable of making lease arrangements for almost anything. In addition to financial organizations, there are companies, which specialize in leasing. Some are engaged in general leasing, while others specialize in particular equipment, such as trucks or computers.

Advantages of leasing

- The obvious advantage to leasing is acquiring the use of an asset without making a large initial cash outlay. Compared with a loan arrangement to purchase the same equipment, a lease usually:
- Requires no down payment, while a loan often requires 25% down.
- Requires no restriction on a company's financial operations, while loans often do.

- Spreads payments over a longer period, which means they will be lower than loans permit.

- Provides protection against the risk of equipment obsolescence, since the lessee can return the equipment at the end of the lease.

- There may also be tax benefits in leasing. Lease payments are deductible as operating expenses if the arrangement is a true lease (and the Internal Revenue Service *agrees* it is). Ownership, however, usually has greater tax advantages through the investment tax credit and depreciation. Naturally, you need to have enough income and resulting tax liability to take advantage of those two benefits.

- Leasing has a further advantage that the leasing firm has acquired considerable knowledge about the kinds of equipment that it leases. Thus, it can provide expert technical advice based on experience with the leased equipment.

- Finally, there is one more advantage to leasing that hopefully you will not be need. In the event of bankruptcy, claims of the lessor to the assets of the firm are more restricted than general creditors.

Disadvantages of Leasing

- Leasing usually costs more because you lose certain tax advantages that go with ownership of an asset. Leasing may not, however, cost more if you could not take advantage of those benefits because you do not have enough tax liability for them to come into play.

- Obviously, you also lose the economic value of the asset at the end of the lease term, since you do not own the asset. Lessees have been known to grossly underestimate the salvage value of an asset. If they had known this value from the outset, they might have decided to buy instead of lease.

- Further, you must never forget that a lease is a long-term obligation. **Usually you cannot cancel a lease agreement.** So, if you were to end an operation that used leased equipment, you might find you would still have to pay as much as if you had used the equipment for the full term of the lease.

Federal Taxes and Leasing

Full lease payments are deductible as operating costs. You can make these deductions only if the Internal Revenue Service finds that you have a true lease. You cannot take a full deduction for a "lease" that is really an installment purchase.

- Although each lease arrangement may be different, there are some general guidelines to meet:
- In no way should any portion of the payment be construed as interest.
- Lease payments must not be large compared with those that would be required to achieve ownership.
- Any renewal option at lease end must be on terms equivalent to what a third party would offer.
- Purchase options must be at amounts comparable with fair market value.

Financial Considerations of Leasing

Accounting Treatment of Leases: The Financial Accounting Standards Board requires that capital leases be recorded on the balance sheet as both asset and liabilities.

Cost Analysis of Lease v. Loan/Purchase: You can analyze the cost of the lease versus purchase problem through "discount cash flow analysis". This analysis compares the cost of each alternative by considering:

- The timing of the payments
- Tax benefits
- The interest rate on the loan
- The lease rate
- Other financial arrangements

To make the analysis, you must first make certain assumptions about the economic life of the equipment, salvage value, and depreciation. If you are in doubt about leasing versus buying, spend the time to talk to your accountant, or to some other professional in the area of financial services before you become tied to a leasing agreement. It could end up costing you more that it would to buy the equipment if you're not careful.

Leasing Property

Before you sign a real estate lease, have an expert check it out and explain the small print to you. You want to know the penalties of canceling a lease and if you can sub-let the property. You may seem sure that the business is doing well when the lease is signed, but with the clothing business it can change with each season. You could find that the cash flow has stopped by the same time next year!

Look Before You Lease

A lease agreement is a legal document. It carries a long-term obligation. You must be thoroughly informed of just what you are committing yourself to. Find out the lessor's financial condition and reputation. Be reasonably sure that the lease arrangements are the best you can get, that the equipment is what you need, and that the terms are what you want. Remember, once the agreement is struck, it is just about impossible to change it.

Read the lease document, it should spell out the precise provisions of the agreement. Agreements may differ, but the major items will include:

- The specific nature of the financing agreement
- Payment amount
- Term of agreement
- Disposition of the asset at the end of the term

- Schedule of the value of the equipment for insurance and settlement purposes in case of damage or destruction
- Who gets the investment tax credit
- Who is responsible for maintenance and taxes
- Renewal options
- Cancellation penalties
- Special provision

Cash Analysis Example

	Sample	MONTH 1	MONTH 2	MONTH 3	MONTH 4	MONTH 5	MONTH 6
STARTING CASH	$2,500						
CASH IN							
Cash Sales	$1,000						
Paid Receivables	$0						
Other	$0						
TOTAL CASH IN	$1,000						
CASH OUT							
Rent	$700						
Payroll	$1,000						
Other	$300						
TOTAL CASH OUT	$2,000						
ENDING BALANCE	$1,500						
CHANGE							
(Cash Flow)	$1,000						

A Simplified Cost Sheet to Be Used for First Year Cash Flow

(Emphasis is on Cash Flow)

Example:

Retail Price .... $ 40.00 / Garment

Wholesale Price .... $ 20.00

Store Discount (8%)...................... $ 1.60

(For Pmt within 30 days)

Sales Commission .... $ 2.21

(12% after store discount)

Cost Fabric, Manufacturing.......... $ 10.00

+ Overhead

Gross Profit.................................... $ 6.19 / Garment

(For more explanation of costing, turn to Chapter 12, 'Product Costing'.)

Example – First Year Cash Flow

Month	Line 1 Activities	Line 1 Financial	Line 2 Activities	Line 2 Financial	Cash Flow Cumulative
Jan	Designing (10 Garments) Patterns Samples				
Feb	Advertising				
Mar	Finished all samples Selling				
Apr	Receive orders for Aug. Delivery 5 garments 400 each = 2000 pieces		Start Line 2 Designing (10 Garments) Patterns		
May					
Jun	Manufacturing	−20,000 (2000 x 10)	Finished all samples Selling		−20,000
Jul			Receive orders for Nov. Delivery 2000 pieces		
Aug	Delivery to Store				*Start Line 3
Sep	Payment (30 days after delivery) store discount + commission	+40,000 (2000 X 20) −7,620 Balance+12,380	Manufacturing	−20,000	+20,000 −7,620
Oct					*Line 3 Expenses Start
Nov			Delivery to Store		
Dec			Payment (30 Days later) Store discount + Commission	+40,000 −7,620	+32,380 +24,760

* Line 3 expenses are not included in cash flow

CHAPTER 5

FINANCING YOUR BUSINESS

"Having a basic knowledge of business finance and available financing options is an essential skill needed by today's small business owner. With this basic knowledge, your business is more likely to be successful. Without it, the failure rate increases dramatically. Lack of adequate capital and failure to apply basic financial management techniques is the number two cause of business failure. Poor overall management and lack of a focused marketing plan are the first and third reasons, respectively, for business failures".

Reviewed by Peter Linington Vice President, CIT Group

This chapter will deal with the debt issue. Does your business need debt, why does it need debt and how do you go about securing debt?

Debt is usually available in one form or another. You have no doubt received numerous applications from companies who want to give you a credit card so that you can incur debt, but the solicitations are not as frequent for a business, especially for a new business.

Every business, large and small needs money. Deciding what combination of money, capital and debt, your company will need can be a time consuming process. It takes time to solicit and negotiate the terms of financial arrangements, and this is in addition to the time you are spending deciding exactly what your business will design, sell, manufacture and ship.

Capital vs. Debt

Capital is the money the business owner(s) contribute to the company. It usually comes from:

- **Savings**
- **Sale of real estate**
- **Sale of stocks/bonds**
- **Money from family and/or friends**
- **Venture capital:** money invested by an outside party for a percentage of ownership in the business.

The money that goes in as capital will not be coming out of the business. What you get in return for capital is the ability to run your business and make a profit. The down side is that you have a partner that is taking part of your equity and sharing your profits.

Debt is money that is borrowed. It has to be paid back, and its cost is interest to the lender. The return to the business owner(s) is the ability to do more business, which leads to additional profits. You incur debt by borrowing from a variety of sources:

- **Bank loans**

- **Factoring your accounts receivable**

- **Loans against your purchase orders (Purchase order financing)**

- **Credit card debt**

- **Loans against your own collateral, including real estate**

- **Loans from family and/or friends.**

Most companies find that at some point in their business cycle they need additional money to help the business grow. Debt is a tool that the business owner can use to help fund new orders, to help with the growth of inventory and the subsequent increase in accounts receivable. Debt can also help a seasonal business through their slow period. It can also off set losses during the start-up phase of a business.

What tells you if you will encounter any of the above situations? Your business plan will be your first step in determining the need for debt, how much, and when. The plan must cover all aspects of your business. The financial section will identify both the capital need and what debt levels the company will need to operate. *(See Chapter 3 Business Plan)* As the company grows so will the need to borrow money. Being able to project your company's growth over a period of three years is important to your business plan. As the company grows you may need to re-think your original business plan and provide up-dated information when applying for a loan. It is rare that a company grows exactly as planned!

There are many ways to borrow money and many types of sources for your business needs. Given this scenario, it is imperative to explore all the options and select the one that best suits your business needs before you go to market and orders are written. Talk to multiple lenders and familiarize yourself with the terms and requirements of taking a loan or later finding a factor. Companies often rush into the process, and select the wrong type of financing. You may find that you are able to fund your initial monetary needs internally, e.g.: family, friends or by sale of valuables or property.

Where to go to find the loan

There are a number of places to start the money search. The first place would be to check out and see what you can find on **www.cashfinder.com**. Or look for other free information on the Web about borrowing money.

Next go to your bank, talk to your accountant, and call your local Small Business Administration office. Each of these places will give you information that you will have to evaluate and make an educated decision. The Small Business Administration has free advice available, and even offers consultations from retired business people. This service should help you stay on track.

Do not overlook the bank or banks with which you already have a personal relationship. Finding the right bank is like getting an experienced partner for your business. Interview as many banks and ask as many questions as it takes for you to feel comfortable with your choice.

Example of Credit Application Requirements for a Loan

Please provide the following information to facilitate our processing of your credit application.

1. Last 3-year business financial statement.

2. Last 3-year business tax return.

3. Current personal financial statement of business principal(s)/guarantor(s), and Addendum to Real Estate Schedule if applicable.

4. Last 2-year personal tax return of business principal(s)/guarantor(s).

5. Five major trade credit references plus three major customers (Name, Address, Contact Person, Telephone number, Fax number).

6. Twelve-month cash flow projection of business.

7. Articles of Incorporation; Statement by Dome3stic Stock Corporation; Fictitious name filing.

8. Current agings of A/Rs and A/Ps and list of inventory. (Account Receivable)

9. Summary totals for twelve months of A/R and A/P agings plus inventory values.

10. Resume.

11. Last appraisal.

12. Copy of most recent real estate loan statement.

13. Business brochures.

14. Insurance agent name, address, telephone and fax.

Selecting a Lender

Obviously the cost of financing should be a factor in selecting a bank or a lender. Different financial institutions may offer different rates because of variations in their cost and availability of funds. At some financial institutions agreeing to maintain a minimum balance in the bank will result in a lower rate. Banks offer variable rate loans, where the interest rate is tied to the prime rate. The rate on the loan will change to correspond with increases in the rate.

Loans are either unsecured, for well-capitalized companies with a history of good performance. Or secured, which means they must be backed by collateral in the form of business or personal assets. Which include: accounts receivable, inventory, marketable securities, equipment, or real estate.

How do you find out how much money you need?

The amount of money you are requesting must be supported by your up-dated business plan. If you ask for too little, you may find yourself with insufficient money for your business operations. On the other hand, if you ask for too much money, you may be increasing your likelihood of being turned down by the banker. Your request must be based on a reasonable factual business judgment.

The following are questions that you will need to answer when presenting your financial plan to the lender for a loan approval.

For what purpose do you need the loan? The purpose for the loan should make good business sense. Such as funds for purchasing additional inventory, financing accounts receivable, taking discounts on purchases, from suppliers, or for the purchase of some type of new equipment or machinery. Generally speaking, the purpose of the loan should contribute to help increasing the profits of the business.

How much personal debt do you have?

The lender will want to know how much personal debt you have. If you are already highly in debt personally, you may find yourself forced to withdraw large sums of money from the business in order to service your personal obligations, and in doing so, jeopardize the financial strength of the company.

How much money have you invested in the business?

Lenders will want to know if you have sufficient capital to operate your business properly, and to protect the business in case there are losses. It is a fact that if there are losses to the business, the losses will decrease the net worth, which in turn will increase your loan requirements, which may jeopardize the lender's loans to the business.

As stated above most start-up companies are initially funded from the personal assets of the owner(s) or with help from family and friends.

What kind of collateral do you have to support your loan request?

Collateral owned by the business, which can be assigned to the bank:

- Accounts receivable
- Inventory
- Equipment and machinery
- Purchase orders
- Real estate

Collateral owned personally by the businessperson, which can be assigned to the bank:

- Cash surrender of life insurance policy
- Savings account
- Municipal, government, or corporate bonds
- Marketable securities
- Real Estate

How much money do I need over the capital invested? This will be a function of the growth of the business and the level of capital invested. If there is enough capital, there may be no need to borrow. This means less expense for the business. If the company's growth cannot be supported by the capital then debt becomes an option. The accounts receivable and inventory, which are the primary assets of most garment companies, can then be used as collateral to secure loans to fund growth.

How and when can I repay the funding? It is up to you as a businessperson to identify specifically the source of repayment for the loan. The repayment can come from a reduction of inventory, the collection of accounts receivable, the transfer of liabilities, such as substituting long term debts for short term debts, or profits from the business operation.

Based on my cash flow, can I afford the cost of the money? The figures will have to be calculated to determine if your company has sufficient cash flow to repay the loan. This is an opportunity to review your costing and profit margins. You may have really good orders, but you may not have built in to the cost sheet enough profit to make it possible to have the added interest expense of borrowing money.

Should I consider selling equity (ownership) rather than a loan (debt)? This maybe a good option if you have the right partner. Finding a partner that will complement you and your business is not an easy match, but if the right partnering occurs it could help save your company and turn it into a successful venture.

Are there other financing possibilities that meet my immediate needs? Sometimes using a credit card for a short-term loan will be sufficient to carry the company over until payment is received from the retailer. Keep in mind, this is an extremely expensive way to borrow money.

Do you have the services of a certified public accountant? If you do not have the services of a CPA, many lenders are reluctant to deal with you. There is a strong feeling among many lenders that an independent third party looking in on the business records, bank records, and operations of a business is necessary in order to obtain an objective evaluation. At a minimum, lenders will require to review quarterly and yearly financial statements from a CPA.

Do you have the services of an attorney? As with maintaining the services of a CPA, an attorney will be an important source of legal information needed to successfully run and operate a business, it is like having insurance. You never know when you will need their services, but should trouble arise, you need to know you have a good relationship with a CPA and must be sure they understand you and your company.

Do you have life insurance? Life insurance is very important to you in order to protect your business in case of death. Insurance will protect your personal assets, estate, and family from creditors.

Do you have business protection insurance? Most businesses require insurance from fire, theft, and water damage. Depending on the size of the business many other types of potential liabilities are required. These include employee death and dismemberment, and vehicles owned and operated by business personnel.

How much do you understand about running a business? Most lenders will want to know how much experience, training, and education you have had in the business that you are operating. Knowing that competent professionals, a CPA and attorney, are advising the new business owner, will be extremely beneficial to the lenders reviewing your loan application.

New businesses will find that obtaining a loan from traditional funding sources is often more difficult, but with a secure financial background and a little investigation, a loan can usually be found.

Established companies have many more options available to them. If they can show a sustained profit or upward growth curve, they will find obtaining financing approval somewhat easier and the actual receipt of the funding will be a bit faster.

Trade Credit It is important to establish trade credit with your suppliers. This will be a very important part of financing your business. Build a good relationship with your suppliers; pay on time so that next time you can ask for a longer time in which to pay the invoice. Delay your payments as long as possible without incurring extra interest on late invoices. Is it possible to pay more for your fabric per yard in order to get some credit? Take it! Sometimes you can pay for part of the shipment upon delivery and the rest in 30 days to 60 days.

If you need help, then be big enough to ask for it.

Factoring

Definition: Factor

- *A person who carries on business transactions for another; commission merchant; agent for the sales of goods entrusted to his possession*
- *An agent, as a banker or finance company, engaged in financing the operation of certain companies, or in financing wholesale and retail sales, through the purchase of accounts receivable*
- *In certain states, a person legally appointed to take care of forfeited or sequestered property*

What is factoring? A factor is a specialized financing company, which loans money to a manufacturer using **accounts receivable** *(retailers' unpaid invoices as collateral)*. Think of factoring in the terms of how a credit card is used. When you present a credit card to a merchant, the information is transmitted to the credit card company and the credit is approved for the amount of the transaction. If the amount is within the purchaser's credit limit, the credit card company provides the merchant with an approval number, and agrees to accept the risk that the purchaser will be financially able to pay.

In other words, the manufacturer sells its account receivable for a cash loan from the factoring company. The factor will usually advance up to 85% of the cash value of the account receivable. The factoring company will collect the money due from the retailer, and after deducting their commission, forward the proceeds to your bank. If an advance loan has been made against the accounts receivable, the collection of the money due will repay the loan. **The longer the retailer takes to pay its invoices, the longer you are paying interest on the loan.** It is therefore very important that the retailer is encouraged to pay in a timely fashion. This is done by building an incentive into the "Terms of Sale", to get your invoices paid on time. The manufacturer will offer a discount to the retailer on the invoice if the retailer will pay within 30 days. *(See Chapter 13)*

The factor's interest rate is usually 0.5% to 1.5% above prime per-annum. The interest rate is dependent on the service cost, as measured by the average invoice size, the credit risk of the client's customer base and the volume of sales factored. Interest is charged on the average outstanding loan balance for the month and is charged at the end of each month. **Think of factoring as a short-term loan that should be paid back as soon as possible.**

EXAMPLE

- Sales $2 million a year
- Factoring commission 1.25%, it would cost the company $25,000 a year.
- For the $25,000, the company would have no bad debts and no expenses for credit and collection departments.
- If the company needs cash before the invoices are paid, the factor will make an advance of 80% to 90% of the outstanding receivable.
- There is an interest charge for money advanced, but the company can minimize the expense by careful cash management and planning.

Types of Factoring Agreements

Factoring agreements are usually categorized based on:

1. Which Party takes the credit risk
2. How the factor pays its clients for the receivable it purchases from them.

Credit Risk

- Some factors, particularly the very small ones, do not take the credit risk on the receivable they purchase from their clients.
- This contract is called *"recourse contract,"* meaning the factor has recourse back to their client's invoices that are unpaid for any reason.
- The larger factors provide what is known as *"old line"* factoring. They take the credit risk under their *"non recourse agreements."*

Non-recourse/borrowing arrangement This is the most common type of factoring. This means that the factor will lend money to the manufacturer against the accounts receivable. Should the retailer default on payment for the merchandise, due to financial inability to pay, the factor will carry the loss. The provisory is that the customer (purchaser) has been credit approved by the factor for the amount of the order, the invoices that are sent to the customer. The factor will make an advance (the loan) against the credit approved sales invoices.

Collection basis contract

- The factor remits payment to the client when the account debt is paid to the factor.
- Cash advances to the client prior to collection of the accounts receivable may be allowed.
- If they are allowed, interest will be charged on the advances until they are covered by collections.

Advantages of Factoring Besides managing the accounts receivable, factors will also offer a number of services to manufacturers that will help a company run more efficiently. Some services include:

- Credit checks on potential customers.
- 100% credit guarantees for orders received from customers
- The freeing of capital tied up in account receivables
- The elimination of the expense of a credit department
- Reports pertaining to receivables, collections and charge backs.
- Additional facilities for inventory financing
- Letter of Credit facilities
- The reduction of bookkeeping expenses
- The expansion of credit and other features

If the factor approves of the customer's order, the manufacturer will receive the advance from the factor at the time the goods are shipped. The invoice is assigned to the factor. Assuming that all is going well, the customer will pay the factor the total amount of the invoices. The payment will repay the loan, the original advance against the invoice, and the balance will become available to the manufacturer.

In short here is the process:

1. Manufacturer obtains P.O (purchase order).
2. Manufacturer calls factor for credit approval for the P.O. amount.
3. Manufacturer produces the goods
4. Goods shipped and invoiced
5. The invoice is assigned to the factor
6. Factor advances money to the manufacturer
7. Customer pays invoice to the factor.

The questions asked in the first part of this chapter would be applicable when applying to a factor for a loan. Here are some other questions that you will need to address when applying to be factored.

- **Are there any hidden fees?**
- **Will there be collection fee?**
- **Will there be sign-up fees?**
- **Will there be termination fees?**
- **Will there be any auditing fees?**

Once the factor has obligated itself to loaning you money, it will usually do all within its power to make the arrangement a success. Your relationship with your factor will hopefully continue for many years to come. Therefore, it will be in their best interest to see that your company succeeds before it is forced to turn to your personal guarantees.

For the smaller start-up company, factoring is not really a viable possibility. Factors will usually only loan money to companies that have proven to be secure and worthy of the risk. Of course there are exceptions to the rule. If there is enough initial capital investment, there will be more of a chance to be factored against your receivables. If your company is short of initial capital investment, you may have to find the funding for your first couple of lines the traditional ways discussed in the first part of this chapter. Traditional bank loans may be all that are needed in the beginning. As the business grows there will be times when the money is going out faster than it is coming in, and you will be waiting for payment on goods shipped.

Most retailers buy from manufacturers on credit; that is, they pay for the merchandise after thirty days, and usually even longer. When you have to buy fabric and trim, and pay for labor and overhead costs, this creates a financial crunch. At this time, most manufacturers turn to banks and factoring firms for financing possibilities.

Loans against the Purchase Orders

One other possibility that should be investigated is borrowing against your Purchase Orders. There are lenders that will lend you money against the orders once they have been written. This is a good option to help finance fabric, trims, cutting and sewing. The downside is, you pay more for the loan and should be well aware of all the costs involved.

If you are denied a loan, you need understand the reasons for the denial. Ask the loan officer to explain why you have failed to secure the necessary help. This will help you understand the requirements so you will be better prepared the next time.

Reasons for denying funding

1. Bad credit
2. Poorly written or no business plan.
3. Insufficient collateral
4. Lack of secondary income
5. High debt-to-equity ratio

A list of factoring companies that cater to the needs of the apparel industry can be found in the appendix. Whether you have been in the business for a short time, or you are a tried-and-true veteran, these companies may have something to offer you in the way of financial service.

Startup Cost Analysis

Revenues	Jan	Feb	Mar	Apr	May	Jun	Jul
Units Shipped:							
Shirts	0	0	900	1200	800	1000	900
Dress	0	0	500	600	600	300	500
Pants	0	0	500	600	500	600	500
Jackets	0	0	500	600	500	400	500
Dollar Sales:							
Shirts (@ $40 each)	$0	$0	$36,000	$36,000	$48,000	$32,000	$40,000
Dress (@ $55 each)	$0	$0	$27,500	$27,500	$33,000	$33,000	$16,500
Pants (@ $60 each)	$0	$0	$30,000	$30,000	$36,000	$30,000	$36,000
Jackets (@ $75 each)	$0	$0	$37,500	$37,500	$45,000	$37,500	$30,000
Total Dollar Sales:	$0	$0	$131,000	$131,000	$162,000	$132,500	$122,500
Cost of Goods Shipped:	Cost includes: Design, Pattern, Fabric, Grading, Marker, Samples, & Production.						
Shirts (@ $50%)	$0	$0	$18,000	$18,000	$24,000	$16,000	$20,000
Dress (@ $50%)	$0	$0	$13,750	$13,750	$16,500	$16,500	$8,250
Pants (@ $55%)	$0	$0	$16,500	$16,500	$19,800	$16,500	$19,800
Jackets (@ $55%)	$0	$0	$20,625	$20,625	$24,750	$20,625	$16,500
Total Cost of Goods Shipped:	$0	$0	$68,875	$68,875	$85,050	$69,625	$64,550
Commissions (@ 10%)	$0	$0	$13,100	$13,100	$16,200	$13,250	$12,250
Returns & Allowances (@ 8%	$0	$0	$10,480	$10,480	$12,960	$10,600	$9,800
Total Net Sales:	$0	$0	$38,545	$38,545	$47,790	$39,025	$35,900
	Total Net Sales = Dollar Sales - Cost of Goods - Commissions - Returns & Allowances						
Operating Expenses							
Owner's Draw / Officer's Salary	$4,000	$4,000	$4,000	$4,000	$4,000	$4,000	$4,000
Salaries-Production	$4,000	$4,000	$4,000	$4,000	$4,000	$4,000	$4,000
Salaries-Operations	$4,000	$4,000	$4,000	$4,000	$4,000	$4,000	$4,000
Taxes & Workman's Comp	$1,500	$1,500	$1,500	$1,500	$1,500	$1,500	$1,500
Benefits	$0	$0	$0	$0	$0	$0	$0
Rent	$650	$650	$650	$650	$650	$650	$650
Utilities	$250	$250	$250	$250	$250	$250	$250
Telephone	$400	$400	$400	$400	$400	$400	$400
Advertising / Marketing	$300	$300	$300	$300	$300	$300	$300
Payroll Services	$200	$200	$200	$200	$200	$200	$200
Accountant	$100	$100	$100	$100	$100	$100	$100
Maintenance Equipment	$60	$60	$60	$60	$60	$60	$60
Office Supplies	$150	$150	$150	$150	$150	$150	$150
Licenses & Permits	$30	$30	$30	$30	$30	$30	$30
Postage	$25	$25	$25	$25	$25	$25	$25
Design Room Supplies	$150	$150	$150	$150	$150	$150	$150
Total Operating Expenses:	$15,815	$15,815	$15,815	$15,815	$15,815	$15,815	$15,815
Net Profit (Loss):	($15,815)	($15,815)	$22,730	$22,730	$31,975	$23,210	$20,085

Net Profit = Total Net Sales - Operating Expenses

Note: Short term financing may be required. Stores pay up to 60 days after delivery of goods.

Revenues	Aug	Sep	Oct	Nov	Dec	Total
Units Shipped:						
Shirts	1000	800	1200	1200	600	9600
Dress	800	600	600	700	400	5600
Pants	700	600	500	500	400	5400
Jackets	500	500	600	500	400	5000
Dollar Sales:						
Shirts (@ $40 each)	$36,000	$40,000	$32,000	$48,000	$24,000	$372,000
Dress (@ $55 each)	$27,500	$44,000	$33,000	$33,000	$22,000	$297,000
Pants (@ $60 each)	$30,000	$42,000	$36,000	$30,000	$24,000	$324,000
Jackets (@ $75 each)	$37,500	$37,500	$37,500	$45,000	$30,000	$375,000
Total Dollar Sales:	$131,000	$163,500	$138,500	$156,000	$100,000	$1,368,000
Cost of Goods Shipped:						
Shirts (@ $50%)	$18,000	$20,000	$16,000	$24,000	$12,000	$186,000
Dress (@ $50%)	$13,750	$22,000	$16,500	$16,500	$11,000	$148,500
Pants (@ $55%)	$16,500	$23,100	$19,800	$16,500	$13,200	$178,200
Jackets (@ $55%)	$20,625	$20,625	$20,625	$24,750	$16,500	$206,250
Total Cost of Goods Shipped:	$68,875	$85,725	$72,925	$81,750	$52,700	$718,950
Commissions (@ 10%)	$13,100	$16,350	$13,850	$15,600	$10,000	$136,800
Returns & Allowances (@ 8%)	$10,480	$13,080	$11,080	$12,480	$8,000	$109,440
Total Net Sales:	$38,545	$48,345	$40,645	$46,170	$29,300	$402,810
Operating Expenses						
Owner's Draw / Officer's Salary	$4,000	$4,000	$4,000	$4,000	$4,000	$48,000
Salaries-Production	$4,000	$4,000	$4,000	$4,000	$4,000	$48,000
Salaries-Operations	$4,000	$4,000	$4,000	$4,000	$4,000	$48,000
Taxes & Workman's Comp	$1,500	$1,500	$1,500	$1,500	$1,500	$18,000
Benefits	$0	$0	$0	$0	$0	$0
Rent	$650	$650	$650	$650	$650	$7,800
Utilities	$250	$250	$250	$250	$250	$3,000
Telephone	$400	$400	$400	$400	$400	$4,800
Advertising / Marketing	$300	$300	$300	$300	$300	$3,600
Payroll Services	$200	$200	$200	$200	$200	$2,400
Accountant	$100	$100	$100	$100	$100	$1,200
Maintenance Equipment	$60	$60	$60	$60	$60	$720
Office Supplies	$150	$150	$150	$150	$150	$1,800
Licenses & Permits	$30	$30	$30	$30	$30	$360
Postage	$25	$25	$25	$25	$25	$300
Design Room Supplies	$150	$150	$150	$150	$150	$1,800
Total Operating Expenses:	$15,815	$15,815	$15,815	$15,815	$15,815	$189,780
Net Profit (Loss) For Period:	$22,730	$32,530	$24,830	$30,355	$13,485	$213,030

CHAPTER 6

PRODUCT DEVELOPMENT

"To create a product is useless unless you know

who wants it and how to reach them."

Reviewed by Cari Vaile "Fleure de Peche"

Cari has a natural style and has used her talent to become a successful designer/manufacturer. She has not had any formal fashion design training but with her talent along with a strong work ethic and a desire to become successful designer, she has made it. She first became a manufacturer when she came up with the innovated idea of turning men's Y-fronts into Junior tops (cut the crotch out and pull it over your head, and you have a great top)! "Wild Cherries" was born and thousands were sold. Her newly formed company became licensed in Japan. She later changed her market niche from Juniors to designing Contemporary clothing due to the competitive price point of Juniors. You need to sell hundreds of thousands of units to be competitive in this clothing bracket.

It is important to add that her success has been partly due to the fact that she is fortunate to have a great mother who has worked beside her through thick and thin.

A successful designer is often born with talent and the drive to succeed. Even without proper training it is possible to become a top designer/manufacturer. There have been many stories of entrepreneurs becoming successful apparel manufacturers without formal training in the field. However, natural talent plus training at a prestigious college are an ideal combination.

Will tomorrow's clothing be sporty or casual, modest or bold, real or fantasy? That's anyone's guess! Designing a line of clothing has to be part gamble. Understanding the principles involved in designing and producing a line of clothing will help you become a more successful manufacturer. In this chapter you will learn to understand the basics of line development. It is important to understand the principles of design, and the elements involved in developing a line of clothing. Take time to study the principals of design, including the principals of garment construction. It's difficult to be an effective designer if you do not understand fit, and the three dimensional aspects of designing. Refer to the many books available at your local library, or if time permits, take a class offered at your local Community College or Continuation College, to learn about designing, draping, pattern making and construction. Most top designers in the fashion world have a good understanding of draping and the way different fabric reacts when cut and sewn into a style.

Only by developing an understanding of design, can one produce clothing that will satisfy the customer's needs. Design can be defined as any arrangement of shape, proportion, balance, lines, value, color, and texture.

Although fashion feeds on new designs and styles, it is not the producers or designers of these styles who determine fashion. No style, or group of styles, can be considered fashion, unless they are accepted by, and bought in substantial quantity, by the public. Acceptance by the public is the very essence of fashion. Designers who have acquired a reputation for creating fashionable clothing, are those who have been outstandingly successful in giving expression to the elements involved with successful designing. All this is easier said than done. Having an eye for fashion is the key to putting together a successful line of clothing! Design talent is often in the blood and seems to be a natural part of successful designer's success. Training will improve abilities and give talented individuals more power, in an industry where training and experience are an essential part of surviving. There is no one rule that a designer can follow to get started. There are fashion school graduates that first work for a company to gain experience, then launch their own line, after careful planning and some hard earned financial backing. Then there is the accidental designer, who starts with an idea and some samples, only to discover that they are able to make a living by designing clothes. Today's designers are starting out, outside traditional methods. There are boutiques and many showrooms that cater to and support hot young designers. There are also special trade shows that reflect the demand for young, edgy, street-inspired garments for which young designers have become famous, and that are not available in traditional department stores. Designers today start by creating their own brand image and a public demand.

Principles and Elements of Design

Here is a brief explanation of the main principles and elements of design that go into developing a clothing line:

Proportion: The relationship of the size of each part of the garment to each other part, and to the whole garment. This includes trims, contrast fabrics and construction details. Proportion is directly related to all aspects of design.

Balance: Related to how symmetrical the design is. Both sides of the garment must be equal; or it could be asymmetrical. This occurs when two sides of a garment are not identical.

Line: It is used to define the outline or edges of the garment and to divide the space within it. Line can create visual illusions such as thinner, heavier, shorter, taller. It can create flattering styles, and unflattering styles. There are two kinds of lines, straight lines and curved lines. Because the eye follows a line, it gives direction to the overall balance of the design. It is possible to attract the eye to certain areas and, at the same time, draw it away from less desirable ones.

Shape: This is the silhouette of the garment, minus detail. There are three basic silhouettes:

- Rectangular (shift, chemise)
- Hourglass (1950's)
- Bell (wedge or lampshade)

These have alternated throughout the history of fashion.

Value: Effective designs use dark and light contrasts between the parts of the garment itself or in contrast trims. It is also interesting to use them in subtle ways, such as with like color values, e.g. black and gray, or black and brown. Usually one value is used to dominate the garment or used to emphasize chosen areas.

Color: Color gives mood to a garment and designers use color as an important part of design. Bright, clear colors are traditionally used for Spring and Summer, darker for Fall and Winter. Reds, gold, silver, and black are Holiday. Color tones can also be used to change the balance and to emphasis the design. Certain colors sell better than others and some should be used with caution.

Texture: Refers to the "hand" and the look of the fabric. "Hand" means the feel of the fabric, soft or harsh, bulky or fine, cold or warm, flat or textured, etc. The look of the fabric could be categorized as: shiny or dull, printed or plain, solid or striped, or the type of weave.

These are some of the principal ingredients for a well-designed line. A designer must incorporate these elements into a pleasing combination, although one of them will usually dominate each design. It is not an easy task to combine them into successful and profitable lines. It takes talent, a natural taste for well-designed clothes and a good head for business, plus lots of luck! Fashion changes continually so there are no hard and fast rules. This makes life in this industry exciting, and ever-changing.

Styling Category

Traditionally manufacturers specialize in a particular target market or classification and a product category, which incorporates their styling, price range, and size of clothing for their target customer. Each season, the design department is responsible for creating a new "line", or seasonal "collection" that the manufacturer will sell to retail store buyers. The term "collection" is used primarily in Europe and for higher priced lines in the United States, while "line" is used more often in the United States for more moderately and popularly priced fashion.

Design Planning

Designers and merchandisers work on two or more lines at once, designing a future line while solving problems of the line that is in production, or about to be shipped. Designers must think ahead to the season when the garment will be sold and worn. For example, a velvet dress to be worn in December must be designed in June or July. Usually, work on new collections begins approximately six to eight months before the selling season for the larger companies and sometimes, the **leadtime** could be even longer. The advantage of smaller manufacturers is that they are able to work nearer to shipping deadlines, and often show samples on a monthly basis. They are able to react to trends more quickly than their larger counterparts, who have the disadvantage of having more departments involved to develop and produce a line This in turn, lengthens the time it takes to produce the line. However most companies produce at least five or six seasonal lines a year: Spring, Summer, Transition, Fall, and Holiday or maybe Resort. These divisions are becoming less distinct; as more manufactures try to fill in their lines with new items, shipping to stores almost monthly. This method of manufacturing and selling, allows the manufacturer to produce consistently and to invoice monthly. The retailers also win because they can plan their merchandising closer to the moment, and cater to their customers' demands. So instead of complete new lines, seasonally fresh items are produced monthly for presentation to retailers and for more frequent new orders. This is ideal for the start-up manufacturer, who should spread out production costs more evenly through the year.

Merchandising Plan

Designing is part of the merchandising plan. The designer's role should encompass the entire planning cycle for the business, from the initial design research, product or design development, sampling, costing, and production to sales and distribution. Merchandising includes every department of the business, a from line development, time and action plans, planning volume and budgets to the merchandising calendar, detailing key dates for planning, selling, and producing multiple lines.. It is essential that designers are familiar with all the various stages of pre-production and involved with producing the finished garment. Each stage will have an impact on the successful retail sales of the garments. It behooves the designers to follow through at every stage.

Groups

In many cases, a line is subdivided into groups of garments. Each group has a specific theme based on the fabric, color, or a particular fashion direction. Ideas for the theme come from trend research and other design sources, color, or fabrics. Sometimes the design for one garment may inspire a whole group. The styling within each group should have variety yet carry out the central theme.

To present a visually pleasing group of "dresses," the line need only have a few elements in common, such as fabric or a color story. Often a manufacturer emphasizes only a few silhouettes (called "bodies or styles" in the trade), interpreting each of them in several prints; or it will feature one print in a variety of styles. Within the group, the dresses must offer a variety of silhouettes, sleeve treatments, necklines, trims, or they should have a certain continuity in stitching details and finishing of the garment.

Example To design "coordinated sportswear", the objective is to have the individual styles mix and match interchangeably. Fabric combinations must be carefully thought out. There should be a variety of coordinating skirts, pants, jackets, shirts or blouses, and tops in each group. There should still be consistency of theme, with color, fabric, line, or detailing to tie the whole group together.

Color and fabrication

The first thing a customer will notice is the color of the garment; the second will be the fabric. People relate to color, usually either selecting or rejecting a garment because of it. This is also true for the fabrication of a garment. The designer must decide which fabric will best work for the design. Choosing a fabric suitable for a particular style is probably the most important aspect of designing. The designer must choose fabric on the basis of fashion trends, quality, and price. The best fabric for a design is one that interprets a design naturally. The "best" is not necessarily the most expensive. The fabric maybe reasonable in price, but the garment labor costs may be intensive. This will raise the cost of the finished product. Quality is often interpreted, erroneously, to mean cost. It is the designer's job to combine all these elements in a pleasing and appealing design.

Sampling

Designers develop many designs for each line, often two to three times as many as needed. From all of these samples the best is then chosen. Design development is challenging and costly. Not only must the designers be creative; they must also know both what sells and the most competitive price. The ultimate blame for a bad season, economic conditions and sales price remaining the same, falls ultimately on the designer.

Line Planning

Before the line is developed and produced, the target market should be thoroughly analyzed. If the market is over-merchandised or saturated with a particular product, then it would be madness to go into a business manufacturing the same thing, which is already out there in depth. Market analysis involves studying the current market trends and anticipated needs for the forthcoming seasons. Styles shift constantly, and minor innovations appear every season, but a full-scale change to a new style is never completed at one time. New fashions usually evolve gradually, the processes by which fashions rise, peak, and decline take several seasons.

Once women would do anything to be fashionable and to wear the correct and dictated styles, now for the first time in history, women are able to wear whatever suits their own personal style. From long skirts to short skirts, from full pants to slim pants, it's all acceptable. Put together correctly, and with added seasonal detailing, they will look brand new and stylish. This makes the manufacturers' life very difficult because they now have to cover all their bases and design for everyone's needs. Creating new fashion is a difficult challenge. You have to do thorough investigation and have a sixth sense for trends.

Whether one is designing, producing, selling, or all three, the first step is to have a clear picture of the customer group that constitutes one's target market. There is no universal group of customers: there is city, suburban, or rural; there is young or not so young; there is blue-collar or white-collar background; there is the middle-income or well to do; there is the conservative or the avant-garde, and so on. With a specific customer group in mind, the next principle is to collect all the facts one can.

Most clothes are purchased from the following:

> Mass Merchants, e.g. Target, Costco, Wal-Mart, Kmart 26%
> Specialty Stores, e.g. Nordstrom, Neiman Marcus, Ann Taylor, Gap 19%
> Department stores, e.g. Bloomingdale's, May Co., Macy's 18%
> Chain Stores, e.g. Sears, JC Penney.. 17%
> Catalogs, e.g. Lands' End, L.L. Bean, Abercrombie & Fitch 8%
> Off Price Stores.. 7%
> Factory Outlets... 5%

Internet retail sales, based on bricks & mortar store, are similar to catalog sales and have the same problems.

- **How numerous are these customers?**
- **What are they buying from day to day?**
- **Where are they buying?**
- **What are they willing to pay for their clothes?**

Find a need and fill it.

Branding

Another consideration for a company is the name or logo it invents and how it is identified as a product. In today's brand-conscious world, companies such as Tommy Hilfiger and Polo are icons of popular culture, and have labels with a certain cachet and overwhelming appeal. Traditionally, the principal way in which a business has sought to distinguish its product among its consumers has been to develop its brand, which in legal terms can be referred to as a trademark. Not surprisingly, brands have become one of the hottest assets that a business may own.

Trend Spotting

The best way for the average person to do an analysis of the market is to "shop" the stores and to walk the streets. Manufacturers and designers are constantly "shopping". That is, they are looking at merchandise in a wide variety of departments and specialty stores. Shopping is a very important part of designing and product development. It is an indicator of social changes and lifestyle shifts, which will in turn affect the buying habits and the spending habits of the general population. This is also one of the best ways to spot trends.

- **With more and more Americans working from their homes as a primary or secondary office, how will this relate to the clothing industry?**
- **What needs to change so that you can provide the customer with what they will need?**

Three trends that are affecting the clothing industry are:

- **Aging Baby Boomers**
- **A desire for natural products**
- **Casual lifestyles**

Trends used to start with the richer sector of society, but the opposite is true these days, with trends often begun in the streets by the younger generation. That is a reason why designers spend time in places where they are able to spot a potential new trend. In L.A., Hollywood and Venice Beach are the "in-places". New York boasts Manhattan; Kings Road and Soho in London are a must for observing fashion trends. They are alive with the beautiful, the weird and the trendy. Each city has a "look" that gives that city a personality all of its own. LA has an important impact on today's market. Designers and manufacturers from around the world fly there to shop the stores and to see what is new and happening in sunny California, with its casual life-style now being adopted worldwide. Not long ago Paris was perceived to be the place to predict future trends; we now watch L.A. and London. Today, Paris fashions are seen more as an "Art Form" that doesn't necessarily relate to fashion trends as much as they used to.

Other sources to help identify future trends are fashion magazines, newspapers, films and TV.

(Go to trade show to see the next trends. Look and experience.)

Professional Predictive Services

Predicting which styles will become fashionable at a particular time, has been called an occupational guessing game for the fashion industry, a game with millions of dollars at stake. The makers and sellers in fashion have their own ways of studying trends and consumer preferences. They spend a great deal of money on examining past trends for clues as to what will succeed today, and they watch today's activities for indications of what will happen tomorrow. These are called "fashion cycles". While some styles are at their peak, their successors are already in the growing stage. Whether or not this money is spent wisely is anyone's guess. Shifts in fashion do not occur at a given time, and it is impossible to pinpoint the exact beginning or end of a specific fashion cycle.

Professional predictive services keep manufacturers up to date as to the new trends in various parts of the world. Predicting trends becomes almost a sixth sense. They learn to study signs that may escape the untrained observer and to forecast which styles are most likely to succeed. Forecasting errors can be costly, so care is taken in analyzing the market.

On-Line Predictive Services

Predictive services can inform us about what is new in Milan, Paris, Tokyo, London, New York, L.A, or any fashion center that has any impact. The newest predictive services are on-line, offering pictures of streets with window displays in all of the top fashion cities. They also have on-line; couture shows from the top designers the very next day after the shows. In addition, they have the textile shows as they are happening. These services even offer color projections of next season's fabrics, and prints. Predictive services are big business, and very useful to manufacturers that do not like to travel in order to do their own analysis of the coming trends. However they do not come cheap!

Forecasting Textiles

Trend forecasting in the textile industry is demanding. Textile designers are required to design and work 6 to 16 months in advance of the finished piece goods being delivered to the manufacturer, who is working 6 to 9 months in advance of delivery to the retail stores. The need to understand both the future demands of the Industry and the buying public's demands is crucial to the success of the textile and fiber producer. Although timing is important, trend information is used for specific product categories and for the many market segments. It is often just as important to recognize a trend that is on the way out, as it is to recognize a future trend.

Color Forecasting

Color plays an important part in attracting the buyer to the product. A consumer's first impression of a new product is largely affected by color. Color forecasting is typically done 20 to 40 months ahead of the targeted market's selling season. To work so far ahead, color experts must combine knowledge of color theories and human behavior with acute observational skills. To accomplish this difficult task, forecasters often have extensive experience in the industry and are required to travel the globe attending trade shows and shopping where new ideas originate. Color is also identified with target markets; for example, bold primary colors are often associated with children's clothing. Trendy and whimsical colors appeal to teens. Colors also change with the seasons, summer colors are brighter than fall and winter. Holiday has typically gold and silver as accents. A list of color trend forecasting services is provided in the appendix.

Merchandising a Line

Stores are an ideal way for you to understand how collections are merchandised, and how clothes in one collection relate to one another. Shopping the stores both in your market and "reach" markets will give you a better understanding of designing and how to merchandise your line. Take note of how different designers merchandise their lines and combine pieces to be worn together. Each successful manufacturer has managed to create their own identity or "look", which customers seek out. This is what you must aim for. Do not have each group within your line look like they are coming from different companies. There must be cohesiveness and follow-through with the finished product. They must relate to one another. Pieces that do not relate will have a problem selling, because they are hard to merchandise. If your line has separates, it is important to have your designs interchangeable so they relate to one another. This way the customer can purchase pieces that can be worn together as an outfit. This is known as "merchandising" and is an important part of designing apparel.

Storyboards

In the early stages of the design process, it is a good idea to put together a "storyboard" that is made up of tear sheets from magazines and other sources. Tear sheets show styles, colors, textiles and other details, which can influence or direct the new collection. The designer may have been to an art show or museum, or may simply have been inspired by a history of costume book. Ethnic costumes may also be used as inspiration for a theme for the season. All these are important sources of information. It is impossible to design in an empty room with blank walls. All inspiration must come from somewhere. There is nothing in fashion that is really brand new; styles are just interpreted in a new way.

Your storyboards would also include fabrics, colors and even accessories as suggestions.

Designers are expected to do this with each new collection. It helps to focus the collection, giving it direction by putting the garments into groups within the collection.

Start by tearing any sheets from magazines or other sources that you feel will be related to the line of clothing being developed for the next season. Color, fabric, texture, styling, or "a look" that gives the line direction: anything that would have an impact on the new line theme.

Example: Vintage cars may be an influence for a print on a shirt, or, some part of a vintage dress could be taken as inspiration; there could be a floral or even a space theme. Anything that would relate to a theme could be torn from magazines or color-copied from a book to help make up the storyboard. Sub-divide these sheets into groups that better relate to one another; e.g. fabric types, colors that could be grouped, styling, and trimmings. All these steps will help clarify your design ideas and help form the groups within your line. It forces you to focus your designing, and hopefully prevents you from producing a line that does not relate. These tear sheets and fabric swatches can then be glued to a board, like a collage, to build a story of your collection. It is an interesting exercise and worth practicing before you seriously begin to work on your line.

Design Development

Once you have focused the line for your type of apparel, season, and the target market or customer you are designing for, and the storyboards have been made, then you have to focus even harder on the actual designs that will be made into samples. Keep the line small and controllable for the first couple of seasons. Design what you know best, and evolve from there. You should have styles that relate to one another and that can be worn inter-changeably: e.g. tops which co-ordinate with bottoms, dresses that co-ordinate with jackets. If you are convinced about a print, and must have it, match it with a plain fabric that will harmonize and complement it. Mix your textures and fabric types to give the line more appeal. If you use a trim, be certain it ties into the rest of the fabrics and styling. Be innovative with construction and finishing. Topstitching should be consistent on all garments in the group or line. The cut of garments must also be consistent; if you have a high cut armhole on one sleeveless dress, make sure you follow through with any other sleeveless styles you wish to include in the line. This type of consistency will eventually give your company an image and hopefully lead you to a recognizable brand identity. Designers are often known for ways that they choose to cut and finish their clothing. The general public identifies with a particular designer for certain aspects of their collections. As a manufacturer you will have to concentrate on building an identity that consumers can recognize and want to be identified with, and most importantly, come back for.

Regional Differences

It is a fact that manufacturers of clothing need to be aware of regional variations in what consumers buy, dependent on what part of the country the product is sold. Obviously, weather changes, from one part of the country to another, will influence the demand for certain types of clothing. That aside, regional differences will also influence sales of certain styles. The West Coast's quickness to accept what is new, and especially what is casual and relaxed, or the mid-west's fondness for shades of blue, go along with the predominately blue-eyed, northern Europeans who settled there. Understanding the regional differences of your target market will help determine the needs and preferences of your target customer, and therefore, how to market your line to them, and where you will have the most success in targeting your product. Information on customers' buying habits and preferences, expressed in their purchases can be found in a number of ways. One important source of information is from salespeople, either from the retailers or from manufacturers' sales representatives who are the first to see what the customer is buying, (wholesale or retail). They see that certain areas are buying certain colors, styles, or fabrics faster or more slowly than others. Another source of information is from fabric producers who are aware of manufacturers' reorders for fabrics and the shades that are selling.

Market Entry

Timing your first line to be ready for showing at the Fall market is thought by some to be a good place to begin. The reason for this is that the selling season is longest from January through to May and you should get more sales. The down side is it will allow your competitors to knock you off. Remember whichever season you are designing for will be shown two to three months before it is put out on the retail floor, and before you will receive any payments for your production. If you are selling directly to your customer, you will be able to produce closer to your sale and hopefully, have a faster turn-around financially.

Seasonal Apparel Markets

Market Opens: **On Sale in Stores:**

July/August ⟹ Paris Fall/ Winter Couture ⟹ October

September ⟹ Holiday/Resort Markets ⟹ November

October ⟹ Paris Ready to Wear Spring ⟹ December/January

November ⟹ Spring ⟹ February/March

January ⟹ New York Summer Sportswear Paris Spring/Summer Couture ⟹ April/May

February ⟹ New York Summer Apparel Paris Spring cont. ⟹ April/May

April ⟹ Paris Ready to Wear Fall ⟹ July/August

May ⟹ New York Fall/Winter Sportswear ⟹ July/August

June ⟹ New York Fall/Winter Apparel Market ⟹ September

Understanding Ready to Wear Sizing

After your investigation of the market is complete and you have made your decision as to which market will be targeted, it is important to understand the various categories of clothing, and the various sizing involved.   There are a number of market categories to be remembered, and which often overlap:

- **Juniors,** 14 years to 20 plus. Odd sizing.
- **Contemporary,** sophisticated updated styling for the age group that has out grown junior clothing. Even sizing.
- **Missy,** usually for 25 years plus. Designed with a more conservative and classic style. Even sizing.
- **Bridge,** is designed for those that want ready to wear designer clothes at below designer named prices. Usually designed by a named designer for their ready to wear lines. Even sizing.
- **Designer,** upper-end clothing from designer names Even sizing.
- **Women's,** for the fuller figure, all ages. Even sizing.
- **Half-Sizes,** for the fuller figured women who are shorter in height. Even sizing.

There are also the cost categories:

- **Budget:** lower-end cost clothing.
- **Moderate:** priced, (self-explanatory).
- **Better/Designer:** higher-end clothing that usually offers more for the money, (fabric and design).

Industry Sizing Standards

Standards are voluntary within the clothing industry. This is the reason that there is no real conformity to size within the apparel industry and why one manufacturer's size will differ from another's. As a rule, the more expensive the garment, the larger the garments become. Whether this is psychological, to give the buyer the feeling that they are smaller than their true size, is unclear.   Standard sizes of yesteryear have gradually become larger and larger; a Size 14 from the 1950's is now a Size 6! Check vintage patterns and their measurements on the back of the package.

There are recommended sizes that have been developed with the Standards Division of the United State's Department of Commerce, and the apparel industry, for the various figure types, sexes, and age groups, but not many manufacturers seem to follow them.

Women's Market

There are four major size classifications for women's clothes:

Missy The average sizes range from 2 – 18 increments of two in even numbers and are designed for the woman with average proportions and height. There are also two subdivisions of the Missy category for the shorter and taller figure: **Petite Missy** and **Tall Missy.** The age group for misses is anywhere from 25 years, to 60 plus. *(There will always be cross over customers in every category).*

Junior sizes range from a 1 to 15 in increments of two in odd numbers and are designed for the more youthful, short, and slim figure. The torso is cut shorter and the bust line is higher than misses. A sub division of the Junior size is the Petite Junior, which is designed for the shorter, Junior figure. The torso, sleeves, and skirt are shorter than their Junior counterpart. Junior clothing is designed for 14 years to 21 years plus, depending on the taste and size of the customer.

Women's sizes range from size 32 to 52 and are designed for the fuller, matured figure of average height. These sizes have usually been graded up to have a longer torso, skirt, sleeves and pants. The average age of this customer is between 25 years and 60 years (plus).

Half-Sizes range from 12 1/2 to 26 1/2 and are designed to accommodate the shorter woman with a full, mature figure. These sizes are cut with a lower, full bust, a larger, but shorter torso, and shorter sleeves.

Men's Market

Sizes relate to style and body measurements, 32-40 Men's sizing is not quite as confusing as it is for women. The measurements tend to be more directly related to the body measurements. Shirt – neck and sleeve length. Pants – waist, inseam, outseam. Jacket – chest and length. Sweaters and other casual items; sleepwear, and underwear may be sized with symbols XS, S, M, L, XL, and XXL.

Infants' and Children's Sizes

Selecting the correct size for a child is as much a problem as it is for women's' clothing. There are sizes that have been recommended by the U.S. Department of Commerce, but again as with women's clothing, few manufacturers adhere to them. The standard measurements that the apparel manufacturer usually uses are the chest circumference, waist circumference, height, and weight of the child. This information is usually provided on labels in the garment or on the packages that hold the garment.

- **Infant** sizes range from 3-24 months. The age of the infant is used along with NB, S, M, L, and XL to denote size. These increments relate to specific height and weight averages, rather than age of the infant, as growth patterns differ.

- **Children's Market - Toddler** sizes range from 2T – 5T girls 4-6X boys 4-7 relate to age, height, chest, hips, waist and body build. Some items are sized as S, M, L, XL, along with the more traditional sizing.

- **Toddler** and **Juvenile** sizes range from 1 through 6X. Some items are sized as S, M, L, XL, along with the more traditional sizing.

- **Girls** range from ages 7– 16 **Boys** range from 8-20. Both correlate to age, height, chest, hips, and waist circumference, as well as body build, (Slim, Regular, or Pretty Plus). As with all other categories and sizes, certain items are sized using the S, M, L, and XL.

- **Pre-Teens** are for girls between the age of 8 years and 13years.

Sample Sizes

When making a first sample, it is wise to make the sample in a middle size. This is normal in the apparel industry. One of the reasons is that the middle size is easier to grade up in size and to grade down in size. It is also easier to cost and make yardage estimates. If you make your smallest size into a sample, and then have it graded for production, it may become distorted in design and proportion, from the smallest size to the largest size. Some manufacturers prefer to make samples in small sizes, they feel the garments present better when shown in a sales appointment.

CHAPTER 7

FLATS, LINE SHEETS AND SPECIFICATIONS

Apparel companies today are utilizing technology to help drive their "Speed to Market" process. As part of a Tech Pack, computer generated flat sketches are one of the key tools used in communicating garment construction details to production teams and manufacturing partners locally and globally. Knowledge of this technology is an important asset, but there is also value in knowing how to draw by hand a good working flat sketch. You may find yourself in front of a buying team that has gone to Europe, purchased samples, and wants to rework them for sale next season. During this meeting, you'll need your drawing skills to quickly and accurately sketch the desired revisions and get those changes to the patternmaker for new prototypes and costing. Your patternmaker will work directly from your flat sketches to put the new season's samples into work. On another occasion, you could have your line sheets and sales samples in the showroom, out for discussion with a key account. Customizing line samples for an account may require sketching their changes so they can be communicated "on the spot". Being able to accurately draw those desired revisions could be the key to getting the good order.

Suzanne Parody Gross, Manufacturer, Owner, Instructor – FIDM

"The devil is in the detail"

What are Flats and Working Sketches?

For those of you who are starting a clothing business without any formal training in the industry, it is important that you learn how to draw a technical flat sketch or a good working drawing with all of the design's details. Flats are used extensively within the industry to explain designs in detail. A technical flat is drawn as if it were laid out flat on a table with all the seams, darts, and construction details. If you have ever seen a drawing on the backside of a commercial store-bought pattern, you will understand what a flat or working sketch is. It is what it says it is, a flat two-dimensional drawing without a figure, drawn to scale. It is used to explain to everyone involved in the construction process, how a garment is designed with all the relevant details pertaining to the design.

Technical Flats

Flats are used for a variety of purposes:

- **Cost sheets**
- **Pattern cards**
- **Line sheets**
- **Specification sheets**
- **Presentation boards**
- **Tech Packs**

Flats are most important for technical packages (sometimes called Tech Packs), which are used to communicate style details to manufacturing partners. *(Tech Packs are used to give the garment's specific full details and should be clear enough for a garment to be made from them without further explanation).* Tech Packs include a Specification sheet, with the style's precise measurements and a precise front and back sketch, a Technical Flat Sketch, including construction details and call-outs, and a Product Details page, listing all of the materials and component specifications. Generally the technical flat is a black and white line drawing, not stylized, but they can be colored with a rendering of the fabrication or a scan of a print or fabric

Computerized Flats

There are some wonderful computer programs that are able to generate flats. Once the user is trained and becomes familiar with operating the program, computer versions of technical flats can be quicker and more precise than hand-drawn flats. These same computer programs can be used to generate line sheets. The results are very professional.

There are a number of types of flats used, but it is important to be able to draw any type of flat clearly and precisely. Here are four by name that people with training will know how to identify:

Stylized Flat

This type of flat is used to emphasize details and style lines with some movement or animation. They are used for buying office bulletins, line description sheets, and as a sales tool, etc.

Technical Flat

The second type has no movement, "flat," precise details, drawn with a ruler, French curve, or on the computer and is often accompanied by measurements and construction "call-outs". A "Technical flat" takes into consideration all the precise technical measurements that are required for production. It goes beyond the style of the design, and shows the points of measure such as the depth of the neck, the length of a sleeve, or the width of a waistband, etc. Each line pays meticulous attention to every detail, such as stitching, gathers, darts, etc. Used for pattern charts, spec sheets, material allocation, general production needs, sales reps and buyers, these flats can also be used to make up a line sheet.

Image Sketch

This is a stylized sketch, often with accessories and illustrated expressing "attitude" of the garment. It may be "camera ready" (reproducible), and is used for advertising, presentations, etc.

Working Sketch

Precise and detail-oriented (like the technical flat) except it is drawn on the body or croquis to demonstrate proportions in relation to the body – hem length, sleeve shapes, silhouettes, fabric texture and body, etc.

If you have no drawing experience it is important to master the skill of drawing a good technical flat. Flats will be used for all of your designs and must be understood in all areas of production. From the designer, pattern maker, and sample sewer, to the sales representatives, in the form of a **line sheet**, and to the retailer, when communicating what they've purchased.

How to draw a good working Flat sketch

Using a Croquis

The best way for you to practice this important part of producing clothing is by using a prepared drawing or croquis, and laying a sheet of tracing paper over it as a guide to the body's proportions. This will teach you to see the body shape, and to understand the shape and lines of a garment in relation to the body. You will find that even for the experienced fashion designer, using a croquis is the best method to achieve a well-drawn flat, and to also save time. Make sure to use the appropriate croquis for your target market, i.e. juniors or women's.

Try drawing one side of the garment, and then fold the tracing paper in half and copy the other side. This will give you a balanced drawing with equal sides. Another method for drawing a flat, is to use a paper with a grid. The grid will help guide you with your drawing, and will make it easier to line up all of the details, in equal sections, between the left hand side of the garment and the right hand side. With practice, you will be able to line up tops and bottoms and keep the flats in proportion to one another.

If you are designing a line that has layers, then you have to be able to draw the garment as if it were on the body, one layer at a time. Does the garment have "functional" ease or does it fit closely to the body? The flat must be drawn with the ease allowed. To give extra information on a style, a blow-up or an enlargement of an area, referred to as a "call out", is a good idea to give specific detailing emphasis.

The more accurate the sketch, the better the final results. Remember, if you need a patternmaker to make the first pattern for your design, then the technical flat may be all there is to go by. It is important to make sure the flat that you give the pattern maker is as clear as possible, with all seams and top stitching details. Do not forget to include the back of the garment or the sides. Often, an inexperienced designer will think of an interesting design, but forget that there is a back to the design, and that the front must relate to back. Give thought to the side seams and where the seams meet. If you make a vague drawing with unclear details, then you will be disappointed with the final result. The patternmaker's pattern will only be as good as your instructions. Unless the flat with the information is clearly described it will be a disappointment to you. Plus, you will have to pay for another pattern and sample to be made. You must try and communicate your vision of what is in your mind. Use either a good technical flat sketch, or a combination of flat sketch plus tear sheets. It is always helpful to show an actual garment that has the fit or other details that you would like applied to your design.

In larger companies, specification sheets are often the job of the assistant designer or assistant patternmaker and they are responsible for making them accurate. This can be a time consuming and exacting job.

Template guide

Various basic silhouettes, also called croquis, of a woman's, man's, and child's body, front and back are included for use as guides when drawing your flats. (See Appendix)

Practice Will Make Perfect

Check out a variety of pattern making books and learn to identify a variety of pattern pieces that go into styling a garment. It will help you with your designs, and in drawing a good technical flat. You will also learn to identify the garment pieces by name.

(See previous chapter, Product Development)

Line Sheets

Line sheets are prepared as sales tools, as soon as the line is finalized. Your sales representative gives them in a brochure format, to the retail buyer to use as extra information about the line. The buyer can then use the line sheet as a reference, and it will help to keep your line fresh in their mind especially when they are preparing to write their orders.

It is sometimes produced in color, and includes all the styles and the colors available in the line. Prices, style numbers, and sizes available should also be included.

Line sheets can be produced in a variety of ways, drawings (flats), photographs, computer aided graphics or fashion illustrated.

Swatching the Line Sheet

Whichever method your company chooses, remember that the line sheet should contain as much information as possible. If color is used, it is important to maintain accurate color rendering of the fabric, - plain or printed. Retail buyers expect the finished goods to match the colors in the line sheet. If producing a colored line sheet is too costly, then having a black and white line sheet is acceptable as long as a swatch of the fabrics is also available.

Computer Programs

These days there are good computer programs available that are capable of producing a line sheet, color cards, or making flats. Remember, the computer is only as good as the person using it. If you are unsure as to how the flat of your design should look, then do not assume that a computer program will be able to design it clearly without help from you.

(I have included examples of various line sheets in the Appendix that should help give you an idea as to how a line sheet should look.)

Specifications

What is a specification sheet?

With more and more production being produced offshore, the purpose of making a good specification sheet and Tech Pack has become much more important.

The specification sheet will always have a well-drawn flat, and measurements of the finished garment. A specification sheet is the responsibility of the Production Patternmaker, or Technical Designer who fill in the specification sheets or forms with exact details and points of measure for the garment. The spec sheet, (as it's known), is given to the domestic contractor or sent to the offshore contractor, who is then responsible for the garment in production. The contractor will follow the directions as best they can and make a first sample to the specs. It should be noted that offshore contractors often have a problem with language. Therefore, the more detailed the specification sheet, the more trouble free it should be in producing the first sample. Once the sample has been completed, it is then returned to the manufacturer for fitting and re-measuring. If the garment is a new item, the process can sometimes be lengthy and it can take up to three months to produce the perfect sample. *(This is more likely the case in offshore production)* To make the process as short as possible, it is important to get the spec sheets as accurate as possible.

Garment Washed Specifications

If the garment is "**garment washed**" after it is sewn, as with jeans, then the specifications become even more complex. Measurements and specs must be taken before the garment is washed and again after washing. Then must be calculated how much shrinkage has occurred so that the patterns can be adjusted to allow for the correct amount of shrinkage.

Over Dyed Garments Specifications

The same is true for "**over dyed**" garments. Dyeing a garment will also incur shrinkage, plus dependent upon the dye used, there will be a different reaction to the fabric. So, each color used will have to have its own specification sheets made, and sometimes a different pattern for certain colors chosen. This can incur a great deal of unexpected costs to the production of a garment if the manufacturer is unfamiliar with these particular problems.

CHAPTER 8

FINDING FABRICS & TRIMS

"Refuse to be abused"

"Tenacity and perseverance will create success"

Leonard Horowitz Past President Textile Association of Los Angeles, Inc. (TALA)

The challenge

Every small clothing company has a challenge at the start of its business to find mills and fabric representatives who will sell to them without stipulating large minimum yardage. It requires some investigation and patience to find suppliers who will sell smaller qualities. Fabric, in smaller amounts, is available. Although it is very limiting, do not be disheartened; with online sourcing information available, this task has been made easier.

Here are some points to remember before choosing fabric for your first line and your fabric search begins:

1. Choose fabrics that are readily available, e.g. plain-colored, popular types of fabric.

2. Try to avoid prints, as it will be hard to order printed fabric without a minimum. If you are lucky enough to find a great print that is available without a minimum, you could be choosing a fabric that another company is using and it's old stock. Prints are a problem even for the larger manufacturer, as they often do not sell as well as the plain fabrics. So for a first line it would be advisable to stay away from prints. If you feel that a print would help your line, and have found just the right print, use it sparingly.

3. Never buy your first fabrics from a mill abroad, a delivery is often a problem. You do not want the retailer to cancel your first orders due to your late shipment, which in turn is due to the fabric arriving late from Italy!

4. Be cautious of bright colors. They are sometimes a problem to sell, and can often be found on the mark down rack.

Textile Shows

Domestic Textile Shows

Textile shows are an important part of finding fabrics. By attending textile shows, you will begin to understand the way business is conducted within the Apparel Industry. They take place twice a year, after the larger European shows. The first is held on the East Coast at the Jarvis Center, IFIE; followed by the West Coast show in LA at the California Mart, International Textile Show. At these shows you will find domestic and foreign representatives showing their latest prints and weaves, plus knits of all kinds, and fabrics made in new and interesting blends of fibers.

Identifying the Major Mills

Designers become energized and inspired when they see all the new textiles under one roof. It is important for designers to attend so they can they can keep abreast of the trends and get some new inspiration for the next season's line. Besides seeing exciting and new fabric designs at these textile shows, you will learn to identify the major mills, and the kind of textiles they produce. It will also help you to identify their image, and the type of product that they produce, when you see their name in any resource directory.

Ordering Sample Yardage from a Textile Show

You will be able to order sample yardage, usually cut in 3 to 5 yard pieces. Textile companies will only send sample yardage if they are sure that there is a chance of getting an order. You must make sure to appear professional; they will want to see your business card. In turn, take their card and keep a reference of the textile companies that you feel would be of interest to your own company. They sometimes forget to send the sample yardage, so you need to be able to follow up with a call. Have all the particular information written down with, the colors that were available, and which color you asked to sample.

International Textile Shows

There are two important textile shows held in Europe twice a year. Textile producers from all over the world display their lines at these textile shows. Clothing manufacturers and textile producers from the US visit these European shows to see the latest directions in fabrics and to place orders. While in Europe they will also "shop" the stores, to gather information on the latest fabrics that have been turned into the latest fashionable styles and to get more inspiration for their designs. *(The need for inspiration is constant).*

Interstoff

This has more than 1,000 exhibitors from twenty-four countries, and is the world's largest apparel textile exhibition. This four-day textile show is held each fall and spring in Frankfurt, Germany.

Premier-vision

Held in Paris, France each fall and spring.

Ideacomo

Presented by Italian textile producers each Fall and Spring season in Como, northern Italy, and is followed by the American exhibitions.

Fabric Sales Representatives

Usually fabric sales representatives, besides showing their line of fabrics at the textile shows, maintain showrooms in the major fashion cities to display and sell their line of fabrics. Each textile company also has sales representatives who visit manufacturers to show their line to the designers and manufacturers. Fabrics are shown on "**headers**" which is the technical name for the pieces of fabric shown, (head ends of the fabrics).

Most fabric representatives are paid in a similar method to clothing representatives. If they represent only one company, they are usually on a salary, plus commission. If they are independent sales agents or representatives who handle several textile lines, they are paid commission.

Textile Firms

Textile firms are known to be in two major brackets:

- **The Mill** is a company that owns machinery that produces fabric. Some mills produce woven fabrics exclusively, others make only knit fabrics, and larger mills produce both. Most U.S. woven textile mills are located in the southeast portion of the United States. The larger knitting mills are located in southern California. Foreign mills are located throughout the world, especially England, France, Italy, Japan, South Korea, India, and Thailand.

- **Vertically Integrated Mills** are a primary source of fabric. They not only make or create the material, but also the yarn, which is in turn woven or knitted into the "greige", also known as Grey, fabric. This is unfinished base fabric that the mills finish and dye dependent on the manufacturer's own creative wishes. The vertical mill may also have its own in-house designers who produce its line of textiles to sell directly to manufacturers. In that case, the vertical mill is responsible for all stages of fabric development, from weaving and finishing to printing and dyeing. However, they do not make their own fiber, *(see Chapter 9)*. Large portions of textile mills are located in the southeastern portion of the United States, with a large percentage in Carolina. These mills tend to produce woven fabrics exclusively, with the larger knitting companies being located in the Los Angeles area. Most of LA mills only produce knit fabrics. However, some of the giant mills manufacture both wovens and knits. Like some of the larger mills in Carolina, some LA based knitting companies are also vertically integrated. The sound of 8,000 giant knitting machines at work can be heard around the city. The corporate headquarters for many of the major mills are concentrated in New York City and Los Angeles.

Converter Textile Companies

These types of companies buy the greige goods from large mills, finish and produce the fabric. These companies have their own designers who will design prints and decide on which dyes to be used.

If you think of the vertical mills as doing everything, from weaving to producing the finished fabrics, and the converter as being the middle fabric producer (converting to the finished goods), that may help make it easier to remember.

Textile firms usually keep their line to one type of fabric, whether it's cottons, woolens, knits or synthetics. Larger companies will have divisions that specialize in one type of textile, and or one type of customer.

Large textile companies usually will not take a small order, this being the function of the jobber. Unless they have left over stock that they wish to unload, then it becomes easier for a start up company to order from the big textile companies.

Fabric Jobber

A Jobber is essentially a middleman who purchases fabrics and resells it. Jobbers may buy from a number of sources and put them together as their own "line," in the hopes of selling later at a good markup during a period of peak demand. Another role of the jobber is to buy unsold goods at great reductions, or the ends of rolls of fabric from clothing manufacturers. This fabric is left unused by the manufacturers who may have over-ordered for production and do not want it left on the shelves as unused inventory. Selling to a jobber at discount is better than having the fabric left in storage as useless inventory. The risk the jobbers take in buying and selling this way enables them to demand a high profit on resale.

Textile Imports

Imported textiles are an important part of the textiles sold in the clothing industry. Japanese silks, Italian wool, polyester from Korea, cottons from India and Pakistan; these have had a great impact on the American textile industry. This is one of the reasons the government began to set quotas on imports to try to protect the American textile industry. However, there are no quotas on silk, flax, and ramie because they are not produced in the United States, and therefore do not compete with American industry. This is the major reason that silk products are so reasonably priced in the stores.

Selecting Sample Yardage

Sample yardage selection will depend on the fabric's price range, aesthetics, season and the suitability for the line you intend to produce. **Keep your first line simple!** It would be nice to have a couple of different weights or textures, blouse weight (top weight) and bottom weight for skirts or pants. You may want to include one knit that can be cut and sewn. Make sure that the fabrics that are chosen complement each other and can be worn together, or interchanged as pieces, this is known as a **Group**. *(See*

Chapter 6) Larger companies will have four or five groups to make up their line. It is all right for you to have one group in your first line.

Sample Yardage from a Jobber

Sampling yardage from a jobber is usually the easiest way to begin your first line. There are jobbers that allow you to buy wholesale, as long as you buy a minimum of twenty yards. The drawbacks with this are, by the time you have sewn the samples, finalized your line and the orders have been written, the fabric may no longer be available. If this should occur, then you contact the sales representative or customer and tell them the problem, but explain that you have an alternative fabric lined up that is just as attractive and of similar quality, only better! The sales representative will do the talking to the retail buyer, who will hopefully be sympathetic, depending on how good your line is and how much they want it in the store. Of course it is up to you to have the alternative fabric lined up. Send a sample (swatch) of this alternative fabric to your sales rep for approval. You must also be cautious with the content of the fabric you decide upon and have the correct care labels available for the garment. Sometimes, jobbers will sell fabrics not knowing their fiber content, and the only resource is to use labels stating "Dry Clean only"! There is a way to test the fabric to discover the fiber content. This is called the burn test, which is used to determine any fabric's content. But it takes some expertise in reading the ashes before you can be sure that the test you have performed

are correct *(See Chapter 8)*. If you decide on a generic type of fabric, then it will be available no matter the size of the orders.

Designer Fabrics

If you should buy designer fabric from a jobber it is wise to first check if it has unlimited commercial use. Ask the supplier or the licensing agent if there are any restrictions on that particular designer fabric. If the fabric has a designer's name and a copyright symbol, do not use that fabric for your production. It is possible that a small amount of designer fabric will be permitted for use in commercial production, but designers are sensitive to how their designs will be used. If you are producing a product that does not match the taste level of the designer's you could find yourself with a legal problem and no product to sell. It is important to avoid the commercial use of any fabric with copyright cartoon characters or NFL logos. You must obtain permission to use such fabric from a licensing agent and pay a percentage for the use of any copyright material.

Interlinings/ Interfacings & Fusing

Interlinings, interfacings and fusing are all terminology for the same thing, they are used for structure in the garment. Finding the correct interlinings for your garment will be an important part of the overall appearance of the finished garment. Because interlinings are not seen, does not mean you do not have to think or worry about them. Interlinings are an important part of your garment, so do not settle for cheap fusing. You will regret it. *(See Chapter 9 for more information on the types of interlinings)*

Resources for sample yardage:

1. Textile shows.
2. Resource directories
3. Trade papers
4. Jobbers (See directories)
5. Converter mills (See directories)
6. Vertical mills that do not require a minimum (See directories).
7. The Web. (See Appendix).

Important Directories

These are the main directories for fabrics, finishers, trims, contractors, and manufacturers in the major cities.

- **TALA Resource Directory:** Published by the Textile Association of Los Angeles, **www.TALAUSA.com**
- **Davidson's Textile Blue Book:** Published by Davidson's Publishing, **www.Davisonbluebook.com**
- **Garment Manufactures Index** Klevins Publications, **www.klevenspub.com**
- **The Designer's Guide** By Susan Powers, Dare Communications, **www.Apparellink.net**
- **Fabric Services & Trims** By Fashiondex, **www.Fashiondex.com**
- **Fabric Stock Exchange** **www.fabricstockexchange.com**

Finding Fabric on the Web

The Web has become an important sourcing method for many apparel manufacturers and designers. This type of sourcing of textiles continues to move online with most of the mills having established a presence on the Web. Previews of the important international fabric shows are to be found there.

There is even a "Fabric Stock Exchange" (*stock referring to the commodity and not the investment*). Information resources vary from the technical to the design, with pictures of the fabric swatches.

Wholesale lots of fabric are being auctioned worldwide. There is a flood of information, and the novice will surely get lost without a map of these vast new territories. Included in the Appendix is a condensed group of some of the sites you could try for information that could help you find fabrics.

Another exciting Web site worthy of a visit is **www.FabricLink.com**. This Web site is an educational link to a number of useful sites that have information about where to find fabrics, and new fiber producers. Plus, there are other educational sites where you will find useful information concerning textile and apparel retailers.

See appendix for more resources.

Swatches

A swatch is a small sample piece of fabric that provides information and a sample of the type of fabric to be used. Swatches are used on:

- Cost sheets
- Pattern cards
- Specification sheets
- Production sheets
- Line sheets

When ordering fabric on the phone or over the Internet, take care not to order without first seeing the fabric. Ask the mill or fabric representative to send a swatch for your approval. Never buy sight unseen, you need to feel and check the quality of any fabric you are thinking of using. What looks good over the Internet, maybe cheap, limp, or poor quality goods.

Fabric Estimation for Production

Deciding on the correct amount of yardage for the first line is difficult for a new company. Should you order the fabric before you know the size of the orders or should you wait? That is the question! This is where good sale representatives will advise you about buyers' reactions to your line. They can help project the sales in order for you to estimate the fabric required for production. Do not over-estimate or you will be left with rolls sitting on shelves, collecting dust, adding to the overhead, and the company's inventory. Having too much inventory should be avoided. It can be the downfall of any successful company! Remember that if you over estimate your fabric requirements, it could end up at the jobbers at a discount price, and will be your loss. Cut as soon as you can after receiving the piece goods. Ship as soon as it is returned from the contractor. You normally have sixty days to pay for piece goods, (although your first line may be paid C.O.D. until you have a good credit rating). The trim is normally paid for in thirty days and the contractor will expect to be paid on delivery of your production. As you grow you may be able to pay within seven days. Keeping open stock of your inventory for reorders is expensive and a manufacturer cannot afford a mistake. Sell any of your left over stock as soon as you can. Do not over cut and finish goods that have not been ordered. This is all wasted stock, which equals loss of profit. Learn to be very cautious with this area of production as many manufacturers have gone broke because of over stocking, and forgetting the costs involved with too much inventory. Do not allow bolt ends of fabric to accumulate. Charge back to the mills for any fabric with flaws or shading. These costs can add up and you should not ignore them.

Use your Web site

If you are left with fabric, it is a new practice to cut and sew into new hot styles and put them onto your website for direct sales to customers or an indirect sale to a retailer *(See Chapter 16)*. The Web is an interesting marketing tool to move inventory and to make up for what would otherwise be sold to a jobber for half the price of the original fabric cost.

Quality Control for Fabric

Checking yardage for problems after it is received is a crucial step in production. Each roll or bolt should be checked for shading and flaws. This of course, costs money, and the price category or price range will determine if checking yardage is a viable process for your company. Having a person check for shading and for flaws can cost more than going ahead and cutting with a few small flaws and rejecting the seconds, which is often the case with budget. If the fabric is too badly damaged, the manufacturer will try to return it to the mill. Timing is crucial to the manufacturer and receiving flawed fabric can cost you the order. It is therefore important to buy from reputable mills where there are smaller risks involved with problem fabrics and with returning flawed goods.

Flaws within fabrics can be anything from holes in the fabric, to color variations and bad printing. It can also happen that the production fabric width is narrower than the sample yardage. This is truly a problem, which will affect the costing of the garment and reduce your profit margin. If the marker has already been made, then a new one will have to be remade to the narrower fabric width. This can be frustrating, costly, and time consuming.

Selecting Findings

Findings are the extra things that go into making up a garment; e.g. zippers, thread, trims and interlinings (interfacings or fusing). When selecting your findings, care should be given to the type chosen. If there is a trim involved, it should be of similar fiber content as the garment, if not a test should be made to check for problems with shrinkage etc. Attention should be given to the type of thread the contractor will use, especially on any of the new woven fabrics or microfibers that have stretch. The thread will have to stretch in the same way the fabric does.

CHAPTER 9

UNDERSTANDING TEXTILES

A good "working knowledge" of textile fibers and fabrics is an important advantage for the fashion designer. By understanding the characteristics of both natural and manufactured fibers and blends, designers have another tool that can be used to set their designs apart. Today, multi-fiber blends are gaining in importance as a way of developing fabrics that not only have more pleasing properties, but also have unique surface effects. For example, instead of using 100% cotton or 100% linen for sportswear or dresses, you could use a blend of 50% linen or cotton, 24% polyester, 24% rayon, and 2% spandex. This will produce a garment that has the look and feel of cotton or linen, but with the durability, wrinkle-resistance, and easy-care qualities of polyester, along with the draping qualities of rayon and the comfort of spandex.

Each fiber has a unique composition and its own set of physical properties. The U.S. Federal Trade Commission has established generic names and definitions for the manufactured fibers, including acetate, acrylic, lyocell, modacrylic, nylon, polyester, polypropylene (olefin), rayon, and spandex. However, all fibers under a generic name are not exactly the same. It is particularly important to keep in mind that all manufactured fibers are NOT alike.

Fiber producers have been able to modify the basic composition of generic fibers, both chemically and physically, to produce variations providing a softer feel, great comfort, brighter/longer lasting colors, better warmth/cooling, moisture transport/wicking, and better properties for blending with other fibers. These improved fibers are given a trademark name and are owned and promoted by the fiber producer.

Knowledge of fabric construction and the effects of how yarns are spun, twisted and finished provide additional ways to develop fabrics with new looks, feel, and functionality. So, always take time to review the basics, and to stay abreast of new technologies. This will give you an important edge in creating designs that will stand out. And, above all, dare to be different!

Kathlyn Swantko

www.FabricLink.com

Fibers, Processing & Finished Textiles

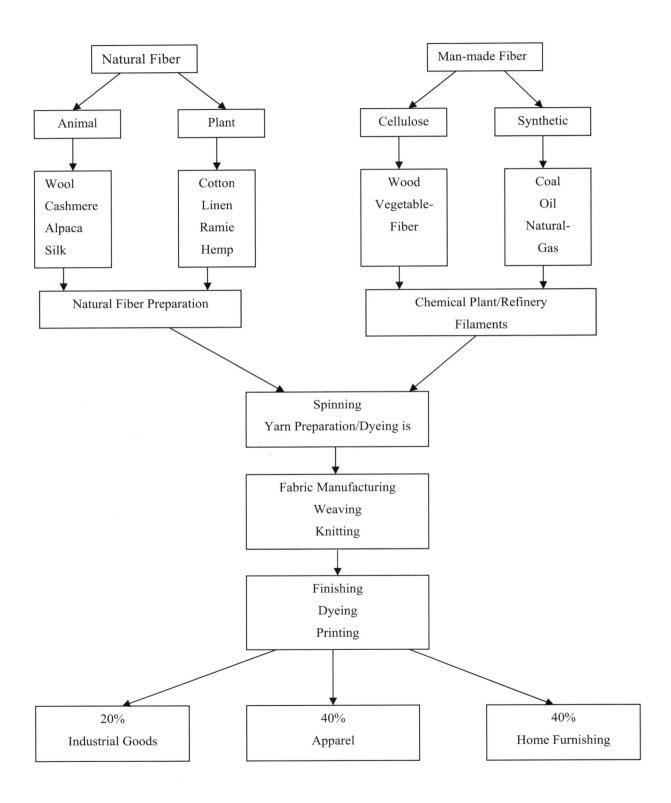

Textiles are comprised of many different raw materials, both natural and synthetic, that require numerous steps in the process of manufacturing a finished textile. Whether the end fabric produced is silk for a ball gown, nylon for active sportswear, or a combination of both, plus other raw materials, the process is lengthy. Reclaimed materials are being recycled by ecology-minded fiber producers, producing some interesting fabrics. (*Some Polo fleece is made from recycled soda bottles!*) The textile market is divided into approximately 40% apparel textiles, 40% interior furnishings and 20% industrial use (see production chain for natural and for synthetic fibers). This chapter will explain very basically the production chain of textiles, from the fibers, yarn, and spinning, weaving, knitting, and finishing of the textiles. See the **Glossary of Fabric Terms** for other textile descriptions.

Fibers

Textile materials commonly consist of fibers in the form of hair-like filaments, which are first spun into long threads before being converted into cloth. Fibers vary in length from one inch to miles. Fibers that are measured in inches are called **staple fibers**. Longer fibers are called **filament fibers**, and are manufactured fibers (except for silk). Silk is the only natural fiber that is a filament fiber and is usually about 1,500 yards long. Filament fibers are often cut into staple lengths, spun and twisted together to be used for the finished textile. Fibers may be either natural or manufactured.

Natural Fibers

Natural fibers are so named because they are taken from a natural source, either animal or vegetable. Animals provide wool, cashmere, mohair, alpaca, silk, etc. (protein base). Vegetable fibers are produced from cotton, flax, linen, hemp, ramie etc. (cellulose base). Natural fibers vary in length; typically a cotton fiber is about 1" in length. In general the longer fibers (over 13/8" in length) are used for finer yarns and fabrics. Silk is produced naturally as a continues filament, which maybe cut up to be used in the same sort of spinning process as other natural fibers or used as a filament.

Natural fibers have a variety of properties, which render them suitable for the production of various kinds of finished textiles:

- **Cotton, linen, ramie, hemp and flax** are associated with finished garments suitable for wearing in warmer climates because they absorb moisture and are comfortable.

- **Wool, cashmere, mohair and other animal fibers** are more commonly worn in cooler climates because they have lofty thick fibers (fleece). Like other natural fibers, wool comes in a variety of different qualities e.g.: fine wool (Merino) and coarser wool (Shetland). Wool has a natural crimp, which prevents the fibers from packing together. This crimp helps to form pockets of air and creates a natural insulation and a warm feeling. Wool has the ability to "felt" under wet conditions, a property exploited in making dense fabrics.

- **Silk** is the thinnest of all the natural fibers, with a luxurious and often soft "hand". It is also the strongest. Like a spider's web, the silkworm produces a long, continuous filament to make its cocoon. Silk is produced from a variety of types of worms and can be processed to produce many types of fabrics with many uses. Duoppioni for example is one of the finest of silks produced from double strands taken from worms that have nested together in one cocoon. The fiber is of varying thickness and can be woven into an exquisite fabric. Silk may also be used for heavier fabrics such as furnishing textiles and carpets. It is a natural thermal insulator and can be comfortably worn in warm or cold weather. Silk is the only natural fiber, produced in continuous filaments. These maybe up to 1,400 yards long.

Natural fibers may be mechanically or chemically modified, e.g. to give crease resistant cotton and lustrous mercerized cotton a fire retardant finish, and many more special effects.

These days, there is a trend with all fiber manufacturers to produce a lighter more trans-seasonal weight of finished textile.

Synthetic Fibers

Synthetic or manufactured fibers such as rayon, acetate, polyester, nylon, and acrylic are derived from various manufacturing processes. Typically, a chemically produced liquid is forced through tiny holes rather like a showerhead, and known as a **spinneret**. The spinneret has hole sizes depending on the fineness of the filaments to be produced. This spinning process creates continuous **"filament fibers"** which can be processed to produce different types of yarns, or cut to produce a **"staple fiber"**. These staple fibers are usually cut into short lengths of around 11/2 inches to 6" in length (depending on the use), and may be chemically or heat-treated before being twisted into yarn. These manufactured fibers may have similar properties to some of the natural fibers, and are often hard to tell apart when woven or knitted into a finished textile.

Synthetic fibers, like natural fibers, have their own unique qualities. They maybe roughly classified under the following headings:

- Rayon, Acetate, and Lyocell (cellulose acetate) formed from wood cellulose.
- Nylon, Polyester, Acrylic, derived usually from a petroleum base.

These are the generic names, but often synthetic fibers are marketed and classified under a trademark e.g. **"Tencel ®"**, **"Anso ®"** (nylon, Allied-Signal).

Viscose/Rayon

Manufactured from cellulose, it was invented at the beginning of the 20th century. Because it is essentially reconstituted cellulose, it closely resembles cotton in its properties. It is a medium-weight fiber with fair to good strength that can be produced inexpensively. Viscose/Rayon is weaker than cotton when wet and should be washed with care or dry-cleaned. It recovers its strength when dry but is rather subject to shrinkage.

Acetate/Rayon

Manufactured from cellulose acetate, acetate/ rayon dates from the early 1920s. Acetate is an inexpensive fiber that gives fabric good draping abilities. Woven acetate fabrics should always be dry-cleaned. They are often used for linings, because of anti-static qualities, but because of their low softening/melting point, must be ironed with care.

Acrylic

Chemically derived fiber from a compound called poly-acrylonitrile (type of plastic). Acrylic was first introduced in the early 1950's as a substitute for wool, and is lightweight, soft, and springy like wool.

Nylon

Chemically derived fiber, of the polyamide family, first introduced in the late 1920's. Nylon is a strong lightweight fiber that is only slightly weaker when wet than in the dry state. It is a resilient fabric that drapes well and can be washed or dry-cleaned without problems. It has a wide range of uses, lingerie, to exercise wear, hosiery, swimwear, outerwear, and carpets, and which also has many industrial uses.

Polyester

First developed post Second World War. Polyester is a fiber with good strength, giving fabrics excellent wash and wear capabilities. It has proved to be the most widely used of all the synthetic fibers because of its versatility. Polyester has low water absorbency and fabrics made from it are quick drying.

Spandex ®

After many years of research, DuPont introduced the first man-made elastic fiber, "Lycra®", in 1958. Lycra® is used widely in all apparel, woven and knitted, and recently in microfibers. It allows the wearer to be comfortable and the fabric is also very durable.

(The fiber types mentioned above are those most commonly used for apparel. There are other industrial fibers such as glass and carbon, but they are not of relevance here.)

Spinning

There is an old saying, "if it has two ends it will spin".

Spinning is the process of aligning fibers, then twisting and drawing them together to produce a yarn, which can then be woven or knitted. Generally, the tighter the twist, the stronger the yarn. Long fibers like linen and silk do not require as much twist as cotton or shorter synthetic staples. A slack twist yarn creates a softer yarn used for fabric with a nap. When a yarn is twisted to create knots along its length, a crepe yarn is the result.

Yarns and Finishes

Yarn can be defined as the result of fibers being twisted and spun together to create continuous threads. Yarns are produced in a variety of thickness. Denier is sometimes used to define the thickness of filament yarns. Once the yarn is woven or knitted, the fabric is then defined by the number of threads per inch (i.e. thread count) or by weight.

There are a large variety of yarns produced from the various fibers, each with their own special qualities and textural properties, from flat and dull, to slubby and lustrous. Yarns are then finished into many types of textiles with thousands of different uses. Yarns used for the warp, (i.e. the yarn which runs lengthwise) are usually spun stronger than the fill or weft yarn. When these are cut, the grain of the fabric should be followed. The term "on grain" is used if a fabric has been cut parallel to the selvage or lengthwise grain. **"Off grain"** refers to cutting the fabric not parallel to the warp or weft. Fabric cut off grain results in skewed or twisted garment (e.g. pant legs or sleeves). Cutting a garment on the wrong grain can result in a garment that will wear out faster than if cut on the warp grain (length grain). **"Bias"** refers to cutting the fabric at 45 degrees to the length and width of the fabric. Bias-cut woven fabric elongates and stretches, which makes it best used for a draped garment.

Woven fabrics are made on a loom so that the woven yarns cross each other at right angles. The manner in which the filling (crosswise) yarns cross the warp (lengthwise) yarns determines the fabric construction, which can determine the strength, weight and feel, as well as the texture and surface of woven fabric.

Yarn Blending

Combining different yarns together, or different fibers in the same yarn, is done for various reasons such as obtaining special properties on the fabric or for reasons of cost. Thus cotton, combined with polyester, will produce a finished fabric with more crease resistant finish than cotton alone. Yarn is often dyed before weaving or knitting; however if the yarn is woven or knitted into fabric before being dyed or finished the fabrics are described as **greige goods**, or **unfinished goods**. The greige goods maybe dyed or printed and finished to produce a whole range of fabrics.

Finishes

To provide finished fabrics, various mechanical and chemical treatments maybe employed to alter fiber and fabric properties. For example, mercerization creates smoother more lustrous cotton. Crimping polyester fiber by heat and mechanical treatment adds resilience, improves the feel, and adds spring to the fibers used in the end product. The laundering of fabric, such as stone washing, using starch, or fabric softeners, will also subtly alter fabric stiffness or softness.

It should be apparent that textile dying and finishing is a vast and sophisticated industry on its own.

Surface Design

Printing a design with dye onto the surface of fabric adds pattern. Designs can create implied texture and give interest to the fabrics. Other patterns may be created by a combination of texture and surface design, or using embossing (a type of printing) on the fabric surface to create textural interest. A good example of this is velour that has been embossed with a decorative pattern, the effect is almost three-dimensional.

High-tech Fabrics or Microfiber

We hear this term a great deal these days, and it is now used extensively in the fashion industry for all types of textiles. **So what is microfiber?** Microfiber is a shortened form of the textile-industry term "microdenier fiber", with "denier" meaning a measurement of fiber size. The smaller the number, the finer the fiber; microdenier is fibers with less than 1.0 denier per filament, as compared with a 1.25 denier for silk. First developed in Japan in the 1980s, microfibers can be derived from polyester, nylon, acrylic or rayon. These fibers are used to produce densely woven fabrics that are strong, water resistant, soft, and drapable. However, because of their density they can be difficult to press. They are often used in permanent press form, as fabrics for finished garments. Can be knit or woven and many are used in knit active-wear. Usually it is possible to wash and dry microfiber goods using low temperatures. Garments usually require little or no ironing. Modern microfibers often have Lycra added to give the finished fabric some stretch.

Understanding Knit Fabrics

(Knitting machines have been around a surprisingly long time. The first knitting machine was built by an Englishman way back in 1589. He finished the first pair of silk stockings nine years later, and presented them to Queen Elizabeth I. The knitting machine has come a long way since, and today computers are employed to program knitting machines.)

Knit fabrics have skyrocketed in popularity in recent years because they offer the conveniences and comfort that modern living demands. Some reports estimate that about 50% of all types of clothing are now knits.

Knits are available in an endless variety of fibers, mixtures of fibers, yarn combinations, (including microfibers), textures, patterns, weights and colors. They feature exciting surface interests such as ribs, piques, jacquards, and crepes, as well as many types of stripes and prints.

Understanding the terms used when referring to knit fabrics, and the differences between woven fabrics will help dispel any hang-ups and enable you to use the necessary terms with confidence. The lengthwise chain of loops is called a "wale" and corresponds to a warp in woven fabrics. The number of stitches or loops (courses) in each inch of fabric determines the thread count of the knitted cloth. The **"gauge"** tells the number of needles per given distance in a knitting machine. In fully-fashioned hosiery and sweater machines, the number of needles per 11/2" represents the gauge. In all other machines it is the number of needles per inch.

Terms related to knit fabrics

Weft Knitting: Weft knits or circular knits as they are generally called, include single knits and double knits. Circular knits are also called tubular knits and are knitted on very large tubular knitting machines and are generally split before shipping. Interlacing yarn loops forms this type of knit, which runs across the width of the fabric.

Warp Knitting: Has interlacing yarn loops, which run in the lengthwise direction of the fabric. Two basic, widely used warp-knits are Tricot and Reschel.

Tricot: French word for knit, which now applies to very lightweight fabrics. It is in demand for lingerie and underwear and as a backing for bonded fabrics. It is also used with a bonding agent added, for interlining. Tricot is a type of warp knitting.

Raschel: Often looks as if it has been hand knitted. It may be knitted in a thin or a thick yarn, to create open work or lacy knits. Raschel is a type of warp knitting.

Single Knits: Also referred to as single jerseys, single knits are made on machines that have one set of needles. They are characterized by v-shaped stitches on the face of the fabric and show semi-circular loops on the back of the fabric.

Double Knits: Are knitted on a machine with two sets of needles. The cloth has the same appearance front and back, that is, the two sides of the cloth are inter-knit together to create the impression of a double knitted plain jersey material.

Interlock: This is the simplest form of double jersey fabric. It is two 1x1-rib fabrics knitted opposite each other resembling the face of a plain fabric on both sides. It is often used for T-shirt knits.

Flame-Resistant Fibers and Finishes

The **Flammable Fabrics Act** was first passed in 1953; it has been amended and updated many times since. The act prohibits the sale of **"torch"** fabrics (fabrics that burst into flame instantly), and that are considered to be dangerous. A tag or label must be attached to a garment to inform the wearer of the fiber content.

Some of the more flammable fabrics and construction are untreated fabrics made of generic fibers such as cotton, rayon, acetate, nylon, and polyester. Fabrics of open, loose construction ignite more rapidly than fabrics that are densely woven or knitted.

There are three classifications of fibers:

- Flameproof fibers that do not burn
- Flame-resistant fibers that have a relatively high combustion
- Flammable fibers which will burn easily ("torch fabrics")

Flammable fibers can be made flame resistant by adding finishes either to the fibers, to the yarn or to the finished fabrics. Unfortunately, the use of these finishes may result in a hardening of the fabric, which adversely affect the draping ability and tends to weaken the fabric.

Strict fire retardant standards have been issued for children's sleepwear, sizes 0-6X and 7-14, large and small carpets and rugs, and mattresses and mattress pads. If you are intending to produce baby wear or children's sleeping apparel, some cities and states have established standards for these textile items, so check with your local authorities to clarify the laws within your city or state. The CPSC has recently redefined the fire retardant standards relating to children's sleepwear to only include loose fitting nightgowns and pajamas. **It is very important that you follow up on the most recent laws and restrictions with regards to the "Flammable Act".**

The construction of fabrics may affect the degree to which oxygen is made available to the fibers. Fabrics that burn quickly are more commonly sheer or lightweight fabrics, napped, pile, or tufted surfaces. Apparel made from these types of fabric ignites quickly, burns with great intensity, and is difficult to extinguish, also called "torch fabrics". Certain styles have been associated with causing tragic accidents e.g.; sweaters made from chenille, fringes on garments, extra long sleeves, flared skirts, ruffles, frills, and flowing gowns.

There are many terms that are used when discussing the ability of a fabric to resist ignition or to burn more slowly than normal. Certain types of fabrics self-extinguish once the source of ignition has been removed from the fabric. Fabrics maybe made flame resistant in various ways, for example:

- Using inherently flame resistant fibers including aramid, modacrylic, novoloid, saran, and vinal/vinyon matrix fibers.

- Fibers in which flame-retardant chemicals can been added to the spinning solution.
- Applying flame-retardant finishes to the fabrics. Flame-retardant finishes are used on cotton, rayon, nylon, and polyester fabrics. They must be durable, withstand 50 washings, be non-toxic, and non-carcinogenic. They should not greatly change the hand and texture of the fabric or have an unpleasant odor. Most finishes are invisible but naturally add to the cost of the finished garment because of the extra processing involved. (Flame-retardant finishes are usually less expensive than flame-resistant fibers or fiber variants).

Before producing a line of children's sleepwear, it is important to check with the Federal Trade Commission and the Consumer Product Safety Commission (CPSC) on any modified laws. Contact **www.CPSC.gov** for specific array of requirements.

What is Interlining / Interfacing / Fusing?

An interlining is a layer of material inserted into certain parts of the garment like plackets and collars. They are used in the inner (lining or facing) and outer (shell) for shape retention, strength and or extra body. Interlinings can be divided into two major categories, sew-in and the type most often used is known as fusible. Sew-in interlinings are held in place by stitching, whereas fusible interlinings are bonded to the fabric using a thermally activated adhesive. The glue is on one side and is fused to the cut pattern piece by heat, or the fabric is block fused and then the pattern pieces are cut.

Some form of an interlining (interfacing or fusing), can be found in most manufactured garments. There are many types of interlining on the market and it is important to choose the correct type for your garments. If the interlining properties do not match the properties of the outer shell, there will be dramatic problems in production and for the wearer. We have all seen jackets that look as if they have bubbles on the surface after the jacket has been to the cleaners. This is due to the manufacturer using the incorrect interlining, or the wrong temperature was used to bond to the self-fabric. The bonding process normally requires a special machine, known as a fusing press, and goods to be fused are usually sent out to an independent service that is specialized in this type of work. It is possible to use a hand iron to adhere the interlining to the garment, but this is very time consuming and not cost effective. Fusing the interlining at the correct temperature is not always possible with a hand held iron and the interlining could begin to pull away after washing if the heat used for this fusing process is insufficient.

Free advice on the correct type of interlinings

The producers of interlining, fusible, and interfacing will often provide their expertise and give free advice on the correct type of interlining to be used for the fabrics you have selected, and the correct type to use for your designs. You provide them with sample yard of the fabric and they will recommend various types of fusing materials for your approval. You can then decide which would have the right properties for production.

Non-woven

Moderately priced and Budget garment manufacturers mostly use interlinings made from a non-woven (paper-like) fabric, in a variety of weights dependent on the fabric's own qualities. Rayon, polyester and nylon are the major fiber components in non-woven structures. Polyester imparts a soft hand; rayon offers a firmer hand with body, and nylon gives superior strength and recovery characteristics.

There are many types and weights of non-woven, fusible interfacings. You will have to be an industry expert to understand their many applications.

Woven Interlining

Better apparel companies often prefer the more expensive fusible woven interlinings for use in outerwear. Woven interlinings have the advantage of strength, stability, good drape and hand. Resiliency is a prime advantage of a woven interlining. The type of fiber used in a woven helps to determine its performance characteristics.

Weft Interlining

This popular type of fusible is a warp knitted fabric with woven-like filling yarns laid into the knitted structure. These types of fusibles offer unidirectional control, which gives drape and softness in the length and resilience in the width. They are usually less expensive than their woven counterparts.

Sewn-in Interlining

Interlinings that are sewn-in are rarely used these days in production. However, they maybe appropriate for more transparent fabric such as chiffon or organza, where a fusible would show through the fabric. Sewn-in interlinings naturally cost more in the production stage.

Interlinings are also used in coats and outerwear to provide extra warmth.

A fusible of any type maybe applied to selected garment parts (as opposed to bonding entire rolls of fabrics) for the following reasons:

- To improve the aesthetics, quality or performance of the garment, by changing the hand, shape or dimensional stability of that part of the garment.
- To aid in the garment's manufacturing process or to improve productivity. Bonding of the entire roll of fabric is sometimes used when the fabric is inexpensive, and by fusing the fabric the finished garment may have a more expensive final appearance at less cost.

Thread Selection

Another often overlooked problem is the manufacturer's use of the wrong type of thread for the fabric. Wrong thread, after washing, will react differently from the fabric causing puckering to occur.

Test your own care instructions!

See Appendix for Resources

CHAPTER 10

SAMPLES, PATTERNMAKING, GRADING, MARKERS AND CUTTING

"As long as CAD Systems are being operated by humans, the operator will remain a deciding factor."

Thomas Baur, President Assyst Inc. USA

Samples

Finding a good sample maker can often be trial and error. Sample makers are often specialized in a certain type of sewing, and you may have to try a couple before you find the right one for your company. However, once the right one is found they are worth their weight in gold. They can teach you a great deal about construction and how the finished garment should look. A good sample maker must be able to communicate with the patternmaker and point out any errors in the pattern; i.e.: notching inconsistencies, seams which do not match, or a collar that is too small. It is essential that the sample maker inform the patternmaker of any problems before the garments go through production, and money is wasted or orders lost. If your contractor is making your first sample, all of the above still applies. Do not be surprised if it takes a few tries to get the sample to your satisfaction. This is normal in product development. It will be important for a company that is in the development stage to spend the extra time and money on developing the perfected sample, which will create an image and build a brand.

Patternmaker

It takes time to create a good pattern, and it takes training and experience to be proficient. To turn a two-dimensional sketch into a pleasing three-dimensional piece of clothing that will hopefully sell in the hundreds of thousands, demands a qualified individual. The patternmaker is not only responsible for making the pattern, but must understand all the components that put a garment together, with construction of the garment being of paramount importance. The patternmaker must be able to give precise instructions to the sample maker on how the garment is to be assembled and finished.

How to find a patternmaker

Finding a good patternmaker can be time consuming and expensive. Trade papers and directories listed in the Appendix will be able to help. Another means of finding a patternmaker is by calling a trade college in your area that offers a fashion degree. They usually have a list of alumni that will have the expertise. Personal recommendations can be very helpful, whenever possible. Grading services and contracting agencies could possibly help by recommending patternmakers and sample sewers that could be suitable for your product.

When interviewing a potential patternmaker it is a good idea to ask to see examples of finished samples they have produced. When employing new patternmakers, it is very common for a manufacturer to ask for a first pattern from a sketch as a test of their skills. To be able to translate a two-dimensional sketch into a three-dimensional garment, a patternmaker needs to develop an eye for design. Their finished work will speak for itself, giving you an idea as to their standard of work, and their interpretive skills. Do not try and cut costs with this important part of producing your line. Like all professions there are good patternmakers, and then there are the others.

What will it cost?

The patternmaking service will have a pay scale as to how long it will take to make a particular pattern, e.g. Jackets would cost more than blouses, and a simple skirt would be priced less than a pair of pants. The price is usually set for certain types of garments; a skirt could cost around $70 but a lined jacket could be as much as $400.

When negotiating with the patternmaker for their rate of pay, you need to find out if they will make adjustments to the pattern if you find it to be unsatisfactory. Pattern revisions are normal and should be included in the cost of making the pattern. If however, it is your mistake you will be responsible for having the pattern re-made at your expense. Therefore, it is important that you know exactly how you wish the finished garment to look. This should include all the stitching details, down to the number of buttons, the size and placement. Patternmakers should not be put into a position where they have to guess what you the designer/manufacturer want. They must be able to fully understand your design in order to translate the flat sketch into an actual garment. *(See Chapter 7)*

Fit Models or Dress Forms?

Do not overlook checking the fit of the finished garment to see if it hangs correctly and has the desired fit. If you need to find a suitable fit model, it is important to inquire about the cost per hour. Fit models do not come cheap! The going price as of 2000 is around $80 per hour. If a fit model is not available, it will be important to purchase a dress form in your sample size, and to check for fit and styling changes. Even if you have a perfect fit model it will be necessary to have a dress form to make minor adjustments. Dress forms come in a variety of shapes and sizes dependent on your company's needs. For a little extra money they can be produced to your own desired specific measurements. They maybe costly, but they are an investment that you will find important to include in your budget. It is sometimes possible to find them used, and have them re-covered and restored to nearly new.

Fitting a Sample

A well-fitted garment feels comfortable, adjusts naturally to the activities of the wearer, is becoming in its design lines. It also has the amount of ease consistent with current fashions. In general, it should be well balanced and hang without wrinkles, sagging, or pulling. Poor sewing and pressing often give the impression of a poor fit. If the sample is poorly executed, it may be difficult to decide what is wrong. It is therefore important to fit a garment with a trained professional who can recommend the required changes to the pattern, and or construction. A tailoring service may be worth seeking. Most drycleaners have a tailor on hand offering alterations and who may be willing to help with fittings, even some sampling. If you are really lucky your first sample could be perfect! But don't count on it; prepare for making your samples at least two to three times.

Basic Blocks and Slopers

Patternmakers will often ask if you have a "**Block**", or as it is sometimes called, a "**Sloper**". Stylized patterns are made from these basic patterns. Each company has its own blocks, and many have spent a great deal of time and money on perfecting the ideal fitting garment for their company. You may have noticed how there are often variations in fit from one company's line of clothing to another. Some lines will fit certain customers well, while others will fit those same customers poorly. Blocks are companies' guarded secrets and are usually locked up with all their other patterns. You should investigate what type of a fit you want your line of clothing to have. Use a model that has the right measurements for your image; try some store clothes on your model to understand the kind of fit you are looking for, and buy them to show your patternmaker.

Numbering your styles

Each design is made into a pattern and then a sample must be given a **design number**. The patternmaker records the number with a sketch of the style and a swatch of the fabric as a reference in a book. The pattern will have a pattern chart hanging with it that will give all the details of the pattern. *(See example of a pattern card at the end of this chapter)* If the style is not used in the line for this season, it may be used in full or in part for a following season. Patterns are costly to develop, so it is important not to throw them out in case they can be used in the future. Some companies save on costs by using pattern pieces that can be interchanged. That is, a sleeve from one jacket will be used for another jacket design, or a collar from one style could be used for another style. This is fine as long as the basic design allows this. In fact, it will give your clothes your own identity and fit as was explained in Chapter 4, Line Development and also save on development costs.

When a garment is approved for the line it will receive a **style number**. The style number is used to identify each new style in the line and to organize the line. Everyone who has any contact with the garment will use this number. The design room, sales representatives, storeowners, contractors, cutters and grader, will all use your style number when referring to any aspect of the order or the garment. You may feel that a name would be sufficient, but numbers are the only logical system used worldwide by all manufacturers. Naming the line or the use of names for a style is fine, but each garment will also have to have its own style number.

Developing a numbering system

Style numbers are made up very specifically, and there are a variety of methods used. Here are some suggestions to help you develop a numbering system when organizing your company's patterns and styles.

You may decide to start with the season the line is designed for, F for fall. H for Holiday, W for Winter, SP for Spring and S for Summer. Then categorize the type of garment to be numbered, e.g. Tops could start with 1, Bottoms with 2, Knits with 3 etc. As most style numbers have four digits you could begin with the following example, W1001. This would translate into the first top styled for winter. You could include the type of fabric used as another digit; it really depends on your line and how you want to customize your numbering system. One word of warning! Do not use a zero at the beginning of the style number. Everyone will know that you

are a new company and possibly inexperienced. Computers are not good at dealing with zeros at the beginning of numbers, which may cause problems in your getting paid on time due to the confusion within the computer's numbering system.

Patterns Made by Computers

Many companies now use computers to make patterns. Computer aided design (CAD) and patternmaking are becoming the norm. *As with everything else, the results are only as good as the operator.* The more experienced the operator/patternmaker, the more successful the results. Computers are useful for making patterns that are repetitive, needing few changes each season. Very large companies like Limited, Express, Gap, use computers for almost everything, from the design to the finished garment. Many better apparel companies such as Givenchey, YSL, also have their patterns made on the computer. After a garment is draped, it is then trued-up on the computer and perfected. After all, the end result of any garment is always a two dimensional flat pattern.

Production Patterns

How do production patterns differ from the first sample pattern?

Production patterns are made from the first pattern by the *"production patternmaker"*. The first pattern is perfected for fit, utilization of fabric and analyzed for production procedures. A production patternmaker is a position that is usually well paid, demanding a person who is capable of saving production costs and fabric yardage without losing the character of the original first sample. They must be experienced in fitting a garment, perfecting patterns, and the many stages of producing a finished garment.

Example: If 2 inches were saved per garment by adding a center back seam, this would allow for a better marker on an order of 2,000 units totaling a savings of 50 yards! If you have paid $10 per yard then that is a savings of $500!

Multiply this with each garment produced, and then you will begin to understand the importance of a production patternmaker's job.

The perfected production pattern is then graded into the other sizes to be produced. The production patternmaker is sometimes responsible for this job, or it is sent out to a grading service, which may also make the marker. Either way the production patternmaker will supervise this important part of production.

What is Grading?

Grading is making the perfected production pattern into the various other sizes that will be available for sale in that style. The production pattern is usually made in the middle size, probably a Size 8 for Missy and a Size 7 or 9 for Juniors. This would mean a Size 8 would then be graded up to a Size 14 and down to a Size 2. A Junior's Size 7 would be graded up to a Size 13 and down to a Size 1 or 3.

A start-up company will contract out to a service that specializes in grading. They will usually also provide the service of making the marker for the pattern. Use the directories and trade papers recommended in the Appendix or the Yellow Pages to find a grader. These days this service is usually done with the aid of a computer, although there are still some very good grading services that do it manually using a grading machine. As with any service, the finished product is only as good as the person responsible for carrying out the task. They are responsible for feeding the computer the information, or the correct *grade rules*, (as they are known in the Industry).

Cost of Grading Service

Whomever you choose, the fee for the service will be quoted by pattern piece. If the pattern piece is a mirrored piece, then there is no extra charge. This means that where you have two sleeves, and the sleeves are identical except that one is left side and the other the right, you will pay for only the one pattern piece to be graded, as they are a mirrored image. If, however, one sleeve has a design detail that is different from the other, they will then be graded separately and you will be charged accordingly. The size of the pattern piece normally does not come into consideration when pricing the graded piece; large or small, the price for the pattern piece to be graded is the same. **Example:** In 2003 the going price per unit is around a dollar per piece, with a minimum cost for grading the whole pattern.

Grading Rules

To establish the rule of the grade you will have to investigate the type of grade that you would like. If you have no experience with sizing a garment then you may have to trust the grading company to do your grading correctly. They will advise you on the normal methods, and explain to you where they make the garment larger and smaller. It would be advisable to look at other graded garments in the stores to see if they are sized, as you would wish. In the States, there is no established set of rules to govern grading or the sizing of a garment. So, when you try on a Size 8, sometimes it is too big and other times too small. When you are lucky, it is just right! In other countries there are rules in place that require exact measurements for each size. It would be less confusing if sizes were more regulated. Each year it seems that sizes get larger. "Better" apparel is cut using more fabric than "Budget". The reason for this is that the manufacturer wants you to feel slim and trim in their clothes. How great it is that you still fit into a Size 6! Over the years a Size 10 has becomes Size 6. Good marketing! The customer is more inclined to buy when they think they still fit into a Size 6. Look at vintage clothing and vintage patterns, you will be amazed at the size difference between 40 years ago and now. An old Size 12 is like a Size 4 in 2003. Of course women have grown taller and naturally larger since the turn of the 20th century.

Garments are now bigger, but paradoxically the sizes have shrunk to keep the market buoyant. *(At the turn of the century the average height for a woman was 4 foot 11 inches, now the average height is 5 foot 5 inches. It makes you wonder what it will be in another 100 years time)!* Women tend to spend more when they believe they are slimmer and when the label reinforces this belief. *(See Chapter 6 for "Understanding Ready to Wear Sizing")*

Here is a simple general rule with regards to grading sizes

Missy sizes are even numbers and graded with a one inch grade up to a Size 10, then the grade may change to a 1½ inch grade. Juniors are uneven numbers and also graded one inch up and down. If there is a break in the grading rules, it will occur at Size 9, when a 1½ inch grade would then be used for all sizes greater than 9. This means that one inch or 1½ inch is added to the circumference of the garment to make it larger. In the case of making it smaller, one inch is graded down or taken off. The length of the garment is also adjusted along with the circumference. Small, medium and large sizes are graded with a two-inch grade. JC Penney uses the best grading rules in the industry so whenever you are in doubt, look at the JCPenney grade rules. Most grading services will help you with this information. Ask them to print out a "nested pattern" so that you can see how the various sizes are graded in comparison with each size. (See example of a nested pattern).

Marker

Once the grading is completed, the pattern is then laid out and the marker is made. There are two kinds of markers created:

- Sample marker - Used for samples and duplicates for sales representatives and showrooms.
- Production marker - Made for all the different sizes offered to the retailer.

The marker is used to cut the pattern pieces out of the fabric. Each pattern piece is laid onto the correct width of paper that is 1" narrower than the width of the fabric chosen (this sometimes depends on the fabric selvage). The pattern is laid out with as little wasted fabric as possible. Making a good marker can be complicated, since sizes are sometimes mixed together for a better yield of fabric; e.g. a Size 2 would be placed with a Size 12 to allow for fabric saving. This is all well and good when the order (**cutting ticket**) has all the same ratio. That is to say, a Size 2 and a Size 8 have the same amount of units ordered. If, as in the normal case, there is a larger order of Size 8's and Size 10's, then a mixed ratio marker can be complicated. This requires some mathematical calculations; it could be a two to one ratio, or a three to one ratio. Using the computer for this type of marker makes the marker maker's job much more straightforward. The marker is then printed out onto special **marker-paper**, and laid on top of the fabric to be used as a guide for cutting the pattern pieces.

Type of Fabric

Markers have to take into consideration the type and width of fabric to be cut. . For each type of fabric with a different width, a new marker must be made. A style may be cut in velvet or other napped fabric, which would require the pattern pieces to be laid all in one direction. Or, the fabric could be printed with a "repeat" design that would require the repeat s be matched. If a plaid is used, the pattern and marker must be carefully arranged in order to match the plaid.

If the marker has been made by the traditional method, a hard copy of the marker is stored, and reprinted for re-use on future orders. If the computer was used, then the marker information is stored for future use.

Cutting

Once the marker is made it is time to roll out the fabric. The fabric is rolled out by **"spreaders"**, onto large cutting tables that may be thirty feet long by 60 inches wide. The fabric is rolled out layer on layer, approximately 12" high. Colors can be mixed in depending on the orders or cutting ticket. Sometimes there are as many as 100 layers or more to be cut at one time, depending on the thickness of the fabric. Large companies use vacuum tables that suck the fabric down so there is a tighter lay and a more accurate cut can be achieved.

Splicing

Rolls of fabric do not come in exact lengths and when the cutter rolls the fabric onto the table, the fabric will have to be spliced or overlaid in parts to allow for this problem. The marker is made to allow for this process. The fabric spreader will plan the cut to match the splice marks. The fabric is rolled out to the exact length of the marker.

Dye Lots

Shading and dye lots are another concern of the cutter. Each roll of fabric will be marked with a dye lot tag and the cutter must plan so that the garment pieces are not sewn with different dye lots. Different dye lots together will result in shading and expensive wastage. Fabric is rolled out in dye lots and layers of different colored tissue paper separate each dye lot to be cut. The person who separates the cut pieces and *"bundles"* them will make certain to keep the dye lots separate for production.

Computer Cutting

As mentioned earlier, patterns can be generated on the computer, as well as grading, marking and cutting. These computer systems are integrated, so once the pattern is digitized into the computer, the rest can all be done with the use of the main server. Lasers are sometimes used to cut, but the laser is not good when a synthetic fabric is used, it fuses the cut edges together. Some companies such as "Levi's" are now using a high-pressure water jet to cut out the fabric. An interesting new use of the laser is in finishing the edges of garments. It fuses the edges of synthetic fabrics, preventing them from fraying and allows the manufacturer to leave the edge without a hem or facing.

Hand Cutting

Smaller companies and the more couture companies have not progressed this far and the older methods are still preferred. Cutting is done by the traditional method of using a vertical vibrating blade, guided around the edges of the marker, to cut out the pattern pieces. Some of the couture houses cut each garment individually, using a single layer of fabric. The cutter uses weights to keep the pattern pieces in place while the pieces are cut out with scissors. Quantity is not the priority, but quality is! This is the opposite of the manufacturer who produces en masse. Because of the intense hands-on work with each garment, couture garments cost much more to produce. The more garments produced the more production costs are reduced.

Cutting Costs

Ask to see the marker and the fabric yield; this will help you understand the process. Discuss the possibility of putting two styles or mixing your sizes on one marker, *(provided of course that the fabric used for both styles is the same).* For a smaller manufacturer this would save on making markers and on the fabric yield. The cutter has to be sure not to waste your fabric. It is advisable to check once in a while to be sure that you have a cutter who is taking care to save on fabric wastage. Unnecessary waste costs can begin to add up and should be addressed before you find that you have a problem.

Cutting Tickets

The cutter's instructions for how many piece to be cut are on the cutting ticket prepared by the production department. As the orders are placed and the orders grow, cutting tickets are written and issued. *(See Chapter 13)*

Quantity to Cut

For the smaller manufacturer, it is a good idea to plan on cutting about 10% - 15% over the orders placed, allowing for more orders and for the inevitable damages that will occur in production.

Price of Cutting

Cutting is priced by the piece. The more units you have, the lower the cost. For a new company with small cuts, the costs will be higher than they would be for a larger company. The expected units to be cut should be given very serious consideration when costing a line. If you cost for a certain number of garments to be cut, and you only get a fraction of the orders, it will cost you more to produce and the profit will be lower. It will be important to consider the risks of producing in such a case. *(See Chapter 9)*

Bundling

After the pattern is cut into the various garment pieces, the pieces are then sorted and bundled ready for production. The garment pieces should have labels to keep the dye lots together and also to help prevent loss or theft. During bundling the cut pieces together, the zippers and trims (**findings**) are also placed into the sorted bundles for the sewing operators. Identification tickets are attached for piecework control. The style number, bundle quantity, individual piecework rate, and operations to be performed are printed on these tickets. The operators will use these tickets as proof of the piecework they have completed. These tickets or labels are then sewn into the garment. If you look at any of your own garments, you will find these labels sewn into a seam somewhere. The cut bundles are distributed to the machine operators in the same factory or sent out to other contractor sewers.

CHAPTER 11

FINDING A GARMENT CONTRACTOR

Words of wisdom from Joe Rodriguez,

Garment Contractors Association Southern California.

*F**or a designer manufacturer, I would recommend that they get to know the product manufacturing side. Try to spend time at the factories where the products are made. If you work for a manufacturer or retailer, find reasons why you have to go visit the factories. Spend as much time as possible learning the issues and concerns of the factory owners and production personnel. If you do this, something magical will happen…you will be able to correctly apply the strengths you bring to the process, like creativity and fashion sense, to the manufacturing process that involves getting logistics addressed and teamwork to take place.*

For a new company establishing relationships with domestic contractors for the first time, learn to price the labor components of your garment correctly. Never place an item in a factory where the contractor does not have enough in your pricing to at least cover its overhead and pay its employees lawfully. PLACE SUCH WORK OFFSHORE! Once you know that your price is fair, you should make it a point to meet with the owner of the contract shop face-to-face and impress upon this person that you never want to hear of any instance of any employee not being paid minimum wage or overtime correctly. Determine if the contractor agrees with this approach. Tell the contractor that you will never do any business with a contractor that engages in illegal practices such as using child labor or homework.

I am convinced that if you do your due diligence up front before you engage a contractor, you can determine whether or not there will ever be problems in that shop. Hiring a monitoring service is not enough. You must deliver with conviction the message of compliance to the contractor. But remember, the price has to be a fair one or else everything falls apart!

Understanding the Contractor

For those of you that may not understand what contractors do and why they are essential to the production process, here are some questions and answers that will help you better understand the roll the contractor plays in manufacturing garments.

- **What is a contractor?** A contractor is a company that provides a service, they contract to do work. In the clothing industry contractors are used extensively to do jobs that are not done by the manufacturer. They may cut and sew, or quilt or pleat, but for the most part, it is the contractor who cuts and sews the garments.

- **Why do manufacturers use a contractor?** The reason that manufacturers choose to contract out their work is mainly cost. To have in-house sewing, the manufacturer must be certain to have enough work to keep the operators busy at all times. They cannot keep hiring and firing machine operators whenever there is a lull in orders. By contracting the work with an independent contractor, they do not have that worry. The contractor is able to keep its operators busy because they work for a number of manufacturers at one time and have a constant turnover of work. The manufacturer will contract with a variety of contractors depending on the type of work necessary for their designs. One contractor may be an expert on sewing knits while another specializes in tailoring jackets.

- **How do you know if they are legal, and not a sweatshop?** By finding a contractor through an association you will only find legal shops. If the contractor has been recommended to you, it would be a good idea to ask to see the contractor's license. Remember, as stated in Chapter 2, it is necessary in some states for a manufacturer to get a license. To date, the states that require licenses are California and New York. The cost for a license is around $250 per year and increases with the size of your production. A small test is given to the manufacturers to make sure that they are aware of the laws regarding contracting and illegal workers before they can receive a license to manufacture. This has all stemmed from having sweatshops producing sewn products, and manufacturers being unaware of having their goods sewn in sub-standard conditions. **California Labor & Standards Tel: 415 703 4848**

- **Can I negotiate the price for the work to be done by the contractor?** Yes, in fact, this is the way it is done and usually the contractor has allowed for some haggling. There will only be room for small adjustments of price so don't be greedy. Operators are normally paid by each piece that they sew, and the quality of the product is important.

- **When will the contractor expect to be paid?** For a start-up company, the contractor will require that you pay for the goods made when they are picked up, or when delivery is made. After a couple of successful seasons working with a contractor, it may be possible to re-negotiate the terms of payment and pay within fifteen days. This will depend on the contractor. Remember they have wages to pay weekly for the work that has been done.

Contracting a Contractor

Many manufacturers contract out all cutting and sewing. Even the larger manufacturer will have to contract out certain stages of producing a garment, from fusing interlinings, laundering, pleating, quilting, embroidery or any other specialty service that requires special machinery or handling. Manufacturers that do their own sewing are referred to as "in-house," contractors are referred to as "outside shop." For the start up company, the important part is not having in-house production, but rather how to find the best contractor for the job at hand. As stated above, you must also make sure that the contractor that you use has the necessary licenses to manufacture. If a contractor is running an illegal shop and it is raided, it will be subjected to a heavy fine and confiscation of goods. In cases of repeated offenses, the penalties will increase dramatically. If you are the manufacturer that has contracted the work with the contractor, you will also have a penalty to pay. It is not worth the gamble. You must make sure to check all the relevant legal papers required by the state and federal government.

Contract Associations

To protect you from the above problems, it is advisable to find a contractor through one of the many contractors' associations around the country. For a nominal fee, or in most cases at no cost to you, they will be able to give you a list of contractors in their association that run legal factories, with legal workers who are qualified to produce certain garments in various categories. It should be noted that the associations only furnish you with names, they do not guarantee the work produced by the contractors. You will find in the Appendix a list of associations that will give you some help in finding a contractor to cut and sew your garments.

Questions to ask the Contractor

It is advisable to first visit a potential contractor, inspect their work place and ask some important questions. The contractor will also want to ascertain some information from you. Be tactful and explain that you are new to the business and want to make sure that every thing is understood. Contractors are often originally from anywhere other than America, so you may find that there is a language problem to negotiate along with any contracts. Here are some suggested questions to ask the contractor:

Do you have a current contractor's license, and may I see it? It is important that any papers or licenses that you inspect are the originals and not copies!

How long have you been in business and whom do you contract for? It maybe a good idea to get some recommendations.

May I see some of the finished sewn goods? This will help you to see the finished product, the quality of the goods, and the type. If they tell you they can sew fine silk and they are sewing sweatshirts, you will need to rethink the arrangement.

What kind of equipment do you have? It would be helpful to have a person familiar with production methods available to help check out the contractor's facilities.

How many garments can your factory produce each week? Of course this would depend on the type of production produced and the quality of the goods made.

Do you meet the deadlines on time? If deadlines are not met, what guarantee or discounts will be given to the manufacturer? If the contractor is late returning work, then the manufacturer will be delayed in shipping their order.

What kind of quality control do you have in place? It is your responsibility to protect the quality of goods produced.

Do you have insurance for fire, loss of goods, damages, etc.? If the contractor is licensed, it is the law that they also carry insurance for lost or stolen goods.

Do you have a basic contract you use for the manufacturers that you sew for? It is useful to read it though and if necessary add or reject where you see fit.

How much would you charge for this garment to be manufactured here? There is usually room for a little negotiation.

Questions the Contractor should ask you

Here are some questions you can expect to be asked by the contractor:

May I see a sample, or do you wish me to make one? The contractor often likes to sew the sample to understand the sewing procedure and to be able to cost the garment.

Do you have specifications, with sewing instructions for your garments? It is important to give as much information as possible so there is no room for mistakes.

How many units are you planning to produce? For start-ups and the smaller manufacturer it is often hard to find a good contractor that will sew small numbers. The number of units sewn will also determine the cost in production.

When do you expect to ship the order? The contractor has to decide if they have the manpower to produce the goods on time, in order to meet the deadline.

Can you guarantee payment? Contractors have to pay their workers at the end of the week and they must know if you are good for the money agreed upon in the contract.

Do you have a state license to manufacture? As the manufacturer you are responsible for the legal documents required by law.

Are your workers legally registered to work in the US? The contractor will be justified in wanting to know who they are contracting to do business with, and if they have all the legal documents.

Contract of Services

Another aspect to consider when using a contractor is having legal documents drawn up to protect you from a number of problems that could occur. Talk to an accountant or the local Better Business Bureau in your city and state. Each state has its own laws with regards to garment manufacturing. "Better safe than sorry!"

Here are some things that you may wish to include in a contract made with your contractor:

- **Late deliveries** The contractor will be penalized for late delivery, and with each day late the penalty will increase.

- **Insurance** against damage due to fire, water etc. It should also include loss of garments in transit, theft of fabric and garments.

- **Workers used are legal** As explained above, if your contractor has illegal workers, you will also be subject to fines along with the contractor. In addition to these penalties, there will be interruptions in your work schedule, which could lead to late deliveries.

Making a Sample

You may have a sample to show the contractors or you may wish them to make a sample for you. Either way they will usually make a first sample for you, and then they are in a better position to accurately cost the garment. If they are making the sample, make sure to provide clear and precise specifications and working flat sketches. You will have to furnish all zippers and trims along with the fabric. The contractor should also make a production sample for you and for them to follow in producing the garments. All garments in production should be as perfect as the production sample. *(See Chapter 12 Production Planning)*

The Right Contractor for the Job

Choosing the right contractor for the job is important to insure that they are able to produce the type of garments you need. Do not assume that the same contractor is able to produce all your production. If your production requires cover-stitching, then make sure that the contractor has enough cover-stitch machines to produce your order. If the contractor only has two cover-stitch machines and all your production requires cover-stitching, then you will have a problem and will have to find other contractor to complete your order on time.

The manufacturer will have to provide the contractor with all the supplies necessary to produce the garment, fabrics, fusing, trims, thread, buttons etc.

Keeping Track of Your Contractors

It is a very good idea to have a file for each contractor with a copy of their garment manufacturing license (California and New York), their worker's compensation insurance and their fire insurance). It is prudent to enter the expiration dates of each onto your general business calendar and get proof of renewal from the contractor when each expires. If any of these three expires and is not renewed it could have very bad financial consequences for you.

Contracting Abroad

As a company grows, so does its production needs, and costing becomes a larger issue. In most cases, sourcing abroad allows the manufacturer to produce with better cost margins. Several types of foreign production packages are found in the Industry. A complete package can be purchased through an agent who will arrange all production; cutting to sewing the whole garment can be completed abroad. The garments will then be classified as imported. It is also possible to cut domestically and have the production sewn abroad.

You may buy Italian fabrics, or other foreign textiles and have the fabric shipped directly to your offshore agent for production without seeing the fabric first yourself. This type of production requires qualified representatives to be on hand in the country responsible for your production to ensure quality control. Offshore production can often add up to some really big headaches, and is one of the main reasons why some manufacturers choose to keep production domestic. Another disadvantage is that the lead-time required will often take too long. With manufacturers working closer to shipping dates, it is usually impossible to send production abroad and have it shipped back on time. The only exception is going south of the Border to Mexico, which allows for better timing to meet the shipping schedules. *(See more on Producing Abroad in Chapter 17)*

How to Calculate Pay Rates for Piece Rate Workers

1. Add employee's **Total Piece Rate Ticket** to determine the **Total Piece Rate Dollars**.

2. Calculate employee's **Total Hours Worked** for the week.

3. Divide the **Total Piece Rate Dollars** by employee's **Total Hours Worked** to determine **RATE** of pay.

$$\frac{\textbf{Total Piece Rate Dollars}}{\textbf{Total Hours Worked}} = \textbf{RATE}$$

4. Multiply **Overtime Hours Worked** by ½ **RATE** to determine **Overtime Pay**.

5. Add **Total Piece Rate Dollars**, plus **Overtime Pay** to determine **Gross Pay**.

Total piece Rate Dollars + Overtime Pay = Gross Pay

EXAMPLE: _Employee Michael Jones is a Piece Rate worker for Brown & Sons, Inc._

1) Jones's Total Piece Rate Tickets, when added, equals $275 Total Piece Rate Dollars.

2) Jones's Total Hours worked equal 45 hours.

3) $275 (Total Piece Rate Dollars)

   $\div$ 45 (Total Hours Worked)

   = 6.11 RATE

4)   5.00 (Overtime Hours Worked)

   x 3.06 (1/2 RATE is .5 x 6.11 = 3.06)

5)   275.00 (Total Piece Rate Dollars)

   +15.30 (Overtime Pay)

   $290.30 GROSS PAY

"Full Package Contracting" _This term is usually applied to a contractor that designs and produces garments for a manufacturer or retailer._

See appendix, for examples of contracts to be used when working with sewing contractors.

CHAPTER 12

PRODUCT COSTING

"Look after the cents and the dollars will take care of themselves"

The "Chargeback" information in this chapter has been added by Joel Stonefield, Co-founder of Stonefield & Josephson, accounting firm to the apparel industry.

Why does a dress cost $300? Is a cotton shirt worth $75? The sticker price of that dress you're considering or the shirt you are saving for can depend on the complexity of the design, the status of the label and whether the clothing is made overseas or domestically. What goes into the clothes you buy can sometimes make the sticker price as high as a luxury vacation or as low as a pizza and a movie. The answer is layered in the long, complex journey a garment makes in the process of creation, production, testing and shipping that brings it finally to the retail store. It also reflects the retailers' overhead costs, for security, real estate and technology etc.

Understanding how to correctly cost a garment will be the key to your company's success. One small miscalculation can be devastating to your profit margins, and could determine the survival of your start-up business. Once you have determined the price bracket that your company will be in, you will have to strive to maintain the quality of styling and construction within the set price structure. For a small start-up company it is very difficult to be competitive with bigger manufacturers in moderately priced and budget clothing. Unless you are investing a few hundred thousand to start your company, the higher price category is usually the best place to start. There is a higher profit margin to the manufacturer and to the retailer in "betterwear". Granted they will be smaller orders, but it is hard to find financing for large orders when you are a start-up company. Most start-ups will not be able to afford to produce large quantities at first, without borrowing money. Start with small orders, then when mistakes are made it will not be too devastating to the company, both financially and emotionally. You will be able to learn by your mistakes.

Major Costs

The major costs involved in manufacturing any garment are for fabric, trims, labor, and operational costs. Becoming familiar with labor costs takes experience in understanding the over-all work involved in the completion of the garment. Direct labor for sewing will be negotiated with the contractor. Marking and grading may be done by one company, and cutting done by another, or in some cases, your contractor may be able to take care of all these steps. All these costs must be calculated by the amount of garments made. For smaller orders there will be a higher price to pay. The more garments sold or the bigger the order, then the labor price decreases. Other labor costs to be included will be design development, first patterns, production patterns, quality control, bookkeeping and shipping. Overhead costs or fixed costs should not be forgotten, including rent, electricity, etc.

Chargebacks & Markdown refunds

One of the more controversial factors in apparel prices is retailers' request for "**chargebacks**" or "**markdown**" money. Chargebacks can be demanded by a store for late deliveries, or for a variety of other reasons. If too few garments sell at full price, sometimes department stores go back to the manufacturer to ask that they share in the losses from discount sales. *(See Chapter 16)* Ironically, markdown money or credit demanded by a retailer adds to the manufacturer's overhead costs and may boost the original retail price of the garment. Another cost that retailers expect the manufacturer to share is the cost of advertising, or promoting the product in store flyers and newspaper advertisements.

Smaller specialty stores are less likely to make such requests, but they have less buying power with the manufacturer. Markdown and chargebacks have become a very sensitive issue and many manufacturers are refusing to do business with larger department stores because of this problem. The wise manufacturer calculates both of these into the costing of the garments.

Importance of correct costing

Incorrect costing can result in losses that will eventually bankrupt the company. If the costing for cutting, sewing, or trims is incorrect, or if the yardage has been under-calculated, then the costing for that garment will result in major losses. Costing is done before the orders are written so it can be difficult to calculate how big the order will be. Therefore, it is important that a start-up company project the size of its production and the money available to produce the orders. You will be out of business in a very short time without an experienced costing person filling in the cost sheets. It is also crucial to have an accurate fabric yield and a precise production cost. **Never guess your costs!**

Market Research

When starting a new company, it is important to assess the market, shop your competition and find out the critical price points of similar products in the market place. To cost too high could mean no orders and to charge too little could result in no profits. Know the three stages of costing:

- **"Actual cost" of production:** This is more or less a fixed price and can only be reduced by modifying or changing the garment.

- **Cost plus your markup percentage**: Deciding on the mark-up will be determined by a couple of factors: How much you need to make in order to make a profit and what the market price will bare. **Retail-selling price:** Having a realistic understanding of the price structure of the market place will help when costing.

Costing for the Start-Up

A simple method of costing for start-up manufacturers is to make the price you sell to the retailer at least twice your cost. This will give you a 100% mark-up, which is a necessary profit margin when you first begin to manufacture and have small orders. The term used for this is "Keystoning".

Example: If your basic cost is $20, you will sell your garment for $40. This is "**Keystoning**" which equals a 100% mark-up. If you go back from the $40 to the cost price of $20 , that will equal a 50% **gross profit margin.**. Understanding these basic terms will help you understand how they should be used.

Never go below 35% gross profit margin, or you will be giving the garments away! Subjective thinking will come into play sometimes when you have to take a smaller mark-up on the pricing of certain styles in order to keep a group together. Hopefully, this will make the group more saleable. Conversely, there will be times when you will mark-up a garment more than 100% to keep the garment in the correct price category. If you do reduce the profit by lowering the wholesale price of a garment, make sure that if the garment sells well and the store wants to reorder, you then adjust the price higher. If not, you may find that this garment will end up losing money for you season after season. Only compromise the cost of a garment if it is to keep a group together and you feel that removing it would harm the overall sales of the group. Your goal is to try and keep the garment at the right price point for maximum sales and profit. To do this you may have to rework the particular garment with the production pattern maker to make it fall in the right price range.

Mass production

For manufacturers producing mass production on a large scale, the mark-up percentage is usually smaller and pricing more competitive, due to the large quantities produced. They can safely work with a 30% profit margin you cannot! Retailers such as The Limited, J.C. Penney's and Sears have a price edge because they can deliver their goods directly from the factory to the public without the independent retail middleman. This is known as vertical production or manufacturing.

(Discount chains such as T.J.Max, Ross or Marshall's usually take lower profits in place of such perks as sales help, personal shoppers, carpets and fancy dressing rooms. Manufacturers often have discounted goods left in stock after the season is finished that needs to be moved rather than added to their inventory

Discount chains can buy this merchandise at a low cost for sale in their stores).

Custom made clothing

When costing a "one-off" garment it is important to establish an hourly worth of the designer/producer. Only when you know this, can you begin to estimate the costs involved of producing a unique, one of a kind, wearable piece of art. Once you have established your hourly worth, double it and add it to all other expenses. This will give an approximate cost of the wearable art piece. If the custom- made piece has been commissioned, it is a general rule to ask for fifty percent up-front, since it is often impossible to sell to anyone but the original buyer. If you know the buyer, it may not be necessary to ask for fifty percent up front, but otherwise protect yourself from being left holding an unclaimed garment. To guarantee payment upon completion, finished pieces may be shipped either COD or Pro forma. *(See Chapter 16)*

Computer programs

With all the new computer programs available for managing your business, it is advisable to get a program customized to your own specifications to cover all the fixed costs of your garments. Then, the yardage, labor costs and fixed costs can be calculated, fed into the program and a correct costing made of each style. Once programmed to your specifications, these programs will calculate the gross profit margin and the net profit margins of each garment. Remember, the computer is only as good as the user, so be sure that the information programmed into the computer is the correct.

Cost sheets

To understand the cost process, start by filling in the cost sheets yourself. This will teach you a great deal about costing. Do not skim over this important stage of producing a garment. Often "designers" are more into creating than thinking about the gross profit margins!

Costs will vary depending on the fabric selected and the amount of work involved in the design. There will be times that an adjustment will be made to the final gross margin to keep garments in the correct price range. If a garment is expensive, it has to look worth the asking price to the consumer. When the fabric cost is high, then a simple design is advisable. When the fabric is reasonably priced, then a more complex design may be chosen. If you have a beautiful piece of fabric, you can stitch it up with two seams. If the fabric is plain, the cut will be important.

The following should be included in a cost sheet: *(See examples of cost sheets in the Appendix)*

- Date
- Style number and design number (name if applicable)
- Fabric yields, (including shipping costs)
- Linings
- Trim cost, including fusing

- Cutting
- Labor & sewing
- Packaging
- Overhead costs
- Actual cost
- Mark-up percentage
- Sales Representative percentage
- Small percentage for "chargebacks" or "markdowns"

With the cost sheet, include a swatch of the fabrics used, trims and a good technical flat sketch of the garment. If anything were sent out for special work e.g. fusing, pleating, embroidery, printing etc, this should be included as well.

Fixed cost

Every cost sheet needs your fixed costs as part of the addition. Fixed costs will always be part of the cost of manufacturing a product, whether one or one thousand pieces are produced. These costs are sometimes referred to as **overhead costs**. They could include product development, office staff, rent, electricity etc.

It is now very easy to work from the home or small office using networking, the Internet, and computers, to produce large amount of goods. Most aspects of producing a line of clothing can be efficiently handled by contracting the work out to experienced contractors. From receiving the fabric, cutting and sewing, to shipping and accounting, all these areas can be controlled by you from an area the size of a desk. Of course you will have to be certain that the service providers are well established and can be trusted to perform their job well. Always investigate the references of the people who work with you, and for you. Do not assume that once they are working for you that they can do the job without supervision. It is important to check the work that is in progress.

Variable costs

These costs are the actual costs in the product, such as materials and labor. This part of costing the garment can vary depending on the costs of fabric and labor involved.

All major parts added to the costing of the product should be evaluated and re-evaluated often to determine if any portion can be reduced in cost. Reducing the costs to produce your garments will yield higher profit margins and more efficient, finished products.

Some companies "load" their cost sheets with every possible item resulting in a smaller gross profit margin. This is fine. To not load the cost sheet, and then discover missed items could be a big blow to your overall financial situation.

Importance of Recosting

For every new style, for every season, rework the cost sheet. Beware of using the same cost sheet when changing fabrication, even if using the same style. There could be hidden costs that you are unaware of when changing the fabrication such as differences in the fabric width, marker, finishing, pressing, etc.

Sales Representatives Percentages

The percentage allowed for your sales representative's sales commission should be worked into the cost sheet after you have calculated the total garment cost and your mark-up percentage. You then add the Terms of Sales to the cost. *(See Chapter 16 for the explanation of Terms of Sales)* If you don't know the value of the terms, which will need to be negotiated, then assume a flat 8% or 10% for discounting or for warehousing and for any other unforeseen eventuality. Add that to the cost sheet as well.

Example of the major costs involved in a cost sheet, including "Keystone "Costing

A blouse takes two yards of fabric

Components:

2 yards @ $4 .00 per yard	$8.00
Freight for fabric @ 15 cents per yard	$0.30
Total Fabric cost	$8.30
Block Fusing	$0.20
7 Buttons @ 2 cents each	$0.14
1 Label@ 2 cents each	$0.02
"Miscellaneous" costs:	$0.36

"Make" Charges:

Cutting	$0.30
Sewing & Labor	$5.00
Marking & grading	$1.00
Total Labor cost	$7.80
Overheads	$1.50

Total cost	$16.46
Keystone: 100% Mark-up	$16.46
Total	$32.92

Wholesale Selling Price

From the above total, you subtract the discount for chargebacks and the sales representative's commission. Costing, using this method will give a margin of profit to work with, when establishing your **wholesale selling price**. A more sophisticated method will have to be developed once the company is paying for employees and other overheads expenses not in your first cost sheet. It is also very important that you understand how to breakdown the charges in the cost sheet and to include all costs in the correct order. One miscalculation in a cost sheet can be expensive and devastating to a company. Once costing is done incorrectly, it is easy to continue on this downward path without fully understanding where you have gone wrong.

There are methods of costing generally used in the Industry that will help you develop a better understanding of the intricacies of costing.   Becoming familiar with these more accurate costing techniques will help you   fine-tune your cost sheets and be on-top-of the important details involved with costing.

You first have to analyze the garment and decide what the market can bare, which will determine your profit margin. This part of costing is subjective and you should be familiar with the market in order to keep the product in the right price bracket. To cost too high will undermine the sale of the garment, and to under cost will undermine your profit.

Sales representatives' commissions and the discounts allowed the buyers are paid off the final price you decide to sell the goods. You have to analyze the garments and decide what that blouse could sell for to the store. If you think it could wholesale for $32.90, and retail for around $70.00, you would then calculate the percentage paid the sales representative and the percentage of allowable discounts to the buyer and subtract them from your final sales price.

Example

True Profit or Net Profit Calculation

Wholesale Price $32.90

Subtract Discounts allowable 10% .... -$3.29

Subtract Sales commission 10% .... -$3.29

Price after discounts and commission $26.32

Subtract Actual Cost of Garment .... -$16.46

True Profit or Net Profit $9.86

Net Profit Margin (True Profit) Calculation

$$\frac{\$26.32 \,(\text{Price after Discounts and Commission}) \, - \, \$16.46 \,(\text{Actual Cost})}{\$32.90 \,(\text{Wholesale Price})} \times 100\% = 30\% \text{ Net Profit Margin}$$

Gross Profit Calculation

Wholesale Price $32.90

Subtract Actual Cost of Garment .... -$16.46

Gross Profit $16.44

Gross Profit Margin Calculation

$$\frac{\$16.44 \,(\text{Gross Profit})}{\$32.90 \,(\text{Wholesale Price})} \times 100\% = 50\% \text{ Gross Profit Margin}$$

You should calculate the percentage of profit and record it on every cost sheet, both the net profit and the gross profit. This will enable you to see at a glance your profit margins. As you can see from the above calculations there is a big difference between the gross profit and the net profit. Don't forget taxes (Your net profit is your taxable income)!

Do not forget

Make sure the fixed expenses from your cost sheets, rent, design, pattern making, administration, telephone etc. are included in your calculations. If you have a 30% gross profit margin, and your fixed expenses are 10% of your net sales, this will undermine your profit. If that is the case, try to reduce your fixed expenses. A realistic percentage for fixed overheads should be around 5% - 7%.

Dilution

This is the difference between what you invoice the retailer (customer) and what you get paid from your customers. There will always be some non-paying customers, chargebacks, and returns. These are calculated into the costing of your garment as part of the chargeback calculations and are real costs. If you choose to ignore them, they could undermine your gross profit so it is necessary to keep a watchful eye on your dilutions and calculate the percentage of them at the end of the season. If your dilution costs are too high, then you should address them. Find out why you are having a dilution problem, and in which area it is most prevalent. Some areas to consider:

- **Is it shipping problems?**
- **Is it quality control?**
- **Is it late shipments?**

If you are selling to department store it is usual to add between 12% and 15% to the cost sheet for the inevitable discounts and charge-backs. If you sell mainly to specialty stores the percentage should be around 6 to 8 percent.

Retailer's Mark-up

Once the retailers buy your product at its' wholesale price, they will then add their profits and overhead costs, which are about 100% to 125% to get to their retail selling price. The blouse we costed previously, may sell in the store for around $70.99

Usually, the retailer will pay for the shipping charges, but work with your sales rep in this regard. They should tell you how the store will expect their shipment, their requirements for packaging details, and if you are responsible for these costs. Anticipate their demands and include them in your cost sheets. ! Do not let the retailers dictate their price, unless you know your profit margin is workable at that price. It is important to protect your profit margin, and stay in control of your product costs. *(See examples of cost sheets in the appendix)*

THREE RULES TO FOLLOW WHEN COSTING

Price = Cost + Profit

PRICE = USUALLY DETERMINED BY MARKET PRICE AT RETAIL

As mentioned earlier, you must investigate your Target market, the competition, and the wholesale and retail price ranges your garments should fit into. Once that is determined they should be kept within the chosen price range. Make sure that the quality and styling is retained. It is good to cost by starting with a retail price and work backwards.

COST = IS THE ONLY VARIABLE WHICH CAN BE CONTROLLED BY YOU!

Understanding the key elements in costing a garment will assure the gross profit margin.

PROFIT MARGIN = PRE-DETERMINED BY YOU. SHOULD NOT BE UNDERCUT

If you have a large, potential order from a department store, and they want you to reduce your profit margin in order to get it, make sure it is possible to take it without losing that profit margin. Just because you get a large order, it is not necessarily in your company's best interest. **You must work out the figures before you accept orders!**

Chargeback advice from Joel Stonefield, CPA and Chargeback Guru.

CHARGEBACKS
What are they?

These are uninvited guests at the apparel manufacturer's picnic. Like ants at one's otherwise lovely party, they ruin everything in sight. Here's an example of how they happen and what they can do to a business, a very extreme example, but not at all unrealistic:

On October 25th, manufacturer ships $1,000 of merchandise at regular price to department store. That merchandise cost $555 to manufacture. On December 10th, store pays the $1,000 invoice, LESS:

- *Damaged goods - $125.00*
- *Penalties for not shipping the goods in accordance with the store's required procedures   -*
  $145.00
- *Un-authorized markdown allowance - $310.00*

Net Check = $420.00 *(This means a <u>loss</u> on the sale of $135.00!)*

Cost of manufacture - $555.00 compared with the Net Check from the store of $420.00, thus a loss of $135.00.

Is each of the above deductions preventable? *SOMETIMES.*

Are these deductions collectable from the store? *SOMETIMES.*

Are these CHARGEBACKS (now the word!) fair or reasonable? *SOMETIMES.*

(ALICE, WELCOME TO THE WONDERLAND OF CHARGEBACKS WHERE 2 AND 2 <u>NEVER</u> EQUAL 4).

Who creates them?

Generally, most department stores and more recently, mass merchandisers, are known to create unauthorized deductions (chargebacks). It is their way of doing business, which anyone selling to them must understand. Which is not to say that one must ACCEPT these stores and their sometimes nasty games, but rather one should UNDERSTAND the process and how to deal with it. Alternatively, smaller stores (specialty shops) do not usually inflict unreasonable deductions on their customers. The much smaller orders placed by these stores involve an entirely different method of doing business – higher selling costs and distribution costs – which may exceed the problem of chargebacks!

WAYS TO LIVE WITH CHARGEBACKS

- **What Works...***Have a line that checks at retail and which makes the store lots of money. None of them are so unwise as to kill the golden goose which....*
- **What Doesn't Work...***Using a factor to prevent chargebacks. Doesn't mean a thing! They'll just pass through   these deductions to you without argument.*
- *Suing the store. You can never win.*
- *Screaming, crying, begging for mercy*

A FEW MORE SUGGESTIONS

(1) Learn in advance the ways of each store and what you should do to comply with its traffic rules, EDI rules, etc.

(2) As to buyers: Learn to argue when you can, and give up when you must.

(3) Know what is going on in your bookkeeping operation. Expect to see every deduction. Understand what is happening with each store. Have a strong bookkeeper or outside chargeback service that will look out for you.

Joel Stonefield CPA

Garment Costing for Success

10 Point Checklist for Profitable Results

1. **Development cost:** Whatever type of garment you manufacture there is always development. These are known as hidden costs and should not be ignored.

2. **First sample or prototype cost:** Check the number of times the average sample is made before the final garment is approved.

3. **Fabric cost for sampling:** Fabric used for samples can begin to add up. Keep a record of this part of development. You may be surprised at the amount of sample yardage ordered.

4. **Pattern development costs:** Pattern making can be more costly than realized. Keep an account of this part of the business.

5. **Yield of fabric costs:** Your fabric expense may be 40% to 50% of the direct cost of the garment. Making sure that you are not wasting fabric and that your markers are good and tight is going to affect the overall profitability of your business.

6. **Trim cost:** Whether it's zippers, labels, embroidery, elastic or other trims, make sure you are aware of the correct amount each garment needs. Waste takes away your direct profit.

7. **Contracting or labor costs:** Sewing is another part of the garment cost that is 30% to 40% and should be fixed early in determining the cost of a garment.

8. **Cutting costs:** Before cutting can begin make sure the fabric is checked on arrival for flaws and for width variations. Chargeback the mills as soon as possible. Timing is important. In-house cutting is ideal to keep a check on wastage. Do not allow a build-up of fabric inventory.

9. **Production overheads:** Real estate prices, electric costs, phone costs, accounting, transportation, quality control, shipping and packaging, even hangers; these are important expenses that should not be ignored.

10. **Quality Control:** Quality of the first production sample and production itself must have continuity otherwise there will be returns. Returns equal reduction of your profits.

Items influencing garment cost

If the garment cost is too high then you must review the situation. Simplification will bring the cost down. This may sound easier than it is in reality, since you have to make sure that the garment retains it originality and its appeal. Here are some suggestions that may help you bring the cost of a garment down.

1. **Total number of pattern pieces.**

2. **Total number of notches**

3. **Total number of steps involved in construction methods**

   - Type of seam finishes
   - Length of stitch
   - Fusing.
   - Hemming
   - Type of buttonholes

4. **Details involved to complete the garment**

   - Fusing
   - Pressing
   - Handling
   - Folding
   - Packing
   - Shipping
   - Inspection
   - Sales commission

5. **Fabrication**

   - Cost of fabric
   - Buying direct from mill *(This is a problem for small companies)*
   - Using a fabric rep
   - Shipping of fabric
   - Number of yards per garment
   - Ease of handling, silk, velvet, matching plaids, spreading, shrinkage under steam iron, pre-shrinking, etc.
   - Color: - dye lots, problem of fading in store windows, washing instructions, etc. Swimwear manufacturers have to test garments when finished.
   - Size of the cutting tickets will also affect the final cost of the garment.

6. **Contracting**

   - In-house or outside contractor
   - Grading
   - Marking
   - Cutting and spreading
   - Sewing
   - Inspection
   - Pick and Packaging
   - Shipping

7. **Construction Costs**

   - Larger lots (outside contractors' costs go down when you have 300 garments or more). Smaller businesses usually have to shop for contractors who specialize in smaller lots.
   - Grading costs are computed on the number of the pattern pieces.

8. **Pattern Stage** Examples that may help cut costs.

- Collar and collar stand in one piece

- Front button placket all in one and tucked and stitched

- Elimination of yoke: *Front yoke cut in one with the back*

    Cuffs, pockets, tabs, extensions, facings, etc., cut in one with the garment.

    Special detail with sleeve using budget cuff and no placket

    Straight hems

    Economy of style lines

    Elimination of darts, seams, waistline seams, etc.

9. **Simplification of construction.**

- One-piece collar instead of two

- Cap of sleeve set in armhole first, then side seam and underarm seam sewn all in one.

- Budget cuffs

- Placket all in one with front, using the tuck method.

- Continuous binding of sleeve placket

- Binding instead of facings

- Less fusing

- Press on embroidery

- Fewer stitches per inch

Quality

More complicated designs can be seen in "Better" priced lines, along with more expensive qualities of fabrics and trims, construction of garment, linings and fusing. Most important, a better fitting garment should be evident in the higher-price range

- **Details of seams**: French, flat felled, slot, topstitching, corded seams, open welt seams, more stitches per inch etc.

- **Details of better fitting garment**: More seams and darts, inner construction and linings. Bigger seams, bigger hems equal more fabric usage, which in turn equals a more expensive garment.

(The final selling price has nothing to do with the worth value of the garment. It is "Perceived Price Value" that you have to consider! This is the niche market that you have so carefully considered. Remember you are not only creating beautiful clothes, you need to make a profit or you are wasting your time.)

CHAPTER 13

PRODUCTION PLANNING,

QUALITY CONTROL AND SHIPPING

"To survive, a manufacturer has to have adequate capital, a loyal customer base – and some luck"

Rob Greenspan, Moss Adams Accounting LA

This chapter reviewed by Professor Jean Gipe, Director of ATRC California State Polytechnic, Pomona.

Planning Production

Controlling the flow of the day-to-day business functions requires an experienced and well-organized person. Often this end of the business receives less attention from the small business owner-manager than it should. Without proper production planning, the manufacturer's efforts can end in disaster. Anyone with experience in the fashion business has had experiences with poor quality construction, damaged merchandise, and late deliveries, to name but a few. The Production Manager for an apparel manufacturer must coordinate and direct all aspects of production so that the garments are carefully executed, and delivery is made as requested on the purchase order. The Production Manager, who, in the case of a start-up business is usually the owner, must learn to say "**no**" to retailers that place orders which are too large and can not possibly be produced to ship "on time". Realistically, lead times for ordering the fabric and trims, the cut and sew processes, finishing and packaging all take careful planning and good execution. Conversely, learning to say "no" to orders that are too small is also very important to your overall profitability.

Personality of the Production Person

Because of the amount of interaction with all the various people involved in producing apparel, it is important your production person be someone who is strong, and yet likable. Vendors and contractors should feel confident about doing business with your company and its representatives so that they will do their best to get your production out on time. It is not a good idea to have a person working for you who insults the contractors involved in your production process. You will never get anything done on time. On the reverse side, having a person who is too timid is also a problem. Look for a pleasant, strong, and knowledgeable person for this position.

Management Plan

This over-all organizational structure should include specific job descriptions, responsibilities, levels of authority and accountability for all involved in making your company successful. Plan this personnel structure fully; it will be good for your company's future growth plans. It also will give the personnel involved something to work for, and to achieve. Never forget all the employees who work hard to make your company profitable. Your neck is really on the line when you own a company, so it is very important that you seek out personnel who are willing to work hard and to work with your best interests at heart. This is one good reason why going into business with a family member often works well.

Major Production Steps Involved to Produce a Garment

Pre-Production

Design Process
Sample yardage
Pre-Production patterns
First Samples
Fittings
Costing
Group and line approval
Technical Package

Production

Marking Grading
Projected Yardage estimates
Order/Receive Fabric and Trim 10%
    standard damage rate (Inspect/QC)
Issue Cut
Pull (Issue) Fabric/Trim

Cutting

Spreading
Plys
Shading
Matching/Nailing
Bundling
Cut/count Blocks
Inspection
Yields Damages/ Splices and Ends/Loss

Send Outs

Embroidery
Special Sewing
Fusing
Bias/Etc
Screen-Printing

Sewing

Knits vs wovens
Different contractors
Different machines
Different threads/needles
Operator's expertise
Bundling (Sobar)
Sewing
Pricing and contact agreements

Shipping Orders

Quality control
Inspection and Hangtags
Pick tickets
Vendor specifications for shipping
Invoice

Differences between Samples and Production runs

Spec Sheets
Sew by sample Machinery
Machine feet
Costing
Piece rate v. Hourly
QC
Finishing QC
Pressing
Buttons
Labels/Etc.

Send Out
Inspection
Laundry
Screen-printing

Finishing
Pressing
Tag/Bag/Hang
Inspection

Pre-Production Planning

This part of production should be planned with precision and is often overlooked.   Good pre-production planning and a merchandising calendar laying out job responsibilities are the keys to timing and meeting delivery dates.   Once the samples are approved for the line and costed, the next step is to plan for market and order fabric for sales rep's samples and production samples.   Here are some of the things to arrange when planning pre-production:

- Order fabric for duplicates

- Begin making production samples and patterns

- Cut and sew sales samples

- Sales rep's receive samples

- Line sheets and swatch cards should be sent along with samples to sales rep's

- Grading

- Specification sheets and Tech Packs

- Sales rep's show the line, styles are ordered and the cutting tickets are built

- Some styles will be better sellers than others; certain styles will have to be dropped from the line because there are not enough orders to make a profit.

- Tell sales rep's which styles are dropped and suggest other styles to replace any orders that will have to be canceled.

- Inform the buyer of any necessary changes to their order; price, styling, color, etc.

Production Planning

There are two ways of thinking with regard to production planning: 1). Cut to order. 2). Cut to stock. The safest method is to cut to order, plus 15% for late orders.   Cutting to stock is very risky business. Many good companies have lost their profits in this way, and been forced out of business.

(Larger companies cut to stock when they know for sure that a particular style has sold well in previous seasons, and are confident it will be selling well next season. Often, they have to order the fabric well in advance if it has to be dyed-to-order, or is a particular print for that style.   For a new company, cutting to stock will only eat away at the money at hand, plus there is a lack of expertise with what is a 'good seller' and you could be left with a large inventory of fabric or sewn production.)

Calculating Size of Production

Computers are often used now to give the manufacturer a report of the daily sales from the sales representatives. This is known as building a cutting ticket. The sales rep who sees the retail buyer, writes these orders. (see Chapter 16) The information received from the sales rep will inform the manufacturer of the number of units ordered, sizes, colors and styles. This information is now computerized, daily sales are tracked, and a cutting ticket is built.

Purchasing Plan

The Purchasing Department is an important part of achieving smooth production. It is good to develop close working relationships with the vendors you choose to assure speedy deliveries and a quick turn around. As soon as the orders begin to accumulate, the Purchasing Department must be informed of the amounts projected for production, so that any potential problems can be dealt with in time. Once the cutting ticket is complete and the size of production is determined, then the fabric yields and trims can be calculated and ordered.

Building Orders

When the orders begin to build, production planning will begin in earnest for the new company. It will then become apparent how important it is to see clearly the sequence of jobs to be completed before shipment, the beginning of next season's line planning, along with fabric ordering and receiving. Keeping a close eye on these tasks will be essential to avoid any cancellations of orders due to late shipments and to your company's success.

Production Flow Charts

When operating a small business, there is often only one person (owner) responsible for all the stages of production, from design development, to fabric buying, to production planning and quality control. Plus, there are many important costing negotiations involved with the various contractors used in the production of the line. It feels like many balls up in the air at the same time and it often becomes more than one person can realistically handle. Development of an effective flow chart or "time and action plan" to show production and shipping dates and job responsibilities will be a useful means to controlling the over all picture involved with your every day production. The use of a visual flow chart for the day to day operations of production will help evaluate what items will be due from the contractor, when they should be shipped, and at what stage each order is on the production chain. Long range production planning in a time and action plan will help control the flow of production, give a better overview of the jobs to be completed, and measure where you are currently in each stage of work for your orders.

(A good and simple visual method is to start with a large calendar, which allows for enough space to write in all the production schedules dates that must be met. The usual way is to note the shipping date that is required by the retailer, and then have a reverse schedule with completion dates, cutting dates, fabric delivery dates and line development schedules for the next season. The first line that is produced is easy compared with having four lines manufactured at the same time; with all the various shipping dates that have to be met it is important to track all the dates carefully.)

Working with a Contractor

Having found a contractor and followed the procedure outlined in Chapter 11, which explains how to legally do business with the contractor, you may find it necessary to have more than one contractor for your line. This will usually depends on the number of styles and the contractor's expertise. There may be woven garments and some knits in the line requiring special equipment and handling. This could mean using different contractors. Also, the cutting may be contracted out to a separate plant. In these situations, the production manager must accurately assess the expertise of possible contractors, so that the appropriate ones are chosen to complete the production orders, on time and satisfactorily.

Diversify sales and workloads

Remember that it is important not to have more than 30% of your business with one customer *That's called having all your eggs in one basket).* This also applies to your supplies and to your contractor. If you have only one supplier then you are putting yourself at risk and at their mercy. This is also a problem when you have only one contractor. As you grow, you should find other contractors to work with so you can diversify the workload. If you have only one contractor, and that contractor is also working with another manufacturer... who pays more for production, has a larger order, or has been a their very good customer for many years, you could be left with all your production being shipped late! However, if you diversify and have your production produced by a number of contractors, you would only have part of your order shipped late.

Negotiating Construction Costs

One of the more important tasks that the production person is responsible for is negotiating the cost of constructing the garment with the contractor. Having some previous knowledge of production procedures would be most advantageous. You must also be aware that a start up company making smaller lots will be subject to a higher production cost. The more garments are produced, the lower the production cost, both for cutting and sewing. Most contractors will evaluate the sample and give you a fair estimate, with a small margin for negotiations. This is one reason why the contractor would first like to sew a sample for your approval, in order to determine the amount of work involved in the garment. The cost of making a sample is usually around two to three times the cost of production.

Cost analyst

The contractor analyses your garment by how many seams and parts there are and the various steps involved with producing it. A sewing specification sheet is then prepared that gives all the details for each garment. How long are the seams, how many stitches to an inch, and type of seam, sewing order and pressing instructions. These are some of the specifications that should be included. Each company will establish their own sewing specification sheets, and as the company grows these specification (spec) sheets become much more detailed.

Sewing Specifications

Often, smaller manufacturers don't think about establishing rules of construction for their product and quality control measures for the company. Sewing specification sheets will establish rules for the sewing process; these rules should be carried through to all other garments produced. *(Remember, bad quality is the number one reason that retailers return your goods, along with late deliveries)* Establishing your standards of quality and adhering to them will help to keep you in business.

Cut, Make & Trim (CMT)

The first two words are self-explanatory, the trim part refers to the extras involved in the production of a garment such as pressing, trimming threads, tagging, quality control, and packaging. For all these important stages there should be paperwork, which will track the garments from the cutting ticket through to the shipping stage. As discussed in the Cutting section of the book, a cut ticket is given to the cutter with all the instructions: size of order, size range to be cut, the ratio of sizes, and colors ordered. The cutter will track all the information on the cut ticket and will then record all other information. An example of information included for tracking would be how many pieces were actually cut. Sometimes the cutter will cut extras to use the remaining fabric, or there could have been a shortage in fabric due to shading or damages, which would cause fewer numbers cut than ordered on the cutting ticket. All this information must be documented in order to have a system in place to track production. This will impact all parts of the company's production flow, and final shipment. If there is a shortage in cutting an order, this will of course mean that the order will be *shipped short*, or more will have to be cut with the next cutting ticket.

Cutting Tickets

A method often used within the industry is to have four copies of the cutting ticket or purchase order (PO). The cutting ticket/PO will have all the information pertaining to the order. The manufacturer will keep one copy; the cutter will document the cutting details on the other three copies; numbers actually cut, any problems with fabric, etc. The cutter will keep one copy, and the other two will remain with the cut pieces and given to the sewers to record sewing problems and damages. The floor manager will keep a copy of this document, along with detailed sewing specifications made for each garment sewn. The final copy is returned to the manufacturer (boss) in order that an exact count of the produced pieces can be made. Calculating shortage is part of the production person's job, and extras should be allowed when writing up the cutting ticket. Between 5%-15% is normal, which will allow for some reorders. If there is more than 5% damage then you should try to track down where the problem most often occurs.

Dealing with Damage

Fabric damages

Try to check fabric for damages, shading or width variations as soon as it is received, in case you need to return the goods. It may seem costly, but it will save in the long run. Leaving inspection until it is cut could be too late. Rolling out the fabric only to find holes or shading problems will mean loss of sales or that the order is shipped short.

Cutting damage or loss

It is amazing how sometimes pieces get lost or walk out the door. Is the cutter experienced in cutting the types of fabrics you require in your line? Each type of fabric may require different handling. The new micro fabrics, woven fabrics with Lycra ®, or knits can be tricky. They do some strange things when layered one on top of the other. Anticipating all the possible problems of certain fabrics will require an experienced cutter.

Sewing damages

Is your contractor sewing fabric they are not experienced in producing and handling? Some contractors are excellent at producing cut and sewn woven goods, but don't have the equipment to sew knit or stretch goods. Make certain that the contractor selected has the correct machines to sew a particular garment. Oil stains can also be a production problem, which can hopefully be cleaned off before shipment.

Fusing Problems

Whether the garment has sections that will require block fusing or piece fusing will depend on the garment. Whichever method used, it is extremely important that the fusing is the correct type for the fabric. Choosing an incorrect fusing will result in problems and returns. Make sure that you get the advice of a fusing company. This service is normally free, as they want you to return to buy their product. *(see Chapter 9)*

Production Samples

The contractor will need a production sample to cut and sew by. This will be used as their guide for how to produce the final garment. Without a production sample you may find that the garment is sewn together with the wrong side of the fabric on the outside of the garment, or topstitching has been forgotten. It is also important to make a production sample for yourself to be used as your own guide of the quality and specifications. Your production sample should **not** leave your possession. It will be needed for reference throughout production, and as a final comparison with the contractor's work. It is also important that the production samples are saved for future reference.

The contractor will also use the production sample to make detailed sewing specifications of each garment. These will include the order of sewing, and the machines to be used, the time allowed for each step in production and the price.

Spot Checks

Driving from contractor to contractor to make certain that the finished product will be satisfactory, meets production requirements, and that delivery will be on schedule demands a great deal of time and further complicates a production person's job. However, it is essential when building a relationship with a new contractor, to make spot checks to ascertain if the work is on schedule and if the quality is up to your required standards.

The production person is usually responsible for overseeing: -

- Negotiations with the contractor for price of garment
- Marking and Grading
- Ordering Fabric
- Ordering Trims

- Cutting tickets for the garment
- Production specifications
- Construction of ordered garments
- Quality Control
- Meeting shipping deadlines
- Meeting deadlines.
- Duplicate Samples.
- Anything to do with production!

Modular Manufacturing

What is modular manufacturing and why is it important to the smaller manufacturer? There are two types of production methods used to produce a finished garment, piece goods method (progressive bundling) and modular. (*It has other names, such as: Cellular manufacturing, Flexible manufacturing, or Just-in-Time (JIT)*)

1) The piece goods method, uses machine operators to sew components of a garment together, e.g. one operator will be used to sew collars together and will be paid for the amount sewn in one hour. The job is priced by a time expert experienced in the amount of time that should be allotted to sew a certain section together, and how many can be sewn in one hour. Some operators will sew more and others will sew less in one hour. Some will sew using better skills and others will not. The work is repetitive and boring for the worker. They are like human robots!

2) The better method, by far, is modular. Modular allows a small team of trained

operators to sew a complete garment together. Operators can be crossed-trained, they are able to work at more than one station, and they move from station to station as required to keep production moving. These operators are paid either by the hour or the amount of garments completed in one day. There are a number of reasons why this is a preferred method. The sewing floor can work on separate projects at the same time. There can be a number of different types of garments produced by a number of teams. This allows the manufacturer/contractor to work on smaller numbers and different styles than would be required by the piecework method. The teams are competitive with one another and they have a sense of pride about their finished work. This makes for a happier worker and better quality!

This is just an overview of the modular method and its benefits. There is information available on this subject, "Apparel Production" By Charles Gilbert.

Quality Control, Shipping & Packaging

Whatever price range your product falls into, there must be set standards. From Budget to Better, every company has to define its own quality control. As often happens, the target market and target price points will have a great deal to do with the kind of quality control the company can afford. The company's degree of quality will be the mark of the product. Each level of production should be the best possible product for the money paid. Quality is not only the finished garment; quality should be part of your whole operation, including:

- Fabric Inspection
- Design Development
- Cutting, Grading and Marking
- Bundling and Shade Matching
- Plant production
- Sewing Management
- Specifications
- Pressing and Finishing
- Trimming and Tagging
- Inspection
- Packaging and Shipping

Just as quality may differ from one firm to another, it may also change from one time period to another. Keeping the quality under control is in fact a difficult task and requires diligence and a high demand for perfection. From fabric, to construction and finishing of the garment, the manufacturer must be cognizant of the problems that could arise, and try to prevent them before the garment is shipped.

Once the garments are shipped there is no turning back! If the goods are not up to standard, there is the risk of having all the garments returned. This means that if the garment is not as perfect as the first production sample that the store approved, it will undoubtedly return all your goods and/or you will be require to pay deductions or chargebacks. *(see Chapter 16)*

A store sets its quality standards in terms of its customers. In prestige stores, durability of merchandise may be of minor importance, but fineness of material and care in workmanship may be important. There is often, a demand for fashion-forward clothing from the higher-end stores, and this type of garment may not be so well constructed. Among stores catering to the middle group of customers, both durability and good fit in merchandise may be important. Customers of mass- produced merchandise may evaluate each piece of merchandise in terms of its price, and stores of this type may have no set standards of quality other than that the goods be represented honestly. It is true that the standard of merchandise in budget stores has increased over the past few years. Their customers are able to find well-constructed garments, made in reasonable quality fabric, for a value price point. This is due in part to the fact that most mass-produced garments are manufactured offshore where the production is cheaper.

Quality Control Inspection Sheets

Once the garments are completed, there are a few options used within the Industry for the final stage of producing and shipment of the garments:

- The contractor will deliver them to the manufacturer for quality control and shipment
- The manufacturer will pick them up from the contractor and spot check before receiving the finished goods for shipment.
- The contractors will be responsible for quality control, and will pack and ship to the stores. (This method should only be used when the manufacturer is certain that the quality standards of the contractor will meet the manufacturer's specifications).

Whichever method used it will be important to establish standard quality control rules. Using a quality control specification sheet will help to set the parameters for each style. This document should include all relevant information pertaining to the final appearance and quality of the garment, e.g. by using quality control specification sheets the manufacturer is able to identify an on-going problem and to track the final shipment. Once the garments are returned from the contractor, the lot should be checked for problems. Each quality control sheet should include the following:

- Order is complete from the contractor
- General sewing; stitches per inch, button placement, hem size, etc.
- Shading or fabric problems
- Size specifications
- Placement of labels and hang tags

- Stains or oil marks
- Fabric problems
- Production problems
- Pressing problems
- Other types of damages

Whatever the size of the order, 500 units or 2,000 dozen, garments have to have some type of quality control in place. Finished garments are checked either totally or by spot-checking, and it is imperative that checking be an on-going process. Quality controllers not only check for hanging threads, but also spot-check measurements against size specifications. This is done as the garments are received from the contractor. If there is a problem, the production manager will have to arrange for the garments to be returned to the contractor for corrections. This will take extra time and could mean a late delivery.

As stated earlier, it is the production manager's responsibility to check contractor's work while it is in production, so that any problems can be corrected before they become too serious.

If stores return garments for poor quality control, not only will the order be lost but also the reputation of the manufacturer will be at stake and the possibility of future sales will be in jeopardy.

Improvements in quality

Creating product uniformity on every garment sold is still in the future, but with the use of technology apparel is produced at a much better standard than formerly, and it keeps improving. Even so, it will always be the manufacturer's job to supervise this important part of production and to ensure that the quality of their merchandise remains consistent.

EDI - Electronic Data Interchange
By Henry Cherner-Aims Software

This is used extensively within the industry, and these days it is a necessary method of communication between companies. When the order is ready for shipment a bar code is used that is scanned into the system. This informs the retailer that the order is being shipped, and a packing list or invoice is sent. This is sometimes referred to as ASN (Advance shipping notice). This method helps speed up payment, and keeps a record of each shipment. The retailer will scan each style as it is sold, this will automatically keep the store's inventory counted and it will also inform the manufacturer of which items have sold.

(For a start-up company EDI software can be expensive, so if you are dealing with a vendor that requires that you use EDI and you are not ready to financially commit to the investment, there are service providers that can perform this process for your company. Many retailers will be understanding with a start-up company and allow you to ship without using EDI. However it will be very important to be certain to ship to their specifications or your goods will be subject to chargebacks if you do not follow their rigid rules and regulations.)

Electronic Data Interchange (EDI) is the computer-to-computer exchange of inter company business documents using a standard, public data format. Instead of relying on the telex, fax machine or mail to exchange documents, EDI users exchange them directly between computers.

What is a trading partner?

Companies that exchange business documents using EDI, are called trading partners. The major retailers you do business with, such as JCPenny, Sears, (there are many others) are your trading partners.

What kind of documents do trading partners exchange?

There are dozens of types of documents exchanged between trading partners. Some of the most common EDI documents that will probably be required by your company are purchase orders, advance shipping notices, invoices, and UPC numbers.

What is an EDI transaction?

An EDI transaction is just another name for a business document. Each type of business document in the EDI public format has been assigned a transaction number. For example, the EDI transaction number for a purchase order is 850. The EDI transaction number of an invoice is 810. There are many other types of transactions, and each has been assigned a unique number.

What is an EDI mailbox and why do I need one?

EDI transactions are sent using computer-to-computer communications, similar to email. The reason you need an EDI mailbox is exactly analogous to your personal email account (mailbox). Rather than trying to make a direct connection to each trading partner, when we want to send data, we send it to a designated mailbox for that trading partner. When we want to receive data, we connect to our own mailbox to "check the mail". That way, each trading partner can send and/or receive data when it is convenient for them.

Several companies such as IBM, General Electric, and Sterling Commerce, to name a few, have established electronic networks for data. These are referred to as VANS, Value Added Networks. Any company requiring EDI can establish a mailbox with one of these networks by becoming a subscriber.

Each network charges subscribers in a manner similar to the phone company. That is, a basic monthly service fee plus utilization. The higher the volume of EDI transactions you send and receive, the higher your monthly service bill.

Do I have to subscribe to many different networks?

Generally not, but there are exceptions. Just as someone using AT&T for long distance can call someone using Sprint, most of the major networks have developed a "pass-through" that permit the networks to interconnect and send data to each other automatically. Therefore, if you do business with multiple trading partners who all use different networks, you can probably subscribe to only one network and still communicate with all or most of your trading partners.

What is EDI integration?

Within the context of computer software, the word "integration" means sharing and managing data between two or more different software applications in some type of automated fashion. This is most commonly done through the use of programs that can import and export data to and from other applications. Each application does its own job, and then passes the appropriate data to the next application.

EDI integration applies to companies that want to automate the process of moving data from the EDI system into the order processing system (AIMS), and from the order processing system into the EDI system.

Without integration, after you receive a purchase order from a trading partner, you have to print it on a report and then manually key enter that same data into your order processing system. Similarly, each time you produce an invoice for a trading partner, you have to print the invoice, and manually key enter the same data into the EDI system so it can be sent to the trading partner.

If you are only processing a few transactions a month, that may not seem like a major concern. Obviously the costs associated with duplicate data entry quickly escalate as your EDI volume increases. This option is also most prone to human error, which often generates charge-backs that increase the costs even further.

With an integrated EDI system, after the trading partner's purchase order is received by the EDI system, the integration software automatically transfers the data into your order processing system. Similarly, after the order is shipped and the invoice is created, the EDI integration software automatically transfers the shipping and invoice data to the EDI system so it can be transmitted to your trading partners.

Translators & Maps

Larger companies with in-house professional IT staff have been exchanging data electronically for many years. These companies developed specifications to meet their business needs and then created proprietary computer programs to implement the exchange of data based on these specifications. Eventually, it became obvious that if these companies created some standard data formats, then many more businesses would be able to participate in data exchange because it would become cost efficient to use standardized data formats to exchange data with many trading partners.

The **Uniform Code Council** is one of the main governing bodies that approves and administrates EDI guidelines and policies. In order to make EDI work for everyone, it is necessary to create a standard that has enough flexibility to meet the complex and ever changing needs of many different businesses. By definition, this flexibility is what makes implementing the exchange of similar business data between trading partners somewhat challenging.

Simply stated, receiving a purchase order from Sears, while very similar, is not exactly the same as receiving a purchase order from JCPenny. In fact, the EDI standards are constantly being revised to meet new and evolving business requirements. This has created a need for EDI software that is both flexible enough to handle all the different ways companies implement EDI transactions, and capable of working even when trading partners are using different versions of standard EDI transactions.

To meet the needs of companies who want to purchase "generic" EDI software, a specific type software known as an EDI Translator has evolved. The job of the translator is to make it possible for a single computer program to deal with all the different versions of EDI data standards as well as each trading partner's individual requirements in a way that enables you to standardize the "translation" of data between your company and your trading partners. This is an enormous task for any software program considering the vastness of the EDI standards, but enough for the purpose of this discussion.

By using a trading partner map, to connect the translator software to the data, it is possible to have a very stable software package that maintains maximum data flexibility. Simply put, the trading partner map is a bridge between the translator program and the actual data that tells the translator program how you want to handle specific transactions for each different trading partner.

Most providers of EDI translators also provide trading partner maps. The maps are available by trading partner and transaction.

In other words, if you want to exchange purchase orders, advance ship notices and invoices with Sears, you would purchase one map for each of those transactions for Sears. If in the future, Sears changes their EDI requirements (for example moving to a newer EDI version), it will be necessary to update the Sears trading partner maps you are using. It will not be necessary to change the actual translator program, only the maps used by the translator. If you are using our service bureau the issue of mapping updates is handled for you.

UPC Barcodes

Barcode Software - Label Matrix™ for Windows

Label Matrix for Windows, software from Strandware, prints bar codes, which is also a big part of EDI. Most trading partners require that you include bar coded price tags on the products they buy. Some retailers even want you to print the bar code tags on labels specifically designed just for their own stores. For example, Sears may require that you ship garments with bar code labels that have the Sears logo.

You will also be required to place bar coded shipping labels on the boxes you ship. These special shipping labels, along with the EDI data you transmit to your trading partners, enable the retailer to use a bar code scanner to record the receipt of your merchandise when it arrives at its destination.

We have chosen to integrate AIMS with Label Matrix. This makes it easy for you to produce all of your bar code labels directly from the data already in AIMS.

Bar Code Printer

The bar code labels required for price tags and shipping labels must be printed on a printer capable of producing an image of high enough quality that it can be accurately scanned with a bar code reader.

Today's low cost laser and inkjet printers designed for desktop computers generally do not measure up to the job. You will need to purchase a special bar code printer for this purpose.

Outsourced vs. In-House Barcodes

Outsourced

Pros	Cons
No major up-front investment to purchase software	Monthly transaction costs are generally higher than operating an in-house system
Pay-as-you-go	
Customer service available to help with problems	

In-House

Pro	Con
Monthly transaction costs are lower. This can result in significant savings to companies with high transaction volumes over a long period of time.	The initial cost to purchase all the required software can be significant. Expect to pay somewhere between $10,000 and $15,000, depending on the system you choose.

Uniform Code Council (UCC)

Before you can do anything with EDI, you must apply for membership with the UCC.

The Universal Product Code (UPC) is a system for uniquely identifying the thousands of different suppliers and millions of different items that are warehoused, sold, delivered, and billed throughout retail and commercial channels of distribution. It provides an accurate, efficient and economical means of controlling the flow of goods through the use of an all-numeric product identification system.

The Universal Product Code (UPC) is a 12-digit, all-numeric, code that identifies the company/product combination. The code uses a six to eight-digit number to uniquely identify each company coupled with a three to five-digit number to identify each of the company's products. The combination of these eleven digits plus a check digit form the 12-digit U.P.C. number which uniquely identifies one and only one item.

Universal Price Code Configuration (UPC)

Company ID	Product Number	Check Digit
6 – 8 digits	3 – 5 digits	1 digit (computed)

To obtain a unique identification number for your company, your company's ID, you must apply for membership to the UCC. When you become a member, you will receive your company ID number which enables you to create UPC numbers for your products. This is the basic fundamental building block for any company involved in retail product distribution and EDI.

Why do I need to use UPC numbers?

As the word "universal" implies, the UPC number that identifies your product is one single part number that can be used world-wide when ordering from your company. That is the whole point.

In reality, when you create a new style, you will assign a style number that has some meaning to you. In the past, many of the large retailers would assign their own SKU numbers to cross reference your style number. If you sold your product to more that one retailer who assigned their own SKU numbers, you would have to keep a cross reference of all the SKU's for each retailer for each of your styles. The use of a UPC number eliminates the need for all that.

How much does a UCC membership cost?

Important! The price of the UCC number can range from $750 to $8000.

The cost of a UCC number depends on how you fill out the application and what criteria you provide. It is based on your annual gross sales volume and the quantity of UPC numbers you will need.

How many UPC numbers will you need?

The quantity of UPC numbers you will require can be calculated as follows. Each style-color-size in your system that will be sold through EDI distribution will require a UPC number. Therefore if you have 100 styles that each come in 10 colors and 8 sizes, you will need 100 x 10 x 8 = 8000 UPC numbers.

The UCC is running out of six-digit company ID numbers. To address this problem, the UCC has created an option to issue seven and eight digit company ID numbers. The problem is that the UPC number is limited to 12 digits, one of which is a check digit, so there are only 11 usable digits in a UPC number.

If the company ID is eight digits, then there are only three digits left for the product code. That means for one eight-digit company ID you could only have 000 – 999 or 1,000 product codes. After that, you have to purchase another company ID number. From the example above, you would need to purchase eight company ID numbers in order to support 8,000 items.

Each time you run out of numbers you must purchase another company ID number. There is also an additional annual membership fee that varies depending on the size of your company.

Sample quotes from the UCC

We called the UCC to get some quotes for obtaining a membership and ID number.

Example1:   Estimating annual sales of $300,000 with 20 styles, 5 sizes and 5 colors each (500 items total), requesting an eight-digit company ID number, the UCC quoted $1500 for the company ID and a recurring annual fee of $400.

Example 2   Estimating annual sales of $3,000,000 with 200 styles, 10 sizes and 5 colors each (10,000 items total), requesting a 6 digit company ID number, the UCC quoted over $8000 for the company ID and a recurring annual fee of over $1400.

To learn more about the UCC, and to apply for membership, visit their web site at: **www.uc-council.org**

Uniform Code Council

8163 Old Yankee Street, Dayton, OH 45458   Tel: 937-435-3870   Fax: 937-435-7317

Quality Grades

Some types of fashion merchandise such as hosiery and shoes are graded by the manufacturer either as "perfect," as "irregulars," or as "seconds." Less-than-perfect goods are graded "irregular" if they have defects that may affect appearance but not wear. "Seconds" are factory rejects that have faults that may affect wear. Depending upon its clientele, store policy may exclude anything except perfect goods, or it may permit irregulars and seconds to be offered in special promotions or by basement departments. It is what customers want and expect that determine policy, as in the many other phases of fashion merchandising.   If customers demand perfect goods, the store offers them; if they accept slight irregularities at concessions in price, the store follows the lead and makes such goods available when possible.

Shipping

Filling orders

Once the garments have returned from the contractors and the quality control has been completed, the garments are divided into groups according to style, size, and color, and put into a storage area where they hang on racks awaiting shipping.

Pulling Orders

The person in charge of shipping pulls merchandise according to the store orders and the date the orders are due for delivery. The garments must be carefully packaged and shipped according to the retailer's instructions.

Packing

Use the original order form to check off when packing.

Packaging Materials

Packaging is not just the product but also the whole presentation, which will include labels, hangtags, logos and the packaging itself. If the retailer requested a specific method of packaging and shipping, and this is not carried out to the letter, this could result in deductions, and even returned merchandise. Some stores request that the garments are folded and put into plastic bags, others will request that the garments be shipped on hangers with plastic bags covering the garments. Hung garments are normally only requested for better stores. They will normally tell you the type of hangers that they require.

Packaging Materials

Buy the packaging supplies from a reputable source, one that is familiar with industry requirements. Keep the product clean; use tissue paper to help prevent creasing of the garments. Stores place orders for a certain quantity of units on an order form that includes the style number, color number, and price per unit. The order form will also include the type of shipping required by the retailer. Garments are packaged into boxes with the packing slips or with the invoice usually on the outside of the box. The boxes are then marked with the means of transportation. The recommended method is to enclose the invoice with the shipment and place the packing slip on the outside of the boxes. This will speed up payment and paper work. Send a copy to the sales representative to inform them that their order has been shipped, whether it was in full or short they should be informed.

Insurance

You should make sure who is responsible for the insurance of the goods shipped, is it you or the retailer? If you are responsible, insure the goods for their full value. If the shipment is under $100 FedEx or UPS will cover the loss.

FOLLOW INSTRUCTIONS!

It is extremely important that the manufacturer follow the specific instructions given by the store about how to pack, label and ship the order. If you fail to comply, the store will deduct part of their payment to you. MORE CHARGEBACKS! Make certain that the delivery time is kept and that the order arrives on time. There will be a window of time in which to ship the goods. Large department stores usually have distribution centers where their goods are shipped, and they will then distribute your shipment to their individual stores. The bigger the store, the bigger their demands are for you to follow their exact instructions as to how your goods should be shipped.

Shipping late or Incomplete Orders

If for any reason you are unable to ship goods on time and you ship them late without having prior approval, **then you can expect to have the goods returned and have the order canceled.** If you have a problem shipping on time, then explain the problem to the retailer and clear the late shipment with them. Making sure you get their authorization in writing via fax or e-mail. If your order is incomplete due to production delays or fabric problems, inform the retailer/buyer and make sure that they still want you to ship what is produced. If the order has coordinated pieces, and only part of the group is ready for delivery, the retailer may want to wait to receive the complete order. If you get the go-ahead to ship incomplete, invoice for the goods shipped and indicate what is back-ordered and when it will be ready for shipment. Communications with the retailer is normally done through your sales representative.

Transportation Terms

C.O.D.

Cash on delivery. This method is used for the smaller retailer or boutique. You may want to ask for a money order to be arranged if you are unsure of the vendor. Once you know the customer then you can accept a check. *(Good checks have been known to be canceled once the order is received!)*

F.O.B. (Free on board)

The buyer pays the transportation and owns the merchandise when it is shipped.

F.O.B. Destination

The seller pays the transportation and owns the merchandise until it is received at the store.

F.O.B. Shipping Point

The seller pays any expense necessary for sending the merchandise to the point where it is turned over to a transportation company. The seller owns the merchandise until it is turned over to a transportation company.

F.O.B. Destination, Charge Reversed

The seller will own the goods until they get into the retail store, however, the buyer will pay the transportation.

F.O.B. Destination, Freight Prepaid

The merchandise becomes the property of the store when it is shipped, but the seller will pay the transportation.

As a rule the retailer usually will pick up the shipping charge.

UPS (United Parcel Service)

You can have your packages picked up from your home. Call one day and they pickup the next. In addition to the shipping charge, you will be charged a small weekly pick up fee that applies to the first pickup of the week and covers all other packages and pickups in the same week. Costs are based on distance, package size, weight and, since most shipments over $100 are insured, the value of the garments. For example, a dozen sweaters by truck from New York may be $6 to $10. Some companies automatically ship Overnight Express and build the charges into the clothing cost. You will need to give the UPS driver a check in the right amount. If you plan to use UPS on a regular basis you can ask for "Ready Customer Pickup Service."

UPS C.O.D. Enhancement Services

NEW important UPS service takes away the risks involved with C.O.D. The checks are made out to UPS and, should they be bad checks, UPS will secure the funds to your account and go after collection. UPS Guarantees when payment will arrive. C.O.D. Secure, posts checks directly to your bank of choice within two business days of package delivery. Funds are guaranteed through UPS Capital Trade Protection Services, Inc. No special bank account is needed, and the record-keeping is simple. You can choose to receive daily C.O.D. remittance statements three ways:

hardcopy, Internet, or fax. Unlike credit cards, you can calculate the costs associated with C.O.D. Secure into the fee you charge your customers. **www.ups.com**

FedEx

Has a very similar service as UPS. You must call and find out which one will offer you the service that best suits your company's needs. They both offer the same service for tracking your order's current status via your computer and the package tracking number. This way it is possible to find where your package is in the delivery cycle in case there is a problem with late arrivals. If the package has been delivered, the sender is able to see who signed for it. Their web site can also provide quotes, pickup times or drop-off locations. **www.fedex.com**

U. S. Postal Service

The Postal Service is beginning to offer better services, and it is advisable to inquire about how they would help with your shipping requirements. The Postal Service should be used when shipping goods to Canada, since provide free customs inspections and deliver right to the customer's door. **www.usps.com**

Keeping track of your Inventory

Having too much inventory can deplete your net worth, whether it's finished goods or rolls of fabric. Some companies count inventory as an asset, apparel manufacturers cannot. Stock that is left on the shelf or in the warehouse should be unloaded ASAP. The sooner it is unloaded, the more chance you have of making a profit from it.

Who wants old apparel inventory?

- Reduce the price and sell to discount stores
- Have your own quarterly sale to move the goods
- Send out fliers and post cards to old customers
- Sell at weekend markets

Just get rid of it!

Remember the four "P's"   *"Proper Planning Prevents Problems"*

Ken Wengrod, Mark Fabrics, LA

Care Labels

Federal Trade Regulations

The Federal Trade Commission regulations have been in existence since 1972. These require manufactures or importers of textiles, wearing apparel, and certain piece goods to provide an accurate, permanent **care label,** which describes regular care instructions for washing, drying, bleaching, warnings, and dry cleaning of that garment or fabric. It must be permanently attached and legible. Instructions for special care treatments are not required. A glossary of care label symbols and terms is included at the end of this chapter.

www3.ftc.gov/bcp/conline/pubs/buspubs/thread.htm

This site is extremely helpful and answers frequently asked questions, it is titled "Threading Your Way Through the Labeling Requirements Under the Textile and Wool Acts"

Care Symbols

These days care labels have evolved into the use of symbols to help consumers understand their cleaning options. As of July 1, 1997, the FTC mandated that all manufacturers must include written explanation of these symbols on garments for 18 months, at which time only the symbol will be used.

Most care instructions fall within five categories: washing, bleaching, drying, ironing, and dry cleaning. Each category shows the basic options for care, as well as one or more warning signs for treatments to avoid in order to prevent damage. *(See Care Label Guide at the end of this chapter)*

Washing Symbols

Instructions should include two basic criteria: whether the garment can be washed by hand or by machine, and whether the manufacturer recommends a normal or delicate cycle. A separate icon indicates items that should be hand-washed.

Does "washable" also mean the garment can be dry-cleaned? Not necessarily, only one method of safe care has to be listed on the label, regardless of how many other safe methods exist. Also, the label does not have to warn about unsafe cleaning methods. For example, clothing labeled "washable" may not dry-clean well. Finally, this category includes symbols to give guidance with the best temperature choice for the garment, along with whether or not it can endure wringing or spinning.

Bleaching Symbols

The triangular symbol shows whether the garment can withstand chlorine bleach on a regular basis or only non-chlorine bleach. If chlorine bleach would harm the garment, but regular use of non-chlorine bleach would not, the label shown will be "Only non-chlorine bleach (when needed)." If the garment should not be exposed to bleach at all, the universal "X" appears through the symbol.

Drying Symbols

This label shows whether the garment can be dried by machine and may suggest a heat setting. Unless regular use of high temperatures will harm the garment when machine-dried; no temperature setting need be indicated. Finally, special drying requirements such as "line-dry" or "lay flat" may also appear on the label. Again, a warning symbol will appear if drying will damage the garment.

Ironing Symbols

In this category, the most important criteria are the temperature and whether the use of steam is permitted.

Dry Cleaning Symbols

These circular symbols are possibly the most confusing of all. A "dry-clean only" label may suggest which type of solvent works best for a garment and may include special notes about moisture level. But if all commercially available solvents can be used, the label does not have to mention a specific solvent. If, however, one or more solvents would harm the garment, a safe solvent option must be listed.

Take extra care when choosing care labels for garments with trims that are metallic, sequined, beaded, or with pearls. Often it is best to inquire about the care of these fancy trims from the supplier.

If you manufacture "separates" and the fabric is identical for all pieces, a care label may only appear on one piece. This label governs the care of all pieces.

The textile firm which supplied the fabric should give you all the care instructions necessary for the fabric supplied. It is also recommended you test for yourself the performance of the finished garment when washed or dry-cleaned. If however you purchase your fabric from a jobber and the exact fiber content is unknown, you can perform a wash test to measure the amount of shrinkage. Measure a 10-inch square and mark the length grain and the cross grain using a felt pen with permanent ink. Wash the square, and then measure the amount of shrinkage. The length grain will usually have more shrinkage. You can work out the exact amount of shrinkage by using this method. *(Make sure that the piece of fabric is ironed in order to measure exactly)* **Example:** if you have ½ inch shrinkage on your 10-inch square, you have 5% shrinkage.

Who is covered by these Federal Trade Commission regulations?

- Manufacturers of textiles and wearing apparel.
- Manufacturers of piece goods sold at retail to consumers, for making wearing apparel.
- Importers of textiles and wearing apparel.
- Importers of piece goods sold at retail to consumers, for making wearing apparel.
- Any person or organization that directs or controls the manufacture or importation of textile wearing apparel, or piece goods, for making wearing apparel.

What is covered by these regulations?

The law applies to most items of wearing apparel. It does not apply to leather, suede, fur garments, ties, belt, and other apparel not used to cover or protect a part of the body.

They also apply to all piece goods for home sewing into apparel.

The exception is for manufacturers using remnants up to 10 yards long, when the content is not known, and cannot easily be determined. Trim up to 5 inches wide is also excluded.

What must be done?

- Provide care instructions to consumers.

- Ensure that instructions and warnings, if followed, will cause no substantial harm to the product.

- Warn consumers about procedures that they may assume are consistent with care instructions on the label, but that would harm the product.

- Ensure that instructions and warnings remain legible throughout the useful life of the product.

Violations and Penalties

Failure to provide reliable care instructions and warnings for the useful life of an item, as required, constitutes a violation of the Federal Trade Commission Act and could subject the violator to enforcement action and penalties of up to $10,000 for the offense.

How to label textile wearing apparel

Manufacturers and importers must provide labels that:

- Are fastened so they can be seen or easily found by consumers at the point of sale.

- If not seen or easily found at the point of sale, will be supplemented by care information that also appears on the outside of the package or on the hangtag fastened to the product.

- Remain fastened and legible during the useful life of the product.

- Say what regular care is needed for the ordinary use of the product.

- Warn consumers about procedures that they may assume are consistent with the care instructions on the label, but that would harm the product.

How to label piece goods for home - sewers

Manufacturers and importers must provide care information clearly and conspicuously on the end of each roll or bolt.

Manufacturers and importers must say in the care information that is on the ends of rolls, what regular care is needed. The information only applies to the fabric on the roll or bolt, and not to additional components that the consumer may add to the fabric, such as linings or buttons.

Country of Origin

A Country of Origin label is required by Customs if the garment is made outside of the United States. The label must say "made in (name of country) or "Made in USA of Imported Fabric," according to the garment.

(A "Made in USA" label is reserved for garments made entirely in the U.S., of American fabric and construction. Items made partially in a foreign country and partially in the United States must disclose

those facts, e.g.; "assembled and sewn in the USA of components made in (name of country)." Recent federal laws also require specific placement of these labels so that they are clearly visible. There have been a number of recent cases where the manufacturer for a large chain store has been advertising "Made in the USA" and in fact the garments were cut and partially sewn in foreign countries and finished in the US. The labels on these garments were fraudulent and misleading.)

Other Types of Labels

Size and Union Labels

Garments will also have size labels and union labels if the garment is produced in an American union shop. In addition, there may be a hangtag to further promote the manufacturer, or the fiber or fabric producer's name.

Private Label

Many garment manufacturers are commissioned to manufacture clothes for large department and chain stores that wish to sell garments under their own brand name or private label. These firms may use the store name as the label for everything, or they may use different names for each line. Mail-order catalogs, specialty stores and large department stores commonly use their own name in garments manufactured by other manufacturers. One example is the Gap - they may have their own label sewn into a pair of jeans when, in fact, Levi ® has manufactured them.

Company Brand

Whether the label is to be used inside the garment or on the outside, the labels used should be designed with as much thought as the design of the business card. A business card and your label are the cheapest forms of advertising and are important in the development of "brand" awareness. Choosing a company name, a business card, and garment labels should be done with consideration of brand and marketing goals, eye-catching graphics and text, and also color, all with a goal of making a memorable impression.

RN (Registration Number)

The Registration Number should also be sewn into the garment, along with cutting lots and which contractor was responsible for sewing the garments. *(See Chapter 2)*

Woven or Printed Labels

Woven labels are the choice for better quality garments. They can be rather costly so call around for the best price. If you are short of cash then printed labels are fine for the first few lines, or until the next label order is placed. A woven label always looks more expensive and professional, but in the long run it will be the styles that sell, not the labels.

Who makes labels?

You will find a label maker by looking in one of the trade papers or trade directories. They will also supply the other labels necessary for the production of the finished garment, e.g. sizes, fabric content, cares labels etc.

As your company grows, you may choose to buy a small printing machine that prints the special labels required for any garment.

Care Label Guide

Wash		Bleach	Dry		Iron	Dry-clean	
Machine-wash normal	Water Temperature 50C/120F (Hot)	Any Bleach (when needed)	Tumble Dry	Heat Setting: High	Iron	Dry-clean	Reduce moisture
Permanent Press/ Wrinkle Resistant	Water Temperature 40C/105F (Warm)	Only non-chlorine bleach (when needed)	Tumble-dry, Normal	Heat Setting: Medium	High	Any solvent	Short cycle
Gentle/Delicate	Water Temperature 30C/85F (Cool)	Warning: Do Not Bleach	Permanent Press/ Wrinkle Resistant	Heat Setting: Low	Medium	Any solvent except trichloroethylene	No steam finishing
Hand Wash	Warning: Do Not Wash		Gentle/Delicate	No heat/ air	Low	Petroleum solvent only	Low heat
	Warning: Do Not Wring		Line Dry/Hang to Dry	Dry Flat	Do not iron	Do not dry-clean	
			Drip Dry	Dry in the Shade	No steam		
			Do Not Machine Dry (used with do not wash)	Do Not Tumble Dry			

CHAPTER 14

THE BUSINESS OF MARKETING & SELLING

"WITHOUT A SALE THERE IS NO BUSINESS"

Marketing encompasses all the activities directed towards the successful sale of your product. This includes planning market research, (customer buying habits), advertising, promotions, public relations, pricing strategies, merchandising, and packaging. Successful marketing of your company will include the ability to identify trends, a strong sense of timing, creativity, and most importantly the ability to grow with the continuing fast changing technological world of sales, all balanced within your financial constraints.

Reviewed by: Ginny Wong Sales Representative California Market Center Los Angeles

Choosing the right strategy to achieve the sales target is perhaps one of the most important decisions you may ever have to make in order to become a successful manufacturer. In many industries, especially the garment industry, (*where Murphy's' law rules*) the best plans may not work, and changes may need to be made so the company can grow. What is planned in concept may not work in reality. Be prepared for changes and to make them.

Channels of Distribution

One of the first choices you will have to make; is what type of distribution is best for your growing company? There are four main channels of distribution to choose from:

1. **Department Stores:** Orders are generally too large for the start-up manufacturer. Once the company is established and is in the "Vendor Matrix" continued sales are likely. However, department stores are risky business for the smaller manufacturer and if too many orders are placed with department stores it could result in **death by chargebacks**!

2. **Specialty Stores:** The chargeback game is beginning to be used extensively by specialty stores, but thankfully, they have not as yet taken it to the level of the department stores. The specialty store is the ideal customer for a small start-up to target for its sales. They like a quick-turn and fashion forward design that will warrant a higher profit margin. The store is usually focused on a well-defined customer. The challenge of the manufacturer is to continually hit on the latest fashion trend. An order

from a specialty store usually has less lead-time and is smaller in volume than a department store's. Re-orders are often made, or "**fill ins**" of the most popular styles and sizes. This requires extra personnel to respond to these extra orders.

3. **Discount Stores:** This market is big volume, which requires a well-capitalized, financially secure manufacturer. These retail giants manufacture their own private-label merchandise and know exactly what each garment should cost to produce. The orders are very large and planning for production is often in the planning stages a year in advance. The larger, efficient manufacturer can do very well with these customers, but they are **not** an option for the smaller manufacturer.

4. **Internet & or Mail Order Sales:** E-tailing is making in-roads into the apparel marketplace. Cash flow is good on the sales side, but inventory stock can be a drain. This is due to the fact that the merchandise must be ready for shipping and therefore, an estimate must be made as to what will sell, and in what quantities. Selling direct to the retailer is an option that will take-off in the next few years and will allow the manufacturer a direct line to the retailer.

Selling Options

There are many different options to sell and market your product. At first, you may choose one, but as your company grows it is possible that you will end up selling your product by a combination of those listed below. You may choose a more traditional method using a sales representative for the bulk of production, but opt to move some of your product via the Internet for a faster turn around. This is a good option if you have inventory that you wish to sell quickly.

- **Direct sales to the consumer**   Via Retail Outlets, Trade Shows, Fairs, Web page, Catalog Sales, Printed Mailers, via electronic or digital media, TV, Fax, E-mail, CD etc. *(See Chapter 15, "Mail Order" and Chapter 16 "Selling on the Internet")*

- **Direct sales via Private Label** As a manufacturer you will produce private label at the request of certain stores.

- **Indirect sales via Private Label** Sales reps will sell a percentage of your merchandise as private label merchandise to retailers.

- **Indirect selling** to wholesalers and distributors, catalog companies or an independent sales rep or agents that are paid on commission of sales.

- **Indirect selling via "in-house"** Sales via sales reps who are employees of the manufacturer.

- **Indirect sales** to the customer via consignment. *(Not a good idea.)* If you have done your homework and have a good product developed, you should have a sale. Consignment is your last resort in sales.

Direct Selling

Selling directly to stores is a good way to start for a new company. It is a way of controlling your own sales and learning more about the business of selling. You will also begin to listen and learn what the customer likes and dislikes. Selling to smaller stores is an effective way of building a good customer base. Once you have them as clients they usually return to buy from you in the future. The down side to showing your line yourself, to potential customers, is that it requires time. This in turn, takes away from your time to run the company and produce your product. If you are running your own business, this would be almost impossible, it demands too much time and energy to travel from store to store to show your line.

Do's and don'ts of direct selling

- Once you have orders from small specialty stores it is a good idea to check that they have a good credit record. This can be done through a Factor who normally offers this service. Otherwise, you must insist on having payment made by a money order or cashiers check for the goods that are received, until the store has proved to be trustworthy. Accepted checks may be good but they can be canceled! Trying to retrieve payment from smaller stores is expensive and time consuming and often costs more than the initial invoice.

- When planning to show your line to a customer, it is important to conduct yourself as a professional. Never stop by to see a customer without first calling to arrange a convenient time to show your line. It is only courteous to check schedules, sales presentations demand time and full attention.

- Before you show your line, learn your sales pitch. Ask a friend to listen to your presentation. Show the items one at a time, explaining the details of each piece. If you have groups within the line, keep the groups separate. Time your presentation so that you are aware of the length of time required to make your presentation. Do not get over-involved with showing your line, explaining every detail. Keep it to the point, the buyer can see if they like the product or not in a second. You may love it and feel that everyone else will, but the hard fact is they won't!

Drawbacks of direct selling

- It is important to try and stay detached from critiques of your line, analyze the comments to learn from them. The truth can be brutal. Be prepared for some honest advice, which in turn is a good way for you to understand what and why different types of garments sell well. Apply all this free advice in a positive way and if possible, improve your product. If your product is well-made, has exciting new styling, interesting fabrication, and the fit good, then you should have a sale.

- It is hard to put yourself out there and then hear negative comments about the product that has taken you so long to develop. If you are unable to handle hurtful remarks and criticism, then find yourself a good sales representative or a partner who can buffer the inevitable critics. You will soon develop a thick skin.

Showing the Line

- Do not arrive to show your product to a buyer or retailer with your goods piled up in a plastic bag. Invest in a garment bag, which allows you to arrange your line in order, and on hangers. Rolling racks are also a worthwhile purchase. They collapse for easy use and can be rebuilt to carry your line for presentation. The storeowner will not be happy to have your line all over their store floor, especially while there are customers in the shop.

- Have each sample tagged with the style number, sizes and colors available. Hand the buyer a "Line Sheet" *(See Chapter 7, Line Sheets)*, with all the relevant information, price, delivery and fabric content, plus an order form for them to complete and send in.

Writing an Order

Understand how to write an order, "Terms of Sale" and shipping arrangements, *(see further in this chapter)*. You can use the order forms found in the back of this book and put your own business stamp on them. You could also design your own order forms with the use of your computer. You will need to have four copies of the order, one for the buyer, one for the sales representative, one for shipping purposes and the other as a record of sales made.

The information on the order form should include:

- **Date of order**
- **Customer and department**
- **Address to be shipped to**
- **Address to be billed to**
- **Number and description of each style ordered**
- **Cost and recommended retail price of each style ordered (optional)**

- **Quantities ordered of each style**
- **Details of color and size in each style**
- **Delivery dates**
- **Cancellation date**
- **Terms of sale**

Remember that writing the order is only part of the final sale. The goods have to be produced and shipped on time, and the quality must be consistent with the samples shown at the time the orders were written. If you are unable to follow through with all that it takes to ship on time, you may find that you have lost a customer forever. A store has to plan their purchases and inventory well ahead of time. Once an order is written, they will plan to receive your goods and will buy other pieces to merchandise with your product. When you are unable to produce, the store will have a problem finding new merchandise to replace yours.

Retailer Buying Habits

Retailers buy in a number of ways to fill their store with merchandise:

- **Market**, usually up to five markets a year. This is the best method to get the best prices and sometimes special deals with the manufacturer.

- **Trade shows**, which are held at various times each year in different locations. (See more information on trade shows further in this chapter).

- **Sales representatives** will visit the buyer's home office or store to present a line. This is done to show newly added styles to a manufacturer's line or to discuss private label.

Private Label

Private label is another method of indirect sales that is used more and more by the retailer. The retailer will commission manufacturers to develop and produce special merchandise just for their store. The merchandise will have the store's own label sewn into the garment. Private label is big business and growing in its use by the retailer. There are normally two types of private label, one is developed to look like designer clothes, and the second is developed to be cheaper, like a bargain brand. Manufacturers are concerned by this trend of marketing because it excludes their own product. However, to keep contact with the department stores, manufacturers agree to include a certain percentage of their product as private label. In exchange for this, the retailer agrees to carry the manufacturer's own label. In effect, the manufacturer is forced to be the contractor for the retailer! Whichever way you look at it, private label is an important moneymaker for manufacturers.

"Virtual Vertical Retailers" are successful retailers who have created their own design, product development, sourcing, and delivery organizations to implement their other traditional contacts with manufacturers. To date, JC Penney's has nineteen private brand labels. Target, Kmart, Wal-Mart all have their own private labels, which play a very significant role in purchasing power. Manufacturers throughout the world create product for Banana Republic, Ann Taylor, Kathie Lee, Martha Stewart, Jacquelyn Smith, to name but a few. Manufacturers can offer packaged, private labels selling directly to the retailer, or by selling through a branded name; e.g. Nike, Cherokee, BeBe, etc. In order to become a successful private label manufacturer, it demands knowledge of the brand and the trends in the market, an understanding of the product development process, with an ability to deliver a product on time. This would be based on organizational skills, along with proper business planning and execution of that plan.

Selling on the Internet

Will the growth of the Internet lead to less demand for retail shop space and traditional methods of shopping? Over time, yes it will!

The Internet continues to make rapid advances as a retail tool and the marketplace will see a growing segmentation of aging "Baby Boomers" and their kids in "Generation Y" (born between 1977-1998). With Internet users currently estimated at one billion, the Commerce Department figures that traffic on the Internet is doubling every 100 days. Online shopping will have an increasing effect on traditional shopping centers, as some retailers capitalize on the trend, others stand on the side lines and ignore these new marketing venues to their peril. When it comes to online buying, it is convenient and enables the buyer to easily browse at will to find the cheapest price. The value and convenience of shopping online is irresistible from a consumer's standpoint. It will eventually change the way most sales are conducted. Traditionally, retailers dictate to the customer the type of product that is available. With online sales, the customer or retailer can go direct to the designer/manufacturer and buy right the creative source.

Technology and selling on the Internet

Technology is changing so rapidly that keeping up with it is more than a full time job.

It is bringing about changes in the way business is usually conducted in sales. Showrooms are going online, and the virtual sales showroom is here to stay. Digital cameras are being used to photograph new styles in the showroom. You can download those new images (styles), and email them on a line sheet, directly to the client. It is a much more efficient and cost effective way to get new products to your buyers on a more frequent basis.

Manufacturers are communicating with retailers and sales representatives through their personal computers daily. This allows the manufacturer to receive all the information instantly from the sales representative, which in turn informs the manufacturer of the building sales.

One of the more interesting advances made have enable customers to feed on-line, their exact shape and measurements that would then enable them to have a virtual image of themselves and then try clothes on their virtual selves, all on-line. This would eliminate the large percentage of returns that manufacturers normally have to allow for when selling to customer's product unseen, as with mail order and the Internet. Larger manufacturers now send swatches of available fabrics and colors to their customers. They ask the customer to feel the quality and to approve the overall garment in advance of shipping, to help cut back on return problems. *(For more in depth information on selling on the Internet read Chapter 16)*

Brand Names

Apparel websites are experiencing the highest percentage of "hits" or growth in # of visitors. This trend tends to apply towards more basic apparel rather than fashion apparel. However, hot brands do well across the board as long as the brand is recognized. A brand name has the greatest influence on consumers' decisions to shop at an Internet-based apparel retailer – with brand recognition, the customer is familiar with the quality, fit, and value for their money.

For a new company, setting up a website could be an interesting and wise move. *(See Chapter 16, Selling on the Internet)*

Catalog Sales

Direct Selling

Selling directly to your customer using catalogs has been a growing trend by manufacturers. If you have investors, and can afford the start-up costs, this can be an effective method of sales. However, for a start-up company with limited means this method is hardly an option. *(See Chapter 15 Catalog Sales)*

Indirect Selling

Start-up companies can sell to companies with catalog divisions, who will sell your product under their name such as JC Penney, Victoria's Secret, and Eddie Bauer. They work directly with manufacturers in developing the kinds of merchandise they want for their catalogs. These companies are so large they have their own detailed specifications about the garments are to be sized and made. Catalog sales is big business, and these companies will often be vertical producers of the whole garment. From the fibers to the design of the fabric, product design and development to the final sale, they control the whole process.

Home Shopping TV-QVC

Home shopping shows combine features of both catalog houses and trade shows. Another name for this marketing technique is "interactive television." The process for selling your idea is similar to that of getting your product displayed in a catalog; sending samples for consideration. If they choose to feature your product, they will work with you to handle processing and fulfillment of orders. Be prepared to handle volume!

Indirect Sales

Sales Representatives

The sales representatives you choose will directly affect your company. They can make it very successful or they can be responsible for its failure. Therefore, it is very important to pay attention to who you choose, or as it happens in some instances, the sales rep who chooses you.

What does a sales representative do for the company? They are responsible for finding the right customers for your product and for presenting your line to the buyers. They are also responsible for writing the orders and negotiating the terms of sales. Good sales representatives are usually well paid for their job, either salary, salary and sales commission, or commission as a percentage of sales. Commission varies from 0% (for salaried representatives) to as much as 25% of sales, depending on the product, territory, and experience of the representative.

Commission

The average percentage of commission for clothing is some where between 10% - 15%, depending on volume. Commission is paid on orders shipped to and accepted by the retailer. *(Not all orders are shipped due to cancellations from the buyer, or because the orders were not large enough for the manufacturer to produce).*

Road Representatives

If they conduct their sales by going to the various stores and boutiques to show the lines, they are referred to as "**road reps**". Most road representatives are paid on a commission basis and are usually responsible for their own expenses; including the cost of operating, and running a car and any other expenses incurred while on the road selling your product.

Showroom Representatives

Sales representatives who run their own showroom, and represent multiple lines "**independent sales representatives**" will sometimes charge some rent to help cover the cost of a showroom, plus a commission fee.

Territory

Sales representatives have their own territory and they will demand exclusive rights to them. If they have a showroom, they will also have a territory, and you should inquire as to what it covers and if they have other showrooms in other cities. It will be important to clarify their territory. If you or any one else representing your company makes a sale in their territory, then the commission may be due in full or the commission split. This type of situation should be discussed and clearly understood by both parties.

In-House Sales Representatives

Larger companies may have their own in-house representative who will only represent their company. Small start-up apparel manufacturers will usually look to independent sales representatives who represent multiple lines.

Benefits of a GOOD Sales Representative

A good representative can help build your company, merchandise your product, and give very helpful business advice. Experienced sales representatives have the "know how" of what sells, and they have direct contact with many buyers, who give feed back on what is hot at the moment and what is not!

Choosing a Sales Representative

It is important that the chosen sales representative has the right contacts for your product. Find out who is their customer base, and if decide if that matches your specific product(s) and target market. All aspects of their client base needs to be considered when choosing a sales representative:

- Type of territory
- Price point
- Sales methodology
- Time frames
- Product mix
- Potential conflict of products
- References

Questions you need to ask your Sales Representative

- *What type of commission and percentage amount?*
- *When is commission due?* This is usually paid the last day of the month for payments received that month.
- *Is commission paid on netshipped orders or gross shipped less returns and allowances*?
- *Number of sales people in the showroom?*
- *Do they do trade shows and the additional cost to you?*
- *Do they charge rent for the showroom on top of the commission?*
- *Do they have other showrooms in other cities that will represent your product and the extra cost?*
- *Can you read their contract agreement, and can they clearly explain it to you?* Make sure to have any contract looked at by a legal expert.
- *How long have they been in business, and their history?*

    Ask to see references and contact their clients' for personal references. It is in your company's interest to find out as much as you can about a potential sales representative.

- *Do they pay for the samples you send them*? Some sales representatives pay for the samples, usually at a 50% discount. Others will hopefully return them at the end of the season to the manufacturer. Samples are expensive to the manufacturer, so if the sales representative does not pay for the samples they should be returned. In this case, an invoice should be sent to the representative and they can pay at the end of the season, or the cost is deducted from their commission. Sample payment or non-payment should be covered in your contract or in a separate contract.

Insurance

Do they have insurance for theft, fire, water damage, earthquake, *(may be classified as an act of God)* and other possible losses? Inquire about the type of insurance the representative carries also, if your samples are covered, and for what cost.

Customer list

It is your right to request the list of customers to which your representative sells. They are not always happy about this, but it is a good idea to fully understand the type of clients they sell to. *(The more that you both understand about one another the easier it should be to work together)*

How do you find a sales representative?

There are several ways to find a sales representative:

- Run an advertisement in a trade paper or circular

- Ask the buyers of your targeted stores.

- Go to the nearest clothing apparel mart and check out the showrooms. Look at the merchandise and talk to the various sales representatives, even show your own line for feedback and advice. You may be lucky enough to find a sales rep that is just right for you and your company, or one that is recommended by another manufacturer.

- Most marts will have notice boards or in- house newssheets that usually carry ads from sales representatives looking for new lines to represent.

- Trade shows are another place to find a representative for your company. If you are there to observe, you should check the sales representatives out and how they present their lines. If you are showing your own line, it is very possible that a sales rep will find you and ask to represent you.

Make sure that the representative you choose has good references

Contact other companies they represent and check their references. Follow up with the stores they sell to, to make sure that they are trustworthy and will work for you and to your advantage. To begin with, try to go with your representative when they visit a buyer, or arrange to sit in and watch them present your line. They are more likely to do a good presentation for you if you are around and keeping an eye out for your own best interest. The majority of sales representatives are honest, and trustworthy, and can make magic happen for your company. *(It's that dangerous minority that you have to protect yourself against!)*

Sales Rep's Samples

Your sales representatives will require a full set of the items that are in your line. Samples are normally made in a middle-size, (Size 8 or Size 7). You should color coordinate your line so all the pieces complement each other, and will merchandise well when the sales representative makes a presentation to a buyer. You will not be required to make a sample of every size and of each color offered. There should be a swatch card to show the colors you will be offering and a line sheet of the complete line with all the relevant information about the garments. *(See Chapter 7 for more information on Line Sheets)*

Duplicates

If you have more than one sales rep, you will need to make a complete line of samples for each sales representative who is showing your line. These samples are called duplicates or sales samples. *(Samples, production samples, and duplicates can begin to add up to a considerable expense for a small company, keep a tight control on this part of your business)*

Minimum Orders

If you require a minimum order for any of your garments, your sales representative should be informed. As a manufacturer, it is in your interest to calculate how many items you will require to be sold in order to make a profit. Buyers don't care if they only order ten items, it does not affect them how large the order is. Before you go to market you need to figure how big the order should be in order to produce it and make a profit. If you require a minimum order of 400 pieces r to cover your fabric and production plus make a 40% mark-up, and your final order is 300 pieces, you will have to decide if it is a profitable order. One of your considerations would be what will happen to the fabric left unused? Sometimes in order to keep the line merchandised so pieces can be sold together, it maybe important to keep an item in the line even if the piece will produce little or no profit. The trick is to remember this for next season and maybe not offer that particular item, or to try and rework the garment in order to cut costs. *(See Chapter 12, Product Costing)*

Too larger an order

The reverse situation is also a problem, it is important that you do not accept too large an order. Growing too fast can be detrimental to your business and will require crisis management. Take control of what you realistically can produce.

Customer Concentration

No more than 30% of your business should be placed with one customer. This might not be possible for the first couple of seasons, as the first big order is the one that will get your company off the ground. However, it should be realized that to be reliant on one customer for your production is an unreasonable risk, and can lead to problems if the retailer decides to sever connections at a later date.

Contract of agreement

You will sign a contractual agreement with your sales representative. This contract is usually for six months to one year, and the dates of this agreement should be part of your understanding. As with any other agreement, do not sign before reading. Clearly understand the content and the terms of commissions to be paid and any other payments that will be required from you. When in doubt consult a lawyer or other legal council, SBA, SBDC or SCORE can also help with contracts. *(See Industry Related Resources)*

Termination

Either party can terminate their contractual agreement in writing and send it via certified mail. It is usual to take sixty days to come into effect. Make sure that the contract agreement does not include commission for sales after the termination of the contract.

Resolving a Dispute

If you have the misfortune to become involved with any unfortunate deeds committed by your sales representative, arbitration is by far the best way to resolve any disputes. Taking matters to court can be excessively costly and no one wins but the attorneys. Build this agreement into your contract and make sure that any arbitration is binding.

Questions a sales representative should ask you:

- Can you ship on time and make the orders?
- How long have you been in business?
- Your experience within the industry?
- Do you deliver on time?
- Price point and target market?
- Standards of quality control?
- Will you send shipping records to the sales representative for proof of sales?

Horror Stories

As with any other part of operating a business, be aware that there are many potential horror stories attached to finding the right representative for your company. Here are a few:

- Loss of samples
- Products destroyed by flood, fire or earthquake
- Not promoting your line as agreed
- Dishonest *(revealing your company's confidential information to a competitor)*

- Personality conflict *(Sales representatives are in the business of persuasion and tend to have overpowering personalities. They work for you and it is important to have this understanding very clear).*

As with any other employee or contractor working for you, bad things can happen, do not be too surprised when they do. Be prepared!

Terms of Payment to the sales representative

Terms of payment to your sales representative will be laid out in your contract. It is normally paid within 15 days of shipment. Make sure that you are aware of when payment is due when making your contract with a sales representative. It is a good idea to forward a copy of your invoice to your representative when the goods are shipped. They will then know actual delivery dates, if the order was complete, and any other information pertaining to the sale they wrote. If there are returns from the retailer or charge backs, this commission will be subtracted from the sales representatives' invoice for the next sales made since commission is not paid on returns.

Advances

It is common practice for the sales representatives to request an advance against the commission due. Be cautious not to pay the full amount of the commission as the final order could be reduced due to returns.

FYI

Sales Representatives in New York or California paid on commission require a written commission agreement with specific terms. Companies that do not have the required agreement are exposed to double damages!

Buying Office

One option for a new company is to be represented by a buying office. There are two kinds of buying offices:

1) Store-owned resident buying office located in an apparel mart that is jointly owned and operated by a group of privately owned stores.

2) Independent buying offices located in an apparel mart, which shows your product to a potential client or recommends your line to for buyers to review. They charge a fee to the store for providing this service and to you for giving you this exposure.

Buying offices can be found in most apparel marts.

Example of a Sales Representative Agreement

Sales Agreement

This Agreement dated the_____, by and between, (*Manufacture's name*) having it's principal place of business located at:_____, hereinafter called the "manufacturer" and (Sales Rep's name), a California business having its principal place of business located at:_____ _____ Hereinafter called the "company".

The Manufacturer does hereby appoint the Company as a Sales Representative for Woman's Clothing and the Company does hereby accept the appointment subject to the following terms and conditions.

Rep Territory: Consists of 13 Western States (California, Oregon, Washington, Alaska, Hawaii, Nevada, Arizona , Colorado, Utah, Wyoming, Montana, Idaho and New Mexico) and 8 Mid-Western States (Texas, Oklahoma, Arkansas, Nebraska, Mississippi, Louisiana, Kansas and Missouri) and all orders written in full price outside Rep's Territory without Company's representation at full commission. All orders written in full price in Rep's territory by other than Rep shall be paid at 6% commission.

Commission: The Manufacturer shall pay the Company commission of twelve percent (12%) on all net sales of line merchandise shipped directly or indirectly by Manufacturer into the territory, irrespective of weather the Company has solicited the sales of such merchandise. There shall be no house accounts and there shall be eighty-five percent (85%) guaranteed shipping on all credit approved orders. Commission to the company for sales of merchandise by the company outside the territory without representation shall be paid at full commission rate as well. Any discounts given to merchandise shipped late due to manufacturer's fault shall have discounts deducted from order and be paid to Company at full commission price. All other discounts shall pay the Company the commission payable, along with invoices, credit memos and statement hereunder by the 15th of the month following the month the merchandise is shipped.

Draw: Manufacturer shall pay the Company a monthly draw of One Thousand dollars ($1,000.00) against commissions, payable by the 1st of each month. The Manufacturer will be required to pay the company a monthly draw only until commissions have been paid. (Approximately 2 to 3 months) at this time the company will no longer require draw.

Samples: At its sole option, the Company may return all or any part of the samples to the Manufacturer at the end of the season(s) for which samples were produced. The Company may purchase all or a part of such samples at its option, at an amount equal to fifty percent (50%) of the wholesale cost of the sample line. In the event the Company purchases any samples, the Manufacturer shall deduct from the Company's commission for each season for which Manufacturer supplies the Company with samples. For example: if manufacturer does not commence until July, the cost of these fall samples shall not be deducted until the July commissions are paid in August to the Company.

Showroom Participation: Manufacturer shall pay to the Company as guaranteed non-refundable showroom participation of $500.00 per month, as agreed by both parties.

Trade Shows: All trade shows the Manufacturer wishes to participate in will be split evenly between such Manufacturers participating. Show fees are to be paid within five days of invoice.

Advertising: The Company shall not be charged with or liable for any advertising allowance granted by the Manufacturer.

Markdowns: The Company shall not be charged with or liable for any monies to be paid back to the retailer (unless otherwise specified).

Duration: Either party upon thirty days written notice may terminate this Agreement. If either manufacturer or the Company terminate, the Company's commissions as provided in paragraph two above, on any orders placed prior to the date upon which the Company's engagements are terminated.

Sales Representative Signature:_____   Date:_____

Manufacturer Signature:_____   Date:_____

Trade Shows

Whether you sell and promote your new company at a trade show or use your sales representative to sell your product, trade shows are big business. Trade shows are held at various times a year in different parts of the country, and in different parts of the world. Trade shows let people in the industry know who you are and what it is that you produce. The Internet may be the newest and fastest way for an established company to sell its product, but the buyers need to feel and to touch the product before they will write an initial order. This is the first important step in establishing your brand. Having a strong presence at a show opens the doors to contacts while allowing you to check the competition out.

The shows are classified as to the type of clothes sold. When planning your product and investigating the market, an important place to spot trends and to see what will be available next season is to attend one of these many trade shows, held in a variety of fashion centers.

Some trade shows require that the apparel manufacturer be "juried" into the show. They require that samples of the product be sent well in advance, they will then inform you if you have been accepted or not. The reason for this is to ensure the quality and to keep the show within a classification, and from having too many items alike.

One of the largest shows in the U.S. is the "Magic show", which is held in Las Vegas twice a year. It began as a men swear show, and has grown to incorporate all types of day clothing; men's, junior's, and women's. Buyers and designers from all around the world fly into Vegas for this important show. It has grown to be so large that it is impossible to get around in one day.

Another important trade show for the smaller manufacturer is the "Boutique Show" out of New York's Jacob Javits Convention Center, also held twice a year. This show incorporates all types of clothing, even jewelry. There are a number of important shows and markets that you will need to learn about depending on your market niche. Call your local apparel mart. *(See listings at the back of the book)*

Selling Season

Trade shows are held in the official selling season *(See Chart of Selling Seasons)*. Remember if your line is for the Spring season, you will be selling your line in the Fall. Make sure that the trade show where you wish to sell your product, is the right type of show, and has the right customers.

Cost of a Trade Show

The price for a small booth at these shows can be a substantial investment. One way to cut cost is to share a booth with another fledgling company, after making sure that there is no conflict of merchandise. You do not want to be in competition with your booth partner, but you will need to be in the same type of clothing category at the show. You can find out about the dates and the cost involved for these shows by calling the trade show sponsors directly. *(See list below)*

Costs of selling at a Trade Show

The cost for a small booth can run in the thousands, depending on the size of the booth and the show. The starting cost of a small booth is around $1,500. Ask beforehand exactly what is included in the cost of the booth. This cost will hopefully include most of the following:

- The basic booth (space)
- Your name in the show directory, with your name and booth number, and the category of your merchandise.
- Floor covering, and walls or curtains (normally bare essentials)
- Basic table and chairs
- Racks, maybe shelves, and maybe risers for your display
- Sign for the booth. *(If you are lucky. You maybe better to bring your own sign along with your own display materials)*.
- You may get help to cart your goods from the loading dock to your space at the beginning of the show and at the close.

Added costs

- Promotional display items.
- Drapes for the table
- Extra lights for a better display
- Shipment of the line to and from the show
- Airfare
- Hotel room and board.

All these costs begin to add up rather alarmingly and should be all calculated into the profitability of deciding to sell at a trade show. Will it be worth the expense?

Trade Show advantages

- Exposure to the market and to buyers is worth a lot. You will learn so much, and network within the right circles, it will be money well invested.

- Keep a business card of everyone that shows an interest in your line, even if they do not place an order. You can put them on your mailing list and send them sales and promotional information. This will remind them of your product, so at the next show they will be more familiar with your line.

- Lastly, because of showing your line at one of the trade shows, you will hopefully get lots of orders.

Display

Make your booth inviting and interesting to visit. Your graphics should communicate who you are, what you do, and how the customer can benefit by buying your line. It is important that your booth creates an impact quickly. Make it easy for people to get in and out of the booth. Make sure that whoever is working in the booth is friendly and out going. **Do not chew gum, drink or eat while selling.** Give away small items with your company's name, to remind the customer of your product. If you can afford a good-looking model to walk around in your clothes, and hand out information and your booth number, this will also be advantageous. Be ingenious, marketing is an important part of the sale of your product, and ultimately the success of your business!

If you show at a trade show and just hand out business cards and appear to make a lot of friends, you have failed miserably. You are there to sell, and if you cannot sell at a trade show, you are not going to sell anywhere.

Can you sell at a trade show where your sales representative is also selling?

Yes, and it is a good idea to be there, to help sell your line. It is advisable to make certain that your line is being well represented, and that all the items in your line are being shown to its advantage. Sometimes sales reps will only promote part of your line. They may have another line that has similar styles to yours, and feel they will have a better chance of selling more styles in that line than in yours.

Some manufacturers will have their sales representative show their line, and rent another booth to show their own line exclusively. Although expensive, it is a great way to give the manufacturer extra exposure, which will pay off with large orders being written. Note that it is normal for the sales representative to receive all the commission on any sales made, even if you made them in your own booth.

Terms of Sale

Terms of sale apply to what type of arrangements is negotiated when the order is agreed upon with the buyer. Terms of Sales normally include a combination of allowable discounts on purchases made by the buyer, and the time allowed for taking such discounts. This is to ensure punctual payment of the invoice. Here are some of the most commonly used terms of sale, which are popular within the industry. For a more thorough explanation, you should talk to your sales representative to get a clearer picture about how your line will be represented and the type of terms that will be offered at the time the order is written. Do not feel shy about asking questions, sales people are usually in sales because they are personable. Terms of sales can be quite complicated, and there are different types used in selling a garment, depending on the buyer. Once you have found the right sales rep for you and your company, he or she will help you by giving you direction as to which customer will expect what kind of terms. Your sales rep will negotiate these terms.

There are four main types of sales for small new companies

1) **E.O.M. (End of Month)** Refers to the time for payment, regardless of shipping/delivery dates, all payments are due at the end of the month.

2) **NET 30** Payment is due 30 days after you ship the goods. There are some times a little confusion about the date you ship and the date the goods are received. Although your terms may be Net Thirty, you will have to keep on top of the larger buyers to insure that your payment is not overdue.

3) **2% -8% 10net30** Is an incentive for the buyer to pay within ten days and receive a discount on that bill, otherwise the full amount is due at the end of the month. Some buyers will agree to these terms, but will pay late and still expect the discount. Stay on top of it and send them a bill for the remaining balance.

4) **C.O.D.** Payment is made when the merchandise is delivered. It should be noted here that if this term is used, then a money order is the best means of payment until the retail store has proved trustworthy. Payment y check has been known to be canceled, once delivery is made.

5) **Pro Forma** This method of payment is used mainly on special orders. You send the invoice for the merchandise ordered, and ship as soon as payment has been received. *(If a check is sent you should wait for it to clear before you ship).*

Discounts

A discount is a deduction expressed as a percentage from the quoted or billed cost of the merchandise, granted by a vendor to a purchaser. Some of the types of discounts allowed are as follows:

- **Cash discount:** a reduction in price allowed by a vendor for prompt payment.

- **Trade Discount:** is a percentage or a series of percentages deducted from the list price or theoretical retail price suggested by the manufacturer.

- **Quantity Discount:** is a percentage off the billed cost that is allowed by the seller of goods when a stipulated quantity is purchased.

- **Seasonal Discount:** a reduction in list price granted to the retail buyer for purchasing goods during the off-season.

Chargebacks

The term "chargebacks" is used for a variety of reasons:

- The retailer will charge back for goods that have been reduced in price or when the garments did not sell. The retailer will sometimes require the manufacturer to take part of the financial loss that is due to poor sales of the garment. This can mean trouble to manufacturers with a low percentage of profit, and many companies have been put out of business because of chargebacks.

- Chargebacks are charged if the goods are not shipped and packaged according to the instruction of the department store. When the order is given, they give exact shipping procedures and requirements for how the garments are to be packed, hanger, flat in bags, etc. It is very important that the manufacturer follows these instructions to the last detail. Not doing so will result in some kind of a penalty, one that the manufacturer will be required to discount from the invoice.

- If the goods have been shipped short, the manufacturer will be "charged back" for the missing goods. This often happens when the goods are being prepared for shipping and are counted incorrectly.

- Late shipment is a big reason that a department store will charge back to the manufacturer, and even cancel orders if the dates agreed upon are missed.

These are the main types of chargebacks that are used in dealing with department store, but if they can think of any reason to charge back a manufacturer, they will. It's their way of saving (making) extra money! *(See Chapter 12, for full explanation of Chargebacks)*

Including the discounts in the costing

It is important for you to be aware of the terms arranged for your order, as they will affect the profits. You have to cost the terms likely to be used and include them in the cost sheet. If the terms of sale are not correctly accounted for, you could be loosing a percentage of your profit. If you are unaware of the type of terms that will be negotiated, or there are various retail buyers with different types of terms, then some type of a discount should be allowed for and worked into the final cost sheet. It is wise to use around an 8% discount, built into the cost sheet. *(See Chapter 12 Product Costing)*

Tracking Deductions

Discounts and other deductions have become an important customer relations' concern. With proper guidance and forethought regarding how to handle this, deductions can be resolved without difficulty. By allowing for deductions in your costing, you make it easier to make a profit. Track deductions by type (i.e., shortage of orders, past cancellation date, incorrect tagging or hangers) and keep statistics to determine which ones can be corrected in the future. Compare these statistics from season to season, and follow the results of the corrective actions taken.

Tracking sales

A week after the goods are shipped to the retailer, the manufacturers will have computer sales results that tells them what's been sold. It is then possible to get a daily count of sales from your sales rep., who is linked to the retailers by phone or the computer. This will give the manufacturer a clear picture of the production, any possible reorders and the bad news of possible chargebacks.

Interest Charged

For late payment of an invoice, there is normally a 1 ½ % per month or 18% annual charge.

Checking Credit

With any new account it is advisable to check a company's credit history. If selling direct to a customer, it will be your responsibility to follow through with a credit history. Use the pre-printed forms provided with this book to track your customer's complete information. If you are a small business trying to check a customer's credit, you can check with the Better Business Bureau to see if there is a record of complaint against a potential buyer.

Dun & Bradstreet is used extensively by manufacturers and by retailers for financial information. D & B is the leading provider of business information for credit, marketing, purchasing, and receivables management decisions worldwide. Their global database has more than 60 million companies to draw from. The D&B D-U-N-S number is recognized internationally as a tool for identifying credit information. **www.dnb.com**

There are many other credit-checking companies that can help you verify a potential buyer's credit for a small fee.

(If in doubt ask for COD).

Bad Checks

Depending on why the check was returned, you will want to take different actions. Checks may bounce because of non-sufficient funds (NSF), a closed account, or no account (evidence of a fraudulent act).

- **Non-Sufficient Funds** If the check is marked "NSF", check with the bank to see if it was presented twice. If not, you can go ahead and deposit it again, but first call the person responsible for writing the check and make sure there is sufficient funds to cover the amount. If the check has been presented twice, you will have to decide if the amount of the check is worth the trouble involved with trying to collect.

- **Account Closed** While this is cause for alarm, people do move and close accounts before all the checks have cleared. Telephone or write to the customer and ask for them to honor the amount due, and ask for a replacement money order. Hold the bad check as evidence of fraud, or return the check when a new payment is received.
- **Customer Refuses to Honor Payment** If you have a customer, who refuses to honor the payment after your polite letters and calls, ask your bank to help collect. There is a charge of around $20 for this service. The bank will instruct the bank that issued the

check, to pay as soon as funds are available in the account. If no funds are deposited during the holding period (usually a month), you will have to try a collection agent.

Collection Agencies

When everything else has failed, to collect on an unpaid invoice you do not have much choice but to turn the invoice over to a collection agency. When choosing an agency, use one that is reputable, there are some dishonest agencies out there. The better agents belong to the American Collector's Association, so before signing with an agent, ask to see evidence of their membership. Members of this association will collect accounts locally or nationally. *(Usually out-of-state accounts are passed on to a member collection agency in an appropriate state)*. The fee for collecting is 40% of a local account or 50% if the collection is made by a member agency. Anything is better than nothing!

Transportation Terms

Who will pay for shipment will depend on the buyer and the Terms of Sale arranged for shipment. Make sure that you are aware of how your goods are to be shipped and who is responsible of the payment. Often the buyer will be responsible for payment for the shipment of the goods. If you are paying for the shipment, remember to include this expense into the cost sheets.

Freight or transportation terms offered by the manufacturer may be expressed as follows:

1) **F.O.B. (Freight on Board or Free on Board) Factory** The buyer pays the transportation.
2) **F.O.B. Destination** The seller pays the transportation and owns the merchandise until it is received at the destination.
3) **F.O.B. Shipping point** The seller pays any expense necessary for shipping the merchandise to the point where it is turned over to a transportation company. The seller owns the merchandise until it is turned over to the transportation company.

4) **F.O.B. Destination. Charges Reversed** The seller will own the goods until they reach the retail store, however, the buyer will pay the transportation.

5) **F.O.B. Destination. Freight prepaid** The merchandise becomes the property of the store when it is shipped, but the seller will pay the transportation.

Cancellation of Orders

A store may cancel an order for justifiable reasons, such as a manufacturer not shipping the designated merchandise by the shipping date specified, or a manufacturer eliminating a style from the order, or changing the fabrication without prior approval. Shipping on time, to a store, is of the utmost importance for prompt payment and meeting the **Terms of Sales.**

Words of Caution

(Do not rely on verbal changes to the customer's written purchase orders. E-mail and faxes should be used to properly document changes in orders. This is especially important where goods are being shipped close to the cancellation date.)

CHAPTER 15

CATALOG SALES

Over a hundred years ago, the first mail order business took off in the states with the sale of fashion plates of popular fashions in Europe. These fashion plates were then given to the local dressmaker, who would drape and sew the garments. At this time, Richard Sears and Julius Rosenwald founded Sears, a small mail-order company that would become a $10 billion corporation, and Aaron Montgomery Ward started his company, which also became a multi-million dollar operation. These three entrepreneurs were the world's first mail-order millionaires. Since then, countless part-time and full-time entrepreneurs have been attracted to the mail-order business. Although many have failed, a surprising number have succeeded in both good times and in bad. Today you can buy everything from clothing, to insurance, to live lobsters from catalogs.

Today's marketing wizards can be highly profitable in the catalog business. Richard Thalheimer built a multi-million dollar company, "The Sharper Image", starting with a chronograph watch and an advertisement in "Runner's World". He now sells not only by catalog, but also through retail outlets across the country and the Internet, a marketing vehicle that is a natural transition for any catalog company. Although everyone cannot expect to achieve the same level of success as these exceptional entrepreneurs, your chances of building a profitable catalog and Internet business *(Chapter 16 Selling on the Internet)* will increase if you possess the following essential qualities:

- **Imagination**

  Imagination is needed to visualize the special appeal that will compel a potential customer to buy your product.

- **Persistence**

  Persistence is required because success is rarely instantaneous; there are always obstacles and setbacks.

- **Honesty**

  Absolute honesty is necessary because a successful catalog business is built on trust, satisfied customers and repeat sales. Cheat your customers, even a little, and you have lost them forever. In addition, Federal, state, and local government agencies, as well as the Better Business Bureaus and consumer groups, constantly monitor advertising and are quick to act against unsubstantiated claims or infractions of law.

One of the most well known laws applicable to the mail order business is the Federal Trade Commission's (FTC) Thirty-Day Delay Delivery Rule. Basically, if you do not mention a specific delivery period in your advertisement, you have 30 days after receipt of an order to ship it. If you cannot make shipment within 30 days or by your stated date, you must notify the buyer of the new shipment date before the original date passes. You also must enclose a self-addressed, stamped envelope, and give your buyer a chance to cancel the deal. This rule is something that should be adhered to, as you could be forced to pay a heavy fine if you do not notify customers of their cancellation rights.

- **Knowledge**

Without proper knowledge, your chances for success are minimal. Success stories like Sears' and Ward's are built around those individuals' constant search for the answer to one important question: What works? You must continually keep learning; you can do this through both reading and experience. Experience can be costly and time consuming; it makes sense to learn through others by extensive reading of other people's experience.

You can learn a great deal by observing successful competitors. Study advertisements in magazines and newspapers and note those that run consistently month after month. Carefully study the catalogs, sales letters, and brochures you receive.

Pricing Structure

It may appear that you can sell almost any product through the mail, but it is not true. You have to find the right product at the right price; it should have a broad appeal to a large, specific segment of the population. It may appear that you will achieve a higher profit by selling direct, but there are two costly factors that must be accounted for when costing your garments:

- **Marketing:** This is the only way of getting a sale, and informing your customer of your product. Getting catalogs, mailers, or brochures printed and mailed is a high percentage of the cost of the product. This is also a problem for a start-up company, it has to come up with the necessary cash at the beginning, before there is any repayment in sales.

- **Returns:** Manufacturers selling clothing by catalog must cost for returns of up to 35%!

To maintain a high enough profit margin, to offset the costs you will entail selling by mail order, you will have to cost two to three times the initial cost of manufacturing. It should be possible to make a sale that is competitive with the normal retail sale because there is no middle person involved. Once you have secured the first sale, it is then much more likely that the satisfied customer will return for further sales. This is another reason why honesty and efficiency in mail order and catalog operations are so important.

Presentation

You may have the right product, at the right price, but still lose customers simply by your presentation. Tests have shown that there can by a vast difference in response depending on the way you present an offer. Unfortunately, because every situation and product is different, no one can tell you which is the best for your company without doing extensive testing.

Forecasting Sales

Always be cautious when forecasting your sales. Your break-even point (the number of units sold in order for a product to stop losing money and begin making money) should be set low, at least until you are sure of your market. For example, if your break-even point is 5% of the names on a mailing list, up to 5% of the people can respond to your offer and you still do not make a profit. Keep your expectations reasonable. For many businesses, one quarter of 1% is an excellent response. Most advertisements don't even bring in .01 of 1%.

Testing the Market

Successful mail order operations test almost everything. They measure the response to an advertisement or to a mailing by testing all advertising variables, such as;

- Offers
- Mailing lists
- Prices
- Headlines
- Formats
- Advertising media

Testing the market is a scientific approach to catalog sales. It permits a mail order entrepreneur to fail with four out of five items, and still walk away with a big profit on the fifth item. Test your product by spending a small amount of money for a test advertisement or mailing list. A complete failure tells you to drop the whole project. Marginal results tell you to experiment and rework some aspects of the line. A major success gives you the green light for a larger investment. This way you can afford to lose money on several dismal failures. When you "get lucky" and your testing indicates a clear success, you can move immediately to capitalize on what you know to be a winner. The idea is not to risk too much money until you are fairly certain of success.

Advertising

Nothing determines the success of a mail order enterprise so much as its advertising, whether it is via magazines, newspapers, radio, TV, direct mail or some other form of promotion. Writing advertising copy, preparing art, selecting media, determining price and other aspects of creating ads usually require expert skills. If you decide to work with an advertising agency, select one primarily on the basis of its successful experience in producing profitable mail order advertising.

Whether you decide to use an agency or go it alone, there are some important points to remember. It is important to recognize that everyone is not a good prospect for your business. A good strategy is to advertise in the same place where similar items are advertised.

What to Put in Your Advertisements

The words (or copy) in your advertisements are critical. They should not be just a casual consideration. Tests have been done on selling the exact garment with different copy and the results have been clear, that how you describe your clothes and how you display them, will make the difference between failure and making a small fortune.

There are many different formulas for developing copy. Initially, you should write your advertisement according to a definite copy structure:

- Get attention
- Develop interest
- Show the benefits and advantages of buying your clothing
- Build and maintain credibility
- Deliver a call to action

Getting Attention

The most important element of your ad and copy is the headline or visual presentation; this is how you gain attention. All headlines have certain things in common. First, they appeal to the reader's self-interest and stress the most important aspect of the product. Use key words that will grab your customer's attention, such as, **"Free" and "New"**: Here is a list of some other power words to use in your copy:

- **Amazing**
- **Bargain**
- **Just arrived**
- **Remarkable**
- **Sensational**

- **Announcing**
- **Hurry**
- **Last chance**
- **Revolutionary**
- **Success**

- **At last**
- **Important**
- **Miracle**
- **Secret**
- **Wanted**

Show good reason for buying

Once you have gained your customers attention with a page-stopping ad, you have to also show the benefits of buying the garment, either with the price or some other detail that is not available using the traditional retail shopping method. The benefits must override the cost of the product and the trouble involved with shopping by catalog.

Encourage Orders

A basic law of sales is that a face-to-face salesperson must ask for an order. As a salesperson selling through mail order, you should call your customer into immediate action. You do not want your customers to wait until another day. You want your customer to order immediately. Research has demonstrated that regardless of initial intent, in most instances, if your prospects do not order immediately, they won't order at all. Include incentives, such as a statement on limited quantities or a time-limited offer.

What does Advertising Cost?

Top quality advertising costs a lot, but it usually brings the best results. However, do not overspend on advertising, direct mail and other promotions. Do not invest in full color printing when one or two colors will do the job. There is no need to print on expensive paper, elaborate art or other extravagances to sell profitably. Show the garments to their full potential, using a professional model.

Special Considerations

Some states require that you include a business (or home) address in your advertisement, even if you want orders to come to a post office number. If you have the choice of using a post office box number or your home address, consider these trade-offs:

- A classified advertisement will probably cost more with a home address as you pay by the word.

- The use of a post office box will allow you to pick up mail seven days a week.

- A prospective customer generally associates lower risk in ordering from a business or home address. Therefore, you are likely to have more returns with a full address than with a post office box number.

- A post office box number protects your personal privacy if you do not want to be bothered at home by customers.

Credit Card Sales

Credit cards sales will increase your returns. This is because prospects who are familiar with your company do know the names VISA & MasterCard. Use of credit cards also means that your customer can order higher priced items easily on credit, with the advantage that the bank grants the credit, not you. Since some mail order companies find that they are able to collect only about 60% of their sales, this may be no small consideration. However, the bank will charge you several percentage points on each order charged against its credit card. If you are new to business, you may also have a problem convincing a bank to let you use its credit card service.

Cash Sales

You should also know that some individuals, who have become mail order millionaires, did so dealing on a strictly cash basis with no credit cards. If you sell expensive items of clothing likely to total a fair amount for each order, credit cards sales may be worth investigating. If you were going to enable your customers to order through a toll-free number, credit cards would make sense.

Toll-Free Numbers

Toll-free numbers allow your customers to order more easily, which will increase your sales. The question is, will it increase your profits? Toll free means that the caller doesn't pay; but you do. Some mail order operators have found that, for their product, use of a toll-free number is not profitable. Others have found that a toll-free service is what makes their business profitable.

(One way to find out whether you should use a toll-free number is to test one. Installation and toll costs vary; you can find out more about toll-free numbers through your telephone company).

Maintain Good Records

A word of caution, as with all businesses in order to succeed, keep accurate records of all figures that are important to the success of your business, such as:

- Results of advertisements
- Advertising costs
- Printing costs
- Cost-per-order

However, do this in the simplest and least time-consuming way possible.

Use a Computer

The computer has revolutionized the mail order business, and it can help you become successful. When you are ready to get a computer, go to your local business software store that will show you many of the programs available. If your town does not have a software store, get a copy of one of the many computer magazines that are published. You will see many programs advertised and described, you can obtain catalogs listing hundreds of programs that promise to help you run and build your business. Below is a list of how different software systems can help you.

Data Base

- Maintain an updated list of customers.
- Find new customers
- Research media
- Track most popular products
- Record ordering information: how frequent, average size, fulfillment dates, etc

Spreadsheets

- Maintain income tax records
- Make "what if" forecasts and plans
- Record price information
- Maintain cash flow information and projections

Desktop publishing

- Write advertisements
- Do your own layouts
- Do your own typesetting for advertisements.

Word Processor

- Write and maintain a file of your business letters
- Personalize your direct mail

Repeat Business – Key to Maximum Profits

Continuous profits come from continuous sales. As already suggested, rarely is a profitable mail order or catalog business established on a one-time sale. You have to keep the needs of the customer always in mind. Your list of customers is your most valuable asset. Once your list grows, you can use it to send additional information. Always remember to include a new catalog or information on special offers in outgoing orders since postage and packing costs have already been paid for when the order was taken. Everyone loves a special bargain, so offer discounts on orders over a specified amount to stimulate larger orders. Gift certificates are another way to spark sales, especially during Christmas and other holidays. When you enclose advertising in envelopes, consider using the envelope itself to feature one or more special offers. Additional printing costs may prove to be insignificant, compared with the extra sales produced.

More Information: Catalog sales can be profitable but remember, as with any clothing business, you will probably lose money before you begin making it. So do not make major investments until you have gained experience and know the right type of product, the right price and the best means of communicating to the most receptive market.

There are many books to be found in the local library that will help give you a much clearer picture of the mail order business. Most libraries have a variety of directories, indexes and encyclopedias that cover many business topics, which can be some of the best-kept secrets in town, and at the right price!

Directories: There are many directories to be purchased that will give you a list of the right customers for your product. Here are a few that will help get you started:

- **United States Postal Service Directmail www.usps.com/directmail/resources/reference.htm**
- **Mail Order Business Directory,** Coral Springs, FL, B. Klein Publications, Inc.
- **Guide to American Directories** (Tenth Edition) Coral Springs, FL, B. Publications, Inc.
- **Mail Order USA,** Dorothy O'Callaghan, Washington, DC.
- **Direct Mail List Rates & Data,** Skokie, IL, Standard Rate & Data Service, Inc. **www.srds.com**

Selling in Other Company Catalogs

If you have your own company that is manufacturing and selling to retail stores, and you would like to try to increase your sales in another direction, selling items in another company's catalog is often done. These companies usually have strict standards to follow and keeping up with them can sometimes be hard work. If you know of a company that has products similar to your own, you may want to call and inquire about the company's policies in this regard. Never send any of your products to the company directly. You may never see them again and there is a possibly that your goods could be "**knocked–off**".

If you are fortunate and receive orders from a catalog company, it will normally give you a test order to see how your item or items sell. If it is well received, you can be sure they will return for more. A "best seller" can be quite profitable to a small company if it has "hot" item that is likely to be reordered.

Catalog companies are a natural for the transition to selling on the Internet. Most of the contents of this chapter would apply to anyone starting their own business on the Internet. *(See next chapter for more information on Selling on the Internet)*

CHAPTER 16

SELLING ON THE INTERNET

With Frances Harder's thorough understanding of the fashion industry and her vision of successful enterprise she clearly defines how to grow your business in the world of e-commerce. In the challenging environment of Internet retailing it is sound business practices that are at the foundation of launching a thriving storefront on the web. Kathy David, Managing Director of JBK designs, Internet Web Site Development www.jbkdesigns.com

QUESTION: WHAT DID THE E-TAILER SAY TO THE RETAILER?

ANSWER: MY FLOOR SPACE IS BIGGER THAN YOURS.

Traditional retailers are becoming limited in their ability to enrich customer choices. Retailers are in a quandary as to what will and will not sell. Customers are frustrated with the lack of choice in stores, and are turning to other ways of buying. The 1980's are over, and the aging baby boomers are weary of shopping malls and are turning on their computers to find things of interest to buy. Enter the Internet, and its near-limitless capacity, which gives retailers and manufacturers a chance to combine traditional selling with new age selling. Being online enables the seller to reach and contact a broad and growing audience with vast displays of merchandise, as well as information about company products. It is possible to inter-act with individual customers or blocs of customers with similar tastes, and tailor promotions or services to their own style. Advances in technology will increase the speed, reliability and convenience of Internet shopping, and make the experience of shopping online well beyond anything we know today.

Netrepreneurs

Like it or not, online shopping is here to stay, we will all learn to live with it and to accept its presence into our daily lives, just as we have fax machines and other modern day inventions! The search engines and on-line directories are refining their tools to improve the consumers' abilities to find exactly what they are looking for. It is expanding at such a rapid rate that it is almost impossible to keep up with the daily developments. Creating effective retail space on the Internet is becoming increasingly sophisticated and effective. There is a word for people developing their own business on the Internet - Netrepreneurs; and some of the success stories are startling.

If you build, will they come?

Web Sites

The number of Web sites doubles every three to five months. It has been estimated that at year-end, 2002, there were over 490 million Internet users or 79.4 per 1000 people worldwide and by year-end 2005, there will be over 765 million users or 118 per 1000 people. As the web sites become easier to find and more graphic-rich, they will attract more and more people. As with outer space, the Internet's potential is limitless-a global economy not limited by real estate constraints.

Marketing Capacity

The Web is a way around the bricks-and-mortar of conventional methods of retailing. The potential of the Internet is clear, and marketing strategies are evolving to match this exciting e-medium. Still, as yet many retailers are not too sure how they fit into the Internet picture and how they will properly exploit such potential. Others are beginning to realize the future selling potential of the Internet and are setting up sites to explore the possibilities of e-commerce. This is just the beginning, like the old telephone system, the Internet has a long way to grow to its full marketing capacity. The customer has to learn to trust buying on the Internet and also the security of the medium itself. By providing secure web solutions and educating the consumer that trust is building.

(Make sure that you have a clear identity of your company and a vision for your site in order to prepare your company to sell on the Internet.)

- Develop an Internet marketing plan
- Obtain the services of online experts
- Register and protect a domain name for your on-line business other than your "real name."
- Establish Internet access and e-mail capability
- Create an Internet presence with a web page, electronic catalog, electronic advertising, and site links.
- Become EDI compliant
- Accept credit cards for electronic payments
- Register site with Internet search engines and directories

Is it For You, and Your Product?

One great advantage of the net is the fact that, as with mail order, you are able to sell directly to your customer and do away with the middle stage of the sales cycle. This will enable you to sell with a larger profit and to offer a better product. Many of the facts covered earlier on "Catalog Sales" *(Chapter 15)* will apply when selling via the Internet. Here are some advantages of investing in a Web site:

- Empowering consumers to comparison-shop.

- Consumer ease of shopping.

- No middle handler or Sales Representative.

- Manufacturer could be linked to other manufacturers and create their own online agent.

- Better mark-up and better quality of product; this makes it possible for the small manufacturer to be competitive with the larger manufacturers.

- A Web site can boost your profits by increasing your sales without proportionately increasing your marketing expenses.

- Allow you to sell directly to retailers in other cities, states, and countries.

The disadvantages of selling apparel on the Internet are basically the same as with a mail order firm.

- Return rates 25% - 35%

- Anticipating the size of the orders.

- Advertisement cost.

Problem Anticipating Orders

Anticipating the size of production is a gamble with mail order where you are selling directly to a customer. This will apply when selling on-line directly to your customer. One item may fly out of the door where you had misjudged the demand. Another could be "a dog" and you are left holding plastic bags full of garments going nowhere. Selling, by these means, can mean trouble financially. You can test the market with small runs and learn as you grow.

Selling Directly to the Retailer

The best possible alternative is to sell to the retailer via the Internet. Once the retailer is familiar with your product and with your business savvy they will be able to reach you via your web site and buy directly from you. You can then build a cutting ticket and order your fabrics when the stores have finished placing their orders through your virtual showroom, this will eliminate most of the gamble involved. There may be less of a profit margin but this is by far the safest method of selling via the Internet for the small manufacturer.

Best of Both Worlds

Once you have shipped your orders and there is inventory left over, it is a great idea to cut up the rest of the fabric in similar bodies as the ones that have been successful. Put them up on the Internet and move your inventory fast. *(Make sure to modify your style somewhat, as the retailer does not want to see your merchandise for sale cheaper than the goods they ordered from you)*

Building a Company Brand

Operating a business within the vastness of cyberspace is not without its problems! Nearly all Fortune 500 companies are victims of copyright and trademark abuse. As your company grows, **your brand will be your most important asset** and will be up for grabs by any other unscrupulous company that decides to "knock you off". Controlling this problem has in itself, created a new business of Internet security services, which scan the net to look for offenders. Selling by traditional methods can open a manufacturer, who is producing cutting edge garments to being knocked-off. This is part of the fashion business however, and although annoying and frustrating, it goes with the territory.

Domain Name Registration

Web sites are identified by their individual domain names on the Internet. It is important to establish your domain name early on and protect it. Online services for domain name registrations are available from a number of Web sites:

- **InterNIC** is a registered service mark of the U.S. Department of Commerce. It is licensed to the Internet Corporation for Assigned Names and Numbers (ICANN). They provide public information regarding domain name registration. They have a complete listing of accredited domain name registration services. **www.internic.com**

- **"Network Solutions"**, **www.networksolutions.com** is owned and operated by VeriSign. This company provides domain name registration services, authentication services and payment services for internet sites worldwide.

- **"Register.com"** accredited registrar with the Internet Corporation for Assigned Names and Numbers

- Some Website Hosting Providers are certified registrars and offer free domain names or discount prices. **www.HostMySite.com** is one such hosting service.

How to pick an Internet Provider?

In addition to the Internet Service Provider Fees, there are several factors to be considered.

- You should choose a provider with stable and reliable connection service. Interruptions in service can cause loss of business for your company. Ask how long the provider has been in business.

- Find out the connection speed. Is it fast or slow?

- What kind of security measures has the provider set up? Are they secure?

- Select a provider with a local phone access or a toll-free number.

- Call to see if a real person is available to answer your questions. You don't want to be waiting for a reply to voicemail when your questions are critical.

- Does your provider monitor traffic at your Web site and give traffic reports commonly referred to as site statistics

- Does your provider offer web-based e-mail and an on-line control panel to manage your e-mail accounts?

- Does your provider offer flexible plans that allow you to upgrade your services easily?

- Does the provider's network include database connections or shopping cart software?

- Does your provider have plans that offer SSL for secure ordering?

- Does your provider offer streaming media plans?

- How frequently can you update your Web page?

- How much assistance will the provider give you in publicizing your site?

- Does the provider offer customer support 24 hours a day?

Web Page

The difference between a bad Web site and a good site is not money, it's creativity. Setting up a good Web site is not expensive, so small company sites can look just as good, or better, than large company sites. Small companies are able to move more quickly, because they are able to make changes without calling endless meetings or securing department approval. On the Web, taking chances and moving quickly pays off. Creative, flexible sites attract the most visitors, who then tell their business colleagues and friends to have a look. The Web is one of those marketplaces where being small is an asset.

The Web site communicates your company's image and your product. *(Therefore, it is important to make it look professional)* Here are some things to keep in mind when designing your company's Web page:

- Keep your Web page or pages simple, and have your site geared towards people unfamiliar with the Internet. Make it easy to navigate. *(A Web site can contain many individual pages, with the front page being called the "home page")*

- Constantly update your site. A Web site is always a work in progress. Like owning a retail store you have to change your "windows" (site) often to keep the customers coming back for new styles. Do not put up a site and then sit back for orders. It takes work and planning to find a customer base and to retain them.

- Identify your clothing with colors and fabrication descriptions.

- Include sizing measurements and highlight new items.

- Give simple instructions on how interested customers can respond with ordering information; don't forget a toll free telephone number. Each page should have this information.

Do-it-yourself Web sites

There are a number of Web site building services available that makes it possible for a novice to create their own site. The user-friendly Web site builders provide numerous templates to choose from, which allow the user to create, add text, and insert photos to their own personalized site.

Examples of Successful Web Sites

Checking out interesting sites across the Net can be rewarding. You may learn from visiting your competitors on the Internet by obtaining new business ideas that will keep you up to date with new business trends. You may also pick up hints about how to improve your own Web site, and begin to understand which business strategies work best and what products sell on the Net. Check the following for interesting sites:

- Lands' End Inc. **www.landsend.com** This clothing catalog company has expanded to the Web and they have reduced printing and mailing costs associated with mail order.

- Internet Mall, Inc. **www.internetmall.com** manages one of the largest online shopping malls, which accommodates virtual stores of many categories.

Publicize your Web site

Anyone can get an immediate presence on-line today. The problem is building a site that will attract your customers. As with mail order you will have to budget for advertising and marketing. Here are some helpful ideas to follow which will promote your Internet presence.

- Market your Web site through advertisements, on your business cards and stationery, and other company material.

- Consider direct mail, bus advertising or radio spots to alert potential customers to your website.

- You will want to register your site with one or more of the top on-line directories like Yahoo and Google.com. This paid submission will cost $299 a year. Establishing a link at Yahoo will help improve your positioning with major search engines like Google, Inktomi and MSN. You can also use Inktomi's paid inclusion services to guarantee that your site is being picked up by this major web crawler and others like it. This will run you about $39 a year for the first web page you submit and $25 for each additional URL you submit. Make sure that you include search engine submission fees into your on-line budget.

- Select carefully the specific categories, keywords or key phrases that search engines use to locate the Web site. There is more to just registering with search engines to gain exposure. Meta tags written into the site's code define descriptive phrases as well as keywords that are needed to achieve a high-ranking position. Recently some of the search engines however have taken meta tag keywords out of their search algorithms because they have been so badly abused. You need to also pay close attention to page titles and web page content including links. Your website developer should be helpful in assuring that your site is optimized for search engine submission. If not there are paid services like **www.submitnet.net** that will provide these services for you.

- These services provide on-line tools to help you optimize your site. Typically, a web-positioning company will review your pages and make suggestions to improve your ranking. There are also software solutions such as Web Position Gold which will help you optimize your site for search engines and also track your progress in improving your position.

- Search Engine Watch is a great web site that has an extensive list of resources related to search engines and how to improve your search engine placement. You may find it helpful to subscribe to their newsletter. **www.searchenginewatch.com**

- Pick an easy to remember domain name for easy promotion.

- Cross-link your site with other popular sites. This is major aspect of your search engine optimization plan. The search engine crawlers figure links back to your site into their algorithm for responding to queries. Linking will give your site an increased chance of improving its search engine positioning and of course more visibility in order for new customers to find you. Make sure anytime you create a link to another site that it opens in a secondary browser window that makes it easy for your users to come back to you. **Make your site stick! You want the user/customer to return for more.**

- Buy an ad on a popular online publication. The on-line yellow page directories often share data with the major search engines and provide you with a chance to create another important link back to your site relative to your industry category.

- Treat site promotions as an ongoing process.

- Buying e-mail lists is not recommended and often can hurt you if the e-mail users are unaware their names are on your list. It is much better to develop your own targeted list by having a "subscribe" button on your web site. Many shopping cart packages provide this feature and there are other e-mail marketing tools such as Roving Software's Constant contact that enable you to add this feature and actually collect your subscribers' e-mails in a managed list to which you can send e-mail newsletters created on-line with their wizards. **www.constantcontact.com** They offer a free trial and are very reasonably priced for the small business owner.

- You will also want to talk to your retail store locations regarding acquisition of their lists. If you are not competing in the sale of the product directly to their customer base they will share their e-mail lists with you. You will most likely need to negotiate a mutual marketing agreement with them in the promotion of your line.

- **Portal malls** These "home page" malls are another way to bring traffic to your site. It is like creating your own shopping district.

For example, a hardware store, grocery store, bank, toy store and apparel store from your town that each have websites might want to link together, pool advertising monies and market as a group. The other option is to join the ranks of existing "malls" such as **www.galaxymall.com**.

- **Banner Ads** You can even generate money by just being online. Your site can charge an impressive fee every time a visitor to your page views an advertiser's banner. One company that sells space, manages the "hit", and provides billing is **www.doubleclick.com**

- **Reciprocal hyperlinks** Build traffic by adding a hyperlink to and from your site from a non-competing site. Simply stated, this is a connection between your site and another in the form of text or a graphic placed on your web page. It is easy to set up and can add visitors you might not have received otherwise.

- **Affiliate programs** Many sites have a direct link to a "buy a specific product page" on a complementary website. When a customer makes a purchase on the target site by going through the link on your site, you get a percentage of that sale. Commission Junction can help you make these connections. **www.cj.com/index.asp**

Keep the Web Site New and Exciting

Of course, if you do not want to be responsible for the Web site promotion yourself, you can always hire a Web promotion agency. Most Web site Administrators up-date their sites at least once a week. This would work well if you have a new item to add to your collection each week. Keeping the site exciting and interesting will make your customers return. Once the customers know that there will be new items added they will return, but do not keep the same Web page for more than two weeks; you will lose your customers. Think of it as your store window. Timing is very important; you have to be the first out of the gate with your product. Like the gold rush of the last century, it is the new frontier, and has become a free for all. **Who can get a piece of it first?** The Internet can be a scary place, but it could be paved with gold for those companies who are willing to practice **"The Three R's."**

- **Relationships** Nothing will happen until you establish relationships with your customers. That entails researching the customers you are targeting and their preferences. The more you know about your customer the more you are able to relate to their needs and provide for them.

- **Reputation** Earn the reputation for quality goods and service. No matter what type of apparel you are producing it is important to retain your customers and to make them feel they are getting a well-made garment for a good price, and that the service they get ordering from your company is hassle free.

- **Reliable** Don't launch your on-line site if you are not ready for the rush! If you are going to spend money to woo customers, be ready to serve them. Once you have lost them they are gone forever. **Your competition is only a mouse click away!**

Virtual Showroom

Commitment, time, and money are necessary for developing, conceiving and executing a solid e-commerce site that will be your own virtual showroom. There are many resources available to help coordinate and exploit all aspects of the Internet. With 100 million people browsing and shopping online today, and a potential of 6 billion surfers, the Internet should be a must for your business.

Protecting Business Names and Trademarks on the Internet

Protecting your business names and trademarks in cyberspace is more important than ever and will become a much bigger issue in the next few years. Cyber-pirates are out there registering trademarked names by the thousands and selling to the highest bidder. Recovering "hijacked" domain names to their rightful owner can be time consuming and costly, (which could include legal and "ransom" money)! Even if someone does not intentionally try to poach on your business names or trademarks, there are numerous examples where unrelated businesses or other individuals share the same or a similar name or trademark in different areas of commerce and in different parts of the world. The first to register a domain name is usually given priority in any legal dispute. It is therefore important that a new company investigate the names taken before introducing the product to the marketplace. This will help to ensure that you do not face unexpected problems related to Internet addresses later. All businesses should register all of their business names and trademarks as domain names. Where possible, domain names containing all relevant important words or phases should be registered in all three addresses (.com .org .net). Although this may add up financially, it is an inexpensive way to protect your business from "cyber-pirates" who might register your business names or trademarks before you.

URL (Uniform Resource Locator)

Avoid changing your URL, which is your Web site address, or service provider. A change in the URL or service provider can cause disruptions in your Internet business. Net users who have your Web address will not be able to reach you. This can lead to loss of business and frustration for your customers. **Important:** If a change in the URL or service provider has to be made, make arrangements so that Net users can be re-routed to your new site.

What is E-Commerce?

E-commerce and on-line distribution will expand product areas, speed product dissemination and updates, and change distribution methods for all areas of selling and producing products of any kind. E-commerce offers incredible opportunities for selling, fitting millions of shoppers into your store and with the right site you can track buying habits and even predict their purchases. Businesses of all sizes will gain a worldwide market, and consumers will be able to shop at any store in the world from the comfort of their own home. When the world is your market, you can always find what you want.

Is E-commerce complicated?

There are more on-line payment services today enabling even computer novices to grasp how to do simple transactions using e-commerce. PayPal and Verisign's PayFlow Services have extensive tutorials on how to implement simple risk free credit card payments on your site. Total e-commerce includes the ability to take secure credit card orders, Web-based shopping carts that track customer purchases, update tax and shipping rates calculations, and develop a Web storefront. However, making a successful transition to e-business is not always that easy. E-business is not just about developing a Web site but rather it is about changing your business model to adapt to the new economy. Putting up a smart front-end site on your current business is unlikely to take full advantage of the opportunities offered by the on-line revolution and may in fact be a prescription for disaster. For example, what you should first do is develop a business strategy that provides a road map for adapting your business to the era of e-business. Just like developing your business plan for the traditional economy, your e-business strategy should start by considering your current position in the market, your strengths and weaknesses, products and distribution channels, the challenges posed by competition, new opportunities in the market, etc. At the same time you should be considering the new opportunities offered by having an e-commerce site and whether your company will truly benefit. The potential to interact directly with your customer and to streamline distribution channels are a couple of extremely important points. Another point to remember is that no matter how good a job you do in developing your site, it's going to be outdated in six months. There is no doubt that within a year the competitive landscape will have changed. This means that you, too, will need to keep abreast of this fast evolving e-business, on-line commerce to survive and prosper.

Is E-commerce expensive?

Not when you consider traditional methods of retailing. Web storefronts can be developed without breaking the bank. Getting in on the e-commerce game will help your firm access new and emerging markets. It can also help save on transactions, administration, printing and marketing costs, and speed up the ordering and payment process. Selling on the Internet is the new frontier and whoever develops a successful online presence first has a head start in succeeding on the World Wide Web. It allows companies of **any size** a whole New World of opportunities, allowing them to sell their goods globally, directly to their customer.

Payment Methods

As a start-up it may be advisable to require C.O.D. on all items shipped, and as you grow and become familiar with your customers, you can assess the need for protected credit card transactions, either in the form of encryption software or a transaction service. Such services process credit-card sales by encrypting them for each customer.

Web TV

The World will be your market! The development of the Web TV technology may be a significant step to widening Internet services by providing easy access from the living rooms of millions of households. The potential success and growth of Internet commerce will depend critically on how much it can meet the customer's needs in various respects.

Provide Quality Goods

As a clothing manufacturer, it will be important to provide quality goods at competitive prices, which will entice users to return and buy as a regular customer. Efficient operations, strong marketing and merchandising skills, and a sincere concern for your customer, these are the things that will boost your business online or off-line.

Virtual World

An interesting new invention out of London will revolutionize selling clothing in cyber-space and possible the way we live. Avatarme Ltd. has made it possible to scan your body and get a computerized image of yourself that will appear on the screen whenever needed. It will have your face and build, it can also run and jump and interact with other "avatars". This will allow you to try e-clothes on your virtual self from the virtual showroom. Your virtual self will eventually be able to attend meetings for you in a beautiful designer suit while the real you is at home on the computer, comfortable in your sweats! It truly is becoming a virtual world.

Your online success will directly reflect the commitment you make to your presence on the web. The web is far more than a contemporary version of the Yellow Pages. With the ability of always providing fresh content, it allows you to give your customers a reason to return to your site regularly and often. Use your web presence to support your offline business with sales and customer support. Your customers will respond positively to your commitment to support their business.

*Arnie Wachman Apparellink.com Webmaster for Fashion for Profit @ **www.FashionforProfit.com** and Fashion Business Incorporated @ '**www.FashionBizinc.org***

CHAPTER 17

PRODUCING & SELLING GLOBALLY

"The world is moving so fast these days that the man who says it can't be done is generally interrupted by someone doing it." Elbert Hubbart

"Revolution in advanced telecommunications is fueling a global marketplace. As a result, this revolution is empowering individuals and small firms as never before. For many small companies, the important question is not whether, but how to globalize. That is, how to survive and prosper outside the narrow confines of a deceptively and familiar domestic market." Ayse Oge

This chapter reviewed by Richard M. Swanson, Jr., Supervisory Trade Specialist, U.S., Commercial Service, U.S. Department of Commerce, Newport Beach, California (Orange County), Member of the national apparel & textile team.

Producing abroad has become common practice, both for the small and for the larger manufacturer, whether it is south of the border in Mexico, or further a field on the Pacific Rim. The benefits are obvious to the garment contractors in the States and have been cause for alarm, both on the West Coast and the East Coast. Weighing the pros and cons of using a domestic contractor or going abroad will be a matter of great importance for a growing company, and its price points. Practically speaking, having the production on the front door step means having more control over the final, finished product. On the other hand, the incentive to move production south of the border or to other foreign countries is strong, particularly when a manufacturer is cost conscious. One of the negotiable areas on a cost sheet is the price of labor. Compare U.S. wages with Mexican wages; there is about a $10 an hour difference. If the product is good and the company has built a strong customer base, it can stand the price differential, which will allow the manufacturer to produce domestically. As a company grows it will often decide to look off shore for part of its production needs, leaving some of the production to be produced domestically. This way they are not purring all their eggs into one basket!

Ultimately, the relationship you have with your contractor will determine whether you stay domestic or go abroad. Another option, of course, is to produce your product, or a portion thereof, from within your own company. If you possess a unique or high margin product then you may have the ability to produce within your company.

Once a company decides to buy fabric from a foreign country or to have garments produced offshore, the Federal government becomes involved. One of the major reasons that the government becomes involved is to protect goods produced domestically. Foreign goods can usually be produced for a lower labor cost than in the U.S., which in turn will affect the final cost of the product. The Federal government tries to protect American businesses in a number of ways. These include establishing quotes on imported goods, imposing tariffs, enacting trade pacts with other nations, and enforcing high standards as a restraint measure.

Trade Pacts & Agreements

World Trade Organization (WTO)
What is the WTO?

The World Trade Organization (**www.wto.org**) is the leading global international organization dealing with the rules of trade between nations. At its core, are the WTO agreements that have been negotiated and signed by the bulk of the world's trading nations and ratified in their parliaments or respective governments. The goal of the WTO is to help producers of goods and services, exporters, and importers conduct their business.

The World Trade Organization (WTO) Agreement on Textiles and Clothing (the Agreement) provides for the phased liberalization and elimination over the transition period of quotas on textiles and apparel imported from WTO member countries. The Agreement was approved as part of the Uruguay Round Agreements Act by the U.S. Congress in December 1994 and went into effect on January 1, 1995. Under this agreement, the U.S. agreed to phase reductions, within a ten-year period, in tariff rates for textiles and apparel products. In 2005 all quota restrictions will be eliminated.

The World Trade Organization has the power to enforce these trade agreements and can assess trade penalties against nations that violate them. Its primary goal is to reduce trade barriers.

In addition to reducing tariffs, the agreement also addresses quotas, by eliminating restrictions on the amount of textiles and apparel that may be imported. These quotas will be phased out in stages, and 2005 will eliminate them all.

NAFTA (North American Free Trade Agreement)

Since NAFTA linked the economy of the United States, Mexico, and Canada, creating the world's largest integrated market of over 360 million consumers in 1995, Mexico surpassed China as the US's leading supplier of imported apparel and textiles. It is predicted that China will again surpass Mexico once quotas are entirely phased out worldwide in 2005. Mexico has gained popularity as a sourcing option because of the reduced or zero duties and the shorter turnaround time as compared with Asian countries.

U.S.-Chile Free Trade Agreement

On June 6th, 2003, the United State signed a historic and cutting-edge Free Trade Agreement (FTA) that, when fully implemented, eliminates bilateral tariffs, lowers trade barriers, promotes economic integration and expands opportunities for the people of both countries.

Textiles and apparel will be duty-free immediately if they meet the Agreements rule of origin, promoting new opportunities for U.S. and Chilean fiber, yarn, fabric and apparel manufacturing. A limited yearly amount of textiles and apparel containing non-U.S. or non-Chilean yarns, fibers or fabrics may also qualify for duty-free treatment.

U.S.-Singapore Free Trade Agreement

U.S. duties on imports from Singapore are less than 1 percent on average, with the preponderance of those duties falling on textiles and apparel. Imports of apparel from Singapore are also subject to quotas that will be removed in 2005 under the WTO Agreement on Textiles and Clothing.

With the subsequent expectation of the worldwide elimination of quotas in 2005 the general thought might be that China will become the "supplier of choice", but there will also be a strong need for apparel companies and retailers to utilize tier 2 supplier-countries for obvious reasons such as quick-turnarounds, mid-season adjustments, niche markets, and trendy fashions.

Off-Shore Production Costs

Roughly half the clothing in retail stores is imported. A garment may be assembled in the United States or in factories in the Far East, India or Third World countries because labor costs are less or because there is a special skill required for a certain technique. A garment may be cut offshore and sewn domestically, or cut and sewn in one or more different countries. Labor in El Salvador, for instance, is much less costly than in Hong Kong or the United States, and expertise varies from country to country.

Questions to Ask

Whatever your reason for going abroad for your sourcing, there are some important questions that you must have answered before you take this big step in your production decisions, and you should clearly understand the answers. If you use an agent to manage your offshore production, take the time to ask the following questions, which will save you from surprises.

What is the cost difference of labor, transportation, customs, and duty? The hidden costs are what you have to look at. Do not think that because the labor is cheaper that your garments will cost out with a higher net profit margin. After you have calculated the true costs, it may be cheaper to produce on home turf.

What is a realistic time it would take to produce a garment or to have fabrics produced? In order to get fabrics, or goods produced abroad, you will have to allow for more lead-time. Shipping your orders late is not an option you can afford to take.

- Inquire how the production will be produced and the type of factory to produce it.

Which freight forwarder, type of insurance, necessary customs' broker, and port of exit and entry will be used for the goods? Make certain that they have experience with handling textiles and apparel goods.

How will payments be arranged? Will you have your bank and the foreign production company's bank arrange **Letters of Credit**? The Letter of Credit is a bank letter or certificate arranged for payment. It entitles the company named to a specified amount of money, which maybe withdrawn from the bank or any of its affiliates when goods are received. This is a secure method of payment arranged by banks for services or goods that have been produced abroad. Follow up with the International Chamber of Commerce (ICC) at **www.iccwbo.org** for additional details on the uses of Letters of Credit.

(When dealing with foreign countries, investigate their country's culture and become familiar with their business habits; this will help if things go wrong and negotiations will be required. You can do this by doing research with a countries' Embassy or Consulate.   In addition, there may be a local office of your government to assist you nearby.)

Advantages of Domestic Production

For some manufacturers there are advantages in staying home in the States. Reorders or changes can be completed within two weeks. The lead-time is shorter and so the manufacturer can produce reorders faster. This is a great advantage for the smaller manufacturer. Large companies must plan months ahead of production. Contractors who are nearby can be watched for quality control, plus overseas production can take up to 4 months lead-time. Balancing against low labor wages, are the tariffs, duty, taxes and freight charges that manufacturers have to contend with, and quality control is, of course, more difficult. There must be people trained to check the work frequently to assure that the work is done as directed by the manufacturer. This is often part of the work done by the agent, contracted by the manufacturer, to supervise production overseas.

Anticipating Orders

Another threat to the ultimate profit of the manufacturer is the orders received may not be as large as anticipated. When producing abroad, it is often necessary to project your sales before an order is written, which adds another element for concern. With shipments of fabric or finished goods arriving from overseas without an order, there has to be an outlet. This means that they usually will be sold at a loss to the manufacturer and end up in a discount store of some sort. Weighing the odds of domestic or offshore production can be a gamble and must be considered carefully. It does not necessarily have to be all or nothing, and diversifying production is often a logical step used by manufacturers. Using a local contractor for part of production and offshore resources for the other is often a natural progression.

Sweat Shops

Recently there has arisen controversy over low-priced laborers working in sweatshop environments in China, developing countries, New York City, and even LA. Exposure of such conditions has triggered legal action and raised consumer consciousness. The government and human rights groups have put pressure on apparel manufacturers and retailers, not to use contractors and suppliers who violate human rights, or who have political policies that violate human rights. In 1996 human rights groups filed a class-action lawsuit against 18 U.S. companies on behalf of apparel workers in Saipan, a central Pacific island. The island is U.S. property and because of this the manufacturer is able to state "Made in the U.S.A" on the label. This has resulted in a number of large manufacturers and retailers implementing guidelines for the regular inspection of foreign contractors, to check that their workers are not being exploited or abused. The sweatshop issue is a problem both legally and morally. It is up to the manufacturers to ensure that their garments are manufactured in a human and legal environment, whether the garments are produced domestically or abroad. There are groups setup to monitor this problem and when factories meet the requirements they will be certified.

U.S. Customs

If you should decide to produce part or all of your production abroad, you should be educated on the laws governing manufacturing offshore. If you cut locally and send the cut goods to be assembled abroad, or you are importing finished **goods**, i.e.: fabric or garments. It is important that documentation be kept for each transaction made. *(There are agents in each international country that will take care of quality control and terms of sale).*

The U.S. Customs Service will want to know all the details:

- Country of origin
- How many garments have been produced
- How much fabric was used

- Type of fabric
- Amount of waste
- Every detail of each garment imported.

It is important to use a broker who is experienced in the exportation of textile goods and who is familiar with the necessary paper work:

- Letters of credit
- Purchase orders

- Invoices
- Suppliers agreements

A customs broker with textile experience will keep you informed as to quotas, where they are applied and on what. Keep all documentation of transactions made for at least five years.

Quotas

Note: Quotas are scheduled to terminate by 2005.

If you produce anything abroad it is important to know about **quotas**. As stated in the vocabulary listing:

Quotas: Numerical limit on a number of products in specific categories that can be imported.

Quotas are usually in units rather than in cash amounts. The U.S. Federal government has established specific quotas to protect manufacturers from unfair competition from abroad.

There are two different types of quotas:

- **Absolute** Any merchandise that exceeds the established limit of a given quota must be disposed of through a variety of means, which is dictated by the U.S. Customs Service.

- **Tariff Rate** Any merchandise that exceeds the established limit of a given quota may enter at a higher rate of duty, or remain in a bonded warehouse until the opening of a new quota.

As a manufacturer who is considering going abroad for any production, it is wise to become educated on the quota system, and to learn which merchandise is subject to such restrictions and which is not. Silk for example, has no quota restriction, because the U.S. does not produce silk domestically. Cotton on the other hand, is produced domestically and therefore has a quota restriction.

Duty

Apparel merchandise imported into the U.S. is subject to duty. The duty is calculated as a percent of the appraised value of each item. The percentage rate varies according to the individual product and the country of origin. American relationships with a particular country will also determine the amount of duty to be paid. Emerging nations are allowed to ship their goods to the U.S. duty fee to help improve their economic situation. These countries have a "Most Favored Nation" (MFN) status, which rewards them with rates lower than countries with no formal trade agreement.

Foreign Production Information

Included in the Appendix is a list of government and private agents who can help with overseas production. If you need additional assistance, try calling the appropriate Consulate General in your city that will put you in touch with the right agencies in your area to help you find sourcing abroad.

Generating Revenue through Exports and Growing Your International Sales

International Marketing

The concept behind "International Marketing" is expanding to include more than just your product, but also your service, including your design, merchandise, licensing, brand, and all other intangible things that come from your creation. The important thing, too, is to be sure to protect your product or service legally before marketing your product or service globally. International Marketing, if done properly, will no doubt create demand and with demand will come sales. However, by getting your product or service into the international marketplace you also place yourself at risk for trademark, copy write, patent, and or brand infringement.

There will always be challenges and opportunities when marketing internationally. The key to marketing globally is the same; serve the consumer, know the shoppers' needs and give them what they want, not what you want. Understand the target market you wish to reach and its culture. Do a top market analysis of each market, including your home market. Look at the most current fiscal year and go back five years if possible to see what trends in sales and shipments have occurred. International marketing is the future, anticipating and serving the consumer's needs, keeping up with changes in the marketplace, developing your virtual e-tailing and e-commerce skills and knowledge will all extend your global marketing expertise.

The concept of purchasing fashion online has never been greater. Though high-end portals exist to purchase many of today's haute couture, the broad base online destinations, such as America's Target retailer, are demonstrating that fashion is as appealing online as it is in-person. In essence, Shopping malls are being created that, in reality, never existed, except on the Internet.

With the world's borders disappearing, exporting your product and or service to Europe, Asia, the Middle East, Africa, and Latin America will become commonplace for the smaller manufacturer in the next few years. It's going to be quite clear that retailing has expanded beyond country borders, and the ebb and flow of products and services now span the entire globe.

"Think globally, market locally".

In the first place, you can make and or sell your product and or service any where in the world, but you will always have to be sensitive to the local consumer. As economies become global and the world begins to become one marketplace, it is still important to keep this phrase in mind. It sums up the challenges of international marketing and what we can expect for the future. Exporting is an important concept, too, because it's changing in the sense that you may create your product or service in one country, make it in another, and export it to entirely different country. With this in mind, whether you actually manufacture your product or service at home or aboard, your export activities promote growth, increase profits back to your company and, ultimately, transform companies into more sophisticated players in their own and worldwide markets. The fashion firms that are involved in international trade tend to be more careful about the product quality, customers service, and different product options. They also make sure they control their destiny. This means that successful global fashion firms control their manufacturing, marketing, and distribution or have a major role in its development, sustainability and growth. This helps the global fashion firm possess a greater degree of competitive advantage in the global marketplace, including the local market. Some benefits of going global include:

- Increasing sales and profits both at home and abroad
- Generating economies of scale in production and supply-chain management
- Exploring previously untapped markets
- Selling excess domestic capacity and inventory
- Eliminating seasonality of products by finding new markets and/or secondary markets
- Gaining competitive knowledge and creative ideas
- Outmaneuvering competitors and getting to market faster and cheaper

- Enhancing the image of the company in the world marketplace
- Creating jobs and prosperity at home and abroad which brings peace through trade

Establishing a company in any global market takes planning, time, resources, and experience before you see a return. Fashion companies have to do extensive research on their target market/country before going global. The first step anyone should take is to develop an international business plan. After a plan has been written out be prepared to follow a short outline of steps needed to increase your revenue streams from abroad and go global:

- Prepare to sell globally
- Research and target markets
- Find and develop buyers, sellers, partners and consumers
- Promote and market your company
- Conduct trade transactions utilizing the help of your freight forwarders and custom brokers
- Finance, protect and insure your product with the help of professionals
- Follow up and monitor transactions
- Continuously improve the process

In order to help you progress successfully through the stages of selling your product globally, there are multitudes of online resources to conduct research, contact trade professionals and meet potential business clientele. We have provided a short list of viable online resources. See appendix as appropriate.

Stat-USA.gov and National Trade Data Bank (NTDB)

This is a great resource for fashion oriented firms to do research and collect trade leads. However, this is a subscription service which is available on a quarterly and yearly basis. In addition, Stat-USA.gov and the NTDB is an important resource that provides trade-related documents, including market research reports, trade leads, trade contacts, statistical information and country reports. Research provides all the pertinent information about the target country, such as size of the market, projected growth, competitors, key players, regulatory environment and established way of doing business, economic and political stability. (**www.stat-usa.gov**).

Is your Business too small to benefit from E-commerce? As the use of the Internet and E-commerce begins to cause a melt down of country borders, there will be much more direct trade transacted using these new technological inventions.

Consumers around the world will continue to buy more and more online and the traditional trade methods will change even more dramatically. The Internet allows even the smaller manufacturer to sell products abroad and have a direct customer base or direct retail contact. This is good news for you, the small manufacturer. E-commerce may seem daunting, and smaller businesses still have many unanswered questions, but everyday there are new advances which will allow the importation and exportation of goods to become commonplace. *(See Chapter 16)*

Customs Forms

This part of trading abroad has also become streamlined and can mostly be done online through the shipping company of your choice. It should be noted that production offshore has strict laws with regards to export of merchandise. Each country has their own laws and you must comply with each foreign country's import and export regulations. It helps to have a relationship in place before selling apparel abroad.

Selling internationally usually falls into one or more of the following methods:

- Direct sales
- Licensing
- Sales through Distributors
- Sales through Agents or Representatives

The pitfalls of each of these markets will vary depending on your experience and the reliable contacts that you have managed to build in your international market of choice. Keep in mind the amount of control over sales and distribution you want to maintain and are able to finance in a foreign market. Everything will be determined on your organizational skills; this will dictate how you do business internationally.

Direct Sales

As with domestic, direct sales, the manufacturer sells directly to a foreign buyer. This allows the manufacturer to have total control over distribution, price point and sales. Direct sales also offer the highest gross profit margin. With direct sales, there are no middle agents to share the profit. The draw back is that you have to find the customer, or if you are lucky, they will find you. However, there will be promotional and marketing expenses, along with handling of returns and customer service issues. This can be very time consuming and difficult to control when in a foreign marketplace with variations from country to country. So, although the profit margin may seem larger, the added overheads involved with direct sales in a foreign market could be eaten away by all the added man-hours. You really need to be an expert on all the issues pertaining to your market niche in the country to which you are exporting.

Licensing

Licensing your brand is an ideal way to enter a foreign market place. When a foreign manufacturer can see a market opportunity within their country they will sign a licensing agreement. Your name will then be licensed to an overseas production company, who will pay you for the privilege of using your name or logo. By licensing your company name, trademark, designs and logos, your manufacturing process has been eliminated. The percentage fee will come from allowing your intellectual property to be used by an overseas manufacturer. It is a low-risk factor for a manufacturer who is not yet ready to enter a foreign marketplace. One major risk to you is the loss of intellectual property. It is also important to understand the local laws and understand the contract before signing any documents. They may be biased to the licensee.

Sales through Distributors

A distributor will be responsible, alone or in partnership with you, for promotion and marketing of your product in their territory. They take possession of your goods, usually paying a percentage below wholesale price, for assuming the burden of delivery, customs, returns, and managing customer service. The manufacture's job is to get the product delivered to the foreign port on time. The credit risk to the manufacturer is lower than using an agent. The distributor is your sole customer and one payment will be made, usually with a ***Letter of Credit.***

Finding the right distributor will be essential to your company's image. It is therefore very important to check credentials and credit-worthiness before entering into a relationship with a foreign distributor.

In Europe, distributors are entitled to compensation if they are terminated. This compensation can be high. Instead of appointing a company a "distributor," it may be better to fill their orders one at a time and avoid using the word "distributor" or "distribution agreement" in your dealings with a European company.

Sales through Agents or Representatives

An Agent versus Representative: An agent is considered a legal member of your corporation and as such, their signature is binding. A sales representative is considered a sales facilitator. In some countries the two are separated and in other countries they are considered one and the same.

As with domestic sales, the problems and the benefits are the same, except that it can be even more problematic choosing the right one! It would be very important to understand the in's and out's of any contractual agreements made in the country where you are engaging an agent/representative. They will work for a salary, commission, or a combination of both in a specific territory. Finding a reliable representative can be very helpful to you, with their expertise on market intelligence and credit information.

Here are some other considerations when selling abroad:

- It will be important to match the order cycle with your own domestic cycle. When in the Northern Hemisphere and selling south of the Equator there will be seasonal differences.

- Certain adaptations to the product will sometimes be necessary, e.g. re-sizing to fit the local target market, colors may need to be changed or quality adjustments made.

- Make certain that when a contract is made with a representative, agent or distributor, that an expert in International law and the local law is available to help you understand the fine print.

- Include in the contract reasonable agreements on the performance of your agents/reps, distributors or partners. If the contract is terminated, be aware of local customs that may hamper the termination.

Developing Overseas Markets

Establishing market exposure is the key to get the awareness of international buyers to your fashion related products. Some of the promotional tools are:

- Company Web-Site. You can design it as virtual company/product catalog with text, images, price sheets, order forms and provide translation into different languages.

- Export Directories – The Commerce Department's Buy USA is a good source for exporters to consider when they are selling overseas.

- Commercial News USA – It is an American export catalog-magazine published by the U.S. Department of Commerce that promotes U.S. fashion products, including fashion products, in more than 150 countries. CNUSA is distributed outside the U.S., free of charge, through U.S. embassies and consulates worldwide.

- Gold Key Service – Experienced trade professionals in the target country arrange appointments for potential exporter with pre-screened and qualified contacts. The GKS includes customized market and industry briefings prior to business meeting, appointments with only qualified buyers, finding interpreters, debriefing with trade professionals to discuss the results of the meetings and appropriate follow-up strategies.

- International Buyer Program (IBP) supports selected leading U.S. trade shows in industries with high export potential. Department of Commerce offices abroad recruit foreign buyers and distributors to attend the U.S. shows while program staff helps exhibiting firms make contact with international visitors at the show. The IBP achieves direct export sales and international representation for interested U.S. exhibitors.

- Multi-State/Catalog - Exhibitions showcase U.S. company product literature in fast growing markets within a geographic region. U.S. Department of Commerce staff and representatives from state development agencies present product literature to hundreds of interested business prospect abroad and send the trade leads directly to participants.

- Matchmaker Trade Delegations "match" U.S. firms with prospective agents, distributors, and joint venture or licensing partners abroad. The Commercial Service staff evaluates U.S. firms' products and services marketing potential, finds and screens contacts, and handles all event logistics. U.S. firms visit the designated countries with the delegation and, in each country, receive a schedule of business meetings and in-depth market and finance briefings.

Terms of Sale

Global Terms of Sale will differ from one country to another and to understand them fully will require that you seek help from an expert in apparel exportation. In connection with practically every international sales transaction, there will arise a number of different costs, which are to be borne by either the seller or the buyer. Because of the differences involved with each country, and the rules that govern exporting, it is impossible for this text to include such information; however this information is available from a licensed freight forwarder. If you need to find a freight forwarder, contact the Federal Maritime Commission or a foreign Trade Association. They should provide you with a list of freight forwarders that have textile experience.

Pricing

It is almost impossible to determine the pricing without primary research *(having someone in the country evaluate the competition and the demand elasticity of the product)*. Exporter can either set premium pricing, or a low pricing/high volume, strategy.

Price is an important factor in determining buying decisions and in international Marketing, it serves as penetration and positioning tool. Price is the only element of marketing mix that generates revenue; all the other factors are cost. Exporters usually take a 10% to 15% markup over cost.

Three Ways of Determining Export Pricing:

- Rigid Cost-Plus: The Company sets export prices three to four percent higher than domestic prices to cover cost of foreign advertising, foreign travel, and shipping.

- Flexible Cost-Plus: The Company offers special discounts to gain market share to offset exchange rate fluctuations.

- Dynamic Incremental: Companies may adjust prices day to day as dictated by the exchange rate.

Enhanced International Company Profile is a detailed report prepared by Commercial Specialist or Commercial Officer in that country that helps U.S. exporters to evaluate potential business partners' financial stability, strength and reliability before they start doing business with them.

Insuring foreign Payment

It will be important to understand how you will be paid for your products before you sell them globally. The primary risk to an exporter is that the buyer may no longer be willing or able to pay. To reduce this risk, it is imperative that the exporter checks the buyer's credit and references, as well as country conditions prior to offering terms. Arranging for **Letters of Credit** with your bank, and with the receiving company's bank, will avoid such complications.

If the foreign exchange rate involves a risk due to unfavorable currency fluctuations, the exporter may find there is not enough profit for the transaction. **It is very important to quote prices in U.S. dollars,** this means that the exchange risk is with the buyer. You may also consider hiring a factoring company that will purchase international account receivables and therefore, assume these risks for a percentage of the sale.

An exporter may reduce the risk of non-payment from the purchaser by purchasing export credit insurance through the Export-Import Bank of the U.S. (Exim bank), and the Foreign Credit Insurance Association (FCIA). That is permitted, provided the product being sold is produced or manufactured in America with 85% U.S. content. If the foreign content is between 16-50%, it covers only U.S. content. Exim bank publishes a schedule of countries where it is open to doing business and the associated premium costs. There are four types of export insurance policies available:

- Protects the exporter against the failure of foreign buyers to pay their credit obligations for commercial or political reasons

- Encourages exporters to offer foreign buyers, competitive terms of payment

- Supports an exporter's penetration of high-risk foreign markets

- Gives exporters and their banks greater financial flexibility in handling overseas accounts receivable.

The Small Business Administration also provides financial assistance for exporters through loan guarantee programs: the Export Working Capital Program, the International Trade Loan program and Export Express.

- **Export Working Capital Program**: This program offers both pre-export financing, such as transactional financing to manufacture or purchase goods or services for export and also post-export financing by financing transactions when they become accounts receivable. Indirect exporters, such as suppliers to exporters, are also eligible.

- **International Trade Loan Program:** The ITL is a fixed asset-financing program. Exporters apply ITL to acquire, construct, renovate, modernize, improve, or expand production facilities, equipment, or permanent working capital and supplies to be used in the United States that will be eventually used to expand their existing export markets or develop new export markets.

- **Export Express Program:** The Export Express program is relatively new. Loan proceeds may be used for most business purposes. For example, loans may provide transaction-specific financing for overseas orders, provide revolving lines of credit for export purposes, and finance export development activities (such as participation in a foreign trade show or the translation of product literature for use in foreign markets). This loan program provides term loans to acquire, construct, renovate, modernize, improve, or expand productive facilities or equipment to be used in the United States in the production of goods or services to be exported to foreign countries.

Office of Textiles and Apparel

The U.S. Department of Commerce Textile and Apparel Team provide a wide variety of export assistance, products, services, and programs for U.S. textile and apparel exporters. Team members are international trade specialists with expertise in textiles and apparel and are located in major U.S. textile and apparel markets in the U.S. and abroad. The function of this office is to assist and protect the interest of U.S. based textile and apparel companies. OTEXA's support is in conjunction and in coordination with the Commerce Department's U.S. Commercial Service domestic and overseas offices. In addition, OTEXA monitors and studies international trade agreements and trade practices between U.S. and other countries. Fashion oriented companies should keep in touch with OTEXA to find out the latest in textile and apparel industry and how it will impact their company and industry.

U.S. Department of Commerce

The U.S. Commercial Service provides timely, customized research on foreign markets and their receptivity to U.S. products. Contact your local U.S. Export Assistance Center for more information. For more information, please visit:

www.otexa.ita.doc.gov

To find information on companies that sell U.S. textile and apparel products, search the EA U.S. Suppliers directory by product, brand name, company name, etc. The directory contains more than 2,200 U.S. suppliers of textile and apparel products. For information on EA U.S. Suppliers:

web.ita.doc.gov/tacgi/suppall.nsf/$$searches? openform

Export Financing

US Export-Import Bank

Exim bank is an independent Federal agency that helps to guarantee the financing of U.S. goods and services to credit-worthy purchases overseas through a variety of loan guarantee and insurance programs:

- Loans to overseas buyers
- Guarantees to commercial lenders
- Working capital guarantees
- Export credit insurance

The Export-Import Bank of the United States (Ex-Im Bank) is the official export credit agency of the United States. Ex-Im Bank's mission is to assist in financing the export of U.S. goods and services to international markets. Ex-Im Bank enables U.S. companies — large and small — to turn export opportunities into real sales that help to maintain and create U.S. jobs and contribute to a stronger national economy. The Export-Import Bank supports the financing of U.S. goods and services, turning export opportunities into real transactions, maintaining and creating more U.S. jobs. They assume credit and country risks the private sector is unable or unwilling to accept.

Contact Information:

Export-Import Bank of the United States

811 Vermont Avenue, N.W., Washington, DC 20571

Tel: (202) 565-3946 (EXIM) or (800) 565-3946 (EXIM) **www.exim.gov**

A bank may finance the export of many types of goods or services provided the product or service is at least 50% U.S.-made content; does not adversely affect the US economy; and the buyer is non-military. Check also with U.S. Department of Commerce, state agencies, International Trade Administration, (ITA) and World Trade associations. Talk with freight forwarders, and banks. There is lots of free help and information available from state and Federal agencies.

U.S. DEPARTMENT OF COMMERCE

The U.S. Commercial Service offers valuable assistance to help your business export goods and services to markets worldwide. From this site you can access a global listing of trade events, international market research, and practical tools to help with every step of the export process. Let the U.S. Commercial Service help your business prosper in today's global economy.

Enter new export markets faster and more profitably with our worldwide network: Four Ways to Grow Your International Sales.

1. Market Research targets the best markets with the world-class research. For example, Country Commercial Guides provide comprehensive information including market conditions, best export prospects, financing, finding distributors, and legal and cultural issues. Also, Industry Sector Analyses offer details on an industry to help determine market potential and size, and foreign competitors for your product or service.

2. Trade Events promotes your product or service to targeted, pre-screened buyers. The International Buyer Program brings thousands of foreign buyers to U.S. trade shows each year. Certified Trade Fair places you in the best international trade shows with access to thousands of buyers and target matching.

3. International Partners meet the best buyers, distributors, and agents for your products and services. The Gold Key service arranges one-on-one appointments with pre-screened business contacts in a targeted export market. International Company Profiles offer low-cost, quick credit checks and due-diligence reports on buyers and distributors.

4. Consulting and Advocacy gets personalized, expert help at every step of the export process. The Platinum Key Service provided customized, long-term support to achieve your business goals. Show time offers in-depth counseling at major trade shows from market and industry specialist.

The U.S. Commercial Service also offers to textile and apparel oriented manufacturers and designers an effective service to keep on top of the latest market research, trade events and trade leads in the global marketplace. The service is called the **Fashion, Apparel & Textile (FAT) E-Market Express (EME)** and allows U.S. based companies the opportunity to receive information via their own email related to the international apparel & textile marketplace on a timely basis. A U.S. based company that is prepared to do business internationally in order to generate revenue streams from foreign markets might be interested in this type of service. The FAT-EME is part of the Commerce Department's National Textile and Apparel Team. You can access this service by visiting **www.buyusa.gov/eme/ta**. If interested in working with a local trade specialist of the National Textile and Apparel Team you can go to **www.export.gov** and enter you zip code.

U.S. SMALL BUSINESS ADMINISTRATION (SBA)

The U.S. Small Business Administration provides export information and development assistance to help small businesses take advantage of export markets, including trade counseling, training, legal assistance and publications. They provide three different loan products for small business exporters and lenders: SBA Export Express, the Export Working Capital Loan, and the International Trade Loan. The SBA Export Express combines lending and technical assistance to help small businesses that have difficulty in obtaining adequate export financing. On the other hand, the Export Working Capital Loan assists businesses with securing the credit they need to close the sales. Under the International Trade Loan program, SBA can guarantee as much as $1.25 million in combined working capital and facilities and equipment loans.

Another interesting place to check is **www.TradePort.org.** Shipping companies, brokers, cargo handlers, transfer agents and consultants of all types are advertising on Trade Port. This gives exporters access to the information they need to expand sales in overseas markets. It was developed to assist exporters at all levels, from beginner to advance; it is a one-stop shopping site for the most comprehensive trade information available on the Internet.

As your company grows internationally, you will need the assistance of foreign agencies that will meet your export and import needs for local marketing and sales activities. It would, of course, help your company to get this international business information before exporting your product, or before producing in any foreign country. Find an expert in international laws to avoid problems, and from being trapped in any unwanted relationships.

Government Resources:

U.S. Department of Commerce: Office of Textiles and Apparel , **otexa.ita.doc.gov**

U.S. Commercial Services, www.export.gov/commercialservice

U.S. Agency for International Development:

Global Trade & Technology Network, www.usgtn.net

U.S. Export-Import Bank, www.exim.gov

(See additional information titled Centers of International Trade, in the Internet Resource Listing)

CHAPTER 18

FASHION RETAILING

Having a retail store for a designer is like a chemist having a laboratory….wonderful, creative explosions happen! There are retail stores and then there are designer owned boutiques where only the designer's clothing is represented. The most important feature is for the designer to see how their clothing fits the average customer. This affords an opportunity to improve and develop shapes, learn the needs of their clientele and hear the feedback on fabrics, colors, style, fit, for example. And, at the end of a long day, when a loyal customer tells you she was the best dressed woman at the party, you'll know you've done something worthwhile.

Hanna Hartnell, Store Owner, Designer, Business Woman. Santa Monica, California

Retailing: The business of buying and selling goods to the consumer

For centuries people have been involved in bartering, trading or selling of goods. Bazaars in the east still trade on the same sites that have used as such for thousands of years. In the mid-1800s, the opening of the first department retail store; the Bon Marché in Paris, was the beginning of modern merchandising as we know it today. However, retailing in the United States evolved in a different way from the European market, meeting the needs of the first settlers who were moving across the country to populate this vast land. General stores and the peddling of wares were the first accepted forms of selling to consumers in America. Due to the vastness of the country and the distances that needed to be covered, mail order quickly became the leading method of retailing. It allowed customers to have a greater choice in the goods they wished to purchase, as the general stores of old had a limited inventory of merchandise. Indeed, mail-order catalogs brought a whole new dimension to the lives of rural settlers.

Today's retailers are constantly evolving to meet the demands of their clientele. In order to survive, a retailer is required to constantly adjust to change. Fashion retailing presents even more of a challenge, as it requires a quick response to trends. A clothing retailer must be able to spot a salable trend and act fast. If the potential retailer is not familiar with the fashion business, they may have the misconception that it is an easy business to enter into. Only after they pick the wrong location, don't have enough financial backing or are not prepared to invest long hours for little return, do they realize that in the long run it would have been wiser for them to remain as consumers rather than enter the world of retail.

The Future of Retailing

Working in industry and in academia, one comes familiar with the highs and lows of fashion retailing. The fashion industry is predictable as a pendulum swings one way, it is bound to return, and swing in the other direction. This applies to fashion by only when a fashion hits the extreme then will it return. For example, mini skirts in high contrast color values such as red and black were *"in"* for Fall 2003 with the return of the Mod Look from designers like Anne Klien, Burberry, MARC by Marc Jacobs and Laundry by Shelli Segal. As fashion moves ahead and prepares for the warmth of spring, pastels and sherbet colors are blooming in every store in softer knits and knee-length skirts. The pendulum is set to swing back – slowly.

This pendulum swing can apply to retailing itself. It was once mom-n-pop and boutique shops, and then the pendulum swung to department stores. Department stores like Nordstrom, Saks Fifth Avenue and Macy's were arising. However, the pendulum has begun to return – department stores are slowly dissipating. Department stores seemed to be impersonal, big, and overwhelming. Retail boutiques are everywhere from Fifth Avenue to SoHo (West Village in New York City) where there are Chanel, Prada and other boutique-like retailers. Rodeo Drive is filled with boutique designers such as Ralph Lauren, Versace, and Ferragamo. Even, on a recent trip to Buenos Aires, Argentina, boutique like shops filled *Avenida de Julio* along with other famous places to shop.

Specialization is the KEY. With internet shopping on the rise, where instant gratification can be obtained, mass customization is the future retailers are providing in order to retain loyal customers. Mass customization is personalization for each and every customer that walks through the retail doors…just as it applies on the internet. As soon as a return customer signs on, the e-Retailer immediately *"knows"* his/her account information, past history of shopping, and preferred choices. Retailers are keeping up (or trying to keep up) with personalization in order to retain the *"walk-in"* customer. Boutiques are one way to personalize and know customers.

Is this the right business for you?

Are you the right person for the job? Simply because you have all of those merchandising classes under your belt does not necessarily mean you will thrive as a fashion retailer. Having an acute business sense, a sincere interest in the clothing business and a significant amount of cash available is more likely to turn your dream into a reality. As I have explained earlier in this book, nothing is sure-fire, and there will be risks attached to starting any kind of business.

Try answering these questions to help you assess your own limitations or dedication to operating a retail store.

- Do you have strong financial backing or know how to get it?

- Are you prepared to gamble with your savings or borrowed capital?

- Do you know the market and have merchandising skills to open and run a successful fashion retail store?

- Do you have an updated business plan? *(Business plans are living things and need continual up dating)*.

- Do you like people? In order to sell to people, you must like them, generally and individually. You need to be a skilled observer of your clients, and be able to read faces and interpret body language.

- Are you prepared to work long hard hours, including nights and Saturdays, often the busiest day of the week for many apparel store owners.

- Do you realize there will be no profit for a couple of years, and you may have months and months without even minimum salary?

- Are you prepared to pay your employee before yourself?

- Are you good at doing lots of busy work, like checking off deliveries, putting stock away, house keeping, ordering merchandise, waiting on customers, lugging cartons, and changing interior and window displays?

- Would you know how to handle shoplifters and worry about burglaries? Even if you are insured it can be devastating to a business to have your store broken into and your entire inventory stolen.

- Would you be a courteous proprietor with difficult customers?

- Can you manage people in a tactful manner?

Fashion begins with an idea, then through the many manufacturing stages, to the sales and marketing, and finally to the ultimate consumer. Whether you decide to specialize in high-end fashion or sporty casual merchandise, you must remember to keep in mind what sets you apart from the department stores and chain stores.

Merchandising, location and store layout will be an integral part of the ultimate success of your retail operation. An old adage among fashion retailers is the five R's, which stands for choosing:

- **The Right location**
- **The Right merchandise**
- **At the Right price**
- **At the Right time**
- **In the Right quantities**

Having all five R's in place will help insure a successful retailing operation. It is very important to realize that you will not want to stock the same merchandise in suburban Kansas as you would on Melrose Avenue in Los Angeles. Knowing the taste of your customers will be a necessary ingredient of a profitable store.

Market Research

Make sure to do your homework and research your targeted community before you decide to move in. Visit the local Chamber of Commerce or U.S. Bureau of the Census, which publish studies on the number of firms in different types businesses and the populations of the community.

Selecting the right Location

Location, Location!

Choosing the right store site within the community is all-important. Just because you open a store doesn't mean they will come. Whether you are locating or relocating, it's always important to look beyond increased sales to the ultimate goal of higher profits.

Buying an existing store

If you are buying an existing store, get as much information as possible from the current owner. Don't be shy to ask questions and to learn from their experiences and more importantly, from their mistakes. Asking questions now will save you money and valuable time. It would also be a good idea to talk to the neighboring stores and ask them how their businesses are doing and what kind of traffic they experience.

Leased Store: Pros and Cons

Usually the landlord will determine the rent by the square foot of the store. The larger the square foot, the more you can expect any discount. Rents can run as high as $40 plus per square foot to as low as $3 per square foot

depending on location. So rent can be in the range of $40,000. The average size clothing retail store is around 1,200 to 1,500 square feet. It stands to reason that rents will depend on location and that will fluctuate between the East coast and the West coast, metropolitan areas to smaller towns. There could be added fees if the store is located near a large department store, you maybe asked to pay a percent of sales above a certain dollar amount. That percentage is usually around 6% of gross sales. If your store is in a mall you may also be required to pay a share of the property taxes. Almost all leases in malls will include charges for maintaining sidewalks and general shared space. These could include parking lots, landscaping and security. You will also need to discuss permission for racks to be placed outside your store during sales. If you have never leased before it would be a good idea to pay for an experienced person to look over the lease. As with any legal document, you must read the small print and look for administration costs or miscalculations. Additional items that would need to be negotiated include remodeling, any liabilities and other duties assumed by you and the landlord. Try to have the landlord remodel before you move in. If he will not agree to paying for the cost of remodeling, you may be able to negotiate for a portion of the rent for an agreed upon time. You may also want to include a bail out clauses in your lease, which will allow you to break your lease for an agreed-upon reason.

Choosing the Right Market Niche

As I previously explained it will be critical to your business to choose the right market niche. This means you should do the market research and decide where the market can bare the need for another clothing store. What type of clothing and who will buy will also be an important part of being a successful retailer. *(Invest the time and effort in answering these important questions and be prepared to do the research before you open your store.)*

- Who is your customer?

- What is the average age of your potential customer?

- What is the average educational level of your customer?

- Where do your customers live?

- What are the types of occupations of your customers?

- What is the average income of your customers?

- Does the store get foot traffic or rely on car traffic?

- Where is your nearest competitor located?

- How is their business? (*Check it out on a regular basis to see what is selling and to calculate the average price point of the merchandise.*)

- Does the market need another store?

Which market niche will you choose?

Men's Apparel

For those of you thinking about opening a men's clothing store, it is important to understand the difference between why men spend money on clothes and why women continually spend on clothing. Men don't change their wardrobe very often, and in fact, usually hate to buy clothes for themselves. They tend to go shopping when they have to, or if their partners make them! The typical male customer is between the age of 18 and 40 years of age, while a small percentage of male consumers are in their fifties. The big spenders are usually single, but typically a wife or a girlfriend will accompany on a shopping trip Thanks to *"Casual Friday"* men have been forced into buying dressier, casual clothing.

Children's Apparel

It is worth noting that parents and grandparents, not children, are the ones who spend the money on clothing for the young ones in their lives. They decide whether or not to go to a store and whether or not to make a purchase. Another important fact is that the bulk of children's clothing sales come from matching tops and bottoms coordinates. Seasonal trends come and go but, for the most part, the traditional colors associated with children's wear are still the top sellers.

Teenage Apparel or Junior

American teenagers typically spend one third of their income on clothing. Companies like Wet Seal, Rampage and XOXO have filled a niche and have responded to the market needs of teenage girls. The price of Junior clothing is traditionally lower than that of Women's, and this makes the market more competitive. Often the garments are manufactured off-shore in order to keep within a certain price point. Junior clothing is cut smaller and fits tighter, and the amount of fabric is usually spare due to the price constrains of the Junior market. Junior sizes range from 1 through 13 and run in odd numbers.

Women's Contemporary

Contemporary clothing sales are continually growing for the specialty store retailer. A hallmark of category is garments innovative in style, fit and fabric, purchased by the 20 to 50 age group. Contemporary manufacturers are typically smaller start-up companies rather than the large corporations that mass-produce apparel found in department stores. Contemporary garments usually have special design features that make them more appealing and different. The price point is higher than Junior clothing, and the cut is more generous. Contemporary sizes range from 0 through 14 and run in even numbers.

Missy Classic

Banana Republic and Ann Taylor are good examples of this category of retailer. As baby boomers age, so unfortunately do their body types. No longer free-spirited hippies wearing bell-bottoms and tie-dye, Missy customers invest in basic classics. The cut of the garments is on the ample side to accommodate the shape of the Missy body. Fabrication is of higher quality. Colors tend to be more on the conservative, solid side with a few muted prints included in the mix. Sizes range from 0 through 16 and run in the even numbers.

Women's and Half Size

This is another market that is growing *(in more ways then one!)* As the women of the Western world have increased in height, so they have in their circumference. Large-size specialty stores are multiplying, and it is a niche that has needed to be recognized for sometime. As with the larger women, clothing for smaller, petite women is also a specialty segment that needs to be addressed. With more and more Pacific Rim and typically smaller-boned females from the Far East looking to find clothes that fit their body types, this is another important market that has tremendous growth potential.

Sports Apparel

In today's market, active sportswear is an important item of clothing for all types and age categories. Whether it is women, men or children's clothing, it makes good sense to include sport attire in the mix of merchandise you choose to sell in your store. Comfort is the overwhelming factor in choosing sports apparel, even for every day clothing attire. However, you should realize that on the whole, younger consumers; 10 to 17 years old, give lesser importance to comfort and more importance to style and the latest trends.

Bridal & Formal Wear

There are some very successful designer/manufacturers in this category, a good example being Vera Wang, who is known all over the world for her sophisticated wedding fashions. Bridalwear has typically consisted of custom-made clothing. The average age increase of brides, as well as the rise of second-time brides willing and able to spend more on attire, has contributed to the popularity of more elaborate, couture styles being sold. The average amount spent on a formal wedding dress is more than $700, and if the gown has any hand beading then the gown could end up costing thousands. Thus, compared to other apparel categories, Bridalwear retailers rely on the one time buyer of a high-end purchase, and less on volume. Bridalwear is typically sold through specialty stores and department stores. Specialty stores will often also carry formal wear or mother-of-the-bride ensembles. Picking out a prom dress has become a ritual in many parts of the country, not unlike the formal "coming out " parties held for debutantes. If you have done your market research or have a client following in this category, it can be lucrative. It is interesting to note that evening wear gets more media coverage than any other category; especially at the Oscars, the Tony Awards, the VH1 Fashion awards and all the many other events that celebrities attend.

Planning stage

Financing/Business Plan

Start-up Investment: You cannot run a successful apparel store without investing money, whether it is from savings, a bank loan or a trust fund. The minimum amount to open and stock a retail store is in the range of $50,000 to $250,000! The more under-capitalized you are, the longer it will take to turn a profit. Money may not buy you love, but it will buy you a certain amount of security for your business. As many new entrepreneurs quickly discover, raising capital may not be easy; in fact, it can be a complex and frustrating process. As I have outlined in previous chapters, you must start with a business plan! Preparing a business plan forces you to think through every aspect of your business. As you address each part of your plan, it will help you and any potential investor to understand where you hope to take your retail store and what steps you will take to get there. *(See Chapter 3: Business Plan)*

Before the Opening

Licenses, Permits, Zoning, Insurance and Tax issues need to be addressed.

Opening an apparel store will require necessary licenses and permits that will need to be applied for. Here is a list for you to follow, but it is still recommended that you call your local Chamber of Commerce and City Hall to inquire if there are other special requirements within your city.

- **Business License:** You will apply for a business license from your city and usually it will be issued right away if you are moving into an existing store. If, however you are applying for the rezoning of a new store, then it can take time and you will need to address this early in your planning stage. Business licenses should be displayed prominently within the store.

- **Sellers Permit:** The State Board of Equalization, the State Sales Tax Commission or the Franchise Tax Board is usually where you will get a seller's permit. The important thing about a resale permit is that it allows you to avoid paying sales tax at the same time you purchase merchandise from suppliers. The sales tax is then added to the clothing when sold to the customer or a final sale is made. This license should also be displayed within the store.

- **Fire Department Permit:** The Fire Department requires you to have a permit if you use any flammable material. Call your City Hall or Fire Department and get the specific requirements for your city.

- **Sign Permit:** Before having expensive signs made, you will need to ask your city officials if they have any ordinances that stipulate the size, location, lighting and type of signs used. It is also wise to check with the owner of the building to find out if they have any restrictions.

- **County Permits:** If your store is outside of the city limits and its ordinance, you may need to apply for another permit from the county in which you are planning to open your store.

- **Federal Licenses:** This is only necessary if you plan to conduct your business across state lines, or if you intend to advertise in other states. Contact the Federal Trade Commission about this particular license.

Payroll & Taxes

Employer Taxes:

- **Federal Identification Number:** Each employer must apply for an **"Employer Identification Number" (Form SS-4)** to comply with Federal Income Tax, Social Security and Unemployment Insurance regulations. (EIN) **www.irs.ustreas.gov**

- **Business Tax Information:** Once you hire an employee, you are required by law to register with various government agencies.

Each employer must apply for a State Employer Account Number (form DE 1) and a Federal Employer Identification Number.

- **State Employer Account Number (EDD):** www.edd.ca.gov (CA for California, for other states you will need to replace the CA with the abbreviation for your state.)

- **Federal Income Tax:** Internal Revenue Service (IRS), 800-829-1040 www.irs.gov

- **Social Security:** Social Security Administration, 800-772-1213

- **Workers' Compensation Insurance:** State Compensation Fund (Call for the telephone number in your state)

- **Safety & Health Regulations:** All businesses with employees are required to comply with state and Federal regulations regarding the protection of employees. OSHA outlines specific health and safety standards adopted by the U.S. Department of Labor. For information contact the Federal Occupational Safety & Health Administration.

Pre-opening check list:

Insurance Issues: Retail insurance protects the contents of your business against fire, theft, and other losses. However, as a business owner it is important to purchase other insurance that will cover:

- Liability
- Property
- Business Interruption
- "Key Man"
- Automobile
- Officer & Director
- Home Office

Business Set-Up:

- "Doing Business As" (DBA)
- Business Bank account
- **Sole Proprietorship:**
- Partnership: *(Remember, each partner is responsible for the actions of the other.)*
- Corporation
- S-Corporation

These issues and more are covered in Chapter 2: Getting Started, Chapter 3: Business Plan, Chapter 4: Bookkeeping for Small Businesses and Chapter 5: Financing Your Business.

Please note: it will be very important to find the right CPA and a trusted legal advisor to assist with critical financial and legal matters when opening and running any business operation.

Operating expenses

Most businesses cannot finance the operating cycle (accounts receivable days + inventory days) with accounts payable financing alone. Consequently, working capital financing is needed. This shortfall problem is typically covered by the net profits generated internally, by external borrowed funds or with a combination of the two. Most businesses need short-term working capital at some point in their operations. For instance, retailers must find working capital to fund seasonal inventory build-up between

September and November for Christmas sales. But even a business that is not seasonal occasionally experiences peak months when orders are unusually high. This creates a need for working capital to fund the resulting inventory and accounts receivable buildup.

Some small businesses have enough cash reserves to fund seasonal working capital needs. However, this is very rare for a new business. If you experience a need for short-term working capital during the first few years of operation, you should identify several potential sources of funding before the need arises. (*The important thing is planning!*) Working capital has a direct impact on your cash flow. Since cash flow is the name of the game for all business owners, a good understanding of working capital is imperative to make any venture successful and profitable.

Financial Budget

For most businesses, the process of budgeting is limited to figuring out where to get the cash to meet next week's payroll. There are so many financial fires to put out in a given week that it's hard to find time to do any short or long-term financial planning. But failing to plan financially might mean that you are unknowingly setting up failure. Establishing a business budget is the most powerful tool available to any small business owner. Maintaining a good short-term and long-term financial plan enables you to control your cash flow instead of having it control you.

In the start-up phase, you will have to make reasonable assumptions about your business in creating your budget. You should ask the following questions to assist you with your budget planning needs.

- How much can be sold in the first year?
- How much will sales grow in the following years?
- How will the goods sold be priced?
- How much inventory will you need?
- What will your operating expenses be?
- How many employees will you need?
- How much will you pay them?
- How much will you pay yourself?
- Will you offer benefits?
- What will your payroll and unemployment taxes be?
- What will the income tax rate be?
- Will your corporation be an S corporation or a C corporation?
- What will be the cost of monthly rent or property payments?
- What equipment will be needed to start the business?
- What payment terms will you offer your customers if you sell on credit?

- What payment terms will your suppliers give you?
- Do you have collateral?
- If you borrow, what will the interest rate be?

Once you begin to tackle these questions you will then have the beginnings of your business plan. (*Chapter 3 Business Plan and Chapter 4 Bookkeeping for a Small Business will assist you with these important steps. There are two types of plans, those that work and those that don't!*)

Maintaining a financial strategy allows you to perform sensitive analysis and make budget changes where they are needed. It is important that you have the advice of a Certified Public Accountant, (CPA) in preparing your initial budget.

Accounting Assistance

Accountants can assist a small business in establishing a sound bookkeeping system, preparing periodic financial statements, preparing state and federal income tax returns, budgeting, forecasting and consulting on various financial aspects of running a retail store.

Costing and profit margins

As with any business, ineffective pricing can drain a retailer's profits. One of the most important financial concepts you will need to understand in running a profitable business is how to calculate your gross profit margins.

The Gross profit on any product sold = Cost of goods sold minus the cost of goods purchased. This will give you a gross profit margin but you should then calculate your net profit margin. *(See Chapter 12)*

Buying

Buying begins with selecting the right product mix. You will need to respond to trends, seasons, and to the economy. What everyone wants this month, you won't be able to give away next month. You must know how much to order and when, and then when to reorder. When something begins to languish on the shelves, you must sense when it's time to drop pieces and cut your losses. You need to see when the sale of an item peaks and respond to trends quickly. You must continually refine and improve your product mix to satisfy your clientele. This will make your store more valuable and important to your customer. Being in the store each day, you will soon notice the items that are selling and the ones that are left on the shelves. This information will prove extremely useful as you buy new product and develop sales strategies.

A best-selling item is sometimes referred to as *"a runner"*. Your never-ending goal as a retailer is to determine next season's runners. You should evaluate the following information to fully understand what makes your choice of merchandise a runner.

- The selling price. Is it worth the selling price?
- The body: Pant, top, dress, shoes, etc.
- The fabric: Print or solid, and in what color?
- The fit: In general, how was the fit of the garment?
- The feel of the fabric or "hand", as it is referred to in the industry.
- The look and finish: Is it well made and with a lot of detail?
- Was it a trendy or classic garment?

One or more of these elements may be what attracts the consumer to the garment and convinces them to make the purchase. You should do your best to determine which element was the reason for the sale. This will assist you in becoming a more valuable buyer for your store.

It helps to have a passion for what you do, and have a hunger for what is new and "in". This means you will need to go shopping in other stores to see what they are selling and how their spaces are merchandised. Good buyers must have a feel for the marketplace, spot trends early, and see the big picture, as well as the details. Watch sell-throughs diligently and respond to information to make educated conclusions. Your knowledge of the market and your keen awareness of what is selling can be the conduit that allows you to cultivate strong relationships with your customers. Your sense of style will help you to plan your product mix wisely and to buy an inventory that will sell.

Selling Accessories

It is always good to include accessories within your store, e.g. handbags, jewelry, socks, etc. They require little space and create more dollars per square foot than anything else that you will carry. Accessories add the finishing touch to a new outfit and give life to old ones. They make nice gifts and are designed to complement the latest fashions. Accessories are very important in today's marketplace.

Consignment

Consignment sales can be a good way to supplement your overhead and bring in some extra money. Consignment selling allows a vendor to place merchandise in your store for sale, with payments to be made after the merchandise is sold. The sale price is usually split 50-50. If you decide to offer consignment, you will need to setup very careful records. A contract or written agreement needs to be prepared for each consignor. The agreement should state when the payments are made, who is responsible for loss or damage (normally the consignor), and how long items should be allowed to remain in the store before it becomes old merchandise! Placement and display of consignors' product can often be an issue, and therefore should be discussed beforehand.

Where, What, and When to Buy:
These are the million dollar questions!

Understanding the tastes and preferences of your customers will be an important factor when venturing out to buy for the store; other crucial factors will include planning your budget and merchandising your store's mix. Finding the right merchandise will be a major step. Below are some of the more common places to find your ideal products. You should begin compiling your "wish list" of labels months before you go buying. This will help you to become familiar with the people that design and produce the garments that you will eventually carry, before you begin writing orders.

- **Market Weeks** Each major city has their own dates for market weeks and it will be important to attend these markets to find the latest lines and the newest styles. *(Reference the back of this book for a list of the major markets).*

- **Trade Shows** Usually, trade shows are held at the same time as market weeks and it will be important to know the dates of certain trade shows. You may want to travel to other cities to find more unusual merchandise.

- **Showrooms** If you live in a large city and within reach of the fashion district, it will be wise to start visiting showrooms in order to become familiar with the lines you would like to buy, and ultimately sell.

- **Road Reps** Once you have opened your store, road reps will seek you out and make appointments to show you their various lines.

Inventory control

Inventory management will be critical to the success of your business Keeping too much inventory on hand will create cash flow problems, and more importantly for the clothing store owner, having too much inventory will increase your risk of obsolete merchandise. Conversely, an inventory that is too lean can cost you important sales. Pay attention to the following:

- Monitoring the items that are typically sold each season is essential. Ordering the right merchandise in the right quantity will also be important. Holding on to old stock will result in depreciation. *Depreciation of aging goods will cost you important profits.*

- Finding manufacturers who can ship quickly and who have inventory available, will allow you to stock on demand. This is often referred to as *"Just in time"* inventory management, and can save a retailer valuable working capital. However, it is also important to note that you should not become overly dependent on one supplier. Any change in the business of a vendor could have a disastrous chain reaction on your retail operation. Manufacturers have been known to abandon small specialty stores when a large order from a department store is received. Remember, that by offering your customer a choice in what you sell, by category and product, you're also protecting your livelihood. Merchandise your store with goods from several suppliers that reflect the diversity of the season and the marketplace.

- Buy stock that sells and don't try to be all things to all people when it comes to inventory management. Focus on what sells!

- Once you have been in business for a while, you will begin to understand the needs of your customers. Mark down the items that don't sell, and when buying for the next season, remember those items and don't replace them.

- Don't hang on to merchandise that has not sold for another year. In order to maintain your operating expenses, it is important to clear the products out as fast as you can. If this means lowering the price to move merchandise quickly, then that's what must be done.

Merchandising

The merchandise that you sell must be different from that of the competition in order to attract new customers. Successful retailers understand that they cannot be everything to everyone! It is important to maintain a level of quality. Understanding what your target market can afford will be important to the success of your retail store. Obviously, what people earn will affect their spending. Where people live will also affect the spending habits of your clientele. By increasing your knowledge of these financial factors, you will be better able to determine the price range of merchandise to be sold.

- Couture or top level: Merchandise in this range consists of the finest materials and workmanship. *To be successful in this category it is crucial to build a customer demand for your product.*

- Intermediate: A high standard of quality and workmanship is maintained, but with an eye to keeping production costs down.

- Affordable: A lower level of workmanship

   However, it is important to note that price point is not always tied into quality of goods sold.

Consistent with product:

- Price points and price range

- The type of branded goods you offer in your store will also help to establish your own market niche. A brand, trademark or logo identifies the product of a specific manufacturer. Branding helps to differentiate one designer from another and in some cases allows the product to be sold for a higher price. For example Donna Karan and Ralph Lauren have acquired a special status that allows them to sell their merchandise for more than an unknown designer. Some manufacturers limit their product to specific stores within a certain area. For example, Nike only allows a few stores in the same county to carry its product.

- When you are buying, you must strive to achieve exclusivity of goods sold in your store. You can sometimes prevail on vendors to confine certain styles to your store, but only for a given period of time. This is usually possible if your order is large enough to make production profitable for the manufacturer. As you expand your retail store, you may ask certain manufacturers to produce your own private label, to your own specifications. Offering your own label is an excellent way to meet price points, build your brand, and achieve exclusivity.

- Breadth and depth of merchandise, or *assortment* refers to the range of stock that is featured in the store. A store may feature a *narrow and deep assortment,* in which it stocks relatively few styles but has them in many sizes and colors. Or, it can stock a *broad and shallow assortment,* in which the store offers many different styles, in limited sizes and colors. Specialty stores will usually choose to be in the broad and shallow assortment range.

Marketing

Before you can become a successful a retailer, you first have to understand how to market your new store. Your marketing skills are as critical to the fate of your business as your management abilities. Having a beautiful new store with a wonderful selection of clothing will **not** be enough. Shoppers must first know that it is there, then you will need to win over customers with the merchandise and service that is offered. There are three important elements to marketing:

- Advertising and publicity are a chief means of communicating with customers, but it can be costly

- Public relations (PR) will be crucial to the long life of your store. Positive word of mouth is the best marketing for your store

- Promotional activities usually entail creating some kind of excitement and awareness that makes people want to visit your store. A good example would be a local street fair that would bring foot traffic into your store

Store Layout & Display Techniques

Sophisticated visual merchandising will be a challenge to anyone without training or experience, and it will be an on-going task that will need to be addressed weekly, if not daily. When planning the store layout it will be important to maintain a visual appeal, ease of movement, and comfort. The design must be attuned to the taste of the target customer, and the environment must not only be pleasant, but also encourage shopping and consumer spending. Placement of fixtures must take into account security issues and discouraging shoplifting. In case of fire, access to fire exits must also be considered. You should consider the needs of disabled customers; certain features such as ramps to ensure wheelchair access maybe required by your local planning office. Meeting all these demands calls for a professional who specializes in store design and planning. Often such a professional will show you a computerized rendition of your new store layout, with a picture of the selling floor merchandise displayed in the best location.

Visual Merchandising

The arrangement and presentation of merchandise both on the floor and in the windows will be a critical factor to keeping the store looking fresh, and an important factor in attracting return customers. Why would shoppers return to buy if the stock is old and the window display is the same? When everything begins to look alike, customers become disenchanted. Remember that the longer a customer spends in your store, the more likely you are to make a sale. Coordinating and accessorized outfits should be displayed to help customers assemble their own wardrobes.

Fixtures

Display fixtures serve the dual purpose of showing and storing merchandise on the store floor. Normally they are purchased at the same time the store layout is being considered. It is important that they enhance the store image and the type of merchandise to be sold. The fixtures will become an important part of the merchandising plan for each new season. There are four types of racks used for hanging clothing:

- **Straight Racks:** are ideally installed against the wall or flat areas, or they are free-standing. Wall racks are used for long garments because they must be fixed high enough to prevent the garments from dragging on the floor. Since they do not show a full frontal view of the garments, they are not ideal for positioning on the store floor.

- **Rounders:** are circular racks that hold a large amount of merchandise, but do not show a full view of the garments. Low rounders are used for tops, skirts, and folded trousers. They take up a significant amount of space, but usually do not block the shoppers' view or make the floor look too crowded.

- **Four-way fixtures:** have two bars crossing at right angles. This allows the customer to walk around the fixture to see four separate outfits with more merchandise hung behind the items in front. This arrangement allows for merchandising and presentation of suggested outfits and how they would look when worn.

- **Waterfall fixtures:** have forty-five degree angled bars that allow the garments to be hung and displayed in tiers. It is a good way to display using a variation of height, and will make for a more interesting presentation.

Another common fixture used in stores is the **_Gondola,_** which is a freestanding island with a flat surface for bins, draws or shelves. It can be used to display folded garments or items such as socks and other accessories.

Housekeeping issues

When choosing racks and fixtures, it is important to remember that you will need to be able to get under and around fixtures in order to properly clean the floor. Maintaining neatness is important for the store image and for the convenience of the shopper. *(Remember, fingerprints on glass windows and doors must be cleaned.)*

Ambiance

Pay attention to atmosphere and the decoration of your store, as this will create the mood and the image. Décor is important, pale colors or off-white will show the clothes off best. Bright colors and patterned wallpapers will distract from the clothing. Merchandise should be attractively displayed on fixtures that relate. Sensory retailing to stimulate your customers' senses has become an art. Playing soft music or mood music in the store will create ambiance and will help customers feel relaxed. Changing rooms should be large enough to include chairs and most importantly, a mirror. It is very frustrating to try clothes on and have to leave the changing room to see how the garments fit. Also, place chairs for seating in the store. Quite often, shoppers bring spouses or friends along.

Creative Selling

If you have the square footage available it maybe a good marketing idea to include space for a small coffee shop in your store. Restroom availability is also very important to women. As a general rule, women shop as a means of enjoyment, and you should try to make their shopping experience pleasurable so they will return, again and again!

Caution! Children in the Store

To avoid damage to your store when children are left unattended as mothers shop, it would be wise to provide some kind of entertainment in the way of coloring books and washable crayons. It is to your advantage to provide a small area of containment for little ones to play peacefully, or even have a TV for watching a video. If a child is running wildly around while mother shops, kindly inform the parent that the child may get harmed if left unattended. You have to hope they take the hint!

Service with a smile!

Customer Service

The marketplace is becoming more and more competitive. Customers are asking for more and have less forgiveness when they don't get what they need. Therefore, it is commonplace for storeowners to offer their customers an array of services designed to increase their competitive edge. Layaway, payment plans, a liberal return policy, free parking, and providing free alterations can help you keep your customers returning. It is important to strive to be the best there is in today's marketplace. People tend not to spend as much time shopping as they used to in the 1980's and early 1990's plus, they demand and expect good service. Department stores have turned people away with their lack of service. It is often impossible to find anyone to help you sort through their racks of merchandise. Specialty stores have the big advantage of offering merchandise that is special and one-of-a-kind, along with outstanding service. Small stores are focused on their community and know their customer's needs. Understanding your customers will be the key to your own success!

Credit card sales

Credit card sales incur a charge to the store by the credit card company. This fee is usually around 2.50% of sales. It will be essential to a retail owner to have credit card capabilities.

Return Policy

In fairness to you as the store-owner and to your customer, it is wise to post a notice with your return policy clearly outlined. Something along these lines: "All merchandise returned in good condition will be accepted within thirty days of the sale with the original receipt. No refunds on sales items."

Bags

To minimize costs, it is a good idea to buy blank paper bags and have stickers made that feature your logo that can then be placed onto the bag. Another option is to have a large stamp made to imprint your logo onto the bags.

Management

To run a business successfully, you need a good business brain but most importantly you will need to understand how to manage people, both your own employees and your customers. Managing people requires combining the psychological and intuitive skills with the ability to communicate directly and effectively. *(In other words, you need to be a people person!)*

Staff & Management issues: As a storeowner you will need to find the right personnel to help you build a solid business. You must understand that you cannot run a retail operation alone. Finding **honest** staff to assist you is always a challenge. The employees you hire can make or break your business, and therefore it is critical for you to spend the time to find the right people. Reflect on your staffing needs before you begin to advertise. What kind of personality, experience and education are needed? Begin by outlining the job and analyzing your requirements for the position.

- What type of physical and mental requirements will be involved?
- How will the job be done?
- Why do you need this employee?
- What types of qualifications are needed?
- Full time or part-time position?

Setting employee policies and giving a clear job description will help you with what you hope to expect from your employees. *(See at the end of this chapter for the forms of application and job description)*

Writing the Ad: The best way to avoid attracting the wrong candidates for the position and thereby wasting everyone's time, is to clearly understand the job requirements. Write the job description for the position you need filled, then look at other ads placed in the classified section of your local news paper to evaluate how best to write it. The following information is important to include when writing your ad:

- Job location this will weed out people who do not live within the area.
- Previous experience, if needed.
- Specify how to contact you; do you want them to fax a resume or call to set up an appointment?

Personal contacts are usually a good place to start, or call your local schools or colleges.

On-line services can also be a valuable resource and you will be able to receive resumes on line.

Pre-Screening Applicants:

There are three important tools in pre-screening your applicants:

- Resume
- Application
- References; important to follow up and check them out. Take the time to call also.

Interview Process:

Once you have narrowed the list down, then begin to set up your interviews. Be prepared and ready to ask important questions, but understand that there are certain questions you are not allowed to ask.

Equal Employment Opportunity Commission (EEOC) guidelines, as well as federal and state laws, prohibit asking certain questions of applicants, both on the application form and or during the interview process.

You cannot ask questions that do not relate directly to the job, including:

- Age and date of birth *(if interviewing a teenager, you can ask if he or she is 16 years old)*

- Sex, race, creed, color, religion or national origin.

- Disabilities of any kind

- Date and type of military discharge

- Marital status

- Maiden Name

- Citizenship status; however, you can ask if he or she has the legal right to work in the United States

- How many children do you have? How old are they? Who will care for them while you are at work?

- Has a psychologist or psychiatrist ever treated you?

- Have you ever been treated for drug addiction or alcoholism?

- Have you ever been arrested? *(You may, however, ask if the person has been convicted, if it is accompanied by a statement saying that a conviction will not necessarily disqualify an applicant for employment.)*

- How many days where you sick last year? Have you ever filed for worker's compensation or been injured on the job?

Interviewing Techniques: Try to put the interviewee at ease. The initial few moments of the interview are the most crucial. As you meet the candidate and shake his or her hand, you'll gain a strong impression of his or her poise, confidence and enthusiasm *(or lack thereof)*. Qualities to look for include: good communication skills, neat and clean appearance, and a friendly and enthusiastic manner. Make a little small talk on a neutral topic. You should then explain the requirements of the job and explain your company's background. Then you may want to ask them about their last job experience. Avoid questions that only require a yes or no answer, you need them to talk to you about themselves. Follow up questions such as "How did that situation come about?" or "Why did you do that?" These require a more in-depth answer and will give you a better insight to their personalities. Watch for "sour grapes" when talking about their last job. They will need good communication skills to work retail. Do they have a job-appropriate appearance; if they have stained or wrinkled clothing for an interview then you know they will not care about their personal appearance on the job! Allow them to ask questions about the job and pay attention to the questions asked. If they have done their homework, they will ask insightful questions about your company, not how long the lunch break will be! At the end of the interview, let the candidate know when you will get back to them. They may have other interviews pending and it is courteous to let them know as soon as possible regarding your final decision. Make sure that you take notes during the interview, as you will need to refer to them when making your final choice. Put resumes and notes in a file just in case your first choice does not work out or some other unforeseen complication occurs.

Checking references: Once you have narrowed the candidates down to three or four then you need to follow up and check those references. *It is interesting to note that one third of job applicants lie about their experiences and education achievements on their resumes and job applications.* A few phone calls up front to check references could save you a lot of hassles, and even legal battles later. Unfortunately, it is not always a straightforward process, as many firms are fearful of reprisal and adopt policies that forbid release of detailed information. However, there are ways to dig deeper if you can avoid the human resource department, which will only supply dates of employment, title and salary. Try calling a person's former supervisor directly. While the supervisor may be required to redirect your call to the human resource department, you maybe able to get them to talk, or least get a good understanding of their feeling toward the candidate.

If the job requires a driver for the company car, it maybe a good idea to check with the Motor Vehicle Department. This may uncover negligence or drug and alcohol problems.

As honesty will be a key factor to finding the right candidate for your position, you may want to do a criminal background check. A third party investigator can do this for a fee of around $100, which could be money well spent. *(If in doubt, it would pay to find out!)*

Federal law requires that you maintain those applications for one year, and for the successful applicant, you must keep it for three years.

Dealing with Problem Employees: Sooner or later you will have to deal with an employee who doesn't live up to your expectations. It maybe a bad attitude, tardiness, laziness, or just plain nastiness, but for one or more of these reasons, the arrangement isn't working out. Everyone deserves a second chance, unless, of course, they have knowingly committed an infraction that constitutes grounds for immediate dismissal. Company policies should be outlined in the employee policy manual. Allow employees an opportunity to correct the error, but make it clear that failure to do so will result in termination. Never reprimand an employee in front of other employees, it is better to take care of business behind close doors, one on one. Explain the problem and how you would like to have it changed. Any employee worth keeping will take the hint. If you feel the infraction is serious, then it should be recorded and documented. If you feel the person is unstable or emotional, it would be in your interest to have another person in the room as your witness.

Firing an Employee: When you have a serious problem with an employee and are forced to fire them, it should be spelled out in a letter as well as informing them in person. If you must, offer them severance pay and let them go. Don't allow them to hang around causing stress and strain on you and other employees.

Resignation of a Valued Employee There will be times when a valued employee will wish to resign, but before accepting their resignation, ask if there is something you can do to make the individual want to stay. It is almost always cheaper to retain a valued employee than have to retrain a new one. If they have made their mind up to leave, always leave the door open for them to return. Don't hold a grudge; remember all the jobs you have had along the way to becoming your own boss.

Part-time Employees: You may not be ready for a full time employee and just need help over the weekends, in which case taking on a part-time employee or two maybe a good way to begin the employee – employer relationship. It will cut your overhead, benefits, costs and allow for flexibility. A traditional source of part-time employees is students. They typically are flexible, willing to work odd hours and don't expect high wages. On the downside, you will need to set ground rules as most students take a job to pay for clothing or entertainment and therefore will often drop work for other more appealing social engagements. Running a clothing store you will find more applicants than you need!

Make sure to understand all the laws and regulations of taking on any employees. Call your local Department of Employment to get a thorough understanding of your commitment as an employer.

Important Record Keeping!

- **Sales Record:** All your income derived from the sales of your store's clothing and accessories can be grouped in one large category called *gross sales* or into several subcategories for different product lines in order to know what merchandise is selling well and what's not.

- **Cash receipt:** These account for all money generated through cash sales and the collection of accounts receivable. This is actual income collected and doesn't include earnings from your sales records, unless you choose to operate a cash-and-carry business. In a cash-and-carry business, your cash receipts match your sales records.

- **Cash disbursements:** These are sometimes referred to as operating expense records or accounts payable. All disbursements should be made by check so that business expenses can be well documented for accounting purposes. If you make a cash payment, include a receipt for payment, or at least an explanation of it, in your business records. Dividing your disbursements into subheadings or categories maybe a good idea for tracking your records.

- **Petty Cash:** A petty cash fund should be established in cash disbursements to cover expenses that are immediate and small enough to warrant payment by cash, such as dinner for your staff when you're working late. Record items purchased from the petty cash fund on a form that lists purchase date, amount and purpose. When the petty cash fund is almost exhausted, total the cost of the items and write a check for the amount in order to replenish the account.

- **Major Purchase:** Any major purchases, like equipment should be accounted for so that its deprecation can be deducted on your tax forms.

- **Insurance:** Keep all records pertaining to your store's insurance policies. This includes life, fire and any special coverage you may obtain to decrease liability in a specific area. List the carriers of the policies, the underwriting agents who issued the coverage and the dates on which you wrote a check for the premiums.

- **Advance Deposits:** Many states require an advance deposit against future taxes to be collected. For example, in California, if you project $10,000 in taxable sales for the first three months of your store's operation, you must deposit 6.5%, in this case $650.

- **Payroll:** If you employ more than one person in your store, you are required to withhold income tax and Social Security tax from each employee's paycheck and send these numbers to the proper tax collection agency. You will also need to obtain an employer tax number from the IRS form 1040 SS-4, and if your state has income tax, from the state as well. You also have to maintain all records pertaining to payroll taxes. All payroll records must be kept for four years.

Additional records of all canceled checks, copies of sales receipts, invoices to customers, cash register receipts, and receiving reports should be kept and stored for tax time. Using an accountant can help you with all the above.

Computer Needs

Technological advances have brought about dramatic changes in the way retailers, manufacturers and buyers are able to communicate and track their merchandise. The computer provides speedy, reliable, and accurate information that facilitates managerial decision-making. Computers are used by store-owners for internal store operations such as inventory control, payroll, credit checking, collections, and order processing. Electronic data processing (EDP), electronic point-of-sale (POS) systems, bar-coding, Electronic Data Interchange (EDI), as well as advances in electronic commerce (World Wide Web) and electronic shopping have opened new opportunities for buyers to reach resources and track sales. Although you may not be in a position to use all of these tools, it is important to understand their importance to the world of retailing.

Electronic data processing (EDP): This system is used for internal operations, such as inventory control, payroll, credit and collections, and order processing.

Electronic point-of-sale (POS): An electronic point of sale system gives the retailer the capability of recording stock sales by keeping track of units sold. It can also provide prices for untagged merchandise, automatically take markdowns, print future sales promotional information on sales tickets, and approve credit cards and bank checks.

Bar Code: A pattern of variable width bars and spaces, representing a code of letters and numbers. They can be found on most products sold and can be scanned at the POS register, which enters the sales on the store's computer system.

Electronic Data Interchange (EDI): Electronic Data Interchange integration applies to companies that want to automate the process of moving data from the EDI system into the order processing system, and from the order processing system into the EDI system. It is a computerized system whereby purchase orders, sales data, invoices, and other business documents can be sent electronically between retailers and suppliers. When tied into the store scanning system, EDI provides an instant link from checkout counter to suppliers, thus enabling the supplier to replenish the depleted inventory. This system is often used to reorder basic or staple items that have a broad assortment of colors and sizes.

The computer system you choose should allow you to take delivery of your products, purchased and track and control your inventory. It is a tool that will help manage your inventory and if used correctly, should streamline your inventory management. As your goods arrive, you will need to issue a code to track your entire inventory through your electronic system. This will allow you to have up-to-the-minute information on every item in your store. This information will include your cost of goods, selling price, a description, the name of the supplier, number of pieces in stock, when a sale was made and when to reorder. A computer can automatically send out invoices and pay bills and update your books. However, it is important to remember that computers are wonderful inventions, but you first have to understand them in order to get what you want from them. They are only as good as their users. If you are not familiar with the various software uses, take classes. It will pay off in the long run.

Retailing Definitions

Consignment: Consignment selling is the practice of allowing vendors to place merchandise in your store for sale, with payments to be made after the merchandise is sold. The sale price is usually split 50-50.

Discount Store: A retail operation that sells goods for less than fully recommended retail prices. They make a profit by keeping their overhead low, self-services and buying large quantities of goods.

Direct Selling: Selling directly to the customer without a freestanding retail store. Avon is one the largest direct sale forces within America. For the most part, direct sellers are independent salespeople who buy from factories directly and make the final sale to customers. This is really a profitable sales method that can cut overhead costs. Many designers do their own trunk shows, or design and manufacture and then sell directly to their customers through their own stores. This allows them to can keep their prices down and be more competitive.

Factory Outlet Stores: Often defined as designer label or discount retailing. Outlet shops are so popular that they are becoming tourist destinations listed in many American guidebooks.

Franchises: Pay a fee plus royalty on all sales for the right to operate a store with an established brand name. The franchiser (parent company) provides the merchandise, advertising material, plus training. Customers often think that a franchise is a chain store. Examples of franchised stores include Benetton and Polo Ralph Lauren.

Leased Departments: Sections of a large, retail store that are leased, merchandised and operated by outside organizations. These outside organizations usually own the merchandise, pay the staff and pay their own advertising. They agree to abide by host store rules, regulations and usually pay a percentage of sales to the department store.

Off- Price Retailer: Sells branded goods or designer label merchandise at lower than normal retail prices when they are past the new or early peak of the fashion cycle. Loehmann's, TJ Maxx, and Marshalls are good examples of successful, off-price retailers in the U.S.

Open to Buy: The retail dollars that the buyer is permitted to spend for merchandise inventory within a certain time period based on a plan. This will avoid having too much stock, which would ultimately end up on the mark down rack. Conversely, it will also avoid under-stocking, which would lead to out-of stock conditions and loss of sales.

Sole Proprietor: Owned retail stores are usually small specialty stores. Owned and managed by the proprietor with an assistant. Once the owner expands to own a few stores they would then become chain store owners.

Specialty Stores: Targets a specific customer with a limited line of merchandise. The GAP, Ann Taylor, and Abercrombie & Fitch, are examples of leading major specialty stores with central buying and distribution. The smaller specialty storeowner may lack the sophistication of these big retailers, but they can offer consumers convenient locations, more personalized service, warmer atmosphere and, often a broader selection of merchandise.

Catalog Retailers/ Mail Order: *See Chapter 15 Mail Order Selling*
Internet Shopping & T.V. Home Shopping: *See Chapter 16 Selling on the Internet*

"In all human affairs there are efforts, and there are results, and the strength of the effort is the measure of the result. Chance is not: "Gifts," powers, material, intellectual, and spiritual possessions are the fruits of effort; they are thoughts completed, objects accomplished, visions realized.

The Vision that you glorify in your mind, the ideal that you enthrone in your heart – this you will build your life by, this you will become." *James Allen*

Appendices

&

References

Example of a Gerber Technology Spec Pack

Concept — A02W101J — **Latitude360**

Womenswear	Style	Description — Blazer w/ Hidden Closure
360	A02W101J	R.Marin
Spring I 2002	Designer — Kiyomi Suzuki	
	Pattern Maker	
	Fabric Content 1 — F1003 95% Wool/ 5% Lycra	

AML Measurement Specification Worksheet

Approved
Created: 01 Jun 01 07:21 AM
Modified: 12 Apr 04 12:06 PM

mission active

Company: Latitude
Product Type: Apron
Sample Size: M
Size Class: Missy
Approval Status: Neither approved nor rejected
Approval Note:
UOM: Imperial(in)
Shown As: Graded

Selected Range: S, M, L, XL

POM	Description	Tol (-)	Tol (+)	S	[M]	L	XL
106	Front Length HPS- Waist	-2	1	16 3/8	16 1/2		16 5/8
106A	Front Length HPS- Hip	-2	1	36 3/4	37		37 1/4
113	Across Shoulder	-2		16 1/4	16 1/2		16 3/4
115	Across Back- 5" HPS	-1/4	1/4	15 1/2	15 3/4		16
118	Across Chest- 5" HPS	-1/4	1/4	15 1/4	15 1/2		15 3/4
142	Sleeve Length CB Neck- L/S	-1/2	1/2	32 1/8	32 1/2		32 7/8
147	Front Neck Drop HPS	-1/8	1/8	10 3/8	10 1/2		10 5/8
148	Back Neck Drop HPS	-1/8	1/8	1/2	1/2		1/2
150	Neck Width	-1/4	1/4	5 7/8	6		6 1/8
219	Bust/ Chest- 1" Below Armhole	-1/2	1/2	38	39		40
220	Waist Relaxed	-1/2	1/2	35	36		37
223	High Hip	-1/2	1/2	38	39		40
227	Sweep	-1/2	1/2	40	41		42
230	Armhole Circumfrence	-1/4	1/4	19 1/2	20		20 1/2
233	Upper Arm	-1/4	1/4	17 3/4	18		18 1/4
236	Cuff Opening Relaxed- L/S	-1/8	1/8	10 7/8	11		11 1/8
302	Collar Height	-1/4	1/4	2	2		2
302B	Collar Point	-1/4	1/4	1 1/4	1 1/4		1 1/4

Printed: 12 APR 04 12:09 PM PST
2. WARPAML.prtWorkSheet (M: 4.1.24, P: 4.1.24)

268

Example of a Gerber Technology Spec Pack

Concept							Latitude360

A02W101J

AML Measurement Specification Worksheet

Womenswear	Style	A02W101J	Description	Blazer w/ Hidden Closure
360	Designer	R.Marin		
Spring I 2002	Pattern Maker	Kiyomi Suzuki	Approved	
	Fabric Content 1	F1003 95% Wool/ 5% Lycra	Created	01 Jun 01 07:21 AM
			Modified	12 Apr 04 12:06 PM

POM	Description	Tol (-)	Tol (+)	S	[M]	L	XL
302C	Lapel Width	-1/4	1/4	2 3/4	2 3/4		2 3/4
303	Shoulder Pad Length	-1/4	1/4	5 1/2	5 1/2		5 1/2
303B	Shoulder Pad Width	-1/4	1/4	10	10		10
303C	Shoulder Pad	-1/4	1/4	1/4	1/4		1/4
303D	Shoulder Pad Placement	-1/4	1/4	1 1/2	1 1/2		1 1/2
*	Test POM	-1/4	1/4	10	9		10

Printed: 12 APR 04 12:09 PM PST
2 WARP AML.rptWorkSheet (W: 4.124, P: 4.124)

Example of a Gerber Technology Spec Pack

Concept	A02W101J		Latitude360
	Design and Cost Specification		

Womenswear	Style	Description	Blazer w/ Hidden Closure
360	Designer	R.Marin	
Spring I 2002	Pattern Maker	Kiyomi Suzuki	
	Fabric Content 1	F1003 95% Wool/ 5% Lycra	Approved
			Created 01 Jun 01 07:21 AM
			Modified 12 Apr 04 12:06 PM

Fit: Missy Color: / Combination:

Item/SubFor	Use	Vendor	Dist:	Dusk 1921	Kiwi 2168	Stucco 2896	Image
LP5035 Plain weave	Full lining	Mainzer Minton Co. Inc. / Mainzer / Taiwan		Canyon Sunset	Jojoba	Pebble	
Lining Materials				95.7488 57.68 YD	95.7488 57.68 YD	95.7488 57.68 YD	
LM5001 Medium weight	See Constructions	Acker & Jablow Textiles, / Acker / Indonesia		Bright White	Bright White	Bright White	
Lining Materials							
TB4000 2-hole horn button	Front	American Button Mfg. / Americanb / United States		DTM|32Lig ne	DTM|32Lig ne	DTM|32Lig ne	
Trim				0.4181 3.03 EA	0.4181 3.03 EA	0.4181 3.03 EA	
TB4000 2-hole horn button	Sleeve vent	American Button Mfg. / Americanb / United States		DTM|24Lig ne	DTM|24Lig ne	DTM|24Lig ne	
Trim				0.5575 4.04 EA	0.5575 4.04 EA	0.5575 4.04 EA	
TS4001 Raglan D-Shaped	Shoulder	Sterling Tex-Trim / Sterling / France		None	None	None	
Trim				0.4264 2.06 EA	0.4264 2.06 EA	0.4264 2.06 EA	
TS4010 Sleeve Head Roll (pre-gathered)	Shoulder seam	Apparel Shaping Textiles / Apparel / Guatemala		None	None	None	
Trim				0.3941 2.04 EA	0.3941 2.04 EA	0.3941 2.04 EA	

Printed: 12 APR 04 12:09 PM PST
5. MAR/PSCA.Report (W: 4.1.24) P:[4.1.24]

Example of a Gerber Technology Spec Pack

Latitude360

A02W101J
Design and Cost Specification

Concept				
Womenswear	Style	A02W101J	Description	Blazer w/ Hidden Closure
360	Designer	R.Marin		
Spring I 2002	Pattern Maker	Kiyomi Suzuki	Approved	
	Fabric Content 1	F1003 95% Wool/ 5% Lycra	Created	01 Jun 01 07:21 AM
			Modified	12 Apr 04 12:06 PM

Fit: Missy

Color: **Combination:**

Item/SubFor	CS	Use	Vendor	Dist:	Dusk	Kiwi	Stucco	Image
					1921	2168	2896	
TH2100 T-18 Spun Polyester Core w/Cotton Cover	CS	Core	Horne & Weiss Horne		Apricot	Jungle Green	Almond Oil	
Trim								
LP1059 Hanger Guard Sizes 8"- 19"		Hanger ends	All World Trading & Import All Italy		None 0.1882 2.1 EA	None 0.1882 2.1 EA	None 0.1882 2.1 EA	
Labeling and Packaging								
LP1081 2 Gauge 9 x 24		Over jacket shoulders	Aikahn Labels Aikahn United States		None 0.09 1.03 EA	None 0.09 1.03 EA	None 0.09 1.03 EA	
Labeling and Packaging								

Example of Specification Sheet

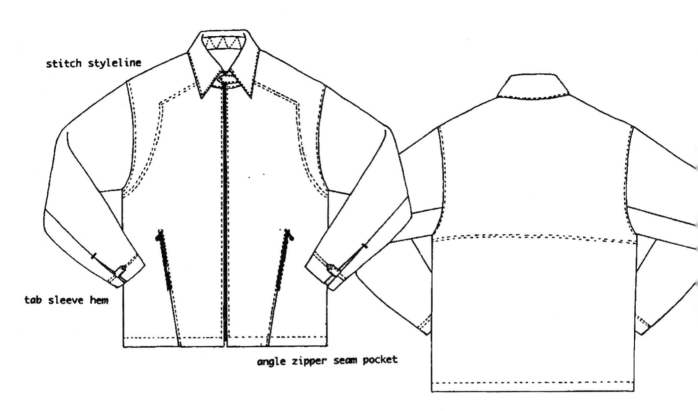

stitch styleline

tab sleeve hem

angle zipper seam pocket

Shirtjacket Style #102
Wholesale Price: $40-45
Fabric: Lt. Weight Wool-Lycra & Flight Satin
Color: Lt. Weight Wool-Lycra comes in Jet Black &
        Millennium Taupe
        Flight Satin- Jet Black

Example of Specification Sheet

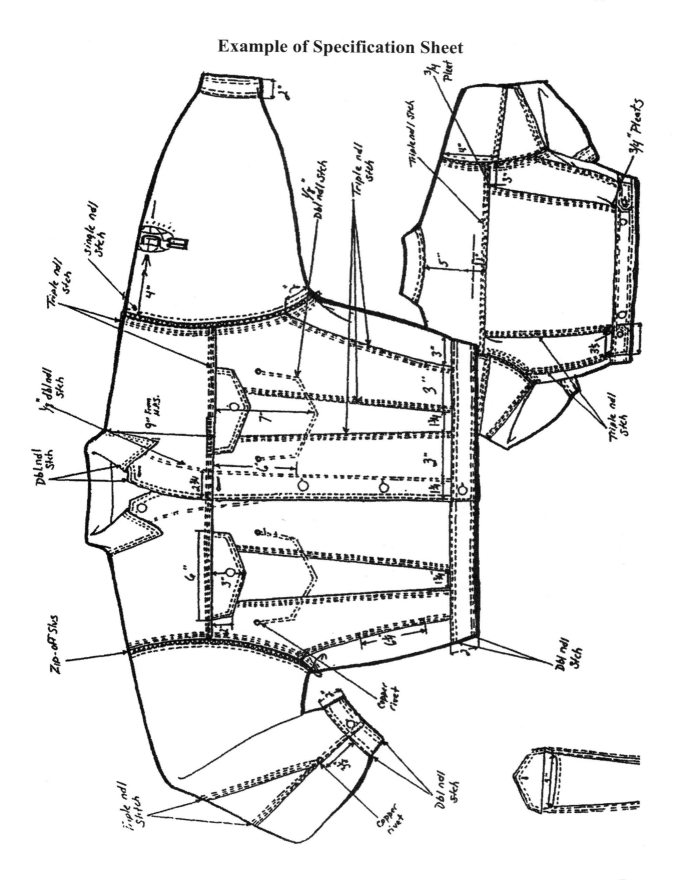

Blank Specification Sheet

Style:

Season:

Fabric / Group:

Gauge / Yarn Cnt: Size

Fit Model: Treatment   Trim

Factory:

Sample Spec Sheet		Spec Measurements / Inches				
Fitting Notes:	A	Waist (relaxed				
	B	W / B Height				
	C	Stretched W / B				
	D	Low Hip (8" below w / b)				
	E	Thigh (1" below crotch)				
	F	Calf				
	G	Leg opening				
	H	Cuff Finish ht				
	I	Front Rise (below w / b)				
	J	Back Rise (below w / b)				
	K	Outseam				
	L	Inseam				
	M	Fly / Zip Length				
	N	Fly / Zip Width				
	O	Pocket Length				
	P	Pocket Width				
	Q					
	R					
	S					
	T					
	U					
	V					
	W					
	X					
	Y					
	Z					

Waist / Elastic Finish:

Cuff Finish

☐ **Correct Pattern**   ☐ **Approved**

Blank Specification Sheet

STYLE: **DATE:**

Description

	SPECIFICATIONS FOR FINISHED GARMENTS	S	M	L
A	BODY LENGTH FM HPS			
B	CHEST 1' BELOW ARMHOLE			
C	SHOULDER- TO SHOULDER			
D	SHOULDER SLOPE			
E	BOTTOM			
F	NECK WIDTH BACK – SEAM TO SEAM			
G	BACK NECK DROP FM IMAG LINE TO SEAM			
H	FRONT NECK DROP FM IMAG LINE TO SEAM			
I	SLEEVE LENGTH FM SHOULDER			
J	ARMHOLE STRAIGHT			
K	WIDTH 1" BELOW ARMHOLE			
L	6" FM CUFF			
M	CUFF OPENING			
N	NECK FINISH / HEIGHT			
O	BOTTOM FINISH / HEIGHT			
P	CUFF FINISH / HEIGHT			
Q				
R				
S				
T				
U				
V				
W				
X				
Y				
Z				

Example of Line Sheet

Style #ap 2379
zip up frt jkt w/ stch detail
content: calf suede
color: taupe
price: $186.00

Style #ap 1056
asymmetrical sheered sleeveless
 top
content: silk matte jersey
color: beige
price: $90.00

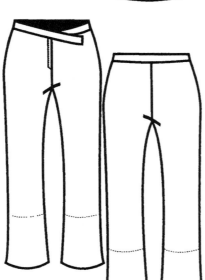

Style #ap 7688
asymmetrical frt fly cropped
 beaded pants
content: poly/silk jacquard
color: taupe/mint
price: $675.00

Example of Line Sheet (Continued)

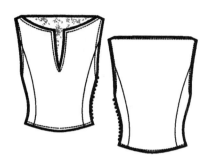

Style #ap 1053
beaded bodice w/ btn down side
content: poly/silk jacquard
color: taupe/mint
price: $130.00

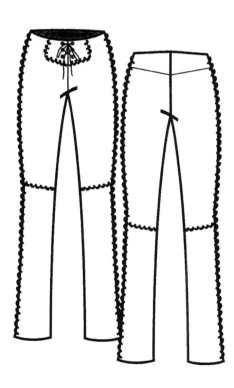

Style #ap 4098
lace up frt pant w whip stch
detailing
content: calf suede
color: taupe (tonal detailing)
price: $230.00

Example of Line Sheet (Continued)

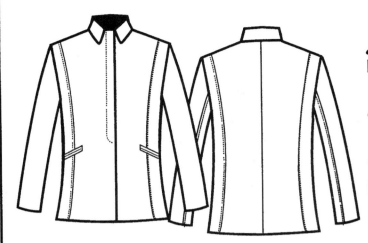

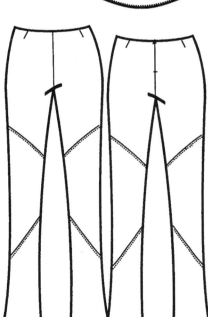

Style #ap 4600
btn down hidden placket frt
    closure fitted jkt
content: snake skin printed
        lamb suede
color: latte
price: $650.00

Style #ap 1745
bustier w/ raw edge & topstch
    detailing
content: calf suede
color: turquoise
price: $160.00

Style #ap 6512
asymmetrical seamed pant
    w/back zip
content: lamb suede
color: taupe
price: $345.00

Croquis

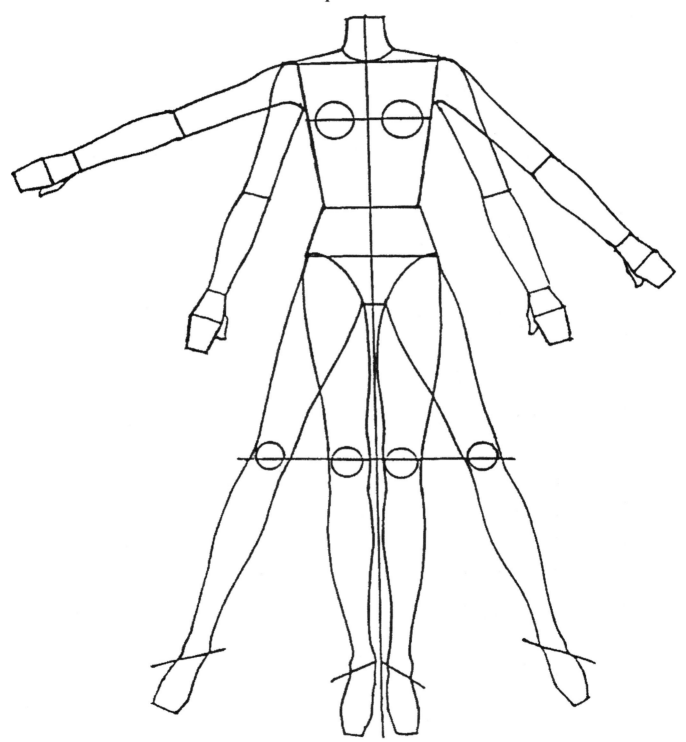

Croquis

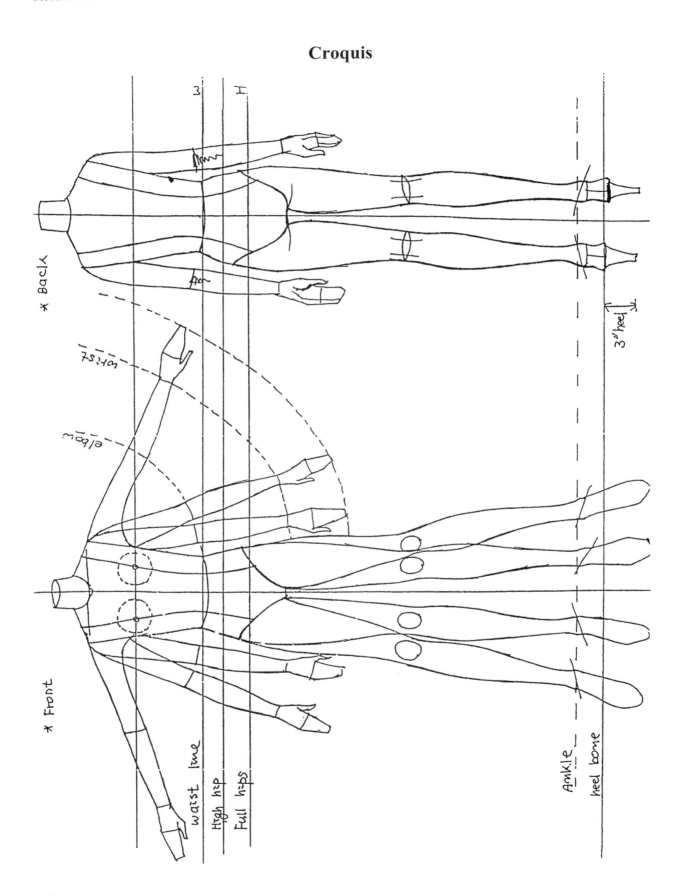

Child's Croquis

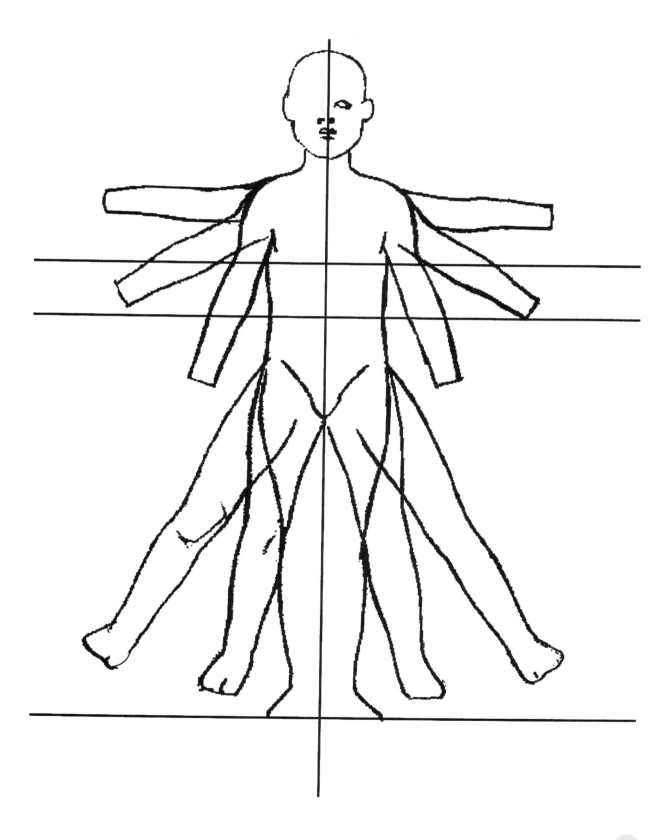

Example of a Marker

Example of a Nested Grade

Style #JA Size Graded 2 4 6 8 10 12 14 16 18 20 22

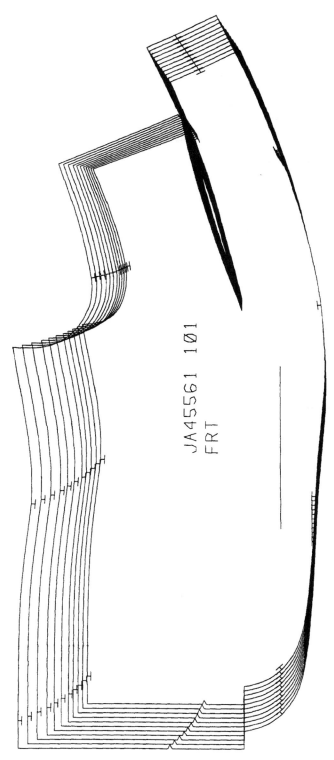

JA45561 101
FRT

Price List for Grading

Sample Marker		
Code	Quantity of Pattern Pieces	Price
SM-150	Per Pattern Piece	$1.00
SM-STD	Minimum Price	$20.00
SM-D	Marker Duplicate (Per Yard)	$1.50

Note: Above price is counted by total pieces in marker
* Over night / 24 hour turn around - Add $25 for each marker

Grading		
Code	Quantity of Pattern Pieces	Price
GR-150	Per Pattern Piece	$1.00
GR-STD	Minimum Price	$50.00

Note: If a pattern piece is cut (2) it is counted as (1) pattern piece
* Over night / 24 hour turn around - Add $25 for each graded pattern

Marking		
Code	Quantity of Pattern Pieces	Price
MM-150	Per Pattern Piece	$1.00
MM-STD	Minimum Price	$50.00
SM-D	Marker Duplicate (Per Yard)	$1.50

Note: Above price is counted by total pieces in marker
* Over night / 24 hour turn around - Add $25 for each marker

Price List for Patternmaking

First Patterns / Knock-offs		
Code	Quantity of Pattern Pieces	Price
FP1-4	1 - 4 Pattern Pieces	$70.00
FP5-10	5 - 10 Pattern Pieces	$100.00
FP11-15	11 - 15 Pattern Pieces	$130.00
FP16-20	16 - 20 Pattern Pieces	$160.00
FP21-25	21 - 25 Pattern Pieces	$190.00
FP26-30	26 - 30 Pattern Pieces	$220.00
FP31-35	31 - 35 Pattern Pieces	$250.00
FP36-40	36 - 40 Pattern Pieces	$280.00

Production Patterns & Revisions		
Code	Quantity of Pattern Pieces	Price
PP1-4	1 - 4 Pattern Pieces	$30.00
PP5-10	5 - 10 Pattern Pieces	$50.00
PP11-15	11 - 15 Pattern Pieces	$70.00
PP16-20	16 - 20 Pattern Pieces	$90.00
PP21-25	21 - 25 Pattern Pieces	$110.00
PP26-30	26 - 30 Pattern Pieces	$130.00
PP31-35	31 - 35 Pattern Pieces	$150.00
PP36-40	36 - 40 Pattern Pieces	$170.00

Note: If Pattern Piece is cut (2) it is counted as (1) Pattern Piece
*Overnight / 24 hour turn around – Add $25 for each pattern

Additional Pattern Copies on Hard paper		
Code	Quantity of Pattern Pieces	Price
PC1-4	1 - 4 Pattern Pieces	$10.00
PC5-10	5 - 10 Pattern Pieces	$20.00
PC11-15	11 - 15 Pattern Pieces	$30.00
PC16-20	16 - 20 Pattern Pieces	$40.00

Templates on Hard Paper		
Code	Quantity of Pattern Pieces	Price
T1-4	1 - 4 Pattern Pieces	$10.00
T5-10	5 - 10 Pattern Pieces	$20.00
T11-15	11 - 15 Pattern Pieces	$30.00
T16-20	16 - 20 Pattern Pieces	$40.00

Example of a Pattern Card

Company	Nelly's Uniforms		
Size Range	XS-XXL	Base Size	M
Rule Table			

Style Number		Date Created	Date Release
		July 28, 1999	
CA123		Date Revised	Approved By
		8/19/99	

Description: V-Neck button front vest with Badge Holder
Cargo pocket & Draw string pocket
Reference #:

Yield	44"	54"	58"	60"
Self				
Self				
Contrast 1				
Contrast 2				
Lining				
Pellon				

Qty	S/O	Piece Name		PN	PC
		Self			
2		Front		1	FT
1		Back		2	BK
1		Back Yoke		3	SLV
1		Right Pocket	RSU	4	RPK
2		Left Pocket	RSU	5	LPK
1		Badge Holder		6	BAH
		Template			
1		Badge Holder Template		7	BAHT
1		Back Template		8	BKT
1		Button Placement	RSU	9	BT
1		Button Hole Placement	RSU	10	BHT
1		Right Pocket Template	RSU	11	RPKT
1		Left Pocket Template	RSU	12	LPKT

Send Out	Fab	Qty	Width	Long	Total	Fin Width	For
S/O	Self	1	1 1/2	24 00	24 00	3/8	Neck Bias
S/O	Self	2	1 1/2	27 00	54 00	3/8	Armhole Bias
S/O	Cord	2	1/4	14 00	28 00	1/4	Draw Cords
S/O	Pel		1 1/4	24	48 00	1 1/4	Front Facing Pellon

Specs	Tol	XS	S	M	L	XL	XXL	
Bust	+ / - 1	41	43	45	48	51	54	
Waist	+ / - 1	0	0	0	0	0	0	
Sweep	+ / - 1	42	44	46	49	52	55	
CB Length	+ / - 1/2	25 3/4	26 1/4	26 3/4	27 1/4	27 3/4	28 1/4	
Armhole	+ / - 1/4	24 3/4	25	25 1/4	25 1/2	25 3/4	26	
	+ / - 1/4							

Trim	Qty	Size	Trim	Qty	S
BTN #1	4	23L	Appliqué #1		
Cord Lock	1	O/S	Appliqué #2		
Sock Cuffs					
Snaps			Rosette		
Twill Tape (cut 2)					
Zipper					
Belt					
Suspenders			Sho Pad	PR	
			Hang Tape		
Silk Screen			Hanger	1	
Embroidery			Label	1	
Embellish					

Pattern Card Blank

Company	
Size Range	Base Size
Rule Table	

Style Number		Date Created	Date Released
		Date Revised	Approved By

Description:

Reference #:

Yield	44"	54"	58"	60"
Self				
Self				
Contrast 1				
Contrast 2				
Lining				
Pellon				

Qty	S/O	Piece Name	PN	PC
		Self		
		Template		

Send Out	Fab	Qty	Width	Long	Total	Fin Width	For

Specs	Tol	XS	S	M	L	XL	XXL	
Bust	+ / - 1							
Waist	+ / - 1							
Sweep	+ / - 1							
CB Length	+ / - 1/2							
Armhole	+ / - 1/4							
	+ / - 1/4							

Trim	Qty	Size	Trim	Qty	Size
BTN #1			Appliqué #1		
Cord Lock			Appliqué #2		
Sock Cuffs					
Snaps			Rosette		
Twill Tape (cut 2)					
Zipper					
Belt					
Suspenders			Sho Pad		
			Hang Tape		
Silk Screen			Hanger		
Embroidery			Label		
Embellish					

Example of Contractor & Sub-Contractor Information

Contractors Name:_____

Address:_____

_____

_____

Phone:_____Fax:_____e-mail_____

Owners Name:_____

State Registration No:_____Exp. Date:_____

City Business Tax No:_____Exp. Date:_____

Federal Employer ID No:_____

Workers Compensation Insurance Company Name:_____

Policy No:_____Exp. Date:_____

Address:_____

_____

_____

Building Owners Name & Address:_____

_____

_____

Page 1

Wages/Reporting/Records/Overtime

Please check the appropriate answer below:

1) Employees are paid by the: hour_____ piece_____

2) Time cards are filled in: manually_____ time clock_____ computerized_____

3) All employees punch in and out for lunch: yes_____ no_____

4) Do you employ any minors (age 17 and under): yes_____ no_____

5) Do you have work permits for all minors who are on the premises: yes_____ no_____

6) Do you have accurate employee records which include all of the following:

   Name, address, occupation, social security number, birth dates, and the proper identity documents (l-9 form) yes_____ no_____

7) Employee payroll accounting is done on the premises: yes_____ no_____

If the answer is no, please supply the name, address and phone number of the service that you use:_____

_____

_____

8) Payroll records are in English and kept on the premises: yes_____ no_____

9) Paychecks always include a receipt listing all deductions made: yes____ no_____

10) All state and federal regulations regarding wages, hours and working conditions (including overtime wages) are practiced and adhered to: yes_____ no_____

Page 2

POSTINGS FOR EMPLOYEE'S BENEFIT

Please check the appropriate answer below regarding the posting (in a visible location) of the following:

1) Fair Labor Standards Act: yes_____ no_____
2) State Industrial Welfare Commission Order No: yes_____ no____
3) OSHA Accident Prevention: yes_____ no_____
4) Federal and state Equal Employment Rights and Protection: yes_____ no____
5) Employment Development Department (EDD) Unemployment & Disability Insurance Notice: yes_____ no_____
6) State Registration Certificate: yes_____ no____
7) Business Tax Registration: yes_____ no_____
8) Worker's Compensation Insurance Policy Notice: yes_____ no_____
9) Illness & Injury Prevention Program: yes_____ no_____
10) State Sexual Harassment Poster: yes_____ no_____
11) Payday/Minimum Wage notice: yes_____ no_____
12) The above posters have a bilingual translation that all employees on the premises can read and understand: yes_____ no_____

POLICY

Please check the appropriate answer to the following:

1) The contractor regularly maintains an accident prevention and emergency training program: yes_____ no____
2) Employees and/or owners allow minors on the premises (i.e., preschool children that do not work in the factory): yes_____ no_____
3) Employer provides rest areas: yes____ no____
4) Meals and lodging are sometimes credited against the minimum wage paid to employees: yes_____ no_____
5) If the answer to #4 above is yes, are the employees notified in advance: yes_____ no_____
6) All cutting, sewing, and trimming is done at the business address: yes____ no_____

FORM COMPLETED BY:_____ **DATE:**_____

(Print name of Production Manager)

Page 3

The undersigned affirms that the foregoing information is true. The contractor acknowledges that any false information supplied is a breach of contract. The Contractor also acknowledges that subcontracting and/or the removal of any of the Company's property from the factory premises is a breach of contract. The company reserves the right to pursue any legal avenues available to prosecute to the fullest extent of the law.

Information supplied by:_____

(Print name of Contractor/Owner)

Signed by:_____ Date:_____

Page 4

Example of a Sewing Contractor's Agreement

```
AIMS HOTLINE                                    PAGE:        1
1633 E. 4TH STREET                              DATE:    05/20/2001
SUITE 260
SANTA ANA, CA  92701-5144
TEL:   (310) 556-2215                           CUT:  600101
FAX:  (714) 973-0907
```

```
        CUTTI                              TEL:   213-629-5768
        CUTTING R US                       FAX:   213-629-2265
        112 W. 9TH STREET
        SUITE 1030
        LOS ANGELES, CA  90015          CONTACT:  MARVIN
```

CONTRACT AGREEMENT

```
Price we will pay to you for each completed garment ....................        $0.25
Charge back rate you will pay for loss and damage you cause ............        $0.00
All work must be completed and garments returned to us on or before .....    05/25/2001

            TYPE OF WORK PERFORMED:     CUTTING

Comments:     CUT ONLY ORDERE
```

STYLE/ COLOR	GARMENT/COLOR DESCRIPTION	SIZE BREAKDOWNS					TOTAL
2950	DRESS	(1)	S	M	L	XL	
BLACK	BLACK	(1)	10	20	20	10	60
2950	DRESS	(1)	S	M	L	XL	
BLUE	BLUE	(1)	5	10	10	5	30
2950	DRESS	(1)	S	M	L	XL	
RED	RED	(1)	5	10	10	5	30
2950	DRESS	(1)	S	M	L	XL	
WHITE	WHITE	(1)	5	10	10	5	30
	TOTAL GARMENTS	(1)	25	50	50	25	150

**My signature below indicates that I have read and agree to all the terms and conditions
of the STANDARD SERVICES AGREEMENT of   AIMS HOTLINE.**

_____   _____

Contractor Authorized Signature   Date

07/10/2001   23:31:34

Example of a Cost Sheet

STYLE COST SHEET

Style: **2950**   DRESS

Color: **BLACK**   BLACK

_____ **Available Sizes** _____

S   M   L   XL

Item	Color	Size	Description	......COLOR......	Job Code	UOM	Quantity Required	Unit Cost	Total $Cost
CT-001	BLACK	S	100% COTTON 10oz	BLACK			3.500	3.000	10.500
								*Subtotal	10.500
CARE01	A/S	S	100% COTTON CARE LBL	AS SAMPLE		EACH	1.000	0.020	0.020
HANGR1	WHITE	S	PLASTIC HANGER 17"	WHITE		EACH	1.000	0.040	0.040
HNGTG1	A/S	S	HANGTAG	AS SAMPLE		EACH	1.000	0.050	0.050
MAIN01	A/S	S	FVM WOVEN LABEL	AS SAMPLE		EACH	1.000	0.100	0.100
PLAS01	A/S	S	PLASTIC BAG	AS SAMPLE		EACH	1.000	0.020	0.020
								*Subtotal	0.230
LABOR		*	CUTTING	CUTTING	(CU)			0.250	0.250
LABOR		*	GRADING/MARKING	GRADING/MARKING	(GM)			0.750	0.750
LABOR		*	OVERHEAD	OVERHEAD	(OH)			0.500	0.500
LABOR		*	PRESSING	PRESSING	(PR)			0.500	0.500
LABOR		*	SEWING	SEWING	(SE)			7.500	7.500
								*Subtotal	9.500

Style: 2950-BLACK	DRESS	Sell 40.00	Markup% 48.78	$Profit 19.77	Fabric 10.50	Trim 0.23	Labor 9.50	Total 20.23

Manufacturing Notes:

1. (3) THREAD OVERLOCK ALL SEAMS
2. POLY COTTON THREAD TO MATCH
3. CENTER BACK NECK LABEL
4. 1" COVER STITCH SLEEVES AND BOTTOM HEM
5. 3/8" COVERSTITCH AROUND NECKLINE W/CLEAR PLASTIC TAPE
6. SHOULDER TAPE W/OVERLOCK.
   CUT SIZES: S=4 3/4", M=5 1/4", L=5 3/4" AND XL=6"
7. NATURAL SHELL BUTTONS: MAKES SURE SEWN ON TIGHT.

Example of Cost Sheet

Design: 7485 Sub-Design: 1   **Line:**

Section: FABRIC

S Fabric	Description	Item Used for	Qty Req'd	Price/ Unit	Variable Cost
1 F100	STRINGTWILL		2.030	10.450	21.2140
1 ZTAF	ACETATE TAFFETA		.280	1.150	.3220
					21.536

Section: TRIM

S Trim

1 BTN	BUTTON 30L	BUTTON J3108	3.000	.070	.2100
					.2100

Miscellaneous Costs:

Description	ID/ Item #	Item Type	Calc Factor		
Trim Allowance	TRMALL	Calc	10.000	.0210	.0210

Section: SENDOUT
Process Description

				Add-On	UOM		
10	BLOCK Fusing Labor	U	LB	.64	1.000	.6400
20	PIECE FUSING LABOR	U	LB	.05	1.000	.0500

Section: LABOR
Process Description

10	Cutting	U	LB	2.00	1.000	2.0000
20	Sewing Labor	U	LB	25.00	1.000	25.0000
30	Misc	U	MI	1.00	1.000	1.0000

Section: MISCELLANEOUS

Selling Price, Net Profit & Marginal Income Analysis

Wholesale Price: $112.127	Gross Margin %: 55.000	Net Margin %: 55.000
Total Cost: $50.457	Total Gross Cost: $50.457	Total Net Cost: $50.457

Budget Cost Sheet

ORIGINAL DATE : 10/04/99
REVISIOIN DATE :10/04/99
SEASON : 1 - SPRING
MARKER :
PATTERN : 1ST
THREAD :

STYLE #   : J2204HP
DESCRIPTION   : 20" SKIRT SIDE SLITS

SIZE RANGE   : S-XL
GROUP   : MICRFIBER PRT

MARKER YARDAGE		SAMPLE ESTIMATES				COLOR COMBINATIONS				
# 1. Materials (Including Freight)	Shrink	Width	Yards	Price	Amount	Colors	Colors	Colors	Colors	Colors
MRP MICROFIBER PRINT	56		0.540	4.90	2.646	TUR	ORG	BRN	PLM	GRN

TOTAL MATERIAL COST ----- ------ 2.646

# 2. TRIMS	Shrink	Qty	Units	Price	Amount	Colors	Colors	Colors	Colors	Colors
TRO5 1/3" ELASTIC		0.780	Yards	0.09	0.070	BLK	WHT	BLK	BLK	BLK

TOTAL TRIMS COST-------- ------ 0.070

4. MISCELLANEOUS	Amount
8% Material Allowance	0.210
10% Trim Allowance	0.010
LABELS, TICKETS, HANGTAGS	0.650

TOTAL MISCELLANEOUS COST---- --------- ------ 0.870

5. LABOR	Amount
Sewing	1.350
Cutting	0.200

TOTAL LABOR COST ----------- --------- ------ 1.550

$5.140

Style	Total Cost	8/10 Sell	Net Sell	8/10 Margin	Net Margin
J2204MP	5.14	10.75	9.89	52.2%	48.1%

Cost Sheet

STYLE #   Generation: Size Category: Size Range:
SEASON: Description:

COMPONENT COSTS:	Yds/Qty	Unit Prc	$ Amt	Front Sketch
Fabrics: Shell				
Lining:				
Other:				
(TOTAL FABRICS)				
Trims: (use back for additional)				
(TOTAL TRIMS)				
CMT COSTS:				
Grading:				
Marking:				Back Sketch
Cutting:				
Make Charges:				
Wash/Type				
Press/Trim				
QE/Bag & Tag				
(TOTAL LABOR)				
PACKING MATERIALS:				
Tissue				
Polybag				
Inner Box				**Comments:**
Outer Box				SEAMS:
(TOTAL PACKING)				
(TOTAL COST):				
WHOLESALE PRICE				
WHOLESALE MARGIN				
RETAIL PRICE				

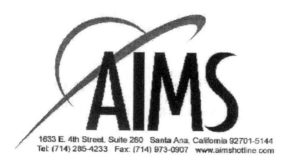

1633 E. 4th Street. Suite 260   Santa Ana, California 92701-5144
Tel: (714) 285-4233   Fax: (714) 973-0907   www.aimshotline.com

Purchase Order

PO Number	Date
50101	**02/08/2004**

Page   1

ECLAT of Universal Channel Inc
250 N.PUENTE AVE

CITY INDUSTRY, CA 91746

Ship To:

AIMS
1633 E. 4TH STREET
SUITE 260
SANTA ANA, CA 92701

Terms	ShipVia	F.O.B.	XCountry/Start	Cancel Date	
NET 30	COMPANY TRUCK	WAREHOUSE		02/29/2004	

Account	Reference	Origin	Confirmation	Vendor Phone / Fax	
	600102			626-961-9889	

Item	Quantity Pattern	Width		Price	Total
CALT01	CALAIS TWILL				
BLACK BLACK	300	58/60	YARD	3.750	1125.000
ORDER TOTAL	300			$	1,125.00

1633 E Fourth St #260
Santa Ana, CA 92701
(310) 556-2215

www.aimshotline.com

ORDER CONFIRMATION

Page   1

Bill To:

FRED SEGAL
8100 MELROSE AVE
LOS ANGELES CA 90046

Ship To:

FRED SEGAL
8100 MELROSE AVE
LOS ANGELES CA 90046

Buyer: RON HERMAN   TEL 323-653-2221   FAX 323-653-2225   Spring   Men

Account	P/O Number	Store No.	Dept	Bulk	Start	Complete	Order	Vendor	Factor
FRE01	LA-1001				03/01/2004	03/30/2004	100101		CITGR

Terms	Ship Via		Special		Dist	Salesrep	Approval
NET 30	UPS Ground		SHIP W/PACKSLIP		100101	001	CIT-9007

Style	Description	S	M	L				Color		Pieces	Price	Total
2905	V-NECK L/S SAILOR			L				WHITE	WHITE	120	$54.00	$6480.00
2906	MOCK TURTLE NECK	S						BLACK	BLACK	60	$59.00	$3540.00
2910	CAPRI PANT	2	4	6	8	10	12	14 BLACK	BLACK	60	$59.00	$3540.00
2914	DRESS	S	M	L				BLUE	BLUE	60	$72.00	$4320.00
2917	V-NECK TANK	S						PINK	PINK	80	$42.00	$3360.00

ORDER TOTAL   380   21,240.00

GRAND TOTAL $ 21,240.00

Authorized Signature   Title   Date

02/10/2004

Invoice Example

1633 E. 4th Street, Suite 260   Santa Ana, California 92701-5144
Tel: (714) 265-4233   Fax: (714) 973-0907   www.aimshotline.com

Page:	1
Invoice	**Date**
200101	**05/21/2001**

This receivable is assigned to, owned by and payable only to: HSBC Business Credit (USA) Inc. P.O. Box 7777-W8720, Philadelphia, PA 19175 or Dept 49941 Los Angeles, CA 90088, whichever is nearer. Any objection to this invoice must be reported to HSBC Business Credit (USA) Inc. at 452 Fifth Avenue, 4th Fl., New York, NY 10018. RF 0009

Bill To:

HENRY'S BOUTIQUE
1540 CARDIFF AVE
LOS ANGELES CA 90035

Ship to:

HENRY'S BOUTIQUE
1540 CARDIFF AVE
LOS ANGELES CA 90035

Acct	Purchase Order	Dept.	Terms	Rep1	Rep2	Ship Via	Order	Apprvl
HEN00	HC-1001		NET 30	002		UPS Ground	100102	

	(1)	S	M	L	XL		Total Units	Price	Total Amt.
2958		(WHITE)	Dress White				6	42.00	252.00
	(1)	1	2	2	1				
						Merchandise	6		252.00
						Freight			4.38

PLEASE CHECK IMMEDIATELY. ALL CLAIMS MUST BE MADE WITHIN 5 DAYS OF RECEIPT OF GOODS. NO RETURNS WITHOUT PRIOR WRITTEN AUTHORIZATION. NO RETURNS WILL BE ALLOWED WITHOUT RA NUMBER AND/OR LABEL. PAYMENT SUBJECT TO TERMS ON INVOICE.

Due Date: **06/19/2001**

Pick Ticket	Ship Date	No. Ctns.	Weight	Start	Complete	Invoice	Pay This Amt.	
000001	05/21/2001	1	6	05/20/2001	05/21/2001	200101		**$256.38**

Customer Copy   Page: 1

CUTTING TICKET

PAGE: 1

AIMS HOTLINE
1633 E. 4TH STREET
SUITE 260
SANTA ANA, CA 92701-5144
TEL: (310) 556-2215
FAX: (714) 973-0907

CUT NUMBER	600101
START DATE	05/20/2001
IN WAREHOUSE	06/22/2001

USE THIS AREA FOR NOTES SPECIFIC TO THE CUT.

2950	DRESS	S	M	L	XL	TOTAL
BLACK	BLACK	10	20	20	10	60
BLUE	BLUE	5	10	10	5	30
RED	RED	5	10	10	5	30
WHITE	WHITE	5	10	10	5	30
Total Garments		25	50	50	25	150

CUTTING TICKET BILL OF MATERIALS

PAGE: 1

AIMS HOTLINE
1633 E. 4TH STREET
SUITE 260
TEL:TA ANA, CA 92701-5144
FAX: (310) 556-2215
          (714) 973-0907

Cut Number	600101
Started	05/20/2001
In Warehouse	06/22/2001

ITEM-CODE		DESCRIPTION	WIDTH	DYELOT	ISSUED	CONSUMED	RETURNED
CARE01	A/S	100% COTTON CARE LBL	1 x 1	_____	150	_____	_____
CT-001	BLACK	100% RAYON	44/45	_____	210	_____	_____
CT-001	BLUE	100% RAYON	44/45	_____	105	_____	_____
CT-001	RED	100% RAYON	44/45	_____	105	_____	_____
CT-001	WHITE	100% RAYON	44/45	_____	105	_____	_____
HANGR1	WHITE	PLASTIC HANGER 17"	17"	_____	150	_____	_____
HNGTG1	A/S	HANGTAG	2x4	_____	150	_____	_____
MAIN01	A/S	FVM WOVEN LABEL	1x2	_____	150	_____	_____
PLAS01	A/S	PLASTIC BAG	45"L	_____	150	_____	_____

1633 E Fourth St #260
Santa Ana, CA 92701
(310) 556-2215

www.aimshotline.com

Ship To:

PICKING TICKET

PICK TICKET	DATE
800101-4	02/07/2004

FRED SEGAL
8100 MELROSE AVE
LOS ANGELES CA 90046

Page   1

		Season	Division
		Spring	Men

Account	Store No.	Dept	P/O Number	Order	Start	Complete	Terms	Ship Via	Salesrep		Approval
FRE01			LA-1001	100101	03/01/2004	03/30/2004	NET 30	UPS Ground	001		CIT-9007

STYLE		DESCRIPTION		S	M	L			PIECES	PRICE	TOTAL
2905		V-NECK L/S SAILOR									
WHITE	WHITE		Picked	2	2	2			6		
									WIP 600102		
			Ordered	20	60	40			120		
			Pick								
2906		MOCK TURTLE NECK		S	M	L					
BLACK	BLACK		Picked	2	2	2			6		
									WIP 600104		
			Ordered	10	30	20			60		
			Pick								
2914		DRESS		S	M	L					
BLUE	BLUE		Picked	2	2	2			6		
									WIP 600101		
			Ordered	10	30	20			60		
			Pick								
						PICKING TICKET TOTAL			18		0.00

Cartons	Weight	Packed By	

1633 E Fourth St #260
Santa Ana, CA 92701
(310) 556-2215

www.aimshotline.com

Invoice	Date
200101	02/07/2004

Please remit payment to:
THE CIT GROUP
COMMERCIAL SERVICES, INC.
P.O. BOX 1036,
CHARLOTTE NC 28201-1036

Ship To:

FRED SEGAL
8100 MELROSE AVE
LOS ANGELES CA 90046

Packing Slip

Acct	Purchase Order	Dept.	Terms	Rep1	Rep2	Ship Via	Order	Apprvl
FRE01	FS-5601		NET 30	001		UPS Ground	100107	

Phone 323-653-2221   Vendor

Style	Description								Total Units	Price	Total Amt.
	S	M	L						12	0.00	0.00
2905	(WHITE) V-neck L/s Sailor White										
	2	6	4								
	S	M	L						12	0.00	0.00
2914	(BLUE) Dress Blue										
	2	6	4								
	2	4	6	8	10	12	14		12	0.00	0.00
2920	(BLACK) Loose Capri Black										
	1	2	2	3	2	1	1				
							Merchandise		36		0.00

Due Date: 03/08/2004

Pick Ticket	Ship Date	No. Ctns.	Weight	Start	Complete	Invoice	Pay This Amt.
	02/07/2004	1	36	02/12/2004	02/15/2004	200101	0.00

Customer Copy   Page: 1

AIMS DEMO
Potential Commission Report
SALESREP COMMISSION POTENTIAL REPORT
COMMISSIONS COMPUTED BY ORDER

** 000   HOUSE

1/2	Acct#	.....Customer.....	Style	Color	Pieces	Gross Booked	After Discounts	Expected Commission
1	HEN01	HENRY'S BOUTIQUE			18	1110.00	1110.00	0.00

000	HOUSE					1110.00	1110.00	0.00

** 001   FASHION BUSINESS INC

1/2	Acct#	.....Customer.....	Style	Color	Pieces	Gross Booked	After Discounts	Expected Commission
1	FRE01	FRED SEGAL			380	21240.00	21240.00	2124.00
1	HEN01	HENRY'S BOUTIQUE			168	9576.00	9576.00	957.60
1	TPN00	TORREY PINES CLUB			24	1476.00	1476.00	147.60

001	FASHION BUSINESS INC					32292.00	32292.00	3229.20

** 002   MR. TEE

1/2	Acct#	.....Customer.....	Style	Color	Pieces	Gross Booked	After Discounts	Expected Commission
1	HLC00	HILLCREST COUNTRY CLUB			66	4206.00	4206.00	420.60
1	PRG00	PRO GOLF			48	2808.00	2808.00	280.80
1	TMP00	TRUMP INTERNATIONAL GOLF			48	3144.00	3144.00	314.40

002	MR. TEE					10158.00	10158.00	1015.80

(*) Do not attempt to balance figures on this report to the open order reports
   because split commissions show booked amounts twice on this report.

Sample Credit Application with Proprietor Authorization/Proprietor Guaranty

This is a suggested sample and is not warranted in any way or for any specific purpose. You may determine whether the information contained here is appropriate for your needs.

Your Company Logo   Date _____

1. COMPANY INFORMATION

Full Legal Name/Business Entity		Phone Number	Fax Number	
Doing Business As (DBA)				
Billing Address (If different from above)		City	State	Zip
Company Type: ☐ Proprietorship ☐ Partnership ☐ Franchisee ☐ Corporation ☐ Other _____				

2. BUSINESS CREDIT INFORMATION

Federal Tax I.D. (if incorporated)	Principal business of firm	Year business established
At present location since	Is business incorporated?	If so, under laws of what state?
Credit line requested	Incorporated for $	

*Please list all branch/affiliate store operations on back of application

3. BANK REFERENCES

Bank Name		Account #		Contact	
Address		City	State	Zip	Phone
Bank Name		Account #		Contact	
Address		City	State	Zip	Phone
Bank Name		Account #		Contact	
Address		City	State	Zip	Phone

4. CREDIT REFERENCES

Company Name		Contact			
Address	City	State	Zip	Phone	
Company Name		Contact			
Address	City	State	Zip	Phone	
Company Name		Contact			
Address	City	State	Zip	Phone	

Page 1

Use either the *Proprietor Authorization* or the *Proprietor Guaranty* to authorize access to the consumer credit information of the business owner/proprietor. To determine whether you need authorization to access the personal credit information on the business owner, see "Do I need authorization to use TRW S*BAR* or TRW SBI?"

This is a suggested sample and is not warranted in any way or for any specific purpose. You may determine whether the information contained here is appropriate for your needs.

1. PROPRIETOR AUTHORIZATION

By signing this Application, I authorize (your company) or its agent to investigate my personal credit and financial records including my banking records. As part of such investigation, I authorize (your company) to request and obtain consumer credit reports on me in connection with the opening, monitoring, renewal and extension of this and other accounts with (your company) and the marketing of other products and services to me and my business by (your company). I further authorize (your company) to share the information received from my consumer credit report with (your company's) parent, subsidiaries, and affiliates [and others if applicable]. If I request, you will tell me whether my consumer credit report was requested and, if so, the name and address of the consumer credit reporting agency that furnished the report.

First Name	Initial	Last Name	Social Security Number
Present Home Address			Home Phone Number
City		State	Zip
Authorized Signature			Date

(If you wish to inquire upon multiple owners, you must have authorized access for each individual)

First Name	Initial	Last Name	Social Security Number
Present Home Address			Home Phone Number
City		State	Zip
Authorized Signature			Date

2. PROPRIETOR GUARANTY

By signing this Application, I acknowledge that I have personally guaranteed the debts and obligations of my business and agree that I am personally obligated to perform all of the terms of, and make all payments to (your company) required by, the agreement of which this Application is a part.

First Name	Initial	Last Name	Social Security Number
Present Home Address			Home Phone Number
City		State	Zip
Authorized Signature			Date

(If you wish to inquire upon multiple owners, you must have authorized access for each individual)

First Name	Initial	Last Name	Social Security Number
Present Home Address			Home Phone Number
City		State	Zip
Authorized Signature			Date

Page 2

305

Apparel Marts in the USA

Atlanta

ATLANTA APPAREL MART
240 Peachtree Street, Suite 2200,
Atlanta, GA 30303, (404) 220-3000
www.americasmart.com

Birmingham

BIRMINGHAM APPAREL MARKET
Birmingham Jefferson Civic Center,
One Civic Center Plaza, Birmingham,
AL 35203,   (205) 871-3305

Boston

Apparel Mart expected to resume sometime
in the future. (*See Domestic Trade Show list*)

Charlotte

**CHARLOTTE APPAREL
MART/MERCHANDISE MART**
2500 E Independence Blvd., Charlotte,
NC 28205, (704) 333-7709
www.Charlottemerchmart.com

Chicago

CHICAGO APPAREL CENTER
350 North Orleans Street, Chicago, IL
60654, (312) 527-7777
**www.Merchandisemart.com/apparelc
enter**

Dallas

INTERNATIONAL APPAREL MART
2300 Stemmons Freeway, Dallas, TX
75258, (214) 655-6100 or (800) DAL-
MKTS **www.dallasmarketcenter.com**

Denver

DENVER MERCHANDISE MART
451 East 58th Avenue , Suite 4270,
Denver, CO 80216, (303) 292-6278
www.Denvermart.com

Kansas City

KANSAS CITY MARKET CENTER
1775 Universal Avenue, Kansas City,
MO 64120, (816) 241-6200

Los Angeles

CALIFORNIA MART
110 East Ninth, Los Angeles, CA
90079, (213) 620-0260
www.Californiamarketcenter.com

NEW MART
127 E. 9th Street, Los Angeles, CA
90015, (213) 627-0671
www.newmart.net

Miami

**MIAMI INTERNATIONAL
MERCHANDISE MART**
777 NW 72nd Avenue, Miami, FL
33126, (305) 261-2900
www.Miamimart.net

New York

FASHION CENTER HEADQUARTERS
249 West 39th Street, New York, NY
10018, (212) 764-9600
www.Fashioncenter.com

Pittsburgh

PITTSBURGH EXPO CENTER
105 Mall Boulevard, Monroeville, PA
15146, (412) 856-8100
www.Pittsburghexpomart.com

Salt Lake City

**SALT LAKE CITY FASHION
EXHIBITORS MART**
230 W 200 So, Salt Lake City, UT
84101, (801) 531-6699

San Francisco

GIFT CENTER & FASHION MART
888 Brannan Street, San Francisco, CA
94103, (415) 861-7733 **www.gcjm.com**

Seattle

**SEATTLE INTERNATIONAL TRADE
CENTER**
2200 Alaskan Way, Suite 410, Seattle,
WA 98121, (206) 441-5144
www.wtcseattle.com

Domestic Trade Shows

Allentown (Pennsylvania)

Eastern Pennsylvania Bridal Expo
www.osbornejenks.com
(800) 955-7469

Atlanta

AmericasMart FirstLOOK
AmericasMart PREMIERE
Gift, Accessories & Holiday Market
Gift & Accessories Market
International Bridal & Special Occasion Market
Men's Market
Women's & Children's Apparel/Accessories Market
www.americasmart.com
(800) ATL-MART
B.A.T.M.A.N.
www.spectrade.com
(305) 663-6635
Gift Fair
www.urbanexpositions.com
(678) 285-3976
Imprinted Sportswear Show
www.issshows.com
(800) 933-8735
North American Shoe & Accessories Market
www.sesta.org
(706) 923-0580
Techtextil North America
www.usa.messefrankfurt.com
(770) 984-8016

Atlantic City

ASD/AMD's Variety Merchandise Show
www.merchandisegroup.com
(800) 421-4511
Imprinted Sportswear Show
www.issshows.com
(800) 933-8735

Billings (Montana)

Fashion Market
(406) 652-6132

Boston

Baystate Bridal Expo
www.osbornejenks.com
(800) 955-7469
Gift Show
www.bostongiftshow.com
(800) 272-SHOW

Boxborough (Massachusetts)

Boston Menswear Collective
www.bostoncollective.com
(508) 655-7158

Chantilly (Virginia)

Gift Show
www.washingtongiftshow.com
(800) 272-SHOW

Charlotte (North Carolina)

The Printwear Show
www.nbmshows.com
(800) 669-0424

Chicago

All Things Organic
www.atoexpo.com
(207) 842-5504
ASI Show!
www.asishow.com
(800) 546-3300
CHICago isŠRED HOT!!!
Fabric & Trim Show
www.aibi.com
(312) 836-1041
Fabric Fair
Gift & Home Market
Men's Wear Collective
National Bridal Market
STYLEMAX
Women's & Children's Apparel Market
www.merchandisemart.com
(800) 677-MART
IFA EXPO
www.formalwear.org
(312) 321-5139

Columbus (Ohio)

Imprinted Sportswear Show
www.issshows.com
(800) 933-8735

Dallas

ASI Show!
www.asishow.com
(800) 546-3300
Bridal & Special Occasion Fabric Show
International Gift & Home Accessories Market
International Western Apparel & Tack
Men's & Boys' Apparel
Men's Apparel
Prom & Special Occasion
Regional Western Apparel Market
Swimwear
SWSTA Shoe Show
The Men's Show
Women's & Children's Apparel & Accessories Market
www.dallasmarketcenter.com
(800) DAL-MKTS

Imprinted Sportswear Show
www.issshows.com
(800) 933-8735

Denver

Apparel & Accessory Market
Gift Jewelry & Resort Show
www.denvermart.com
(800) 289-6278
International Western/English Apparel & Equipment Market
www.denver-wesa.com
(800) 295-1041
Jewelry, Gifts & More
www.helenbrett.com
(630) 241-9865

Ft. Washington (Pennsylvania)

Philadelphia Gift Show
www.urbanexpositions.com
(678) 285-3976

Galveston Island (Texas)

Gulf Coast Gift & Resort Merchandise Show
www.urbanexpositions.com
(678) 285-3976

Gatlinburg (Tennessee)

Apparel & Jewelry Market
Gift & Variety Show
www.nortonshows.com
(865) 436-6151

Hartford (Connecticut)

Connecticut Bridal Expo
Hartford Bridal Expo
www.osbornejenks.com
(800) 955-7469

Honolulu

Hawaii Gift & Apparel Retailers Expo
Hawaii Market Merchandise Expo
www.douglastradeshows.com
(800) 525-5275
Hawaiian Mainland Pacific Apparel Show
mgarmento@aol.com
(510) 531-6392

Houston

ASD/AMD's Variety Merchandise Show
www.merchandisegroup.com
(800) 421-4511

Huntington Beach (California)

ASR Fall
www.asrbiz.com
(949) 376-8144

Indianapolis

The Printwear Show
www.nbmshows.com
(800) 669-0424

Key Biscayne (Florida)

Electronic Retailing Conference & Trade Expo
www.retailing.org
(800) 987-6462

Las Vegas

ASAP Global Sourcing Show
www.asapshow.com
(888) 564-6263
ASD/AMD Jewelry Show
ASD/AMD Trade Show
ASD/AMD's Gift Expo
ASD/AMD's Merchandise Expo
www.merchandisegroup.com
(800) 421-4511
ASI Show!
www.asishow.com
(800) 546-3300
Electronic Retailing Convention & Expo
www.retailing.org
(800) 987-6462 fabric@MAGIC
www.fabricshow.com
(877) 554-4834
Global Sourcing
www.appareland footwear.org
(703) 797-9055
GlobalShop
www.globalshop.org
(770) 569-1540
International Apparel Show
www.discountapparelshow.com
(866) 746-9432
International Lingerie Show
KID Show
WWIN
www.spectrade.com
(305) 663-6635
International Textiles & Sewing Products Expo
National Sewing Show
www.sewing.org
(516) 596-3937
ISAM
www.isamla.com
(818) 566-4044
MAGIC
MAGIC kids
the edge
WWDMAGIC
www.magiconline.com
(800) 421-9567
Off-Price Specialist Show
www.offpriceshow.com
(262) 782-1600

POOL
www.pooltradeshow.com
(323) 666-5587
PPAI Expo
www.ppa.org
(888) 492-6890
SIA SnowSports Show
www.thesnowtrade.org
(703) 556-9020
West Coast Exclusive
www.westcoastexclusive.com
(310) 439-1548
WSA Shoe Show
www.wsashow.com
(949) 851-8451

Long Beach (California)

Action Girl Sports
www.actiongirlsports.com
(800) 335-7721
Imprinted Sportswear Show
www.issshows.com
(800) 933-8735
The Printwear Show
www.nbmshows.com
(800) 669-0424

Los Angeles

Agenda Show
www.agendashow.com
(213) 622-6523
Brighte Companies
www.enkshows.com
(212) 759-8055
California Gift Show
www.californiagiftshow.com
(800) 272-SHOW
D&A Annex
Designers & Agents
www.designersandagents.com
(212) 302-9575
Fashion Week
www.californiamarketcenter.com
(800) 225-6278
www.cooperdesignspace.com
(213) 627-3754
www.gerrybuilding.com
(213) 228-1988
www.newmart.net
(213) 627-0671
Gift & Home Market
International Textile Show
Junior & Contemporary Majors Market
Shoe Show
Urban/Suburban Show
www.californiamarketcenter.com
(800) 225-6278
Gift & Home Furnishings Market
www.merchandisemart.com
(800) LAMART4
Mercedes-Benz Shows LA
www.mbshowsla.com
(212) 253-2692
West Coast Exclusive
www.westcoastexclusive.com
(310) 439-1548

Marlboro (Massachusetts)

New England Apparel Market
www.neacshow.com
(781) 326-9223

Memphis

Gift & Jewelry Show
Mid-South Jewelry & Accessories Fair
www.helenbrett.com
(630) 241-9865

Miami

B.A.T.M.A.N.
www.spectrade.com
(305) 663-6635
Florida Fashion Focus
www.floridafashionfocus.com
(888) 249-1377
International Gift & Decorative Accessories Show
www.urbanexpositions.com
(678) 285-3976
Men's & Boys' Apparel Market
www.geocities.com/ssesite
(561) 967-6040
SMOTA Shoe Show
www.smota.com
(305) 262-7673
Swim Show
www.swimshow.com
(305) 262-4556

Miami Beach

citystyle
www.citystyleusa.com
(954) 476-5761
Fashion Week of the Americas
www.fashionweekamericas.com
(954) 476-5761
Material World
Technology Solutions
www.material-world.com
(800) 318-2238
SPESA Expo
www.spesaexpo.com
(919) 872-2924

Minneapolis

Market Week
www.northstarfashion.com
(800) 272-6972

Myrtle Beach (South Carolina)

Grand Strand Gift & Resort Merchandise Show
www.urbanexpositions.com
(678) 285-3976

Nashville

Apparel, Jewelry & Gift Market
www.nortonshows.com
(865) 436-6151

New Orleans

Gift & Jewelry Show
International Jewelry Fair/General
Merchandise Show
www.helenbrett.com
(630) 241-9865

Newport Beach (California)

California Resortwear Show
www.calresort.com
(800) 947-7873

New York

Accessorie Circuit
Fashion Coterie
Intermezzo
The Collective
www.enkshows.com
(212) 759-8055
Accessories The Show
www.accessoriestheshow.com
(800) 358-6678
Action Girl Sports
www.actiongirlsports.com
(800) 335-7721
American International Designers
at the Waldorf
www.americaninternationaldesign
ers.
com
(312) 627-1720
ASD/AMD¹s Variety Merchandise
Show
www.merchandisegroup.com
(800) 421-4511
Atelier Designers
www.atelierdesigners.com
(505) 982-9112
China Textile & Apparel Trade
Show
International Lingerie Show
www.spectrade.com
(305) 663-6635
Clear Collections
Sole Commerce
www.enkshows.com
(212) 759-8055
D&A Annex
Designers & Agents
www.designersandagents.com
(212) 302-9575
Direction
www.directionshow.com
(973) 761-5598
European Preview
www.europeanpreview.com
(203) 422-0473
FAME
www.fameshows.com
(877) 904-FAME
FFANY Collections
FFANY Shoe Expo
www.ffany.org
(212) 751-6422
IFFE-International Fashion Fabric
Exhibition
www.fabricshow.com
(877) 554-4834

IFJAG Show
www.jewelrytradeshows.com
(914) 761-9019
Industry (212)
www.industry212.com
(877) 554-4834
International Gift Fair
www.nyigf.com
(800) 272-SHOW
INTIMA America
Intimate Apparel Salon
www.usa.messefrankfurt.com
(770) 984-8016
I-TexStyle
www.i-texstyle.com
(212) 980-1500
Latin Fashion
www.agriflor.com
+31 20 6622482
Licensing International
www.licensingshow.com
(800) 331-5706
Lingerie Americas
www.lingerie-americas.com
(203) 618-0092
Moda Manhattan
www.modamanhattan.com
(800) 358-6678
National Retail Convention & Expo
www.nrf.com
(800) NRF-HOW2
Off-Price Specialist Show
www.offpriceshow.com
(262) 782-1600
Olympus Fashion Week
www.olympusfashionweek.com
(212) 253-2692
Pacific Designer Collection
www.pacificdesignercollection.com
(415) 461-1960
PanTextiles
www.pantextiles.com
886 2 2341 7251
Printsource
www.printsourcenewyork.com
(212) 352-1005
Project Trade Show
www.projectshow.com
(212) 614-7324
SOURCES
www.sourcesny.com
(800) 272-SHOW
Surtex
Surtex Gallery
www.surtex.com
(800) 272-SHOW
TBC-To Be Confirmed
www.2beconfirmed.com
(212) 965-1146
The Evening Show
www.the-evening-show.com
(954) 476-5761
Turkish Fashion Fabric Exhibition
www.turkishfabric.com
(212) 398-6241
Women¹s Apparel Market
(212) 289-0420
Workshop
www.workshopsalons.com
(212) 925-2507

Yarn Fair International
www.yarnfair.com
(212) 925-6349

Ocean City (Maryland)

East Coast Resort Gift Expo
www.urbanexpositions.com
(678) 285-3976

Orlando

Action Girl Sports
www.actiongirlsports.com
(800) 335-7721
ASD/AMD¹s Variety Merchandise
Show
www.merchandisegroup.com
(800) 421-4511
ASI Show!
www.asishow.com
(800) 546-3300
Florida Gift & Home Accessories
Market
www.americasmart.com
(800) ATL-MART
Gift Show
Jewelry & Accessories Expo
www.urbanexpositions.com
(678) 285-3976
International Lingerie Show
www.spectrade.com
(305) 663-6635
PGA Merchandise Show
www.pgaexpo.com
(800) 840-5268
Surf Expo
www.surfexpo.com
(800) 947-SURF
The Super Show
www.thesupershow.com
(800) 327-3736

Panama City Beach (Florida)

Gift & Resort Merchandise Show
www.urbanexpositions.com
(678) 285-3976

Pittsburgh

Fashion Mart
www.pittsburghfashionmart.com
(888) 366-4660

Portland

Gift & Accessories Show
www.portlandgift.com
(800) 346-1212
Northwest Apparel & Footwear
Materials Show
www.americanevents.com
(800) 343-1822

Prior Lake (Minnesota)

Northwest Shoe Traveler¹s Show
(651) 436-2709

Rosemont (Illinois)

TransWorld's Fabric, Trimmings & Services Expo
www.transworldexhibits.com
(800) 323-5462

Salt Lake City

Outdoor Retailer
www.outdoorretailer.com
(949) 376-6200

San Diego

Agenda Show
www.agendashow.com
(213) 622-6523
ASR
www.asrbiz.com
(949) 376-8144
PGA Fall Expo
www.pgaexpo.com
(800) 840-5268

San Francisco

Fashion Market
www.fashionsanfrancisco.com
(800) 536-4422

International Gift Fair
www.sfigf.com
(800) 346-1212

Sarasota (Florida)

Women's Apparel & Accessory Market
www.geocities.com/ssesite
(561) 967-6040

Seattle

Gift Show
www.seattlegift.com
(800) 346-1212
Trend Show
www.seattletrendshow.com
(206) 767-9200

Tampa

Imprinted Sportswear Show
www.issshows.com
(800) 933-8735

Virginia Beach (Virginia)

Surf Expo BTS
www.surfexpo.com
(800) 947-SURF

Warwick (Rhode Island)

IFJAG
www.jewelrytradeshows.com
(914) 761-9019

West Springfield (Massachusetts)

Springfield Bridal Expo
www.osbornejenks.com
(800) 955-7469

Wethersfield (Connecticut)

Connecticut Men's Apparel Show
www.bostoncollective.com
(508) 655-7158

White Plains (New York)

Westchester County Bridal Expo
www.osbornejenks.com
(800) 955-7469

International Trade Show Sponsors

Amsterdam

Mode Fabriek
www.modefabriek.nl
31 020 4421960

Anglet (France)

ASR Europe
www.asrbiz.com
(949) 376-8144

Bangkok

International Fashion Fair
International Leather Fair
www.thaitrade.com
662 511 6020 30

Barcelona

Moda Barcelona Bridal Week
Moda Barcelona Fashion Week
www.moda-barcelona.com
34 93 209 36 39
Pielespaña
www.pielespana.com
34 90 223 32 00

Beijing

Intertextile
www.interstoff.com
(770) 984-8016
Yarn Expo
www.messefrankfurt.com
(770) 984-8016

Berlin

BREAD & butter
www.breadandbutter.com
49 030 400 44 0
Premium
www.premiumexhibitions.com
49 030 629 08 50

Birmingham (England)

Footwear UK
www.dewevents.co.uk
44 0 1707 648330
MODA UK
www.moda-uk.co.uk
44 0 1707 648330

Bologna

Fashion Shoe
www.bolognafiere.it
39 051 282111
Lineapelle
www.lineapelle-fair.it
39 028 807711
Simac
www.assomac.it
39 038 178883

Brno (Czech Republic)

KABO
STYL
www.mdna.com
(312) 781-5180

Brussels

4th Avenue
Kids¹ Fashion
Women¹s & Men¹s Wear
www.bff.be
32 2 370 60 13

Cairo

Egytex
www.egytex.com
202 7365311

Calcutta (India)

International Leather Goods Fair
www.indiatradefair.com
(212) 370-5262

Calgary (Canada)

Mode Accessories Show
www.mode-accessories.com
(416) 510-0114

Cernobbio (Italy)

Ideabiella
www.ideabiella.it
39 015 8483242
Ideacomo
www.ideacomo.com
39 031 513312
Shirt Avenue
www.shirt-avenue.com
39 026 6103838

Chennai (India)

India International Leather Fair
www.indiatradefair.com
(212) 370-5262

Cologne

IMB Forum
Kind + Jugend
www.kolnmesse.de
(773) 326-9920

Copenhagen

CPH Vision
www.cphvision.dk
45 3964 8586
International Fashion Fair
www.ciff.dk
45 3252 8811

Damascus (Syria)

International Fair of Shoes & Leather
www.dltafair.com
363 11 3337408

Dongguan (China)

China Shoes
China Shoetec
www.chinashoesexpo.com
(312) 781-5180
International Dyeing & Finishing Expo
International Knitting & Embroidery Expo
www.adsale.com.hk
(408) 737-2820
MATECH CHINA
www.aplf.com
(609) 452-2800

Dubai (UAE)

International Fashion Jewellery & Accessories Fair
www.intexdubai.com
971 4 3438884
Motexha
www.motexhaonline.com
971 4 3365161

Düsseldorf

cpd fabrics
cpd woman€man
www.idego.com
(312) 781-5180
GDS International Shoe Fair
www.mdna.com
(312) 781-5180

Edmonton (Canada)

Alberta Fashion Market
www.albertafashion.ca
(780) 484-7541
Gift Show
www.albertagiftshow.com
(888) 823-7467

Florence

ModaPelle
Pitti Immagine Bimbo
Pitti Immagine Filati
Pitti Immagine Uomo
www.pittimmagine.com
39 055 36931
Prato Expo
www.firenze-expo.it
39 0574 455280

Frankfurt

Fur & Fashion
www.furfashion.
de/english/index.html
49 69242635 0

Gaziantep (Turkey)

GAPTEX
www.gatemach.com
90 342 2206985

Guadalajara

ANPIC Guadalajara
www.anpic.com
52 33 3616 5804
Intermoda
www.intermoda.com.mx
33 3122 4499
Modama
www.modama.com.mx
52 3824 6040

Guangzhou (China)

International Shoes & Leather
Exhibition
www.toprepute.com.hk
852 2851 8603

Guatemala City

CBI Apparel Sourcing Show
www.apparelexpo.com

Guayaquil (Ecuador)

Modatex Ecuador
www.agriflor.com
31 20 6622482

Hong Kong

APLF Fashion Access
APLF Materials, Manufacturing &
Technology
www.aplf.com
(609) 452-2800
Asia's Fashion Jewellery &
Accessories Fair
www.jewellerynetasia.com
852 2516 2110
Fashion Week
World Boutique
www.tdctradefairs.com
(213) 622-3194
Interstoff Asia
www.interstoff.com
(770) 984-8016

Istanbul

AYMOD
AYSAF
www.rdf.com.tr
90 212 251 2328

CANT€SA Leathergoods Fair
Deri Gunleri-International Leather
Days
FUR'IST
www.ezgiajans.com
90 212 284 9420

Johannesburg (South Africa)

SA Fashion Week
www.safashionweek.co.za
27 11 442 7812

Leon (Mexico)

ANPIC
www.anpic.com
52 33 3616 5804
SAPICA
www.sapica.com
(888) 525-8812

Lille (France)

Future by Tissu Premier
Tissu Premier
www.promosalons.com
(888) 522-5001
Indigo
www.lille.cci.fr/indigo/
33 03 20 63 78 32

Lima (Peru)

Peru Moda
www.perumoda.com
511 2210602

Lisbon

Exponoivos
www.ecorex.pt
351 21 254 82 00

London

Fashion Week
www.londonfashionweek.co.uk
44 020 7636 7788
For Attention Of
www.forattentionof.com
44 020 7377 1312
London Front Cover
Londoncentral
Londonedge
www.londoncentralshow.com
0208 257 1985
Off-Price Show
www.offpriceshow.co.uk
0208 675 4745
Pure London
www.idego.com
(312) 781-5180
TBC-To Be Confirmed
www.2beconfirmed.com
(212) 965-1146
Turkish Fashion Fabric Exhibition
www.turkishfabric.com
(212) 398-6241

Lyon (France)

Interfilière Lyon
Lyon, Mode City
www.promosalons.com
(888) 522-5001

Madrid

International Gift, Jewellery &
Fashion Jewellery Week
International Leather Week
SIMM International Fashion Week
Textilmoda
www.ifema.es
34 91 722 51 80

Medellín (Colombia)

Colombiamoda
Colombiatex
www.inexmoda.org.co
574 3115915

Melbourne

L'Oréal Melbourne Fashion
Festival
www.mff.com.au
61 3 9510 8870
PGA Merchandise Show
www.pgaexpo.com
61 2 9422 2565
TCF International
www.ausexhibit.com
61 3 9261 4500

Milan

Bijoux
MICAM Shoevent
Mifur
Milano Moda Donna
MilanoVendeModa
Mipel
Moda In
Modaprima/Esma
Sposaitalia Collezioni
www.fieramilano.it
(888) 343-7264
FILO
www.filo.it
39 015 404032
Intertex Milano
www.intertexmilano.it
39 02 48015026
nextex
www.nextex.it
39 02 76018402
Ready To Show
www.readytoshow.it
39 02 48015026
un-dress
www.iniziativefieristiche.com/undress
39 02 34984405

Monte Carlo

**Electronic Retailing Conference &
Trade Expo**
www.retailing.org
(800) 987-6462

Montreal

Fashion Week
www.mfw.ca
(514) 392-0500
Gift Show
www.montrealgiftshow.com
(888) 823-SHOW
NAFFEM
www.furcouncil.com
(514) 844-1945
NSIA Snow Show
www.nsia.ca
(800) 263-6742

Moscow

CPM Moscow
www.idego.com
(312) 781-5180
Moda Moscow
www.moda-expo.ru
7 095 935 7350
Mosleather
Mosshoes
Mosshoes Technology
www.mosshoes.com
095 124 6404

Munich

ABC Salon
Moda Made In Italy
www.moc-muenchen.de
49 89 32 35 30
Fabric Start
www.munichfabricstart.de
49 89 419 43 316
Fashion Fair
www.munichfashionfair.de
49 89 340 80 950
ISPO
www.ispo.com
(312) 377-2650

New Delhi (India)

Tex-Styles India
www.indiatradefair.com
(212) 370-5262

Novo Hamburgo (Brazil)

Courovisão
Fenac
Fimec
www.fenac.com.br
5511 3897 6100

Offenbach (Germany)

ILM
www.messe-offenbach.de
(212) 974-8830

Osaka (Japan)

International Gift Show
www.giftshow.co.jp
81 3 3843 9851

Paris

Atmosphère
Avant-âge
FATEX
Made In France by FATEX
Paris Sur Mode
Who¹s Next
www.comexpo-paris.com
33 01 49 09 60 00
Casabo Homme/ŠBy Casabo
Pick & Mix
www.pretparis.com
33 1 44 94 70 00
Eclat de Mode (Bijorhca)
Interfilière
Interselection
Lingerie Paris
Prêt-À-Porter
Salon Génération Bébé
Silmo
www.promosalons.com
(888) 522-5001
Expofil
www.expofil.com
(212) 925-2507
Haute Couture
Mode Masculine
Ready-to-Wear
www.modeaparis.com
33 01 42 66 64 44
Journées Fournisseurs
www.journeesfournisseurs.com
33 01 47 56 32 32
Kids¹ Fashion
www.bff.be
32 2 370 60 13
La Maroquinerie Française
www.ff-maroquinerie.fr
33 1 42 44 22 44
LE CUIR A PARIS
www.lecuiraparis.com
33 01 43 59 05 69
MIDEC
www.midec.com
33 01 44 71 71 71
Mod¹Amont
www.modamont.net
33 01 44 71 71 71
Premiere Classe
www.premiere-classe.com
33 01 40 13 74 70
Première Vision
www.premierevision.fr
(203) 861-2082
Texworld
www.messefrankfurt.com
(770) 984-8016
Workshop
www.workshopsalons.com
(212) 925-2507

Porto (Portugal)

Expocouro/Fipele
Exponoivos
MAQUITEX
www.exponor.pt
351 229 981 400
MOCAP
www.apiccaps.pt
351 22 507 41 50
MOD¹tissimo
www.modtissimo.com
351 22 610 87 32

Poznan´ (Poland)

Fashion Week
www.mtp.com.pl
48 61 869 2297

Puebla (Mexico)

EXINTEX
www.exintex.com.mx
(800) 667-3736

Quito (Ecuador)

Modatex Ecuador
www.agriflor.com
31 20 6622482

Riva del Garda (Italy)

Expo Riva Shoe
www.palacongressi.it
39 0464 520000

San Juan (Puerto Rico)

**Caribbean Apparel, Shoe &
Accessories Show**
www.tradeshowcaribe.com
(787) 781-3050

San Salvador (El Salvador)

Speed to Market Summit
www.elsalvadorworks.com
(503) 210-2500

São Paulo (Brazil)

Streetwear & Skate Show
Surf & Beach Show
Surf & Beach Tex Preview
www.surfbeach.com.br
(949) 492-3747
Couromoda
www.couromoda.com
55 11 3897 6100
Feimaco
Fenatec
Fenit
Salão Infanto Juvenil e Bebê
SIM-International Fashion Show
www.alcantara.com.br
55 11 4197 9111
FRANCAL
www.francal.com.br
55 11 56 69 5050

Shanghai

All China Leather Exhibition
China International Footwear Fair
Moda Shanghai
www.aplf.com
(609) 452-2800
Cinte Techtextil China
www.messefrankfurt.com
(770) 984-8016
Dessous China
Fashion China
www.idego.com
(312) 781-5180
Intertextile
www.interstoff.com
(770) 984-8016
SpinExpo
www.spinexpo.com
33 1 39 76 96 70

Sharjah (UAE)

Al Hida'a
Texpo
www.expo-centre.co.ae
9716 5770 000

Taipei

TITAS
www.titas.com.tw
886 2 2341 7251

Tokyo

Active Collection
www.activecollection.com
81 3 3813 3601
Designers & Agents
www.designersandagents.com
(212) 302-9575
International Fashion Fair
www.senken.co.jp/iff
81 3 3263 6881
International Gift Show
www.giftshow.co.jp
81 3 3843 9851
Intima Japan
www.interstoff.com
(770) 984-8016
JAPANTEX
www.japantex.jp
81 03 3433 4521
JITAC European Textile Fair
www.premierevision.fr
33 04 72 60 65 00
TBC-To Be Confirmed
www.2beconfirmed.com
(212) 965-1146
Workshop
www.workshopsalons.com
(212) 925-2507

Toronto

Imprint Canada Show
www.imprintcanada.com
(905) 856-2600
International Gift Fair
www.torontointernationalgiftfair.com
(888) 823-7469

Luggage, Leathergoods,
Handbags
& Accessories Show
www.llhashows.com
(800) 896-7469
Mode Accessories Show
www.mode-accessories.com
(416) 510-0114
Ontario Fashion Exhibitors
www.ontariofashionexhibitors.ca
(800) 765-7508
PGA Golf Merchandise Show
www.pgaexpo.com
(888) 322-7333
Shoe Show
www.torontoshoeshow.com
(888) 443-6786

Tunis (Tunisia)

Promocuir
www.fkram.com.tn
21671730111

Vancouver

Gift Show
www.vancouvergiftshow.com
(888) 721-4403

Zhejiang (China)

International Exhibition on
Hosiery
& Garment Industries
www.adsale.com.hk
(408) 737-2820

World Trade Information / Foreign Trade Information

HONG KONG TRADE DEVELOPMENT COUNCIL
They have branch offices in various cities around the U.S. To find the one nearest to you call, or fax their New York office, or find them on the Web.
Phone: 212 838 8688, Fax: 212 838 8941, **www.tdctrade.com**

TEXTILE CONSULTING GROUP (Cutting, Sewing, & Finishing)
Mexico: 619 280 0129, **www.netsv.com/almeida/**

US COUNCIL FOR INTERNATIONAL BUSINESS
Phone: 562 495 9273, Fax: 562 590 9564, **www.uscib.org**

WORLD HONG KONG (Better-wear, Tailoring)
New York Production Farm out.
501 7th Ave., #1307, N.Y. 10018
Phone: 852 258 4333, **www.hkenterprise.com**

Trade Publications

AMERICAN SPORTSWEAR & KNITTING TIMES
386 Park Ave South, NY. NY. 10016, Tel. 212 683 7520 Fax 212 532 0766 **www.asktmag.com**

APPAREL STRATEGIST
PO Box 406, Fleetwood PA 19522, Tel. 610 944-5995 **pblack@prolog.net**
www.apparelstrategist.com

BOBBIN MAGAZINE
P.O. Box 1986, Columbia, SC 29202, Tel. 800 845 8820 Fax 803 799 1461 **www.bobbin.com**

CALIFORNIA APPAREL NEWS
California Mart, 110 E.9th St., Suite a 777, Los Angeles CA. 90079 1777, Tel. 888 304 6397
Fax. 213 623 5707 **Webmaster@apparelnews.net**

NATIONAL REGISTER DIRECTORIES
Marche Publishing, California Mart, 110 E. 9th St., AL19, Los Angeles, CA 90079,
800 347-2589 **www.thenationalregister.com**

STITCHES MAGAZINE
PO Box 12960, Overland Park, KS 66282-2960, Tel. 913 341 1300 Fax. 913 967 1898
www.stitches.com

WWD WOMEN'S WEAR DAILY
Fairchild Publishing, 7 West 34th Street, NY. NY. 10001-8191, 212 630 4231 or 800 289 0273
www.wwd.com

Industry Related Resources

ACRYLIC COUNCIL
1285 Avenue of the Americas New York, NY 10016   (212) 554-4042
www.Fabriclink.com/acryliccouncil

AMERICAN APPAREL MANUFACTURERS ASSOCIATION (AAMA)
2500 Wilson Blvd., Suite 301 Arlington, VA 22201 (800) 520) 2262 **www.americanapparel.org**
Membership is of major manufacturers.

AMERCIAN APPERAL PRODUCERS NETWORK (AAPN)
Box 720693 Atlanta, GA 30358. (404) 843-3171, **www.aapnetwork.net** Membership of producers
and contractors or quality authentic American apparel.

AMERICAN ASSOCIATION FOR TEXTILE TECHNOLOGY, Inc.
347 Fifth Avenue New York, NY 10016 (212) 481-7792   Fax: (212) 481-7969

AMERICAN ASSOCIATION OF TEXTILE CHEMISTS AND COLORISTS
P.O. Box 12215   Research Triangle Park, NC 27709   (919) 549-8141 **www.aatcc.org**

AMERICAN FIBER MANUFACTURERS ASSOCIATION
1150 17th Street NW Washington D.C. 20036   (202) 296-6508   Fax: (202) 296-3052
www.fibersource.com

AMERICAN FUR INDUSTRY
363 7th Avenue New York, NY 10001

AMERICAN LEATHER ACCESORY DESIGNERS (ALAD)
Kleinberg Sheriff, 392 Fifth Avenue   New York, NY 10018   (212) 971-0906

AMERICAN PRINTED FABRICS COUNCIL
45 West 36th Street   New York, NY 10018   (212) 695-2254 Fax: (212) 947-0115

AMERICAN TEXTILE MACHINERY ASSOCIATION
7297 N. Lee Highway, Suite N Falls Church, VA 22042   (703) 533-9251 **www.atmanet.org**

AMERICAN TEXTILE MANUFACTURERS INSTITUTE
1801 K Street NW Suite 900 Washington, D.C. 20006 (202) 862-0500 Fax: (202) 862-0570
www.atmi.org

AMERICAN WOOL COUNCIL
6911 South Yosemite Street Denver, CO 80112   (303) 771-3500 Fax: (303) 771-8200
New York Office: 50 Rockefeller Plaza, Suite 830 New York, NY 10020
(212) 245-6710 **www.americanwool.org**

AMERICAN YARN SPINNERS ASSOCIATION
P.O. Box 99   Gastonia, NC 28053   (704) 824-3522 **www.aysa.org**

APPAREL EXCHANGE
571 Creekview Drive Stone Mountain, GA 30083-4019, (800) 241-2463, email:
skohler@mindspring.com. , **www.fabric.com** Fabric clearinghouse: who has what fabric to sell;
usually odd lots. Annual subscription of $120 allows you unlimited access to all areas of website for
constantly updated information.

APPAREL LINK SADDLE STITCH GROUP
(818) 353-1876 **www.apparellink.com**

ASSOCIATED CORSET & BRASSIERE MANUFACTURERS Inc.
1290 Avenue of the Americas, New York, NY 10104 (212) 757-6664

ASSOCIATION OF TEXTILE DYERS, PRINTERS & FINISHERS OF SOUTHERN CALIFORNIA
2833 Leonis Blvd., Suite 316 Los Angeles, CA 90058 (213) 589-5833 Fax: (213) 589-1731
www.atdpf.com

BUREAU DE STYLE
California Market Center 110 West 40th Street New York, NY 10016, (212) 947-4600,
Fax (212) 391-4218, T.I.P. (TRENDS IN PROGRESS) RESOURCE GUIDE is a national directory of suppliers, services, and information sources. It indicates which suppliers will sell in small quantities. SOURCING NEWS is a quarterly newsletter with current information about fabric, fashion trends, suppliers, etc. JUST PRINTS is a supplement to Sourcing News which focuses on new prints and trends.

CALIFORNIA APPAREL NEWS, CALIFORNIA MARKET CENTER
110 E. 9th St., Suite A-777, Los Angeles, CA 90079-1777, (213) 627-3737, Fax: (213) 623-5707
www.Apparelnews.com

CALIFORNIA FASHION ASSOCIATION
444 South Flower Street, 34th Floor, Los Angeles, CA 90071, (213) 688-6288, Fax: (213) 688-6290.
California fashion industry forum consisting of manufacturers, suppliers, allied associations and professional support people. **www.californiafashionassociation.com**

CAMEL HAIR AND CASHMERE INSTIRUTE OF AMERICA
230 Congress Street Boston, MA 02110 (617) 542-8220 Fax: (617) 542-2199 **www.cashmere.org**

CARPET AND RUG INSTITUTE
P.O. Box 2048 Dalton, GA 30722 (706) 278-3176, (800) 882-8846 **www.carpet-rug.com**

CLOTHING MANUFACTURERS ASSOCIATION
1290 Avenue of the American, New York, NY 10104 (212) 757-6664

COTTON, INC.
1370 6th Avenue New York, NY 10019, (212) 586-1070, and California Market Center 110 East 9th Street, suite A-792, Los Angeles, California 90079, (213) 627-3561, Fax: (213) 627-3270
www.cottoninc.com They provide information about cotton, its qualities, specific sources, color forecasts.

COUNCIL of FASHION DESIGNER of AMERICAN (CFDA)
1412 Broadway, New York, NY 10018 (212) 302-1821

CRAFTED WITH PRIDE IN THE USA
1045 Avenue of the Americans, New York, NY 10018 (212) 819-4397 **www.craftedwithpride.org**

DIRECTIVES WEST BUYING OFFICE, CALIFORNIA MARKET CENTER
110 East 9th Street, suite A1126, Los Angeles, California 90079-2827, (213) 627-5921
www.directiveswest.com

DISCOUNT FABRICS USA
108 N. Carroll Street, Thurmont, MD 21788 (301) 271 2266 Fax (301) 271 4488

DOWNTOWN PROPERTY OWNERS ASSOCIATION
California Market Center 110 E. 9th Street, Suite C625 Los Angeles, CA 90079 (213) 488-1153
Fax: (213) 488-5159

FABRIC MARKETING RESEARCH
16 Catalipa Lane, Valley Stream, NY 11518, (212) 686-2345, Fax: (516) 791-6114
www.fabricmarketing.com   Daily updates of information for apparel, textile, and soft goods industries.

FABRIC STOCK EXCHANGE
Textile Broker, 34 Rocking Horse Way, Holland, PA 18966 (215) 579 2791 Fax (215) 579 2813
www.Fabricexchange.com

FAIRCHILD PUBLICATIONS
7 West 34th Street, New York, NY 10001, (800) 289-0273, (212) 630-4000 **www.fairchildpub.com**

THE FASHION ASSOCIATION (TFA)
475 Park Avenue South, New York, NY 10016 (212) 683-5665

FASHION BUSINESS INCORPORATED
New Mart Building, 217 E. 9th Street, Suite #212
Los Angeles, CA 90015 (213) 892 1669, Fax: (213) 892-8595 **www.FashionBizinc.org**
Educational non-profit that provides business training and resource information to start-ups and apparel manufacturers.

FASHIONDEX
153 West 27th Street Suite 700 New York, NY 10001,   (212) 647-0051, Fax (212) 691-5873,
www.Fashiondex.com   Publisher and distributor of apparel industry information.

FASHION FOOTWEAR ASSOCIATION OF NEW YORK (FFANY)
870 Seventh Avenue New York, NY 10019 **www.ffany.org**

FASHION GROUP INTERNATIONAL Inc.
597 Fifth Avenue New York, NY 10017 (212) 593-1715 **www.fgi.org**

FUR FARM ANIMAL WELFARE COALITION, Ltd.
405 Sibley Street St. Paul, MN 55101 (612) 293-0349

GARMET CONTRACTORS ASSOCIATION OF SOUTHERN CALIFORNIA
California Market Center110 E. 9th Street., Suite A701 Los Angeles, CA 90079   (213) 629-4422
Fax: (213) 629-4517

HEADWEAR INSTITUITE OF AMERICA
1 WEST 64th Street New York, NY 10023   (212) 724-0888

INTERNATIONAL ASSOCIATION of CLOTHING DESIGNERS
475 Park Avenue New York, NY 10016   (212) 685-6602 **www.iacde.com**

INTERNATIONAL ASSOCIATION OF SKATEBOARD COMPANIES
(949) 589-8863 Fax (949) 589-3604 **www.skateboardiasc.org**

INTERNATIONAL LINEN PROMOTION COMMISSION
200 Lexington Avenue New York, NY 10016 (212) 685-0424 Fax: (212) 725-0438

INTERNATIONAL SWIMWEAR & ACTIVEWEAR MARKET AND THE SWIMWEAR ASSOCIATION
110 East 9th St. Los Angeles, CA 99079   (213) 239-9347

INTIMATE APPAREL COUNCIL
150 Fifth Avenue New York, NY 10011   (212) 807-0878

KLEVENS PUBLISHING COMAPANY
7600 Avenue V Littlerock, CA 93543, (805) 944-4111 **www.Klevenspub.com**
email: **klevensPub@aol.com**

GARMET MANUFACTURERS INDEX
Nationwide sources of fabric, trim, supplies, factory equipment and sewing contractors.

LEATHER INDUSTRIES OF AMERICA
1000 Thomas Jefferson Street NW Suite 515 Washington, D.C. 20007 (202) 342-8086
Fax: (202) 342-9063 **www.leatherusa.com**

MASTER OF LINENS
200 Lexington Avenue Suite 225, NewYork, NY 10016
(212) 734-3640 and (210) 725-0483.   They represent linen mills and supply information about and
sources of linen yardage.

MEN'S APPAREL GUILD OF CALIFORNIA (MAGIC)
100 Wilshire Blvd. Santa Monica, CA 90401   (310) 393-7757

MOHAIR COUNCIL OF AMERICA
36 W Beauregard Street Room 516, FNB Bldg. San Angelo, TX 76903   (915) 655-3161
Fax: (915) 655-4761 **www.mohairusa.com**

NATIONAL ASSOCIATION OF FASHION AND ACCESSORY DESIGNERS
2180 East 93rd Street Cleveland, OH 44106   (216) 231-0375 **www.nafad.com**

NATIONAL ASSOCIATION OF HOSIERY MANUFACTURERS (NAHM)
3623 Latrobe Drive, Suite 130, Charlotte, NC 28211   (704) 365-0913 **www.nahm.com**

NATIONAL ASSOCIATION OF MEN'S SPORTSWEAR BUYERS (NAMSB)
500 Fifth Avenue New York, NY 10110   (212) 391-8580 **www.namsb-show.com/na-assoc.htm**

NATIONAL COTTON COUNCIL OF AMERICA
P.O. Box 12285 Memphis, TN 38182 (901) 274-9030 **www.cotton.org**

NATIONAL FASHION ACCESSORIES ASSOCIATION
330 Fifth Avenue New York, NY 10001 (212) 947-3424

NATIONAL KNITWEAR & SPORTSWEAR ASSOCIATION
386 Park Avenue South   New York, NY 10016   (212) 447-1234

POLYESTER COUNCIL
1675 Broadway New York, NY 10019 (212) 527-8941 Fax: (212) 527-8989

SAN FRANCISCO FASHION INDUSTRIES (SFFI)
1000 Brannan Street Suite 206 San Francisco, CA 94103   (415) 621-6100 Fax (415) 621-6384
www.sffi.org The membership of this industry organization consists of manufacturers, suppliers,
production services and professional services in the Bay Area. They will provide information on the
phone to help you locate who and what you need. The directory is published in February and August
of each year.

SIMA Surf Industry Manufacturers Association
120 1/2 South El Camino Real, Suite 204, San Lemento, CA 92672, (949) 366-1164,
Fax: (949) 366-1147, **www.sima.com**

SOUTHEASTERN APPAREL MANUFACTURERS & SUPPLIERS ASSOCIATION (SEAMS)
1900 Broad River Road Suite 100 Columbia, SC 29210-7047 (800) 476-5289 **www.seams.org** A
non profit organization of garment manufacturers and suppliers in the Southeastern U.S. working for
the survival of the domestic sewn products industry by providing referrals, consultations, benefits
packages, training and lobbying

STYLE SOURCE CUSTOM APPAREL SOURCING
1633 Hanover Ave., Allentown, PA 18109 (610) 740 1633 Fax (610) 740 5860
www.Style-Source.com

T.C.F. RESOURCE CENTER OF WESTERN AUSTRALIA
7 Fairbrother Street, Belmont, WA 6104 61 8 9479 3777 Fax 61 8 9479 3888 **www. TCFWA.com**

TECHNOLOGY EXCHANGE
iMagine That! Consulting Group Inc.   2229 Sherwood Ct. Minnetonke, MN 55305
(612) 593-9085 **www.techexchange.com** Searchable database of software and hardware,
consultants, service bureaus for apparel, textile, and home furnishings industry.

TEXTILE ASSOCIATION OF LOS ANGELES (TALA)
110 E Ninth Street Suite C765 Los Angeles, CA 90079   (213) 627-6173   Fax: (213) 627-0015
www.talausa.com   Resources, sources, suppliers, etc They also publish a directory annually.

WOOL BUREAU Inc.
330 Madison Avenue New York, NY 10017   (212) 986-6222 Fax: (212) 557-5985
www.woolmark.com

Fashion and Color Trend Forecasting Service

THE COLOR ASSOCIATION OF THE UNITED STATES (CAUS)
409 West 44th Street, New York, NY 10006, Tel: 212 582 6884 Fax: 212 757 4557

DESIGN OPTION
Cal Mart B-731, 110 E. 9th Street, Los Angeles, CA 90079, Tel: 213 622 9094, Fax: 213 622 9050
www.design-options.com

THE DONEGER GROUP
463 Seventh Ave., New York, NY 10018, Tel: 212 564 1255 Fax: 212 564 3971
www.doneger.com

ESP TRENDLAB
12 West 37th Street, New York, NY 10018, Tel: 212 629 9200, Fax: 212 629 0040
www.esptrendlab.com

HERE & THERE
1412 Broadway, New York, NY 10018, Tel: 212 354 9014 Fax: 212 764 1831
West Coast Office: 127 E. 9th St., #410, Los Angeles, CA. 90015
Tel: 213 622 5001 Fax: 212 622 2701 **www.hereandthere.net**

MARGIT PUBLICATIONS
1412 Broadway, Suite 1102, New York, NY 10018, Tel: 212 302 5137 Fax: 212 944 8757
www.mpnews.com

PANTONE COLOR INSTITUTE
590 Commerce Blvd., Carlstadt, NJ 07072, Tel: 201 935 5500 Fax: 201 896 0242
www.pantone.com

PAT TUNSKY INC
1040 Avenue of Americas, New York, NY 10018, Tel: 212 944 9160 Fax: 212 764 5105
www.rtwear.com

PROMOSTYL (Paris headquarters, with subsidiary offices in NY, London, Tokyo)
80 West 40th Street, New York, NY 10018, Tel: 212 921 7930 Fax: 212921 8214
www. Promostyl.com

THE TOBE` REPORT
40 East 42nd Street, New York, NY 10017, Tel: 212 867 8677 Fax: 212 867 8602
www.tobereport.com

WORTH GLOBAL STYLE NETWORK, WEST COAST (London based Internet predictive service)
110 East Ninth Street, Suite C247, Los Angeles, CA 90079, Tel: 213 629 5234
Fax: 213 629 5355 **www.worthstyle.com**

Major Factors

BAY VIEW FUNDING
15233 Ventura Blvd., Suite 310, Sherman Oaks, CA 91403 Tel: 818 382 2444: (888) 781 2444
Fax: 818 382 3737
Territory served: United States via 8 loan production offices.
Services: They provide a full range of factoring services, accounting, check processing, access to credit information, credit guarantees and financing. Part of Bay View Capitol Corporation, an over $3 billion financial service company.

CAPITAL FACTOR INC.
700 S. Flower St., Suite 2001, Los Angeles, CA 90017 Tel: 213 891 1320 , ext. 231;
Fax; 213 891 1324
Annual sales revenues: $3 billion nationally; $1 billion Los Angeles
Territory: Chicago and west
Services: Full-service factoring

THE C.I.T. GROUP/COMMERCIAL SERVICES
300 S. Grand Ave., Los Angeles, CA, 90071 Tel: 213 613 2400
Annual sales revenues: $7 billion
Territory: 13 most western states and Hong Kong market through an affiliated joint venture with State Street Bank.
Services: Notification and non-notification factoring, as well as accounts receivable financing, credit protection, accounts receivable management, inventory and equipment financing, letter of credit financing, and term loans to assist in either working capital needs or real property acquisitions.

CONTINENTAL BUSINESS CREDIT
16027 Ventura Blvd., Suite 610, Encino, CA 91436 Tel: 818 385 2738 Fax: 818 501 3039
Territory: Western United States
Services: Factoring with and without recourse as well as accounts receivable and purchase orders financing. They also provide inventory and equipment financing.
Start-up with annual sales of $500,000

DEMMITT & OWENS FINANCIAL INC.
2199 Norse Drive, Suite B, Pleasant Hill, CA 94523, Tel: 925 602 2775,
Fax: 925 602 2763
San Francisco: 800 378 3863, Chicago: 800 323 0156, Detroit: 800 583 7311

FINOVA
New York Office:
111 W. 40th St., 14th Floor, New York, NY 10018 Tel: 212 403 0700, Fax: 212 403 0418
Los Angeles Office:
355 S. Grand Ave., Suite 2310, Los Angeles, CA 90071 Tel: 213 253 1522, Fax: 213 625 3501
Annual Sales Revenues: $10 billion
Territory: Serves clients throughout the U.S. from offices in New York and Los Angeles.
Services: Offers a full array of factoring and accounts receivable management services, including accounts receivable and inventory financing; letters of credit; purchase guarantees; and term loans secured by equipment and real estate.

GENERAL BUSINESS CREDIT

110 E. 9th Street A-1131, Los Angeles, CA 90079, Tel: 213 244 9500, Fax: 213 244 9606
www.gbcfactor.com
Services: Factoring, Trade Finance, Purchase Order Finance.

GOODMAN FACTORS INC.

3003 LBJ Freeway, Suite 200, Dallas, TX 75234 Tel: 877 4-GOODMAN, toll-free: 972 241 3297,
Fax: 972 243 6285 **www.goodmanfactors.com**
Annual Volume: $120 million
Territory: Nationwide
Service: Factoring service for business with monthly sales volumes of $10,000 to $1 million.
Services include invoice and cash posting, credit and collection service and cash advances on invoices
upon shipment. **Start-ups OK!**

HANA FINANCIAL, INC.

1055 Wilshire Blvd., Suite 1717, Los Angeles, CA 90017-5600, Tel: 212 977 7298,
Fax: 212 482 1214 **www.hanafinancial.com**

REPUBLIC BUSINESS CREDIT CORP.

1000 Wilshire Blvd, Los Angeles, CA 90017 Tel: 213 312 3600, Fax: 213 312 3630
www.us.hsbc.com
Annual Volume: $5 billion
Territory: West of Mississippi
Services: Factoring; inventory and A/R financing; export factoring; and A/R management.

Fabric Mills and Fiber Products

AMERICAN TEXTILE MANUFACTURERS INSTITUTE
1130 Connecticut Ave, N.W. Suite 1200
Washington, D.C. 20036
Tel: 202 862 0500 Fax: 202 862 0570
Web Site: **www.atmi.org**

BURLINGTON INDUSTRIES
www.burlington.com is a quick source for the company's product information (in dozens of categories) and contact names.

CELANESE ACETATE
www.celaneseacetatefiber.com offers a convenient explanation of their famous biodegradable fashion fabrics. Converters (East and West Coast) are listed.

CONE MILLS
www.cone.com is the most up-dated of the mills on line. Details products in the news.

COURTAULDS
www.courtaulds.com is another corporate site with its various divisions, including "Tencel" (under "fibers"), which is a blend of wood pulp and man's ingenuity. Especially popular in the Far East.

DUPONT
www.dupont.com/mictomattique is a microfiber polyester blend website
www.dupont.com/lycra for their Lycra website

DYERBURG
www.dversburg.com. Here you will find "mill direct" sportswear fabrics.

GUILFORD MILLS
www.guilfordmills.com. Clear presentation of their ready to wear fabrics, and their innovative "microdenier" range is explained.

SPRINGS INDUSTRIES
www.springs.com. Fire-retardant fabrics are among the products highlighted.

THE APPAREL EXCHANGE
www.apparelex.com. This goes beyond just textile sourcing and is the most comprehensive site currently online. You can also access the well-respected Davidson's Blue Book of Textile Sources at this site.

LARKIN
www.larkingroup.com has free access to searchable sourcing directories that link apparel manufacturers with trimming and textile suppliers worldwide.
Companion site, **www.sourcingtradeshow.com.**

THE TEXTILE ASSOCIATION OF LOS ANGELES, (TALA)
www.textileassociation.org. is a non-profit organization that has been in existence for more than 56 years They co-support the LA International Textile Show with the LA California Mart. They also publish the TALA resource directory, which is updated annually with over a thousand active, and associate apparel industry professionals.

FABRIC STOCK EXCHANGE
www.fabric.com live auctions are conducted

TEXTILE INDUSTRY AFFAIRS

121 East 24th Street, 12th Floor, New York, NY 10010, Tel: 212 677 1450, Fax: 212 505 3300
www.textileaffairs.com

T.I.M.S. (TEXTILE INFORMATION MANAGEMENT SYSTEM)

www.unicate.com Features worldwide company and item search, online catalogs with product pictures, client showcases (including built-in e-mail links) and employment opportunities.

GLOBAL TEXTILE NETWORK

www.gtn.com, This may be too pricey for the start-up company, at over $100 dollars a month it promises to be the most comprehensive information on-line. This service allows member to negotiate sales and order on-line.

SOURCING WEB

www.sourcingweb.com, allows vendors to post free listings for products, including specifications and pricing.

TEXINFO

www.texinfo.com. Has a clear, logical series of directories and categories about everything textile related.

Contract Associations

AMERICAN APPAREL CONTRACTORS ASSOCIATION
P.O. Box 720693, Atlanta, GA 30358-2693, Tel: 404 843 3171 Fax: 404 256 5380, Web Site:
www.usawear.org

ATLANTIC APPAREL CONTRACTORS ASSOCIATION, INC.
95 Highland Ave., Suite 114, Bethlehem, PA 18017-9424, Tel: 610 837 4220, 800 237 9777 (NY),
Fax: 610 861 8069 **www.atlanticapparel.com**

BETTERWEAR TAILORED
(200-300 Units)

CHINESE BAY AREA APPAREL CONTRACTORS ASSOCIATION
950 Stockton Street, Suite 402, San Francisco, CA 94108, Tel: 415 989 1907 Fax: 415 9891907

GARMENT CONTRACTORS ASSOCIATION OF SOUTHERN CALIFORNIA INC.
110 East 9th Street Suite A701, Los Angeles, CA. 90079, Tel: 213 629 4422   Fax: 213 629 4517
www.garmentcontractors.org Email **gcasc@earthlink.net**

INTERNATIONAL GARMENT ASSOCIATION
5572 Walter Circle, Westminster, CA 92683, Tel: 714 893 1163, 800 327 5551, Fax: 562 865 6913

KOREAN AMERICAN GARMENT INDUSTRY ASSOCIATION
1830 W. Olympic Blvd., Suite 219, Los Angeles, CA 90006, Tel: 213 389 7776
Fax: 213 389 6093

KOREAN APPAREL MANUFACTURERS ASSOCIATION
420 East 11th street, Suite 312, Los Angeles, CA 90015, Tel: 213-746-5362, Fax: 213-746-0728,
www.kamausa.org

KOREAN GARMENT WHOLESALERS ASSOCIATION
420 E. 11th St., Room 312, LA. CA 90015, Tel: 213 746 5362 Fax: 213 746 0728, **www.kgwa.org**

NATIONAL KNITWEAR & SPORTSWEAR ASSOCIATION
386 Park Ave., South, New York, N.Y. 10001, Tel: 212 366 9008 Fax: 212 366 4166
www.asktmag.com

SAN FRANCISCO FASHION INDUSTRIES
1000 Brannan St., Suite 206, San Francisco, CA 94103, Tel: 415 621 6100 Fax: 415 621 6384
www.SFFI.org

SOUTH EASTERN APPAREL MANUFACTURERS ASSOCIATION (SEAM)
1900 Broad River Road, Suite #100, Columbia, SC 292107047, Tel: 803 772 5861 Fax: 803 731 7709

WORLD HONG KONG
501 7th Ave., # 1307 New York, NY 10018, Tel: 212 354 2255 Fax:212 921 2509

If the above does not help then try the yellow pages for extra listings.

Helpful Internet Resources

THE FASHION GROUP
International industry news, trend reports and forecasts, directories of professional services, job listings, and events calendar.
www.fgi.org

VIRTUAL RAGS
Links to international apparel industry sites.
www.virtualrags.com/links.htm

AMERICAN TEXTILE MANUFACTURERS INSTITUTE
Textile news, publications, products, and manufacturers directory. **www.atmi.org**

APPARELLINK.NET
Full resource site for the apparel industry.
www.Apparellink.net

APPAREL NEWS
California based trade paper.
www.Apparelnews.net

CAMEL HAIR AND CASHMERE INSTITUTE
Facts about these fibers and products manufactured from them.
www.cashmere.org

COTTON INCORPORATED
All about cotton, from crop economics to consumers; includes the Cotton Works Fabric Library of mills, knitters, and converters relating to woven fabrics, knits, home furnishings, and trimmings.
www.cottonincorp.com

FABRIC LINK
Technology, terminology, history, and care of fabrics and textiles. **www.fabriclink.com**

FASHION BUSINESS INCORPORATED
(formally The Fashion Business Incubator) FBI
Not for profit educational organization that provides business training, resource information, promotional opportunities and discounted marketing space for smaller designer driven manufactures.
www.fashionbizinc.org

FIBER SOURCE
All about man-made synthetic and cellulose fibers: fiber facts and history, economic statistics, industry news, and careers, plus the events calendar for **American Fiber Manufacturers Association.**
www.fibersource.com

SOUTH CAROLINA ELASTIC
History and use of "narrow fabrics" in apparel and home fashions.
www.scelastic.com

TEXTILE WEB
News and global links regarding yarn and fiber, fabrics and textiles, and textile manufacturing and sales.
www.textileweb.com

THE WOOL BUREAU
Beautifully designed site about wool, from yarn through apparel. **www.woolmark.com**

WOMEN'S WEAR DAILY
Fashion industry's daily news source.
www.wwd.com

APPAREL EXCHANGE
Apparel/textile links, services, and trade associations. **www.fabric.com**

DNR
Premier news magazine of men's fashion and retail. **www.dailynewsrecord.com**

THE BOBBIN SHOW DAILY NEWS
Information about Bobbin World (the International sewn Products Expo).
www.bobbin.com

DALLAS MARKET CENTER
News an exhibition dates for over 50 annual markets held at the world's first and largest wholesale and merchandise mart.
www.dallasmarketcenter.com

IGEDO
Fashion fair calendars for Düsseldorf, London, Miami, Hong Kong, and Shanghai.
www.igedo.com

MAGIC INTERNATIONAL
Event information for the world's largest market of women's, men's, and kid's apparel.
www.magiconline.com

MONTREAL FASHION MART
Canada's most expansive listing of fashion retailers. **www.montrealfashionmart.com**

CNN STYLE
Interactive Web site for news about fashion and home decór. **www.cnn.com/style**

THE FASHION CENTER
Industry links within New York City, including a map of the Garment Districts.
www.fashioncenter.com

FASHION-ICON
Fun site of fashion news from street style through leading designers. **www.fashion-icon.com**

GUPPY 22
Fastest-growing teen clothing site.
www.guppy22.com

HOME SHOPPING NETWORK
HSN's online shopping site, including their own company news and job openings.
www.hsn.com

JANE
Lifestyle magazine for confident, media-savvy, 18-34 year old women.
www.janemag.com

AMAZON.COM
Bookstore site for fashion-related titles.
www.amazon.com

BARNES & NOBLE
Bookstore site featuring new and used books about the fashion industry.
www.barnesandnoble.com

FAIRCHILD BOOKS
Online catalog for Fairchild Publications' books and visual media.
www.fairchildbooks.com

FASHION FOR PROFIT (Book and 2hour seminar DVD)
From design concept to selling a line. A professional's guide to entering the apparel industry.
www.FashionforProfit.com

FASHION PLANET
Award-winning magazine-style Web site about the businesses and personalities of the New York fashion industry. **www.fashion-planet.com**

ANGEL OF FASHION
www.fashionangel.com/linkpages

WEBPROMOTE.COM
www.webpromote.com

SEARCH ENGINE WATCH
www.searchenginewatch.com

DNS REGISTRARS DOTSTER
www.dotster.com

NETWORK SOLUTIONS
www.networksolutions.com

HOST MY SITE
www.hostmysite.com

ITPAPERS.COM
www.itpapers.com

THE APPARELLINK INDEX
For delivering apparel industry professionals to your site. **www.apparellink.net**

TEXTILE & APPAREL TRADERS
Free services such as apparel industry classified advertising, resource directories and apparel industry expert forums that generate repeat visits from industry professionals.
www.textileandappareltraders.com

Business Related Resources

FASHION BUSINESS INCORPORATED
(formally Fashion Business Incubator)
Small apparel business resource information center with their own model incubation agency.
www.Fashionbizinc.org

SOUTH COAST AIR QUALITY MANAGEMENT DISTRICT
www.aqmd.gov

SOUTHERN CALIFORNIA GAS COMPANY
www.socalgas.com/erc

SMALL AND HOME-BASED BUSINESS LINKS
A cornucopia of reference info, news group access, and links to business marketing tips.
www.bizoffice.com

SMALL BUSINESS ADMINISTRATION
Jump start your business with SBA assistance. **www.sba.gov**

SMALL BUSINESS FOCUS
This search engine focuses exclusively on SOHO sites. **www.sbfocus.com**

SOHO AMERICA
Enjoy some of the same support, benefits, and other resources that big-business honchos take for granted. **www.soho.org**

SWITCHBOARD
Find people, businesses, Web sites, and phone numbers. **www.switchboard.com**

YAHOO BUSINESS
Strong search directory provides topic-based links. **www.yahoo.com/business**

Fashion Vocabulary

Understanding the words and terms used within the fashion industry will be an important part of conducting every day business. Using these words and understanding them correctly will help when dealing with people in the industry, and will show that you are familiar with related terms and vocabulary. It will save you from feeling ignorant, and people familiar with the business will not know you are fresh on the scene. Being new to the game is one thing, but ignorance can lead to trouble. Spend some time to become familiar with these terms and the vocabulary. Learn a few words each day you will not regret it.

Accessories: Articles worn or carried to complete hats, handbags, and shoes.

Active sportswear: Clothing designed to be worn while participating in an active sport, e.g.: soccer, basketball, running, etc.

Adaptation: A design that reflects the dominant features of the style that inspired it but is not an exact copy.

Advertising credit: A mention of one or more store names, in connection with the advertisement of a vendor, as being the retail source for the merchandise advertised.

Advertising director: The person in charge of the personnel and activities of the advertising department.

Advertising plan: A forecast for a specified period of time, such as a season, quarter, month, or week, of the advertising that a store intends to employ to attract business.

Advertising: Any paid message in the media used to increase sales, publicize services, or gain the acceptance of ideas by potential buyers.

Apparel contractor: A firm whose sole function is to supply sewing services to the apparel industry.

Apparel industry: The manufacturers, jobbers, and contractors engaged in the manufacture of clothing, (also known as the rag trade).

Apparel manufacturer: A firm that performs all the operations required to produce a garment.

Artisans: People who do skilled work with their hands.

Ascot: A long scarf worn looped at the neck.

ASN/Advanced Shipping Notice: Electronically transmitted invoice.

Asymmetrical: A design that has a left and a right side, which are different, not identical as with a normal garment.

Atelier: French word for designer workshop.

Avant-garde: French term describing a design that is ahead of its time or unconventional.

Bodies: The basic shapes or silhouettes of a garment.

Base goods: Main solid fabric of a group.

Base stock: An item of fabric or merchandise that is in consistent demand throughout a year or season.

Bespoke: Refers to custom-made apparel, especially men's tailored apparel.

Bias: The diagonal cut of fabric or 45% degrees to the length or width of the fabric.

Block: A base pattern, from which new styles are created, sometimes referred to as a *sloper*.

Blocking or boarding: The application of heat to create the final shape in the finishing process for knitted goods.

Booth: A rented space used to show and to sell your product at trade shows.

Boutique: Small shop with unusual clothing.

Branch store: Store owned and operated by a parent store; generally located in a suburban area under the name of the parent store.

Brand name: A trade name that identifies a certain product made by a particular producer.

Budget: "Budget clothing" refers to the lower price range in garments, mass-produced for the budget clothing stores.

Bundling: The process of disassembling the stacked, cut fabric and reassembling pieces, then grouped by garment size, color dye lot, process of assembling, (the pieces that are first sewn together), and quantity of units ready for production.

Buttonhole Contractor: A contractor who specializes in making buttonholes, (keyhole or straight).

Button-stand: The area that extends beyond the true center front of the garment, to overlap and allow for buttons.

Buyer: A merchandising executive responsible for planning, buying, and selling merchandise

Buying office: An independent or store- owned office that is located at a market center and buys for one chain or for many stores.

Buying plan: A general description of the type quantities of merchandise a buyer expects to purchase for delivery within a specific period.

CAD: Computer Aided Drafting; Computer software programs that are used in pattern making and grading.

Carryover: Garment styles repeated in a line from one season to the next.

Cash discount: The percentage of premium allowed by a manufacturer off an invoice if payment is made within a certain specified period of time.

Caution: A fee charged for viewing a couture collection; as a preventive measure against copying, but which may be applied to any purchase.

Chain Store: A group of retail stores owned and operated by a central organization, all selling similarities of merchandise.

Care Labels: All manufacturers are required to include information on washing, drying, ironing, bleaching, or dry cleaning on all textile wearing apparel.

Charge-back: A store's invoice for claims against and allowances made by a vendor.

Chic: French word meaning stylish.

Classic: A fashion that is long lasting.

C.M.T.: *Cut, Make and Trim*, production steps used to produce a completed garment.

Collection: A group of apparel items presented together to the buying public, usually by the higher end designer.

Color Coding/Patterns: Helps to organize pattern pieces. Each type of fabric is color coded on the pattern.

Color story: Each group within a line of clothing will be grouped into a color story, either of like colors or with colors that complement one another.

Color-forecasting Prediction of future color preferences; research conducted by color forecasting companies, and textile and apparel companies to determine color trends.

Color-way: The variety of three or four seasonal color choices for the same solid or prints fabric available for each garment style.

Computer integrated manufacturing (CIM): The integration of computers, linked together produces finished produce.

Confinement: The sale by a producer or manufacturer of a fabric, line, label, or style on some exclusive basis, becomes exclusive to the buyer.

Conglomerate: A group of companies that may or may not be related in terms of product or marketing level but which are owned by a single parent company.

Consolidation: The combination of two companies to form a new company.

Consumer demands: The quality and quantity of goods or service the consumer is willing to buy.

Consumer: A user, sometimes used to denote a person who makes a buying decision.

Consumerism: The right of consumers to have protection against unfair marketing practices.

Contemporary styling: Sophisticated updated styling; originally designed for the age group that grew out of junior clothing.

Contour: The outline of the body.

Contractor: Company that specializes in sewing and finishing goods.

Contrast: Fabric of a different color or texture to create surface interest.

Converter, textile: A producer who buys fabrics in the greige and contracts to have them finished (dyed, bleached, printed, or subjected to other treatments) then sells it to a manufacturer.

Cooperative advertising: Advertising costs shared by a textile producer and/or a manufacturer and /or a retailer.

Copyright: Allows the copyright holder the exclusive right to use, perform, or reproduce written, pictorial, and performed work.

Corporation: Company established by a legal charter that outlines the scope and activity of the company.

Cost (wholesale cost, or cost to manufacture): The total cost to manufacture a style, including materials, sundries, labor, and such auxiliary costs as freight, duty, and packaging.

Cost sheet: Is used to calculate the total cost of manufacturing a garment, and will include yardage used, amount of sewing needed, plus any other overheads.

Cotton: A vegetable fiber from the boll of the cotton plant.

Counterfeit goods: Products that incorporate unauthorized use of registered trade names or trademarks.

Couture: French word meaning "high sewing" it refers to the highest-priced apparel produced in small quantities, made of high-quality fabrics and sized to fit individual clients' bodies.

Couturier: Male designer/dressmaker. *Couturiere:* women designer/dressmaker.

Croquis: A French term that refers to a figure outline used as a basis to sketch design ideas. Also called an under lay figure.

Custom-made: Apparel made to a customer's special order, cut and fitted to individual measurements, and opposite of ready-to-wear.

Customs broker: A person licensed by the Customs Office, to assist apparel manufacturers gain customs clearance to import goods produced offshore.

Cut to order: This term is used for couture clothing when there is only one garment to be made to order.

Cut, make, and trim (CMT): Apparel contractors who cut, make, and trim the garments for the apparel manufacturer.

Cutter: The person who cuts material into the pieces to been sewn, during the manufacturing process.

Cut-up trade: Manufacturers who produce belts for apparel manufacturers to add to pants, skirts, and dresses.

Dart: An angular seam sewn into a garment to shape for fit.

Dating: The period of time allowed by a vendor for the taking of cash discount.

Department store: Large retail establishment that departmentalizes its functions and merchandise.

Delivery Dates: Retailers requested dates for the delivery of the orders placed, usually within a two-week period. If the goods are not received within the give time the order will be canceled.

Design reports (Predictive): Reports and ideas available by subscription to manufacturers and retailers: - for example, I.M. International, Faces, Nigel French, Promostyl, Here and There, Tobe`.

Designer resource: Any resource from which a designer obtains ideas; can be trade papers, design reports, fashion magazines, museums, historic-costume books, nature, theater, films, fabrics, etc.

Designer: Person who creates ideas for garments or accessories in the fashion industry.

Design Specifications: A sheet that gives precise information on a design, from fabric, (swatch must be included), sizing, to the detailed sketch of the finished garment.

Die cutting: A piece of metal with a sharp edge similar to a cookie cutter tooled to the exact dimensions of the shape of the pattern pieces (the die). The die is positioned over the fabric to be cut, and then a pressurized plate is applied to the die to cut through the fabric layers.

Diffusion line: Designer's less-expensive line (e.g., Armani X, DKNY).

Digitizer: A table embedded with sensors that relate to X and Y coordinates (horizontal and vertical directions) which allow the shape of the pattern piece to be traced and converted to a drawing of the pattern in the computer.

Dilution: Difference between what you invoice and what you are paid

Direct marketing: Marketing by which manufacturers sell directly to the consumer. No middleman.

Direct-mail advertising: Any printed advertising distributed directly to specific customers by mail.

Discount: Is a term used in sales for the amount of discount allowed to a retailer.

Discretionary income: Income left after basic necessities have been paid for.

Display: Visual presentation of merchandise or ideas.

Disposable income: The amount a person has left to spend or save after paying taxes.

Distribution strategy whereby manufacturers sell their merchandise through their own stores as well as through other retailers.

Distributor: Middle person between the manufacturer and the retailer.

Domain name: Name that is selected by you for use on the Internet.

Downward-flow theory: The theory that fashion is first adopted by people at the top of the social pyramid. The style is then accepted at lower social levels. Also called the "trickle-down theory."

Draping: A process of creating the initial garment style by molding, cutting, and pinning fabric to a mannequin. This drape can then be made into a pattern.

Duplicate: A copy of the prototype or sample style used by the sales representatives to show and sell styles in the line to retail buyers (also called sales samples).

Dye House: The place where the fabric or piece goods are dyed.

EDI: Electronic Data Interchange; Computer-to-computer communications between companies.

Embroideries: A contractor specializing in embroidering goods. These days they usually use specialized computers that drive and sew the machines to produce the embroidered pieces.

Empire: A dress or top with a high waistline, named after Napoleon's empire, made famous by Empress Josephine of France who wore the high waistline dress popular at this time.

Ensemble: Refers to the complete outfit worn, including the shoes and accessories.

Estimated yardage: The estimated yardage for a garment or garments.

Fabric/Textile Shows: Trade shows, which show new designs of textiles to manufactures at, wholesale prices.

Fabrication: Selection of the appropriate fabric for a garment.

Factoring: Providing loans to manufacturers based on orders received (accounts receivable). Factor.

Fad: Short lived fashion.

Fallout: The fabric that remains in the spaces between pattern pieces on the marker, representing the amount of fabric wasted.

Fashion consultant: A person who gives professional fashion advice or services.

Fashion coordinator or director: The fashion expert of an organization, who keeps it current with fashion developments and works with designers or buyers to form the fashion image of the company.

Fashion cycle: Fashion changes; refers to the introduction, acceptance, and decline of a fashion.

Fashion editor: The head fashion reporter at a magazine or newspaper, who analyzes the fashion scene and interprets it for readers.

Fashion forecast: A prediction of forthcoming fashions.

Fashion Group: An international association of professionals in the fashion business; founded in 1931.

Fashion innovation: New ideas in fashion styling.

Fashion merchandising: The planning required to have the right fashion-oriented merchandise at the right time, in the right place, in the right quantities, and at the right price.

Fashion season: Name given to lines or collections that correspond to seasons of the year when consumers would most likely wear the merchandise; e.g. spring, summer, fall, holiday, and resort.

Fashion trend: The direction in which fashion is moving.

Fashion: The prevailing style accepted and used by the majority of a group at any given time.

Fiber: A hair-like unit of raw material from which textile fabric is made.

Fiber Content Labels: Most textile items are required by law to provide fiber content by predominance of weight. This information is not required to be sewn in with a label, but the fiber content must be available at the point of sale.

Fictitious Business Name/ DBA (Doing Business As): Your registered business name in the state that you are doing business. (Usually renewable every five years, check your own states laws). Required to open a business checking account, obtain a local business license or resale license.

Filament: A continuous strand of fiber.

Findings: Trade term for such as zippers and elastic.

Finishing: The last treatments given to fabrics; the final handwork or final touches done to a garment.

First cost: The wholesale price of merchandise at place of origin.

First pattern: Trial pattern made in the design department for the sample garment.

Fit model: The live model whose body dimensions match the company's sample size and who is used to assess the fit, style, and overall look of new prototypes.

Fixtures: Used for displaying purposes in trade shows, showrooms, and retail stores.

Flat pattern: The pattern process used to make a pattern for a new style from the base block or sloper.

Flat-knit: Goods that are knit, as compared to goods knit in a tube (tubular knit).

Foundations: The trade term for such women's undergarments as bras, girdles, panty girdles, garter belts, and corsets.

Franchise: A type of contractual arrangement, to provide the franchisee with exclusive distribution of a well-recognized brand name in a specific market area as well as assistance in running the business in return for a franchise payment.

Freight Charges: Shipping costs.

Freight forwarding company: A company that moves a shipment of goods from the country where the goods were produced to the United States.

Full-fashioned: Goods knit with shaping along the edges to conform to the body contour.

Full Package Manufacturer: Producing the total garment, from design through to shipping.

Fusible: *Interlinings or Interfacings*, used to give extra body or control to the garment, often referred to as **fusing** as it is fused to the surface of the fabric used for the garment by using heat.

Fuse: Heat-setting fusible interfacings into place, to give extra body to a garment.

Garment dyed: Apparel produced as white or colorless goods, then dyed during the finishing process.

Garment Manufacturers license and Registration Laws: Required in some states to protect the labor laws. Payment of a fee, and requiring a simple test based on the labor law.

Garment specification sheet: A list of vital information for the garment.

Girth: Measurement around the body.

Godet: Triangular piece of fabric used to make a garment wider on one end, for better fit or for design purposes.

Gore: A tapering piece of fabric used to make a garment wider on one end, often used in skirts.

Grading/Grader: A person or contractor who is trained to size the base size pattern up and down to the other sizes that will be produced. This is done either manually or by computer programs, CAD.

Grain: The woven thread making up the fabric.

Grain-Line: Direction of warp and weft threads in the fabric; lengthwise and crosswise grains.

Greige/Grey goods: Unfinished fabric bought by the converter to convert to the finished goods.

Gross margins: The difference in dollars between net sales and the net cost of merchandise during a given period.

Group: Coordinated apparel items using a few colors and fabrics within an apparel line.

Gusset: Fabric piece of various shapes set into a garment to make it easier to move.

Hand: The feel of the fabric.

Hang Tags: Attached to the finished garment to provide information: Manufacturer, Care, and Fiber content, Size, Style, and Color.

Haute couture: Fashion term for high fashion clothing, sold in small quantities, generally at high prices.

Header: Technical name for a sample of fabric used by the textile sales rep. to show their line to the designer or manufacturer. (Head-ends of the fabric).

High fashion: The newest fashion designs worn by fashion leaders.

Hot item: A best selling item.

House Account: The manufacturer has made the contact and sale; no commission is paid to the sales representative.

Hue: A color tone.

Ideacomo: Italian fabric trades fair, held each November and May in Como, Italy.

Image: The public impression that your company conveys.

In-house/Inside shop: An apparel company that does all its manufacturing process in its own factory.

Intensity: The brightness or paleness of a color.

Interlinings/Interfacing: *Fusible*, stabilizer used in garment construction.

Interstoff: German term meaning "interfabric"; international fabric trade fair, held each November and May in Frankfurt, Germany.

Intimate apparel: The trade term for women's foundation, lingerie, and loungewear.

Inventory: All stocked goods, fabric, trims, finished goods.

Invoice: The bill, which is shipped with the merchandise.

Item house: Contractor who specializes in the production of one product.

Item: One of a group or line.

Jacquard: A weave of elaborate patterns, such as damask, brocade, or tapestry. Thought to be the first step to the invention of the computer.

Jobber: A middleman between the producer and the commercial consumer. **Fabric Jobber:** buys end lots or odd rolls of fabric from mills, converters, wholesales, distributors and manufacturers.

Junior: Size scale of female apparel; odd size range, 1 to 15.

Keystoning: A method used to determine the final cost of your goods. The manufacturer and the retailer usually double the basic cost to arrive at a selling price.

Knock-off: A copy of an existing garment.

Lab dip: The vendor-supplied sample of the dyed-to-match product, such as fabric, zipper, button, knit collar or cuff, or thread.

Last: A form made from wood, metal or plastic that is used to shape shoes when being made.

Lay ends: The section on either end of the marker that is waste material.

Lengthwise grain: Threads parallel to the fabric selvedge.

Licensing: Giving a manufacturer permission to use a designer's mane or design in return for a fee or percentage of sales.

Ligne: (French) Line: Refers to the size of a button.

Line brochure: (line catalog, or line sheet) A catalog of all the styles available in the line, used to market the line to the retail buyers.

Line: A group or several small groups of apparel items developed with a theme that links them together.

Linen: A vegetable fiber from the woody stalk of the flax plant.

Lingerie: Undergarments. Slips, camisoles, nightgowns and panties.

Logo: A symbol or graphic used to identify a product, usually trademarked.

Long-range forecasting: Research focusing on general economic and social trend related to consumer spending patterns.

Long-run fashion: A fashion that takes more seasons to complete its cycle than what might be considered its average life expectancy.

Loss leader: An item sold at less than the regular wholesale price for the purpose of attracting retail buyers to other merchandise.

Man-made fibers: Synthetic fibers made in chemical plant.

Marker: Pattern lay out of all the pattern pieces marked onto paper the width of the fabric, and used by the cutter to follow when cutting the garment.

Market: Specific times throughout the year that manufacturers sell, usually in a trade mart in a key city.

Market Fees: Fees charged to sell in a mart for temporary space.

Marketing: A business interaction that includes the planning, pricing, promotion, and distribution of goods.

Market Niche: A product type targeted for a specific customer.

Mark-up: Difference between cost price and selling price.

Mart: Center or building that houses showrooms in which sales representatives shows the clothing lines to buyers.

Mass production: The production of garments in large quantities.

Merchandising: Planning required by the retailer to insure the merchandise is targeted for the right customer, at the right price, in the correct quantities, and at the right time.

Microfiber: A manmade fiber two or three times thinner than human hair, it has the touch and feel of silk or cashmere, but is wrinkle resistant.

Mill: Where textiles are woven or knitted.

Millinery: Hats, and especially hats made by hand.

Minimum order: Number of garments or dollar amount the manufacturer requires the retailer to buy before the order is accepted.

Missy: Female size range in even numbers.

Mode: Used mainly in Europe, meaning fashion.

Muslin: Unbleached cotton used to drape a garment or to sew into a first trial sample.

Nap: Corduroy, Velvet, Suede etc, all have a nap and must all be cut in one direction, to avoid shading.

National brands: Brand name that is distributed nationally and to which consumers recognize and attach a specific image.

Natural fibers: Cotton, silk, wool, flax, etc. All fibers that are grown or produced naturally.

Non-store retailer: Distribution of products to consumers through means other than traditional retailers.

Notch: A small cut in the pattern or fabric to show dart placement and seam allowance, which aids the operator in sewing up the garment.

Off-price retailer: Retailer who specializes in selling national brands or designer apparel at discount prices.

Offshore production: Production outside the United States.

Open-to-buy: The amount of money a buyer can spend on merchandise to be delivered within a given period, minus the amount allocated to merchandise on order.

Order Form: The sales person writes the order from the customer. This information is used to produce, ship and bill for the goods.

Out-side shop: Contractors used by manufacturers to cut, sew, or other special services.

Out-Sourcing: Services or goods form outside the company.

Overheads: The cost of operations that do not vary from month to month, (Fixed Costs).

Packing list: An itemized form, which is included in the shipment of goods. The list should also include any items on back order or sold out goods. This list is either included in the box or can be attached to the outside.

Partnership: Business owned by two or more persons.

Patent: Legal process to ensure original idea is protected with exclusive rights.

Pattern Design System (PDS): A computer hardware and software system that is used by the patternmaker to create new patterns.

Physical inventory: A count of the stock.

Pick-Tickets: The term used for the method of pulling the orders for shipping to the customers.

Piece dyed: The process of dyeing the fabric after weaving or knitting. Manufacturers often use this method to have customized colors dyed.

Piece goods: Trade name for fabric.

Piecework: Construction method used in the industry, and a method of calculating pay for work done.

Ply: A thickness of fabric or of fiber.

Pre-Packs: Goods pre-packed for sale in: sizes, colors, or assortments thereof.

Prêt-a-Porter: French term used for the ready to wear shows and exhibitions.

Price point: A specific price at which an assortment of merchandise is offered for sale.

Price range: The range between the lowest and the highest price for a clothing line.

Private label brand: Brand name that is owned and marketed by a specific retailer for use in its store.

Private label: Merchandise that includes a retailer's label on a product for which the retailer has some, or full control of the garment that is manufactured.

Product Development Department: A group of experts, within large companies who develop new lines. The team will include, a designer, a merchandiser and head of product development.

Production cutting: The production fabric is laid open along the entire width and many yards long in length, it is stacked in multiple layers with the marker resting on top as a guide for the cutting.

Production pattern: The final perfected pattern used to make the marker for cutting.

Production schedule: Used in producing a garment and getting it shipped on time.

Production: The construction process by which the garment is made.

Production Patterns: The perfected first pattern, ready and graded for production.

Production Sewer: A power machine operator who sews garments together, either as a piece worker or producing the whole garment.

Product Line: The type of product your company produces for resale.

Profit: Why we are all doing what we are doing!

Proportion: The relationship of one part of a design to another, an important principle of garment design.

Prototype: The first sample garment of a new style.

Pulling & Packaging: Pulling goods to be shipped and packaging them, according to the order.

Punch holes: Small holes to mark the end of a dart, pocket placement etc.

Purchase Journal: A monthly or semimonthly report listing all invoices for merchandise received, transfers of merchandise, or returns to vendors as entered in the inventory book.

Quality Assurance/ Quality control: Area of a company that focuses on inspecting finished products and making sure they adhere to specifications of a company's quality standards.

Quick response: The concept of filling orders as quickly as possible.

Quota: Numerical limit on the number of products in specific categories that can be imported.

Ready-to-wear: Apparel that is mass-produced.

Receiving: the area of a company where packages are received, opened, and checked.

Registration Number (RN#): The manufacturer is required to display their RN # or their full name on each garment that they manufacture.

Re-Orders: Goods that are reordered by the customer.

Repeat Bodies: Successfully styles that are re-cut in other fabrications: may have variations of detailing.

Resource: Place to find articles needed in manufacturing.

Retail price: The wholesale price plus a markup covering the retailer's operating costs and its profit.

Retail store/direct market brands: Brand names on merchandise that is also the name of the retail store, e.g., The Gap, Banana Republic.

Retro: The return to a fashion look of recent decades, (abbr. Retrospective).

Return-to-vendor: A store's invoice covering merchandise returned for cause to its vendor.

Risers: Fixtures used raise displays, used at trade shows, showrooms, and retailers stores.

Road Reps: Sales representatives that travel to the customer to make a sale.

Sale representative: Individual who serves as the intermediary between the apparel manufacturer and the retailer, negotiating sales of the apparel line to retail buyers.

Sales Sample/Duplicates: Samples made for the sales representatives to show to the buyers.

Sales Terms: How the payment for the order will be paid.

Sample cut: A three to five yard length of fabric purchased from textile firms by the apparel manufacturer to use in making a first sample garment.

Sample Sewer/Maker: A designer's assistant who is expert in constructing a garment and who is familiar with production methods used in the industry.

Sample: A prototype of a garment.

Savile Row: Famous street in London known for men's tailors.

Screen Printer: A person that makes a screen for a design, and prints it onto a finished garment, or onto a cut pattern piece that is then sewn into a finished garment.

Selling Seasons: Time when the garments are shown to the buyer for ordering. Traditionally three months before shipping dates.

Seventh Avenue: The garment district in New York.

Sew by: Also known as a sample garment sewn by a contractor to use as a guide in production.

Shipping & Distribution: The method used to deliver goods to the buyer.

Shopping the market: Looking for new styles and fashion trends in the retail market that may influence the direction of the apparel industry.

Short-range forecasting: Determining fashion trends of the coming season.

Showing: Formal presentation of styles, usually in connection with showing the season's new merchandise.

Showroom: A place where sales people show a line of merchandise to potential buyers.

Showroom Fees: The amount of rent money paid to the sales representative for the space used to show a line.

Silhouette: Outline of a garment.

Silk: A fiber produced from the cocoon spun from a silkworm.

Size specifications: The actual garment measurements at specific parts of the garment, which are set by the production sample.

Size standards: Proportional increases or decreases in garment measurements for sizes produced by a ready-to-wear apparel manufacturer.

SKU #: A number used to track a garment and for ordering purposes.

Sloper: *Block:* A basic pattern that is used to make other patterns for new styles.

Snap Setters: Usually contracted to set special snaps on garments using special machinery.

Soft goods: Fashion and textile goods.

Source: Company from which textile producers, apparel manufacturers, or retailers purchase products necessary in their production and distribution (e.g. fiber sources, fabric sources, apparel product sources).

Sourcing: Decision process for determining how and where textile and apparel products or their components will be produced.

Specifications/Specs: Used extensively in the industry to give precise details on a garment: - measurements, fabric, colors and any other details.

Spinning: The process of drawing and twisting fibers together into yarn or thread.

Split Commission: Commission of sales is divided, when more than one sales representative is involved with a sale.

Sportswear: Clothing intended for casual wear. Not to be confused with active sportswear, or athletic clothing.

Spreading machines: Equipment designed to carry the large rolls of fabric, guided on tracks along the side edges of the cutting table, to spread the fabric smoothly and quickly.

Spreading: The process of unwinding the large rolls of fabric onto long, wide cutting tables, stacked layer-upon-layer, in preparation for cutting.

Staple goods: Goods for which there is a continuous demand over many seasons. Staple goods should always be in stock.

Staples: Clothing that is basic in style and is always in demand, e.g. t-shirts, jeans, underwear etc.

Start Date: A period of time to begin shipping and delivering to a customer.

Statement: A bill of outstanding charges that is sent to a customer, usually every month.

Stock turnover: The number of times a store's merchandise stock is sold and replaced in a given period.

Structured apparel: A garment whose construction involves many different operations that give it a shape of its own, as in tailoring.

Style: A characteristic or distinctive way a garment looks, and features that makes it different from other garments, often thought of as elegant.

Style boards: Used to show design direction for the next season.

Style name: This is the name that best describes a garment, e.g. shift dress, or tub top.

Style number: A number (usually four digits) assigned to each garment style that is coded to indicate the season/year and other style information.

Style range: Categories of style that appeal to different consumers.

Stylist: A fashion expert; generally selects colors, prints, or styles for presentation or prepares merchandise for advertisement or catalogs.

Sub-contractor: If the contractor needs special operations to be done on a garment, it can be sub-contracted out to another contractor. At times a contractor can have too much work and will need to contract out the work, this is *sub-contracting*.

Swatch: A small sample of fabric, used to show the intended fabrication for a style.

Sweatshops: Apparel factories known for poor working conditions, long hours, and low wages.

Tagboard: sometimes referred to as manila: A heavy weight paper used to make patterns.

Tanning: The process of transforming animal skins into leather.

Target market: A group of consumers for whom a manufacturer, or retailer aims products.

Taste: Good taste in fashion implies sensitivity not only to what is artistic but also what prevailing fashion says is appropriate for a specific occasion.

Technical drawing: A drawing of a garment style as viewed flat rather than three dimensionally on a fashion figure. It could also include details of a garment.

Terms of sale: The combination of allowable discounts on purchases and the time allowed for taking such discounts.

Textile fabric: Cloth made from textile fibers by weaving, knitting, felting, crocheting, laminating, or bonding.

Textile mill: Company that specializes in the fabric construction stage of production (e.g. weaving, knitting).

Textile/Apparel Linkage Council (TALC): Formed to establish voluntary electronic data interchange between apparel manufacturers and textile companies.

Texture: The look and feel of all types of material, woven or non-woven.

Theme: A line should be designed with a theme to tie it together and give it a cohesive flow.

Thread count: The number of yarns or "threads" in one square inch of fabric.

Toile: A French term used to refer to a first sample, or muslin trial garment.

Tolerance: The acceptable dimensions, plus or minus in inches (or metric measurements) from the size specifications.

Torso: The body from the neck to the hips.

Trade associations: Nonprofit associations made up of companies designed to promote, research, or provide educational services regarding an industry or a specific aspect of an industry.

Trade shows: Sponsored by trade associations, apparel marts, and/or promotional companies. Trade shows allow companies to promote their newest products to prospective buyers who have the opportunity to review new products from a number of companies in one show.

Trademark: A company's individual registered mark, and name for a product.

Trend: The direction of fashion both in styles, color, fabrics, and accessories.

Trend research: Reading appropriate trades publications or fashion magazines to determine directions for color, fabric, and styles.

Trendsetter: A designer or fashion leader who sets a fashion direction that others follow.

Trimmings: Also referred to as findings e.g. zippers, bindings, buttons.

Trunk show: Designer clothes that are shown from store to store often accompanied by a personal appearance by the designer.

Underlining: Fabric sewn to each pattern piece before the garment is sewn together, to give added support or shape; often seen in vintage clothing.

Unit control: Systems for recording the number of units of merchandise bought, sold, in stock, or on order.

Units: Each manufactured garment or piece is referred to as a unit. Some companies produce more units than another.

Universal Product Code (UPC): One of several barcode symbols used for electronic identification of merchandise. A UPC number is twelve digits that identify the manufacturer and merchandise item for stock keeping of units.

Unstructured apparel: Garments whose construction involves few steps and takes its shape from the wearer.

Upward-flow theory: The theory that a style is created on the streets of lower income families, and is then adopted by all other income brackets as a new fashion trend.

Usage: The number of yards (yardage) of fabric(s) required to make a garment. It usually refers to the most economical layout, which uses the least amount of fabric.

Value: The lightness or darkness of a color.

Variable costs: This cost fluctuates; depending on how many units is sold, e.g. sales reps commission.

Vendor: A seller, resource, manufacturer, or supplier.

Vertical integration: The joining of companies at different levels of production and marketing, such as a fiber producer with a fabric mill.

Vertical mill: From the fiber to weaving, to printing and dyeing of the clothing.

Warp: Lengthwise thread of fabric that forms the foundation for the *weft*.

Warp knitting: Knitting fabric in loops running vertically.

Weaving: The process of forming fabric by interlacing yarns on looms.

Weft: Crosswise thread of fabric.

Weft knitting: Knitting fabric in loops horizontally or in a circle.

Wholesale market: Market where commercial consumers buy directly from producers.

Wholesale price: Price paid by commercial consumers for supplies and product, which are then sold to the customer for the retail price.

Women's Wear Daily: Trade publication of the women's fashion industry.

Wool: An animal fiber, which is from the hair of sheep or other animals.

Working sketch: Same as technical drawing or specification.

Yarn: A continuous thread produced by twisting or spinning fibers together, long enough and strong enough to use in fabric.

Yarn-dyed: The dyeing of the yarn before weaving or knitting; this results in deep rich colors.

Yoke: A shaped piece in a garment (shoulder or hip) from which the rest of the garment hangs

Glossary of Fabric Terms

Acetate: This synthetic man made fabric is manufactured from cellulose fibers and usually used in linings. It is an inexpensive fabric with poor washing abilities, and should be dry-cleaned. *(See Chapter 9)*

Acrylic: Often used in place of wool as a cheap synthetic substitute. It is warm and lightweight, it washes well, and is less expensive than wool. (See Chapter 9)

Alpaca: The lower grades of alpaca were originally used as linings, and the better grades for fine dress goods. True alpaca cloth of alpaca hair is soft and lightweight.

Antique Satin: a reversible satin-weave fabric with satin floats on the technical face and surface slubs on the technical back created by using slub-filling yarns. It is usually used with the technical back as the right side for drapery fabrics and often made of a blend of fibers.

Astrakhan: Rough fabric with closely curled face resembling Astrakhan lamb's pelt. Woven or knitted usually with base yarns of cotton and pile of wool, mohair, acrylic or modacrylic fibers.

Barathea: Smooth-faced worsted uniform fabric constructed of an indistinct twilled basket weave of fine two-ply yarns.

Bathrobe Blanketing: Double-faced fabric woven with tightly twisted warp and two sets of soft spun filling yarns. Usually napped to produce soft, thick, warm material. Made of cotton, wool, polyester, acrylic, and blends of these fibers.

Batiste: an opaque, lightweight, spun yarn plain-weave fabric with a smooth surface. When made of cotton or cotton/polyester, the yarns are usually combed. It can be made of all wool, silk, or rayon.

Bedford cord: a heavy, warp-faced, unbalanced pique-weave fabric with wide warp cords created by extra filling yarns floating across the back to give a raised effect.

Bengaline: a lustrous, durable, warp-faced fabric with heavy filling cords completely covered by the warp.

Blanket Cloth: Plain or twill weaves. Thick, soft-filling yarns heavily napped both sides. Often yarn-dyed in plaids or stripes.

Boucle´: A fabric woven or knitted from curled or specially twisted yarn, which has small loops on the surface, giving a kinky appearance. The curls do not cover the entire surface but occur at intervals, distinguishing it from astrakhan. Often made in coating weights but also in lighter weights for dress goods and sweaters.

Broadcloth: a close plain-weave fabric made of cotton, rayon, or a blend of either cotton or rayon with polyester. It has a fine rib in the filling direction caused by slightly larger filling yarns, filling yarns with a lower twist, or a higher warp-yarn count. High-quality broadcloth is made with plied warp and filling yarns. The fabric may be mercerized. It has a soft, firm hand. The term *broadcloth* is also used to refer to a plain- or twill-weave lustrous wool or woo-blend fabric that is highly napped and then pressed flat.

Brocade: a jacquard-woven fabric with a pattern that is created with different colors or with patterns in twill or satin weaves on a ground of plain, twill, or satin weave. It is available in a variety of fiber contents and qualities.

Buckram: a heavy, very still, spun-yarn fabric converted from cheesecloth gray goods with adhesives and fillers. It is used as an interlining to stiffen pinch-pleated, window-treatment fabrics.

Bunting: (See Cheesecloth)

Burlap: a coarse, heavy, loosely woven plain-weave fabric often made of single irregular yarns of jute. It is used in its natural color for carpet backing, bagging, and furniture webbing. It is also dyed and printed for home-furnishing uses.

Calico: A low-count or medium-count cotton or cotton/manmade print-cloth with small early American designs. Used for aprons, dresses, curtains, and quilts.

Cambric: a fine, firm, plain weave balanced fabric with starch, and has a slight luster on one side.

Camel Hair: In undyed form, camel hair is light tan and with a soft nap. Fabrics that merely have this distinctive color cannot be correctly called camel hair. The best grade is very expensive, and even then, camel hair is sometimes mixed with sheep's wool or other fibers.

Candlewick: Muslin base fabric tufted with heavy plied yarns providing fuzzy designs.

Canvas: a heavy, firm; strong fabric often made of cotton or acrylic and used for awnings, slipcovers, and covers for boats. It is produced in many grades and qualities. It is made in plain or basket weave.

Cashmere: Real cashmere fabric is woven only from the hair of the Cashmere goat. It is of fine close twill weave, napped and extremely soft. The total amount of cashmere hair available is severely limited.

Cavalry twill: a steep, pronounced, double-wale line, smooth-surfaced twill fabric.

Challis (shal´i): a lightweight, spun yarn; plain weave, balanced fabric with a soft finish. It can be made of any staple fiber or blend of fibers.

Chambray: a plain-weave fabric usually of cotton, rayon, or a blend of these with polyester. Usually chambray has white yarns in the filling direction and yarn-dyed yarns in the warp direction. Iridescent chambray is made with one color in the warp and a second color in the filling. It can also be made in striped patterns.

Charmeuse: Silk, rayon, or cotton satin weave fabric with semi lustrous surface and dull back. Used for dresses, gowns, and pajamas.

Charvet Silk: Diagonal rib weaves with stripes. Soft, drapes well. Used for neckties.

Cheesecloth: a lightweight, sheer, plain-woven fabric with a very soft texture. It may be natural colored, bleached, or dyed. It usually has a very low count. If dyed, it may be called *bunting* and could be used for flags or banners.

Chenille: Fluff or fuzzy-faced fabric made with a chenille filling yarn that has a fuzzy pile protruding from all sides. Some imitations made by tufting, using no chenille yarn. Other versions are knitted with or to imitate chenille yarn.

Chiffon: a sheer, very lightweight, plain-woven fabric with fine crepe twist yarns of approximately the same size and twist used in warp and filling. The fabric is balanced.

China silk: a soft, lightweight, opaque, plain-weave fabric made from fine-filament yarns and used for apparel.

Chino: a steep-twill fabric with a slight sheen, often made in a bottom-weight fabric of cotton or cotton/polyester. Often it is made of combed two-ply yarns in both warp and filling and vat-dyed in khaki.

Chintz: A cotton print cloth, of high-count plain weave, with bright, attractive floral or geometric designs, both large and small. Often given a permanent or semi-permanent glaze; then known as glazed chintz. For draperies, slipcovers, and dresses.

Cloque fabric: a general term used to refer to any fabric with a puckered or blistered effect.

Corduroy: a filling-yarn pile fabric where the pile is created by long-filling floats that are cut and brushed in the finishing process. The ground weave may be either a plain or twill weave.

Cotton: a white vegetable fiber grown in warmer climates in many parts of the world and which has been used to produce many types of fabric for hundreds of years. Cotton fabric feels good against the skin regardless of the temperature or the humidity and is therefore in great demand by the consumer. *(See Chapter 9)*

Crash: a medium- to heavyweight; plain-weave fabric made from slub or irregular yarns to create an irregular surface

Crepe: Has a pebbly or crinkled surface produced by use of special crepe yarns. Can be crepe, granite, or plain weave. Generally, mixed-twist crepe yarns used in both warp and filling; occasionally crepe yarns used only in the warp or the filling. Crepe effects can also be obtained by chemical treatment and embossing.

Crepe-back Satin or Satin Crepe: Satin weave of silk or manmade fiber with a crepe-twist filling. As the fabric is reversible, interesting effects can be obtained by contrasting the surfaces. Used for dresses, blouses, and linings.

Crepe Charmeuse: Smooth, soft luster fabric of grenadine silk warp and filling, with latter given crepe twist. Body and drape of satin. Used for dresses, and eveningwear.

Crepe (Wool): Wool crepe is a lightweight worsted fabric with a more or less crinkly appearance, obtained by using warp yarns that are tightly twisted in alternate directions. The term is often applied to lightweight worsted fabrics for women's wear that have little or no crepe surface.

Damask: a reversible, flat, jacquard-woven fabric with a stain weaves in both the pattern and the plain-weave ground. It can be one color or two. In two-color damasks, the color reverses on the opposite side. It is used in apparel and home furnishings.

Denim: a cotton or cotton/polyester blend, twill-weave, and yarn dyed fabric. Usually the warp is colored and the filling is white. It is usually left-hand twill that is commonly available with a blue warp and white filling for use in apparel. It is available in a variety of weights.

Doeskin: Two different types: (1) Fine quality, close compact wool fabric, satin weave, smooth face, light nap finish. Used for suits and coats. (2) Rayon twill or small satin with face nap. Used for suits, coats, and sportswear.

Double cloth: a fabric made by weaving two fabrics with five sets of yarns: two sets of warp, two sets of filling, and one set that connects the two fabrics.

Double knit: a general term used to refer to any filling-knit fabric made on two needle beds.

Double weave: a fabric made by weaving two fabrics with four sets of yarns (two sets of warp and two sets of filling yarns) on the same loom. The two fabrics are connected by periodically reversing the positions of the two fabrics from top to bottom. Double weave is also known as *pocket cloth* or *pocket weave.*

Drill: a strong, medium- to heavyweight, warp-faced, twill-weave fabric. It is usually a 2/1 left-handed twill and piece dyed.

Duck: a strong, heavy, plain or basket weave fabric. Duck comes in a variety of weights and qualities. It is similar to canvas, usually made from cotton.

Embossing: a fabric with a design with heated, engraved calendars creates embossed fabrics. Often print cloths are embossed to imitate seersucker, crepe, or other structural-design fabrics.

Faille (file): a medium- to heavyweight, unbalanced, plain weave fabric with filament yarns, warp-faced, flat ribs created by using heavier filling yarns. It has a light luster.

Felt: a fiberweb fabric of at least 70 percent wool made by interlocking the scales of the wool fibers through the use of heat, moisture, and agitation.

Flannel: a light- to heavyweight, plain- or twill-weave fabric with a napped surface.

Flannelette: a light- to medium-weight, plain-weave cotton or cotton-blend fabric lightly napped on one side.

Fleece: Fabric with deep, soft nap. Term properly applied to flat woven or knit fabrics as well as to those woven on the pile principle. The long nap or pile provides many air spaces, resulting in a fabric with high insulative properties.

Frieze´: a strong, durable, heavy-warp yarn pile fabric. The pile is made by the over-wire method to create a closed-loop pile.

Gabardine (gaberdine): a tightly woven, medium- to heavyweight, steep- or regular-angle, twill-weave fabric with a pronounced wale. The fabric can be wool, a wool-blend, or synthetic-fiber content designed to look like wool. Gabardine can also be 100 percent-texturized polyester or a cotton/polyester blend.

Gauze: a sheer, lightweight, low-count, plain- or leno-weave balanced fabric made up spun yarns. It is often cotton, rayon, or a blend of these fibers. *Indian gauze* has a crinkled look and is available in a variety of fabric weights.

Georgette: a sheer, lightweight, plain weave fabric made with fine-crepe yarns. It is crepier and less lustrous than chiffon.

Gingham: a yarn-dyed, plain weave fabric that is available in a variety of weights and qualities. It may be balanced or unbalanced. It may be made of combed or carded yarns. If two colors of yarn are used, the fabric is called a check or checked gingham. If three or more colors are used, the fabric is referred to as plaid gingham.

Gossamer: Very soft, gauzelike veiling originally of silk.

Granada: Fine, face-finished fabric with a granular surface. Made of worsted yarn. Often dyed black.

Gray goods (grey goods or greige goods): a general term used to describe any unfinished woven or knitted fabric.

Grosgrain: (grow´grain) a tightly woven, firm, warp-faced fabric with heavy, round filling ribs created by a high-warp count and coarse filling yarns. Grosgrain can be woven as a narrow-ribbon or a full-width fabric.

Habutai: a soft, lightweight silk fabric. It is heavier than China silk.

Handkerchief linen: similar in luster and count to batiste, but it is linen or linen-look with slub yarns and a little more body.

Herringbone: a broken twill-weave fabric created by changing the direction of the twill wale from right to left and back again. This creates a chevron pattern of stripes that may be or may not be equally prominent. Herringbone fabrics are made in a variety of weights, patterns, and fiber contents.

Hessian: See *Burlap*.

Homespun: a coarse, plain weave fabric with a hand-woven look.

Hopsacking: a coarse, loosely woven suiting-or bottom-weight; basket-weave fabric often made of low-grade cotton.

Houndstooth check: a medium- to heavyweight, yarn-dyed twill-weave fabric in which the interlacing and color pattern creates a unique pointed-check or houndstooth shape.

India Silk: Very thin, soft, hand-loomed plain weave fabric made chiefly in India.

Interlock: a firm, double filling knit where the two needle beds knit two-interlocked 1 x 1 rib fabrics. Both sides of the fabric look like the face side of jersey.

Irish Poplin: Two types: (1) Originally a fabric constructed with silk warp and wool filling in plain weave with fine rib. (2) Fine linen or cotton shirting also made in Ireland. Sometimes used for neckwear.

Khaki: Tan or dusty colored warp face twill, softer and finer than drill. Name derived from East India word meaning earth color. Fabric made of cotton, linen, wool, worsted, or manmade fibers and blends.

Lace: an openwork fabric with yarns that are twisted around each other to form complex patterns or figures. Lace may be hand or machine made by a variety of fabrication methods including weaving, knitting, crocheting, and knotting.

La Coste: a double-knit fabric made with a combination of knit and tuck stitches to create a mesh-like appearance. It is often a cotton or cotton/polyester blend.

Lame': Fabric in which flat metal threads form the pattern or the background. Used chiefly for eveningwear.

Lawn: a fine, opaque, lightweight, and plain weave fabric usually made of combed-cotton or cotton-blend yarns. The fabric may be bleached, dyed, or printed.

Leno: refers to any leno-weave fabric in which two warp yarns are crossed over each other and held in place by a filling yarn. Leno weaves require a doup attachment on the loom.

Linen: can be classified in a variety of classifications, from fine and lightweight used for fine shirts to a heavier more durable weight used for pants and jackets. Linen has the tendency to creasing and needs ironing often.

Lining twill: an opaque, lightweight, warp-faced twill of filament yarns. It may be printed.

Loden Clothe: Heavily fulled or felted fabric originating in Austrian Tyrol. Wool may be blended with camel hair or alpaca. Thick, soft, waterproof without chemical treatment. Sometimes given fine nap. Used for coats, sportswear.

Lycra: (See Spandex)

Madras: Cotton fabric of plain weave of coarse yarns. Usually comes in stripes, checks, or plaids. Colors may bleed. Used for shirting.

Marble Silk: Lightweight silk fabric of warp-printed yarn or multicolored filling, which imparts mottled appearance. Used for dresses.

Marquisette: a sheer, lightweight; leno-weave fabric usually made of filament yarns.

Matelasse': A fabric having a raised figured pattern in a blistered, quilted effect. Woven on a Jacquard or dobby loom. Double warp-face material stitched together in warp and filling. Face of cloth has a fine warp and filling, the back a fine warp and heavy filling. Comes in various weights and used for blouses, dresses, upholstery.

Melton: Well-fulled or felted overcoating fabric with smooth, hard finish and close-cropped nap. Generally in plain colors. Coarser meltons similar to mackinac cloth, but sometimes made of fine, soft wools to produce smooth coating fabric with finish like broadcloth. Also made with wool blends.

Microfiber: Shortened form of the term "microdenier fiber", with "denier" being a measure of fiber size. Synthetic fiber, which is extremely fine and can be spun from polyester, nylon, rayon, acetate, or a combination of these. Can be blended with natural fibers to produce a strong durable fabric that is soft and water-resistant. *(See Chapter 9)*

Milanese: Warp knitted fabric with distinctive diagonal. Made of any filament fiber. Used for gloves, lingerie.

Mohair: Yarns and fabrics of mohair are bright and lustrous. Warp yarns of cotton or worsted generally used in flat mohair fabrics. Mohair pile fabrics used in automobiles and for upholstery usually have pile introduced as warp, but in such a fashion that the special system of threads is not subjected to severe tension.

Moire´: Watermark designs embossed on plain-weave fabrics that have crosswise ribs. Usually of silk, rayon, acetate, or nylon. Marking permanent on the thermoplastic fibers. Cotton moire´ is made with compact plain weave and given finish that is permanent if washed with care in lukewarm water, mild soap, and no bleach.

Moleskin: a napped, heavy, strong fabric often made in a satin weave. The nap is suede-like.

Monk's (Druid's) Cloth: Basket weave, a variation of the plain weaves. Made with heavy rough yarns. Can be a 1 x 1, 2 x 2, 4 x 4, or 8 x 8 thread; the best known is the 4 x 4. These four threads in warp and filling are placed flat together and woven over and under in a plain weave; the resulting appearance is that of a basket. Used for drapery and upholstery.

Mummy Clothe: Two different types: (1) fine, closely woven linen fabric used in Egypt for wrapping mummies. (2) Dull crepe fabric of silk or cotton warp and wool filling.

Muslin: a firm, medium- to heavyweight, plain weave cotton fabric made in a variety of qualities. Muslin made with low-grade cotton fiber with small pieces from the cotton plant is often used in apparel design.

Nacre Velvet: Velvet with pile of one color and back of another, giving a mother-of-pearl, changeable appearance.

Net: a general term used to refer to any open-construction fabric whether it is created by weaving, knitting, knotting, or another method.

Nylon: a lightweight manmade synthetic fabric with excellent strength and durability, suitable for many different uses. Often blended with natural fibers to give extra strength and better washing qualities. *(See Chapter 9)*

Oilcloth: Sheetings or printcloth that are printed, bleached, or dyed, and given a special linseed oil and pigment preparation. Used for table coverings, waterproof outerwear; now largely replaced by plastic-coated and vinyl materials.

Oilskin: Cotton linen, silk, or manmade material treated with linseed oil, varnish for waterproofing. Used for rainwear.

Organdy: a transparent, crisp, lightweight; plain-weave fabric made of cotton-spun yarns. The fabric has been parchmentized to create the crisp, wiry hand.

Organza: a transparent, crisp, lightweight; plain-weave fabric made of filament yarns.

Ottoman: Heavy, plain weave fabric with wide, flat crosswise ribs that are larger and higher than in faille. Sometimes comes with alternating narrow and wide ribs. When made of narrow ribs only, it is called *soleil*. Warp may be silk or manmade fiber; filling may be cotton, silk, wool, or manmade fiber. Used for dress coats, suits, and trimmings.

Outing flannel: a medium-weight, napped, plain- or twill-weave, spun-yarn fabric. It may be napped on one or both sides. It is heavier and stiffer than flannelette.

Oxford: A plain basket weave of medium or heavy weight. Made with a variety of cotton, rayon, or polyester/cotton yarns. The majority of oxfords are of combed yarns, with heavier filling than warp yarns. Cheaper grades are mixed carded and combed yarns, and sometimes all carded yarns. Two warp yarns, placed flat next to each other, are woven over and under one heavier filling thread. Usually mercerized. A number of variations of this weave are on the market. For shirting's, dresses, and similar purposes.

Panama: Lightweight summer suiting. Plain weave, usually with cotton warp and worsted filling. Skein or piece-dyed.

Panne Satin: Lightweight silk or manmade fiber satin fabric with very high luster achieved with aid of heavy roll pressure. Crushes easily. Used for eveningwear.

Panne Velvet: A velvet with a special luster produced by pressing the pile in one direction.

Paper Taffeta: Lightweight taffeta with crisp, paper-like finish.

Penne Satin: Lightweight silk or manmade fiber satin fabric with very high luster achieved with aid of heavy roll pressure. Crushes easily. Used for eveningwear.

Percale: a plain weave, medium-weight, piece-dyed or printed fabric finished from print cloths of better quality. Percale is usually a firm, balanced fabric.

Pigment Taffeta: Taffeta woven with pigmented yarns. Surface has dull appearance.

Pique': Two different types: (1) Medium- to heavyweight fabric that has a warp or filling wale or cord, usually warp. A heavy stuffer yarn is used in back of the cloth; this heavy yarn is caught at intervals by a filling thread. Groups of fine warp yarns are woven on the surface over the back stuffer yarn, forming a rib. Many of the cheaper or lighter versions are woven without this stuffer yarn. Other versions of pique' are irregular or novelty wales, woven dots, bird's-eye, diamond, square, and ladder effects. (2) Double-knit fabric usually with fine dots in the stitch pattern.

Plisse': a fabric finished from cotton-print cloth by printing with a caustic soda (sodium hydroxide) paste. The paste causes the fabric to shrink, thus creating a three-dimensional effect. The strip that was printed usually is darker in piece-dyed goods because the sodium hydroxide increases the dye absorbency.

Plush: Compactly woven fabric with warp pile higher than that of velvet. Made of cotton, wool, silk, or manmade fiber, often woven as double face fabric and then sheared apart. Higher pile gives bristly texture. Usually piece-dyed but may be printed. Used for coats, upholstery.

Polished cotton: a medium-weight, plain weave fabric that has been given a glazed-calendar finish.

Polyester: a medium weight man made fiber that is strong and can be found in many types of fabrics. *(See Chapter 9)*

Pongee: a medium-weight, balanced, plain weave fabric with a fine regular warp and an irregular filling. It was originally a tussah or wild-silk fabric, but now pongee is used to describe a fabric that has the general appearance of fine warp yarns and irregular filling yarns.

Poplin: a medium- to heavyweight, unbalanced, plain weave, and spun-yarn fabric that is usually piece dyed. The filling yarns are coarser than the warp yarns. Poplin has a more pronounced rib than broadcloth.

Power net: a Raschel-warp knit in which an inlaid spandex fiber or yarn is used to give high elongation and elasticity.

Print cloth: a general term used to describe unfinished, medium-weight, plain weave, and cotton for cotton-blend fabrics. These fabrics can be finished as percale, embossed, plisse´, chintz, cretonne, or polished cotton.

Raschel knit: a general term for patterned, warp-knit fabric made with coarser yarns than other warp-knit fabrics.

Ramie: Similar to flax with a high natural luster. Fine, absorbent, and quick drying fiber, used for apparel, some interior furnishings, rope, and other industrial uses.

Rep (Rep) Plain weave: Has a rib running across the fabric. The rib stands out more than in poplin. Usually given a high luster, although not always.

Rayon: the first synthetic fiber produced from mostly cellulose, which greatly resembled cotton in its chemical properties. Rayon is weakened by water and often shrinks after washing. It can be woven and knitted into many types of fabrics and used for many purposes. *(See Chapter 9)*

Sailcloth: a bottom-weight, half-basket-weave (2 x 1) unbalanced fabric. It may be made of spun- or textured-filament yarns. It can be piece dyed or printed.

Sateen: A cotton fabric usually woven so that the surface is smooth and the finish lustrous, resembling satin. Can be either a strong, warp-face sateen or softer filling-face sateen. Often, though not always, filling sateens have a softer finish than warp sateens.

Satin: Originally silk, now also of filament manmade fibers with a highly lustrous surface and usually a dull back. Made in different weights according to its uses, which vary from lingerie and dress goods to drapery and upholstery fabrics. May be made with a cotton back. Sometimes double-faced for use as ribbon.

Scrim: A durable plain weave. Generally play yarns and low thread count. Somewhat similar to voile but a much lower thread count. Cheesecloth with a stiffening finish is often referred to as scrim. Comes in many variations. Usually has a selvage. Generally carded, but a few combed varieties.

Seersucker: Light-to medium-weight fabrics, of cotton or manmade fiber, of plain or crepe weave, with crinkled stripes in cloth made by alternating tight and slack twist warp yarns. Usually with dyed wrap yarn producing stripes. Imitations are chemically treated or embossed plisse´. Used for summer suits, dresses, or bedspreads.

Serge: a general term used to refer to twill-weave fabrics with a flat, right-hand wale. The interlacing pattern is 2/2. The fabric is often wool or wool-like.

Shagbark: usually gingham with an occasional warp yarn under slack tension. During weaving, the slack-tension yarns create a loop at intervals giving the fabric a unique surface appearance.

Shantung: Plain weave. Has a rib effect formed by slub-filling yarns. Certain parts of the yarn are not given the usual number of twists. These places form the slub in the rib. Made of cotton, silk, rayon and other manmade fibers. Low in luster, heavier and rougher than pongee. Sometimes used to describe a heavy grade of pongee made in China. Also sometimes called: *nankeen, rajah, and tussah.*

Sharkskin: A term descriptively applied to wool fabrics woven in two and two right-hand twill, with a one and one color arrangement of yarns in the warp and filling. This combination of weave and color results in color lines running diagonally to the left, opposed to the direction of the twill lines, and a distinctly sleek appearance and feel that suggests the texture of the skin of the shark. Also made of rayon, acetate, triacetate, other fibers, and blends. Used for suiting, sportswear.

Sheers: General classification for thin, lightweight fabric, of any one of several open weave constructions. May be made of any natural or manmade fiber.

Sheetings: Plain weave. Mostly carded but occasionally combed yarns in all weights; light, medium, and heavy. Generally about the same number of yarns in warp as in filling, but often warp yarns are heavier than filling. Sheetings come in both wide and narrow widths. Yarn sizes range from 10s to 30s. Maybe made of cotton or any other major natural or manmade fiber.

Shetland: Three different types: (1) originally, soft, napped fabric made of wool from the Shetland Islands. Herringbone twill is common. (2) Soft, knitted fabric of Shetland wool. (3) A woven or knitted fabric with a soft hand resembling that of Shetland but does not contain that wool.

Silesia: Generally, lightweight cotton twill lining with a calendered glaze.

Silk: A natural fiber produced from the silk worm. First made into beautiful exotic fabrics by the Chinese hundreds of years ago. There are many different types of silk fabrics produced from this fine natural fiber. *(See Chapter 9)*

Slipper Satin: Compactly woven, strong fabric originally used for women's evening shoes. Made of silk or manmade filament fibers in white, solid colors, and brocade designs.

Spandex: generic name for synthetic fibers of a segmented polyurethane composition. Spandex fiber threads are man-made elastic threads with properties better than natural rubber, which has been developed into many new stretch fabrics.

Suede cloth: a plain weave, twill-weave, or knitted fabric that is napped and sheared to resemble suede leather. Suede cloth can be napped on both sides. Any suitable fiber can be used. Suede also is used to refer to brushed leather.

Suiting: a general term for heavyweight fabrics. Suiting can be any fiber content or fabric construction that works well in men's or women's suits.

Surah: Originally of silk, now also made of manmade filament fibers. Soft, supple fabric of twill weave. May come in plaid or printed pattern. Used for neckwear, scarves, blouses, and dresses.

Taffeta: A smooth, closely woven fabric in a plain weave. Originally of silk, now often of manmade filament fibers. Often weighted to produce its characteristic crispness. Solid colors, but sometimes of one color warp and another color filling to give iridescent, or changeable color effect, sometimes called "shot taffeta." May also be striped for plaid, occasionally printed. Sometimes has a moiré pattern. Used for dresses, suits, coats, and lingerie.

Tapestry: a firm, heavy, stiff, jacquard-weave fabric made with several warp and filling yarn sets. Tapestry is also the term used for fabric made by hand in which the filling yarns are discontinuous. In hand-made tapestries, the filling yarn is used only in those areas where that color is desired.

Tarpaulin: Waterproofed canvas. Sometimes of nylon or other manmade fiber.

Terrycloth (terry): a slack-tension, warp-yarn pile fabric. Terrycloth may have loops on one or both sides of the fabric. Terrycloth may have a jacquard pattern and may be made with plied yarns for durability. There are also weft or filling-knit terrycloths.

Ticking: A variety of fabrics are known by this name. The main weave is a closely-woven, thick yarn twill. Spaced, colored, and natural or white yarns repeated in the warp, and all natural or white in the filling, forming a stripe. Several color combinations used, as blue and white, brown and white, red and white. Heavy warp-face sateens as well as heavy sheetings are printed and sold as ticking. Jacquard damask ticking woven in damask effects also sold for this purpose as well as other fabrics, such as drills.

Toile: Three general types: (1) broad (French) refers to many plain or twill linen fabrics: (2) sheer cotton or linen fabrics; (3) design printed on fabric or woven in lace.

Transparent Velvet: Lightweight, soft sheer velvet of silk or rayon pile and silk or rayon back. Drapes well. Used for evening gowns, negligees.

Tricot: Warp-knit fabric with fine vertical wales on face and slightly angled coursewise rib on back. May have stripes, mesh, or patterns in structure. Mostly manmade filament yarns. Used for gloves, lingerie dresses.

Tropical Weights: Lightweight, clear finish plain weave fabrics of wool or wool/polyester 2/60s or better worsted yarns, usually the latter, used for men's and, less frequently, for women's summer suits. The weave should be firm but open, because the fabric is especially designed for hot-weather wear.

Tsumugi Silk: Made in central Honshu, Japan. Characterized by yarn-dyed striped or plaid patterns. Has somewhat coarse, homespun quality and handsome appearance.

Tulla: Fine, lightweight, stiff net of hexagonal mesh. General made of silk, rayon, or nylon. Used for ballet costumes, bridal dresses, and veils.

Tweed: A term broadly applied to the sturdier types of fabrics made of the coarser grades of wool. Tweed fabrics originally derived their interest from the color effects obtained by mixing stock-dyed wools. More recently the term includes monotones, which derive their interest from weave effects. The most popular weaves for tweeds are the plain, the twill, and variations of the latter. Now also made of other fibers.

Ulster: Heavy, overcoat material, loosely woven with right-hand twist warp, and left-handed twist filling. All types of fiber used, quality varies accordingly. Given a long nap that is pressed down.

Ultrasuede: Trademark of an imitation suede fabric composed of polyester microfibers combined with polyurethane foam in a non-woven structure. Hand and appearance resemble sheep suede.

Velour: a general term used to describe pile fabrics. Velours tend to have dense, long, or deep pile. Velours can be woven or knitted.

Velvet: Compact short warp pile of silk or manmade fiber and usually a cotton or, perhaps, rayon back. Similar to plush but shorter pile and softer.

Velveteen: a filling-pile fabric made with long floats that are cut in the finishing process. The ground fabric can have a plain or twill weave. The pile in velveteen is short. Velveteen is usually a spun-yarn fabric.

Vicuña: Short, soft, exceedingly fine hair fiber, very valuable because of the limited supply. It is rarely used by itself, although a few vicuña coats are manufactured each year. Sometimes mixed with wool to produce special soft coating fabrics. The term and certain derived and coined names have been much misused.

Viyella: Trademark for lightweight British napped fabric usually of two-up and two-down twill of 55/45 blends of wool and cotton. Some variations in fiber content, qualities, and weights. Used for shirts, dresses.

Voile: A soft yet firm sheer fabric of plain weave. Generally made of combed hard-twisted single yarns, although ply yarns are also used. About the same number of yarns in warp as in filling. Has clinging effect. Occasionally dots are woven in, and a crisp finish given the fabric; then is sold as dotted Swiss. Used for children's wear, blouses, and dresses.

Waffle Cloth: Similar to pique´ in texture. Honeycomb weave made on dobby loom. Usually of cotton.

Whipcord: Compact, medium-weight fabric of prominent right-hand 63° warp-faced twill. May be made of cotton and may be mercerized. Often made of good quality woolen or worsted yarn. May be of rayon, nylon, other manmade, or blends. Very serviceable. Used for suits, coats, and uniforms.

Wigan: Usually made of printcloth or lightweight sheetings. Dyed in dark colors and starched and calendered. Used mostly for interlinings.

Wool: a natural fiber that is clipped from a sheep *(fleece wool),* which is then washed, combed, and spun into yarns of various qualities and used for a variety of different types of uses. Wool has been produced in many countries for hundreds of years and because of its warm comfortable feel against the skin has many clothing uses. *(See chapter 9)*

INDEX

D

E

F

G

H

I

J

K

L

M

N

O

S

X

Y

Z

NOTES

NOTES

NOTES

NOTES

NOTES

NOTES